ROYAL TAXATION
IN FOURTEENTH-CENTURY FRANCE

MEMOIRS OF THE
AMERICAN PHILOSOPHICAL SOCIETY
Held at Philadelphia
For Promoting Useful Knowledge
Volume 116

ROYAL TAXATION
IN
FOURTEENTH-CENTURY FRANCE

The Captivity and Ransom of
John II, 1356–1370

JOHN BELL HENNEMAN

University of Iowa

THE AMERICAN PHILOSOPHICAL SOCIETY
Independence Square • Philadelphia
1976

In Memory Of
my late grandmother
Margaret Olmsted Ogden (1874–1952)
whose encouragement of a boyhood
enthusiasm led me to become a historian

CONTENTS

Preface

This book is written as a sequel to my earlier work, *Royal Taxation in Fourteenth Century France: The Development of War Financing, 1322–1356*. Both volumes originally were planned as part of a series that would examine in detail the development of royal finance during a critical century in which most of the essential institutions of the early modern French state took form.

The destruction of the French financial archives for this period makes it impossible to treat royal taxation from a statistical point of view. French scholars like Gustave Dupont-Ferrier have studied it as an administrative problem, treating the subject topically, but not making clear how taxation actually developed or how its development related to political theory. Very early in my research, it became clear that taxation developed in a complex military, political, and social context and that external factors sharply affected the attitudes of both the government and the governed towards taxes. To understand these factors, one must study the subject chronologically, and what I have written is, in effect, a political history of taxation.

My first volume dealt with the thirty-five years of the fourteenth century which were the most obscure from the point of view of royal finance, and my purpose was to assemble as much information as possible and indicate the major trends in taxation. It became evident that after 1356 a change occurred in the level and continuity of taxation, in attitudes about taxes, and in the role of central assemblies. The purpose of this volume is to document and explain this change and to show why the years 1356–1370 established the fundamental pattern of royal finance that would prevail in the next few centuries. I shall examine in detail the political crisis of the later 1350's and the circumstances in which, during the 1360's, France first submitted to regular peacetime taxes. I shall conclude with a brief general survey of the years 1370–1440, showing how the fiscal system of the 1370's, after vicissitudes and interruptions, became established permanently.

This book, like its predecessor, makes substantial use of unpublished manuscripts, but there will be less emphasis on bringing to light new facts and more emphasis on reorganizing and reinterpreting existing information. Much more has been published about the years after 1356 (although not about taxation as such). Narrative sources and certain kinds of administrative documents are more abundant and more complete. Yet as earlier regional diversity gave way to greater uniformity in taxation, the documents are less distinctive and are more apt to duplicate each other. Ironically, the records of the royal treasury are most sparse for the period 1350–1370, leaving us without the statistical information that would be so valuable.

I have attempted to conform to the usages of my previous book, using interchangeably certain words and expressions for reasons of style (king, crown, government; pounds, *livres*, l.; bourgeois, burghers, townsmen). I have also followed the same general principles regarding names, generally anglicizing royalty and place names outside France, while leaving in French the names of lesser personages and places inside France. Once again, institutions have been anglicized except where clarity of meaning required that the French names be used.

I have received a great deal of valuable assistance in preparing this book. Financial assistance from McMaster University made possible trips to France in 1966 and 1968. When the latter trip was cut short by the strikes and revolutionary activity that occurred in France, I was able to obtain microfilms through the kindness of Professor Philippe Wolff and the archivists of Toulouse and the departments of the Tarn and Haute-Garonne. The library staffs of McMaster University and the University of Iowa also gave valuable assistance in obtaining material via interlibrary loan and in securing microfilms of manuscripts. A Research Assignment from the University of Iowa in 1974 gave me the opportunity to carry out additional research.

My enormous debt to other scholars will be obvious to the reader, but I should like to single out the individuals to whom I am particularly grateful: Charles Taylor, who trained me in the historian's craft and encouraged me to study French

taxation; Gaines Post, whose legal studies and helpful suggestions have greatly enriched my perspective; Joseph Strayer, the
mentor of many distinguished medievalists, who has been so
generous with his time whenever I asked for assistance or
critical comments on my work. I deeply appreciate the many
useful suggestions of Thomas Bisson and my friend and
colleague Donald Sutherland, both of whom are skillful
judges of historical prose.

In looking ahead to the fifteenth century, I have ventured
into the field of other specialists, and I have been saved from
many errors thanks to the advice of J. Russell Major. I
am especially indebted to Martin Wolfe, whose study of
royal finance in Renaissance France is a model of how the
subject of taxation ought to be treated. Professor Wolfe gave
enthusiastic support to the publication of this book, and
his valuable suggestions led to many improvements in the
manuscript.

Above all, perhaps, I owe thanks to Raymond Cazelles and
Elizabeth Brown. M. Cazelles, whose deep understanding of
fourteenth-century French politics has been demonstrated in a
succession of provocative articles, has for more than a decade
been of great help to me. Without the benefit of his scholar-
ship and encouragement, it would have been impossible for
me to undertake this study of taxation in a political context.
Professor Brown has shared with me her unpublished papers
and her vast store of notes, has helped me obtain microfilms of
manuscripts, has directed me to important sources, and has
been a trusted critic and adviser throughout this project.

I am also much obliged to several younger medievalists.
Charles Radding and Jan Rogozinski have offered valuable
suggestions and have permitted me to use some of their
unpublished research. These two scholars will add greatly to
our understanding of fourteenth-century France when their
current projects are completed and published. I have also
profited from the work of four distinguished graduate students
at the University of Iowa, whose writings are cited in the
bibliography—Armand Arriaza, Robert H. Gore, Sarah H.
Madden, and Thomas R. Prest. My research assistants, Robert
Gore and Jill Harsin have helped with proofreading,
and I owe a great debt to my wife, Gerry, for the many

ways in which she has helped and encouraged me over the years.

All these persons have contributed to whatever merit this book may have. I alone am responsible for its errors and imperfections.

John Bell Henneman

Iowa City, Iowa
December, 1975

Abbreviations Used Throughout in the Footnotes

AD   Archives départementales

AM   Archives municipales (communales)

AN   Archives Nationales, Paris

BN   Bibliothèque Nationale, Paris

Foedera   *Foedera, conventiones litterae et cujuscunque generis acta publica inter reges Angliae et alios quosvis imperatores, reges, pontifices, principes vel communitates.* 1727-1735 (2nd. ed., 20 v., London).

Gr. Chartrier   *Archives de la ville de Montpellier, Inventaires et documents: Inventaire du Grand Chartrier redigé par Robert Louvet.* 1895-1955 (2 v., Montpellier).

HL   *Histoire générale de Languedoc avec des Notes et les pièces justificatives.* 1872-1904 (new ed., 16 v., Toulouse).

INV   *Inventaire sommaire des archives . . . .*

Mandements   L. Delisle, 1874. *Mandements et Actes Divers de Charles V (1364-1380), recueillis dans les collections de la Bibliothèque Nationale* (Paris).

NAF   Nouvelles Aquisitions Françaises

Ord.   *Ordonnonces des roys de France de la troisième race recueillis par ordre chronologique.* 1723-1849 (21 v., Paris).

Petit Thalamus   *Le Petit Thalamus de Montpellier.* 1836. *Sociètè archaeologique de Montpellier* (Montpellier).

P.J.   Pièces justificatives

P.O.   Pièces originales

RTF 1322-1356   J. Henneman, 1971. *Royal Taxation in Fourteenth Century France: The Development of War Financing, 1322-1356* (Princeton).

THE FRENCH ROYAL FAMILY

Philip III
1270–1285

├─ Philip IV 1285–1314

│   ├─ Edward II = Isabella of England
│   │   └─ Edward III
│   │   └─ Edward the Black Prince
│   │
│   ├─ Philip V 1316–1322 m. Joan of Artois and Burgundy
│   │   ├─ Margaret, m. Louis I of Flanders
│   │   │   └─ Louis II of Flanders, 1346–1384
│   │   │   └─ Margaret, heiress of Flanders, Burgundy, Nevers, Artois
│   │   └─ Joan, m. Eudes IV of Burgundy
│   │
│   ├─ Charles IV 1322–1328
│   │
│   └─ Louis X 1314–1316
│   └─ Joan, q. of Navarre
│   └─ Charles II "the Bad" king of Navarre 1349–1387

├─ Louis, ct. of Evreux
│   └─ Philip, ct. of Evreux ══ Joan, q. of Navarre
│   ├─ Charles II "the Bad" king of Navarre 1349–1387
│   ├─ Blanche of Evreux, 2nd wife of Philip VI
│   ├─ Philip of Navarre, ct. of Longueville
│   └─ Louis of Navarre
│   └─ Joan of Evreux, 2nd wife of Charles IV

└─ Charles, ct. of Valois
    ├─ Philip VI 1328–1350
    │   └─ John II 1350–1364
    │   ├─ Charles V 1364–1380
    │   │   ├─ Charles VI 1380–1422
    │   │   │   └─ Charles VII 1422–1461
    │   │   └─ Louis, dk. of Orléans
    │   ├─ Louis, dk. of Anjou
    │   ├─ John, ct. of Poitiers and dk. of Berry
    │   └─ Philip the Bold, dk. of Burgundy, m. Margaret, dgtr. Louis II of Flanders
    └─ Charles, ct. of Alençon
        └─ Peter, ct. of Alençon

I. The State of French Taxation by the End of 1356

1. Introduction

O N 19 September, 1356, at Maupertuis, near Poitiers, the army of King John II of France suffered a disastrous defeat at the hands of an outnumbered force of English and Gascons under the command of Edward, Prince of Wales. Many French nobles were killed; others fled, and many more, including the king himself, were captured.[1] This battle is a famous landmark in European military, political, and diplomatic history, but it was even more decisive for French fiscal and constitutional history.

It has become traditional to regard the sixty years before 1355 as years of "preparation" or experimentation in royal finance, while the years 1355–1370 were those in which regular taxation was established and the years 1435–1445 were those in which taxation became permanent and ceased to require consent from central assemblies.[2] In fact, however, such assemblies hardly ever were involved in consent to taxation, and the Estates of 1355 bore too much resemblance to the meeting of 1347 to be considered a landmark. Furthermore, the decade 1435–1445 merely marked the re-establishment of what had been done in the 1360's. Throughout the fourteenth and fifteenth centuries, continuity was more important than decisive or sudden change, but a major turning point in

---

[1] E. Perroy, *The Hundred Years War* (tr. W. B. Wells, London, 1951), pp. 130–131; R. Delachenal, *Chronique des règnes de Jean II et de Charles V* (2 v., Paris, 1910) 1: pp. 70–74; R. Newhall (ed.), *The Chronicle of Jean de Venette* (tr. J. Birdsall, New York, 1953), pp. 64–65; R. Delachenal, *Histoire de Charles V* (5 v., Paris, 1909–1931) 1: pp. 227–243.

[2] F. Lot and R. Fawtier, *Histoire des institutions françaises au moyen âge* (3 v., Paris, 1958–1963) 2: pp. 201f and 256f, speak of "la préparation à l'impôt" (1285–1355) and "l'éstablissement de l'impôt" (1355–1370). M. Wolfe, *The Fiscal System of Renaissance France* (New Haven, 1972), p. 24, states that "it was the great reforms of the 1430's and 1440's that finally gave the king 'absolute' power over the imposts. . . . These reforms should not be regarded as continuing trends of the late Middle Ages."

French fiscal history did take place when the French began paying annual taxes without regard for the state of war or peace. This turning point was a direct result of the battle of Poitiers.

From 1294 to 1356, French royal finance was dominated by the war subsidy, an "extraordinary" but increasingly regular royal tax, levied in time of war for military purposes. Taking many different forms, this tax had been known before 1294, but the frequency and persistance of warfare after that date gave it a new importance. The increased tempo of taxation aroused many complaints, but the taxes remained light. Generally regressive in nature, they continued, with rare exceptions, to be collected by the existing, and increasingly outmoded, domainal administration. They were always brought to a halt in time of truce or peace treaty, except in localities that felt a continuing sense of military danger.[3]

Many characteristics of the preceding generation survived after 1356, but the defeat and capture of John II had three major consequences. In the first place, his subjects had to pay a large ransom to obtain his release, and this ransom necessitated, for the first time, substantial annual taxes in time of peace with England. In the second place, France was left in 1356 with a discredited nobility, an empty treasury, civil war in Normandy and Brittany, and a leaderless government that had to face the public demand for scapegoats. These circumstances made it much more difficult to effect during reforms in the government and much easier for self-seeking adventurers to exploit governmental weakness for their own advantage, discrediting central assemblies in the process. In the third place, John's capture led to a suspension of Anglo-French hostilities during the truce of 1357–1359 and the treaty of Brétigny (1360–1369), leaving thousands of professional soldiers stranded on French soil without a livelihood. Turning to brigandage at a time when the government was too weak to discipline them, these *routiers*[4] soon taught the French taxpayers that "peace" could be more terrible than war. People developed a conception of "evident necessity" that differed sharply from that which had been held before the 1350's. They

---

[3] *RTF 1322–1356*, chap. IX.

[4] The soldiers were organized into companies, or *routes,* hence the term *routier* which is so often applied to these brigands.

began to perceive that taxation, however distasteful, could be justified in time of peace as a necessary requirement for order and stability. Because of these consequences, the battle of Poitiers ushered in a new era in French financial history.

Taxes lost their earlier diversity of form and began to be collected by an administrathon specifically established for this purpose. The three main types of tax that emerged in the decade after 1356—the *aides, gabelle,* and *fouage* (later,

MAP 1.   France in the 1360's.

Names in capitals = Bailiwicks, seneschalsies, or major fiefs
Names in small letters = towns

taille)—were eventually to become a permanent part of the financial structure of early modern France. Despite the setbacks and disorders of the ensuing sixty years, the period of 1356–1370 proved decisive—for taxation, for financial administration, and for the history of representative assemblies in France. Thus the captivity and ransom of John II brought an end to the "age of war subsidy," which gave way to a period in which regular royal taxation was established.

2. The Hundred Years' War and French Society

Of all the factors influencing the development of French royal finance, the most important was war, not merely because of its impact on royal financial needs and on the willingness or ability of royal subjects to pay taxes, but also because the attitudes and behavior of the military class did much to determine the politics of taxation.

The king's captivity and the subsequent treaty of Brétigny brought to a close the first two decades of the Hundred Years' War, in which supremacy shifted strikingly from France to England. The English king, as duke of Guyenne, was a peer of France whose claim to the French throne placed him at the head of those French lords who defected from the Valois monarch. Among these were the Harcourt family of Normandy, the Montfort branch of the ducal house of Brittany, Count Gaston III of Foix, and the Evreux branch of the Capetian dynasty itself. We should include also the many connections of Raoul de Brienne, constable of France prior to his summary execution by John II in 1351.[5]

Both French politics and English strategy were strongly influenced by the existence of this important anti-Valois faction within the French aristocracy. The Anglo-French struggle was, in a sense, also a French civil war.[6] Whether

---

[5] E. Meyer, *Charles II, roi de Navarre, comte d'Evreux, et la Normandie au XIVe siècle* (Paris, 1898), p. 33; D. F. Secousse, *Mémoires pour servir à l'histoire de Charles II, roi de Navarre et comte d'Evreux, surnommé le Mauvais* (2 v., Paris, 1755–1758) 2: p. 31 (hereafter cited as *Charles le Mauvais*); K. Fowler, *The King's Lieutenant: Henry of Grosmont, First Duke of Lancaster, 1310–1361* (New York, 1969), p. 78; J. d'Avout, *Le meurtre d'Etienne Marcel* (Paris, 1960), pp. 12–13; R. Cazelles, "Le parti navarrais jusqu'à la mort d'Etienne Marcel," *Bulletin philologique et historique* 1960: pp. 845–846.

[6] J. le Patourel, "The King and the Princes in Fourteenth-Century France," *Europe in the Later Middle Ages* (ed. J. Hale, J. Highfield, B. Smalley, London, 1965), p. 183; P. S. Lewis, *Later Medieval France: The Polity* (London 1968), p. 40.

Edward III really considered the French throne his main
objective, as some have argued recently, or whether his claim
was merely a tactic, it permitted dissidents to oppose the house
of Valois without opposing French kingship as such. The
succession question distinguished the period of English victories after 1337 from the French hegemony of the preceding
generation.[7]

After the Breton succession crisis broke out in 1341, Edward
III began to conduct coordinated military operations on
several French fronts. In 1345–1347, armies under Derby,
Northampton, and Edward himself won victories in Gascony
and at Crécy and Calais.[8] A decade later, similar strategy
produced new gains for the English, who profited from the
most important of all the French defections, that of Charles
the Bad, king of Navarre and count of Evreux, whose family
controlled strategic lands in Normandy and the Ile-de-France.
In this campaign the Prince of Wales ravaged Languedoc and
then won his great victory at Poitiers, while Lancaster operated in the west and Paris was threatened from the Evreux
possessions.[9] John II had twice tried to patch things up with
the king of Navarre, but in April, 1356, he lost his patience
and imprisoned Charles, executing four of his prominent
followers.[10] This action turned Charles into a martyr around
whom malcontents rallied, and much of Normandy deserted

[7] J. Le Patourel, "Edward III and the Kingdom of France," *History* 43 (1958): pp.
173–177; K. Fowler, *The Age of Plantagenet and Valois* (New York, 1967), pp. 50,
62–66. Le Patourel believes that Edward's prime objective was the French crown,
noting that he campaigned in regions other than Guyenne, and that it was always the
French who insisted that the war was over Aquitaine. Other scholars tend to think
that friction over the legal status of Guyenne was the main reason why England went
to war. B. Wilkinson, "A Letter to Louis de Mâle, count of Flanders," *Bull. John
Rylands Library* 9 (1925): p. 180, says that Edward's claim to the throne "was a
diplomatic move whose hollowness nobody realized more clearly than he himself."
G. Templeman, "Edward III and the Beginnings of the Hundred Years' War," *Trans.
Royal Hist. Soc.*, 5th ser., 2 (1952): pp. 69–76, surveys the bibliography on the war,
most notably the work of Déprez and Perroy, and concludes that historians generally
agreed (in 1952) that the question of English Gascony was the basic cause of the
conflict. See also G. Cuttino, "Historical Revision: The Causes of the Hundred Years'
War," *Speculum* 31 (1956): pp. 463–472.

[8] Fowler, *Plantagenet and Valois*, p. 59. *Cf.* Fowler, *King's Lieutenant*, pp. 54–65;
and Perroy, *Hundred Years War*, p. 118.

[9] Fowler, *King's Lieutenant*, pp. 147–148; Fowler, *Plantagenet and Valois*, p. 59;
Avout, *Meurtre*, p. 55.

[10] *Chron. Jean II et Charles V* 1: pp. 62–66; L. Delisle, *Histoire du château et de sires
de Saint-Sauveur-le-Vicomte* (Valognes, 1867), pp. 77, 80f; H. Denifle, *La désolation
des églises, monastères et hôpitaux en France pendant la guerre de Cent Ans* (2 v.,
Paris, 1899) 2: p. 109.

John. Leaders of the Navarrese party there, Godefroy d'Harcourt, lord of Saint-Sauveur, and Philip of Navarre, count of Longueville, now gave homage to Edward III as king of France and duke of Normandy.[11]

Recognition of Edward enabled these people to legitimize actions that otherwise would have been mere rebellion.[12] This was important to the European aristocracy, for whom chivalry was no empty charade but the embodiment of a code that was taken seriously. Members of the aristocracy, and also professional soldiers of lowlier origins who wished to be considered noble, were anxious to observe the letter of the "law of arms" and be able to justify their actions on moral or legal grounds.[13] This desire gave rise to considerable casuistry, and the behavior of these fighting men towards the civilian population raises the complex question of "brigandage," which was to have an important effect on French taxation.

The problem of brigandage has not been given the systematic study it requires, but it is related to the broader economic and social dislocations of the fourteenth century. Assorted vicissitudes had weakened the manorial economy seriously by 1356,[14] and seigneurial purchasing power suffered. The degree of inflation in this period remains conjectural, but it does appear that the price of military equipment rose more quickly than did military salaries.[15] Recurrent plagues left labor shortages in the depopulated towns and a contracted market for foodstuffs. Peasants migrated from their villages, leaving the rural seigneuries short of labor and the

---

[11]*Ibid.*, p. 143; *Foedera* 5: pp. 851, 854, 867–868; Delisle, *St. Sauveur*, pp. 86–89; Le Patourel, "Edward III and France," pp. 183–184; J. Le Patourel, "Edward III, 'roi de France et duc de Normandie,' 1356–1360," *Rev. hist. droit fr. et étr.*, 4e sér., 31 (1953): pp. 317–318; S. Luce, *Histoire de Bertrand du Guesclin et de son époque* (Paris, 1876), pp. 256–261.

[12]Lewis, *Later Medieval France*, pp. 79, 376.

[13]M. Keen, *The Laws of War in the Late Middle Ages* (London and Toronto, 1965), *passim*, but especially pp. 15–24, 63–100, 254–257; Luce, *Du Guesclin*, pp. 326–327, 340. Luce condemned the lack of patriotism of those engaging in brigandage, but their international class loyalty did insure that most fighting men treated each other according to a recognized code. See Lewis, *Later Medieval France*, pp. 187–188; Fowler, *Plantagenet and Valois*, pp. 36, 102.

[14]G. Duby, *Rural Economy and Country Life in the Medieval West* (London, 1968), pp. 298–309, 319f; Avout, *Meurtre*, pp. 12–13; *RTF 1322–1356*, pp. 13–15.

[15]Fowler, *Plantagenet and Valois*, pp. 36, 138; P. Contamine, *Guerre, état, et société à la fin du moyen âge* (Paris, 1971), pp. 96–97.

remaining peasants in a better bargaining position.[16] Warfare in the countryside inflicted personal misery on many peasants, but also destroyed the capital of manorial lords.[17] Taxes were light in the first half of the century, particularly for the rural upper class, but the levies became increasingly frequent and gradually heavier. Nobles became increasingly class-conscious, seeking to maintain their separate identity as a military class. To claim this special status, they avoided bourgeois occupations and depended increasingly on plunder and military employment.[18] Other ways of replenishing their finances, such as borrowing money or selling off lands, were hindered by royal policies toward usury and the acquisition of fiefs, policies that tended to constrict credit and drive down property values.[19] Even more aggravating to the upper class was the royal policy on the coinage.

For centuries, coinage had been regarded as a prestigious and profitable seigneurial right, but royal currency now circulated far more widely than the surviving non-royal coins. When a mint purchased silver (by the "mark" of 4608 grains), it generally issued coins valued at more than the purchase price. The resulting profit (*monnayage*) paid for the costs of minting and provided income for the lord who controlled the mint. If a shortage of bullion forced the mints to pay higher prices for specie, the lord's *monnayage* declined unless he altered his coins to maintain the level of profit.[20] This process was known as "weakening" the currency. It could be accomplished not only by debasing the alloy, but also by increasing the number of coins struck (or "cut") from a mark, or by raising their official value (*prix* or *cours*). These different

---

[16]H. Miskimin, *The Economy of Early Renaissance Europe, 1300–1460* (Englewood Cliffs, N. J., 1969), pp. 9–10, 51–57; *RTF 1322–1356*, pp. 13–14 and notes.

[17]Duby, *Rural Economy*, pp. 297, 312.

[18]A. Coville, in E. Lavisse, *Histoire de France* (9 v., Paris, 1900–1911) 4, 1: p. 152f; G. Dupont-Ferrier, *Etudes sur les institutions financières de la France à la fin du moyen âge* (2 v., Paris, 1930–1932) 2: p. 175; P. Timbal, *et al.*, *La guerre de Cent Ans vue à travers les registres du Parlement (1337–1369)* (Paris, 1961), pp. 19, 342–343. See *RTF 1322–1356*, pp. 12f and 316f. On the unemployment of nobles in time of truce or treaty, see Luce, *Du Guesclin*, p. 327.

[19]J. Henneman, "Enquêteurs-Réformateurs and Fiscal Officers in Fourteenth Century France," *Traditio* 24 (1968): pp. 312–313 and notes; J. Henneman, "Taxation of Italians by the French Crown, 1311–1363," *Med. Stud.* 31 (1968): p. 34f.

[20]T. Prest, "Policy and Protest: The Search for Monetary Reform in France" (unpubl. M.A. thesis, U. of Iowa, Iowa City, 1971), p. 14f.

characteristics of a given coinage were embodied in a formula that yielded a figure called the *pied de monnaie*. The *pied* divided by four equalled the value of the minted mark in *livres tournois*.[21]

The French long considered the ideal currency to be the "strong money" of Louis IX, whose silver coinage was the 12th *pied*, meaning that a mark of minted silver was valued at 3 l. t. Under Philip IV, and again in the 1320's, the monarchy weakened the royal coinage and collected large sums as *monnayage*. A reform in 1329 restored the 12th *pied*, but after 1337 came new weakenings, and the money was on the 60th *pied* in 1343 when public indignation forced an abrupt return to the 15th *pied*. This last measure dislocated prices and aroused so much criticism as to end for all time the nostalgia for the money of St. Louis. New mutations of the currency began in 1349, and John II sought to maximize his profits from *monnayage* by raising the *pied* in a series of steps and then abruptly lowering it.[22] As this cycle was repeated, the currency tended to grow weaker, reaching the 120th *pied* late in 1355. At that point the Estates demanded and obtained a revaluation, but John's financial needs forced him to abandon the reform in the months before the battle of Poitiers. He weakened the coinage to the 60th *pied* and collected a *monnayage* of more than 50 per cent.[23]

As a result of all these manipulations, the royal coinage had become a bitter political issue. Critics of the king's policies now called for "sound," or consistent money, rather than stressing the old demand for "strong," as opposed to "weak" money.[24] The seigneurial class still condemned the weakenings as inflationary, but other interests were offended by the frequency of the mutations and their evident use for royal profit. *Monnayage* was one tax that clearly bore more heavily on the rich than on the poor, and since frequent mutations

---

[21]*Ibid.*, pp. 8–11. See also *RTF 1322–1356*, pp. 332–333.

[22]R. Cazelles, "Quelques réflexions à propos des mutations de la monnaie *royale française (1295–1360)*," *Le Moyen Age* 72 (1966): pp. 94–95, 257–263; Prest, *Policy and Protest*, chaps. 2–4; *RTF 1322–1356*, 340–344.

[23]*Ibid.*; Prest, "Policy and Protest," pp. 121–127. See also L. Balas, *Une tentative de gouvernement représentatif au XIVe siècle. Les états-généraux de 1356–1358* (Paris, 1928), p. 104, for the relationship between coinage mutations and insufficient taxes.

[24]This distinction has been made by Prest, "Policy and Protest," pp. 12–13, and it seems more accurate than my use of the term "sound money" in *RTF 1322–1356*, Appendix I, to describe coins of a relatively low *pied*.

could also disrupt business, it is not surprising that burghers
with substantial movable wealth were becoming the leading
critics of the policy.[25] Poor people lacking in economic
sophistication were alarmed by sudden reductions in the *pied*,
which reduced the supply of money and left them with the
impression that they had been swindled.[26] Nearly everybody,
therefore, now objected to the king's manipulation of the
coinage, and people were receptive to the ideas of Nicole
Oresme, who declared that the currency belonged to the
public and could be altered only with public consent in cases
of necessity.[27]

Because the fourteenth century was a time of war, economic
trouble, and social tension, popular grievances naturally went
far beyond the coinage.[28] As various factors caused the royal
domain to decline in financial importance, the royal government demanded more frequent taxes for military purposes,
only to suffer military defeat. The crown came under attack,
not for tyranny, but for corruption and waste.[29] Individual
regions became more jealous of their traditional rights, more
solicitous of their own defense. People who gained advancement in the royal service were resented and criticized by those
who felt excluded. Thus the critics of the government were
impelled by many fears, frustrations, interests, and principles,
but all were related to a common issue, the royal financial
policies and those who determined them. The capture of the
king ignited the crisis that faced the monarchy at the end of
1356, but the crisis had been building up during the period we
have called the age of the war subsidy.

---

[25] See Delachenal, *Charles V* 1: p. 293, and Balas, *Tentative*, 100–102. *Cf.* Cazelles,
"Quelques réflexions," pp. 262–263, for the efforts of John II's government to
minimize the economic dislocations occasioned by the mutations.

[26] *Ibid.*, pp. 94–95.

[27] E. Bridrey, *La théorie de la monnaie au XIVe siècle, Nicole Oresme* (Paris, 1906),
pp. 45–54, 183–297.

[28] P. Wolff, "Les luttes sociales dans les villes du Midi française, XIIIe-XIVe
siècles," *Annales: Econ., Soc., Civ.* 2 (1947): pp. 448–449; *RTF 1322–1356*, pp. 15–16
and notes. According to Avout, *Meurtre*, pp. 37, 41, however, the artisans and *haute
bourgeoisie* of Paris were drawn together, rather than divided, by the financial
measures of the crown.

[29] The importance of the domain will be discussed in chapter VIII. See *RTF
1322–1356*, p. 309; M. Rey, *Le domaine du roi et les finances extraordinaires sous
Charles VI, 1388–1413* (Paris, 1965), pp. 91–92. For one expression of public irritation
at alleged royal waste, see *Venette*, p. 63.

3. Theory and Practice in the Age of the War Subsidy

In 1294 a long period of relative peace had given way to one in which war or threat of war became the usual state of affairs in France, forcing the monarchy to search for non-domainal sources of revenue. Each interval of peace was shorter and more precarious than the one before; each period of war seemed more intense, involved more parts of the realm, and proved less successful for French arms. Military defense was expensive, the economy less prosperous, and ordinary revenues less adequate. Seeking ways to justify extraordinary taxation, royal advisers trained in Roman and canon law perceived the possibilities inherent in the legal doctrine that "necessity knows no law." According to this concept, the king had the right to suspend traditional privileges and take extraordinary or unprecedented subsidies for the "common profit" or the "defense of the realm" in times of "evident necessity" or cases of "evident utility."[30]

As expounded by the lawyers, such theories conferred great power on the king, but they were slow to gain acceptance from the public. For a time at the end of the thirteenth century, Philip IV did levy subsidies based solely on the royal assertion that the kingdom was in danger and that all subjects had to contribute to its defense. Beginning in 1302, however, the crown employed the more traditional device of proclaiming the *arrière-ban* which summoned the kingdom to arms, then levying subsidies as fines in lieu of personal military service.[31] The change probably was dictated by a general reluctance to pay taxes purely on the basis of a royal declaration of emergency, which was too readily abused. It was more customary to treat taxes as a substitute for service, and a call to arms offered some indication that the king was sincere about the military danger. Taxpayers had their own ways of defining or describing "evident necessity." One community promised a tax if the king maintained in the field an army of specified

---

[30] G. Post, *Studies in Medieval Legal Thought: Public Law and the State, 1100-1322* (Princeton, 1964), especially pp. 15-19, 310-332, and 436f. See also the discussion in *RTF 1322-1356*, pp. 22-24 and notes 56-57.

[31] *Ibid.*, p. 29; J. Strayer and C. Taylor, *Studies in Early French Taxation* (Cambridge, Mass., 1939), pp. 45-56; Contamine, *Guerre*, p. 38.

size.[32] Another wished him to lead in person the army he had summoned,[33] while another refused to pay unless the king of England personally led the expected enemy attack.[34] On another occasion, the king was required to show his concern for the defense of a region by sending his son as royal lieutenant.[35] Finally, after the defeats at Crécy and Poitiers, the expression *arrière-ban après bataille* was used for a call to arms after a major disaster, thereby implying a distinction between "ordinary" emergencies and "extraordinary" ones.[36] It seems clear that throughout the age of the war subsidy the king was not conceded the right to declare on his own what justified a tax.

When people considered it justified, a subsidy could produce large sums, like the 735,000 *livres tournois* collected in 1304,[37] but most subsidies seem to have yielded much less, and any tax based on the commutation of military service was laborious to collect. The cumbersome system perpetuated the principle of personal military service that encouraged the nobles and clergy to claim exemption from paying. Still worse, it tied taxation rigidly to a state of outright military conflict, thereby conforming to popular conceptions of "evident necessity" but not to the realities of the early fourteenth century.

The weakness and inflexibility of the system became apparent in the years 1305–1339, a time of endless war scares and border incidents. The government collected subsidies when it could, but sometimes felt it wise to return them if military action did not materialize.[38] To the royal financiers, these were years of financial straits when it was difficult to meet essential military costs, but to much of the population it was a time of endless, and often pointless, taxation. The government and the governed could not agree as to what constituted the public

---

[32] AM Cordes CC 29, no. 267 (early 1325).

[33] *Ord.* 1: pp. 602–603, 785–786. The fiscal/military obligations of some abbeys were expressed in the same terms: 200 footsoldiers if the king does not lead the army, or 400 if he goes to war in person. AN JJ 91, nos. 509, 510.

[34] *Gr. Chartrier*, no. 2375.

[35] *HL* 10: cols. 1112–1120.

[36] *RTF 1322–1356*, p. 225, citing a text for 1347 from Normandy; *Ord.* 3: p. 138, a document of March, 1357; Contamine, *Guerre*, p. 38.

[37] Strayer and Taylor, *Studies*, pp. 59–75; *RTF 1322–1356*, p. 349.

[38] *Ibid.*, pp. 30, 33, 131.

interest. The crown turned to fiscal expedients: fines for acquisition of noble fiefs, usurpation of royal rights, violation of the coinage ordinances, lending money at interest, or malpractice in office; sale of rights, privileges, pardons, or patents of nobility; and at times, mutation of the currency. Such measures were technically within the king's rights, but people found them increasingly irritating and they did not bring in enough money to meet the king's needs. On occasion, however, commissioners empowered to seek funds from these sources were enough of a nuisance to collect large sums from communities willing to buy them off.[39]

In using such methods to supplement revenues when "necessity" was not "evident," the kings were following a course that was politically safer than forcing a showdown on the issue of taxation. In avoiding peacetime subsidies so scrupulously, they were motivated by political prudence, but also perhaps by conviction. Many of the writers who claimed broad power for the monarch by asserting the doctrine of necessity also warned him against tyranny and unjust extortion. They invoked the old maxim, *cessante causa cessat effectus*: when the need for extraordinary taxes ceased, so also should the taxes.[40] In 1313 Philip IV endorsed this principle explicitly by returning a subsidy when the anticipated conflict was averted by negotiation.[41] Philip V tried in 1321 to obtain a tax in peacetime to finance reforms that he claimed were for the common profit. The proposal failed because his subjects were unwilling to define the common profit in any but military terms.[42] As late as 1338, the towns of Languedoc persuaded Philip VI to return their tax when the realm was not actually invaded.[43] This attitude, however, could work both ways. After a truce was concluded late in 1340, the crown continued to collect a sales tax of four *deniers* per *livre* (1⅔ per cent) in much of Languedoil, where the English threat from Flanders and Brittany remained sufficient to meet local criteria

[39] Henneman, "Enquêteurs," *passim*.

[40] E. Brown, "*Cessante Causa* and the Taxes of the Last Capetians: The Political Applications of a Philosophical Maxim," *Studia Gratiana* 15 (1972): pp. 565–587.

[41] *Ibid.*, pp. 576–577.

[42] *Ibid.*, p. 583; C. Taylor, "French Assemblies and Subsidy in 1321," *Speculum* 43 (1968): pp. 217–244; E. Brown, "Subsidy and Reform in 1321: The Accounts of Najac and the Policies of Philip V," *Traditio* 27 (1971): pp. 399–430.

[43] *RTF 1322–1356*, p. 131.

for "evident necessity."[44] The renewal of this tax was not accompanied by the formalities we associate with the term "consent," and it is with regard to consent that we find a major divergence of practice from theory during the age of the war subsidy.

Theorists recognized the principle that "what touches all" (*quod omnes tangit*) must be approved by all.[45] Those whose rights were affected by extraordinary subsidies were supposed to concur in their levy, and although this could be a mere procedural formality, it was a potential limitation on royal power. The crown often sought and received consent, but often collected taxes without this formality. Sometimes these taxes were opposed, but generally on other grounds, and taxes sometimes met resistance even when consent had been obtained. Resistance to taxes was frequent enough, but it rarely focused on the question of consent.[46]

The apparent lack of interest in the principle *quod omnes tangit* during the age of the war subsidy requires an explanation. The taxpayers were not theorists, but they knew that collection of taxes, then as now, required their cooperation, a *de facto* consent that had nothing to do with legal theory. They were more interested in whether a true emergency existed, as they defined it. If it did, they did not quibble over the formalities of consent; if it did not, they resisted taxes on other grounds like precedent or privilege, which only an emergency could override. Kings who were scrupulous in observing the principle of *cessante causa* may have disarmed opposition, for they appeared to share their subjects' view of what circumstances justified extraordinary taxation.[47]

Perhaps a more important reason for this lack of emphasis on consent was that people perceived a distinction between this term and "counsel," in the feudal sense of advice. These two terms had different meanings in the thirteenth century,[48] and Philippe de Beaumanoir mentioned *conseil* in his writings, but not consent. In the first half of the fourteenth

---

[44]*Ibid.*, chap. V.

[45]For some of the bibliography on this principle, see *ibid.*, p. 23, note 57. See especially Post, *Studies*, pp. 113, note 96; p. 123, note 118: pp. 170–172, 209, 231–232.

[46]*RTF 1322–1356*, pp. 324–329.

[47]*Ibid.*, pp. 25–26, 325; Brown, "Cessante Causa," pp. 584–585.

[48]G. Langmuir, "Counsel and Capetian Assemblies," *Stud. Presented Int'l. Commission* 18 (1958): p. 28.

century, people still seem to have found the right to give consent much less meaningful than the duty to give counsel and the king's duty to request it.[49] With respect to taxes, to give counsel was to agree that a subsidy was justified, that an emergency existed, that the common profit was at stake, or that a proposed military venture was necessary. Consent, on the other hand, implied a binding commitment to a specific tax. Those whose rights were affected, or their fully empowered representatives, had to be informed of the tax and be given an opportunity to raise objections. Such consent did not imply a vote; it could be largely passive in nature, but it was supposed to bind those whose representatives consented.

For most of the age of the war subsidy, consent in this sense was obtained locally if it was obtained at all—generally at the level of town or *viguerie*. The system was inefficient, and there is evidence that the crown would have preferred to obtain definite grants of money from assemblies representing larger areas. In 1339 and 1340 the crown did obtain such grants from assemblies representing several bailiwicks, but intermittent truces slowed the development of such assemblies until after 1346. More years would pass before the pattern of locally negotiated taxes was really broken.[50] Central assemblies, later known as the Estates General, convened with some frequency in the early years of the century, but mainly to give counsel. When the king asked for representatives with full powers, these still declined to make commitments that their constituents considered binding, and the early Valois kings stopped demanding full powers. When assemblies in 1321 gave only *petit conseil* and declined to endorse a tax in peacetime, the crown abandoned the use of central assemblies for fiscal purposes for two decades.[51]

The most important period in the history of the French Estates General was the quarter-century beginning in 1343. In that year Philip VI sought a tax in commutation of the unpopular *monnayage* and called the Estates after advertising his proposal in advance. Most of the representatives consented to the scheme, but the towns who had instructed their proctors to refuse consent did not consider themselves bound by the

[49]*RTF 1322–1356*, p. 327.
[50]*Ibid.*, pp. 139–140, and chaps. VI–VIII.
[51]Taylor, "1321," pp. 218, 239, 243.

majority.[52] The Estates General met in separate sessions for Languedoil and Languedoc in 1346 and 1351, but since no royal proposal was advertised in advance, they merely gave counsel on the need for taxes. The Estates of the whole realm met in 1347 and did consent to a large subsidy in return for certain royal promises; important details, however, were left to subsequent local meetings. In 1355 the Estates not only consented to a specific subsidy but even assumed responsibility for its management. Unfortunately for both the royal budget and the future of representative assemblies, the work of the Estates of 1347 was nullified by the Black Death, while that of the assemblies of 1355–1356 was thwarted by the refusal of the populace to pay the taxes.[53]

In short, the kings had become discouraged from seeking consent from central assemblies, and when it was given it did not produce substantial taxes. Assemblies remained useful for giving counsel, but only those that were very local in nature were effective consenting bodies. The public inverted the legal theories, not insisting on the right to consent, but demanding that the king receive counsel if the justification of a tax was in doubt. For most of the age of the war subsidy, there were such doubts, because people defined the common profit in very local terms and associated it with a clash of armies. Localism of outlook and lack of interest in consent stunted the growth of central assemblies.

Despite the problems caused by localism, taxes did become more uniform in character after 1340. The sales tax of 4 d./l. was levied through most of Languedoil for six years or more, while the *gabelle* on salt, established in 1341, was collected throughout the realm until suppressed in 1346–1347. Local variations lasted longer in Languedoc, but the apportioned hearth tax (*fouage*) was a preferred method of paying.[54] Beginning in 1345, Philip VI proposed that the whole kingdom pay a tax computed in the salaries of men-at-arms. Each region would determine what form of tax to use in paying its share and would appoint the persons to collect it. This plan met with little enthusiasm at first, but it had real advantages. It divorced taxation from the cumbersome procedures of the

[52]*RTF 1322–1356*, pp. 172f.
[53]*Ibid.*, pp. 231f, 291f, and 328–329.
[54]*Ibid.*, chaps. V–VI.

arrière-ban while retaining the close connection between taxes and military necessity. It required royal subjects to act within a framework of national needs, but catered to local preferences as to form and administration of taxes and bypassed unpopular royal officials. It was this plan that the Estates General adopted late in 1347. The disruptive effects of the Black Death were unfortunate in their timing,[55] for the plan would not be revived until 1355. Following the plague, Languedoil reverted to the system of regular indirect taxes, now generally granted for a year at a time by assemblies of Estates at the bailiwick level. In Languedoc assemblies usually limited to town representatives met two or three times a year, granting small, short-term hearth taxes as the military situation dictated. These were apportioned among the seneschalsies on the basis of pre-plague enumerations of hearths.[56]

When the scheme for a nationwide grant of troops was revived in 1355, Frenchmen had gained valuable experience in these regional assemblies and knew how to bargain with the king and his officials. While the regional assemblies had increased the pretensions and self-confidence of the Estates, however, they had also reinforced local particularism, since they had dealt with all issues within a local or regional perspective. When the Estates of Languedoil tried to collect indirect taxes early in 1356 through a network of *élus* and *généraux*, the taxes were bitterly opposed and could not be collected until ratified by the more familiar and trusted local assemblies. A nationally coordinated grant of troops again proved unfeasible, this time because the Estates moved too far in the direction of centralization.[57] The actual taxes of 1356 reflected a discontent with the recent past. In Normandy, where indirect taxes had long been the rule, a hearth tax was tried. Languedoc abandoned the traditional *fouage* for a sales tax. The Estates of Languedoil withdrew their sales taxes in favor of a levy on incomes.[58] Given the French tradition of devotion to precedent and suspicion of novelties in taxation, this general rejection of traditional taxes is very striking. It

---

[55]*Ibid.*, pp. 182–238, 306. See also J. Henneman, "The Black Death and Royal Taxation in France, 1347–1351," *Speculum* 43 (1968): pp. 405–428.

[56]*RTF 1322–1356*, pp. 239–282.

[57]*Ibid.*, pp. 289f, 328–329.

[58]*Ibid.*, pp. 300, 310.

suggests that an era in royal finance was already coming to an end in early 1356. The king's capture in September brought the crisis to a head and ultimately determined the future course of taxation.

4. Political Factions and Governmental Reform

In comparing the political crisis of the later 1350's with that of the later 1340's, Raymond Cazelles has noted significant parallels. On both occasions, the crown was attacked for inefficiency and corruption. A purge of financial officers and a halt to coinage alterations were demanded. Reformers sought the leadership of a prince of the blood and expressed their will through the Estates General. These similarities are indeed striking, and all the more so since the Estates met at the beginning of December in both 1347 and 1355 and each time granted a large tax in men-at-arms, to be raised by *élus* who were not part of the regular royal administration.[59]

There also were differences between the late 1340's and the late 1350's. Representatives to the Estates were more experienced in the latter period and the military situation was different. The Estates of 1347 met in the aftermath of military defeat, while those of 1355 did not. The Estates of 1356 did follow a military disaster, but by that date they had spent ten months trying, without success, to produce taxes for which they had assumed responsibility. The recurrent failure of central assemblies to deliver adequate revenues was a factor that weighed heavily on the political events of the next two years. The most critical differences, however, between the late 1340's and the late 1350's, lay in the form taken by political dissent. Cazelles has argued that the clamor for reform in 1347 aligned itself behind the heir to the throne.[60] The future John II was then twenty-eight years old and a man of some experience. He was an ideal figurehead for a reforming movement because, through him, reformers could attack the government without attacking the dynasty.

---

[59] R. Cazelles, *La société politique et la crise de la royauté sous Philippe de Valois* (Paris, 1958), pp. 253-261, 427; Henneman, "Black Death," pp. 405, 427-428; J. Henneman, "The French Estates General and Reference Back to Local Constituents, 1343-1355," *Stud. Presented Int'l Commission* 39 (1970): pp. 44-51.

[60] Cazelles, *Soc. politique*, p. 214f.

In 1355 some of those who criticized the government attempted to follow the earlier precedent and use the king's son as a leader, but the Dauphin Charles was then only a teenager without political experience. Intrigues against the government, which involved him briefly, seem to have been engineered mainly by his older cousin and brother-in-law, Charles II of Navarre.[61] This prince—Charles "the Bad"—was an attractive young man with a strong claim to the throne and an influential following, but he nevertheless was a renegade. His murder of the constable, Charles of Spain, in 1354 had earned him the hatred of John II. His security subsequently depended on the continuation of Anglo-French hostilities, with the result that the rest of his career was marked by duplicity towards his friends and disruption of peace-making efforts. Despite his doubtful qualifications as a leader for a reforming movement, his incarceration by John II in April, 1356, won him considerable sympathy. For a time, at least, genuine reformers rallied to his cause with as much zeal as the malcontents and adventurers who were permanently attached to his party.[62]

There were various reasons for opposing the royal government in 1356. To understand the impact of this opposition on taxes, we must consider the interests and motives of the principal critics, and the changes that they demanded. Cazelles, the most careful student of political factions in the fourteenth century, writes of a "Navarrese party" which he defines very broadly as embracing everybody who sought changes in the government and aligned themselves with Charles the Bad while pursuing this end. The nucleus of this party consisted of (1) the Evreux family and those allied to it by marriage; (2) the families of both of John II's wives,

---

[61]*Ibid.*, pp. 258–259, blames this intrigue primarily on the bishop of Laon and doubts that Charles of Navarre was the central figure. The latter, however, received considerable blame, and the incident embittered his already difficult relations with John II: Avout, *Meurtre*, p. 48. Royal letters pardoning both the dauphin and the king of Navarre for their apparent conspiracy against the king have been published by Secousse, *Charles le Mauvais* 1: pp. 45–49.

[62]Cazelles, *Soc. politique*, p. 429; Cazelles, "Parti navarrais," pp. 852, 866. Among the strong critics of Charles the Bad are Denifle, *Désolation* 2: p. 172, and S. Luce, "Examen critique de l'ouvrage intitulé Etienne Marcel et le gouvernement de la bourgeoisie au XIVe siècle, par M. Perrens," *Bib. Ec. Chartes* 21 (1860): p. 279. Luce, *Du Guesclin*, p. 240, goes so far as to say that "One searches history in vain for a person more repulsive than Charles II, king of Navarre. . . . Charles the Bad was perfidy personified."

especially the house of Boulogne-Auvergne, which was connected by marriage to the Evreux and formed part of an
important pro-Navarrese element in the aristocracy of the
Massif Central; (3) a strong Norman group representing all
classes of society and including many connections of Raoul de
Brienne, the executed constable; (4) certain families of Champagne who believed that the descendents of Louis X were the
true heirs to the country; and (5) a large group of Picard
families, many of whom had opposed the crown during the
disputed succession in Artois some decades earlier and had
been given pensions by the Evreux family since the 1330's.[63]

Beyond these major centers of support, the "Navarrese
party" gained the temporary, and more limited allegiance of a
strong reforming movement in Languedoil. The members of
this group may perhaps be called the "true reformers," those
whose desire to change the character of the government grew
out of some sense of the kingdom's welfare and was less clearly
tied to family connections, personal grudges, or obvious self-
interest. It is not easy to isolate members of this group, since
some of them had connections with pro-Navarrese families or
stood to gain from the widespread ouster of existing fiscal
personnel. Cazelles seems insufficiently discriminating when
he labels as a reformer anyone who joined the government
when it was revamped in 1347–1348.[64] The impulse for reform
in the government had a long tradition going back to the
reign of Louis IX. A major objective of mid-fourteenth-
century reformers was to bring an end to the anarchy that
characterized the royal currency. Almost as pressing was a
broader issue, which Cazelles has underscored clearly—the
monarchie de structure encore domaniale, still geared to the
thirteenth century and no longer adequate to govern a large
realm in time of extended warfare.[65]

What, then, did the reformers wish to achieve? Again,
Cazelles suggests the answer: "a change in the methods of
government and finance and the maintenance of a certain
local autonomy."[66] If these words appear imprecise, it is
because this goal of the reformers was not put into any precise

---

[63]Cazelles, "Parti navarrais," pp. 839, 842–849.
[64]*Ibid.*, pp. 850–851. See below, at note 122.
[65]Cazelles, "Parti navarrais," p. 850.
[66]*Ibid.*, pp. 851–852. *Cf.* Contamine, *Guerre*, p. 74, for further insights into the
demands of reformers.

manifesto. What they had in mind, however, was probably a
plan like that adopted late in 1347, when the Estates obtained
changes in governmental personnel and a stabilization of the
coinage, and then granted a large subsidy. This tax, it will be
recalled, was based on the principle that the entire kingdom,
regardless of privileges, would contribute to the upkeep of an
army of specified size. Collections would be in the hands of
élus, rather than the overworked, obsolescent, and untrustworthy domainal administration. The form of tax, the nomi-
nation of the *élus*, and certain other details would be left to
individual regions. This plan was ruined by the Black Death,
but it seemed to represent that combination of updated
financial administration and local autonomy to which Cazelles refers. It also suggests that "bureaucratic decentralization" by which Russell Major has characterized the "Renaissance Monarchy" of Charles VII, when France embarked on a
period of regular taxes, stable coinage, and military success.[67]
In short, it does not seem reckless to assert that there was a true
reform program in the mid-fourteenth century and that much
of this program would, in time, become royal policy and
achieve some of the successes for which its advocates had
hoped.

Like most programs for reform, however, this one had to
surmount obstacles. Success depended on a combination of
favorable conditions. In 1347 the kingdom was chastened by
recent defeat but not yet decimated by plague. The nobles were
politically vulnerable but not yet gravely discredited. The
bourgeoisie was ready to support reform but not yet experienced or confident enough to make an aggressive bid for
leadership that might antagonize the nobles. The dissenters
found their leader in the mature son and heir of an aging
monarch, not a rival to the reigning dynasty. This apparently
favorable set of circumstances underscores once again the
decisive importance of the Black Death's timing.

When the next opportunity for reform presented itself in
1355, it was missed. The absence of a strong and trustworthy
figurehead to lead the reformers may have been a factor. The
absence of a recent military defeat may have prevented na-

[67] J. R. Major, "The Renaissance Monarchy: A Contribution to the Periodization of
History," *Emory University Quart.* 13 (1957): pp. 112–124; J. R. Major, *Representative Institutions in Renaissance France, 1421–1559* (Madison, 1960), pp. 3–7.

tional concerns from overcoming local ones. The widespread discontent with existing taxes made any large subsidy a difficult thing to impose. Above all, however, the need for catering to local sensibilities was greater than in 1347 and yet the Estates General failed to retain the crucially important decentralizing features of the subsidy of 1347-1348. Did the royal government, on grounds of speed and efficiency, talk them out of it? Or did the representatives themselves, more experienced and self-confident than eight years earlier, arrogantly assume that their constituents would support their actions? We shall probably never know.

The Estates which convened in October, 1356, after the battle of Poitiers were presented with still another opportunity for effecting the sort of program which reformers desired. This time, however, they had no king to deal with; they were too easily dominated by adventurers who pursued narrowly partisan interests; and they had to contend with a measure of class antagonism that would hinder unified action in the coming year.

Who made up the party of "true reformers"? It seems possible to point to three main groups: (1) the University of Paris; (2) the upper bourgeoisie; and (3) a miscellaneous group, mostly clerics but including some nobles who had been in royal service, men of experience who advocated reforms without anticipating any direct personal reward from changes in the personnel of the government. Many members of this last group were jurists, and they would be among the first defectors when the Navarrese party began making demands that put personal or partisan interest ahead of governmental reform. This group included the archbishops of Reims and Sens, and Philip VI's former chancellor Guillaume Flote.[68]

As to the role of the university in the crisis of the later 1350's, opinions have ranged from Perrens's claim that its members held Charles the Bad in high esteem, to Denifle's assertion that it was devoted to the dauphin.[69] Jourdain, eager to disassociate the university from the leaders of the Navarrese

---

[68] Cazelles, "Parti navarrais," pp. 857-859, 866-867; cf. Luce, "Examen critique," pp. 258-260.

[69] Ibid., p. 276; A. Coville, review of Denifle, Désolation, Le Moyen Age 13 (1900): p. 526.

party, went out of his way to stress its neutrality, and in the
process probably minimized its role too much.[70] One member
of the faculty of theology, Robert de Corbie, was one of the
king of Navarre's most avid Picard supporters.[71] As a whole,
the university would not profit from extremism, and its leaders
took care not to show signs of faction.[72] The faculty of arts, in
general, demonstrated more sympathy to the government,
while that of theology leaned towards Charles the Bad.[73] The
most influential reformer in the university was probably
Nicole Oresme who, in October, 1356, was confirmed as rector
of the Collège de Navarre, which enjoyed the special patron-
age of the house of Evreux. A Norman, who had studied since
1348 in this pro-Evreux college, Oresme may be counted a
member of the Navarrese party, albeit one of its more disinterested adherents.[74]

We have said that the upper bourgeoisie furnished the third
major component in the body of the "true reformers." The
role of this group, however, is very easily misinterpreted. It
would be a mistake to claim for the bourgeoisie a sweeping
plan for constitutional reform or a deep hatred for the
nobility. It is very unlikely that the most famous bourgeois
spokesman, Etienne Marcel, continuously reflected the prevailing views of the burghers of Languedoil. Marcel himself
was not a democratic leader, nor really a constitutional
reformer.[75] It is equally erroneous to describe him as a
Navarrese partisan before the end of 1357, but in his earlier
years he was motivated by jealousy and personal ambition as

---

[70] C. Jourdain, "L'université de Paris au temps d'Etienne Marcel," *Rev. Quest. hist.*
24 (1878): pp. 549–565; Cazelles, "Parti navarrais," pp. 860–861. Cazelles notes the
occasions on which the university attempted to mediate the political crisis of 1358.

[71] Jourdain, "Université," p. 549; Secousse, *Charles le Mauvais* 1: pp. 157–158.

[72] Jourdain, "Université," p. 554.

[73] Cazelles, "Parti navarrais," p. 860.

[74] *Ibid.,* pp. 861–862; Avout, *Meurtre,* p. 86.

[75] Balas, *Tentative,* p. 95, is generally sympathetic to Marcel, sees him as the effective
head of the bourgeoisie, but reproaches him for having been exploited by the
intrigues of others, presumably the king of Navarre and the bishop of Laon. Lot and
Fawtier, *Institutions* 2: p. 570, call him a constitutional leader, not a democratic one.
On the other hand, Paul Viollet, "Les Etats de Paris en fevrier 1358," *Memoires de
l'Académie des Inscriptions et Belles-Lettres* **34**, 2 (1895): pp. 261–262 referred to a
"great democratic movement," while J. Castelnau, "Etienne Marcel, a-t-il trahi?"
Revue des Deux Mondes 1956: p. 301, refers to a true bourgeois revolution. None of
these writers have interpreted Marcel's career accurately.

much as by principle.[76] What, then, are we to say about the bourgeois element in the reforming movement?

The wealthier bourgeois had long resented taxation, except when they perceived a clear case of necessity. In such cases, their concern was that privileged persons join in paying, and that the money be used efficiently to meet the crisis. Being inclined to define issues in local terms, they were sensitive to the needs of local defense. Long a target of royal fiscal officers and *réformateurs*, the municipal oligarchs distrusted the existing royal administration. Thus they were inclined to support a scheme like that of 1347–1348, which entrusted the collection of taxes for defense to locally appointed *élus*. They may have resented the nobles for engaging in brigandage or seeking to escape taxation, but their main resentment was directed at the king's officers. This resentment contained elements of envy, since royal service offered the bourgeois a chance for social prestige and perhaps a patent of nobility. Merchants who favored a stable coinage and the restoration of public order would be likely to attack corruption and seek to obtain the king's release.

Critics of the monarchy, like Marcel or the partisans of Charles the Bad, could count on widespread support from the bourgeoisie as long as they pursued, or appeared to pursue, these objectives. But once the burghers no longer perceived a common interest with the anti-government forces, they shrank from opposing the monarchy, which seemed to be the best guarantee of order and stability. It has been observed that the towns which showed the greatest and longest sympathy to the anti-Valois movement were those in the area dominated by the navigation of the Seine. This was precisely the region with the largest number of pro-Evreux nobles and some of the more strategic fortresses in Navarrese hands, and it was dominated economically by the hanse of the water merchants of Paris, led by Marcel.[77] Even in this area, however, the towns would gradually desert the opposition during 1358.

Even the best and most recent study of the crisis of the 1350's has preserved the tradition of earlier scholars when consider-

[76] On Marcel and the king of Navarre, see below, chapter II. For various opinions on this subject, *cf.* Balas, *Tentative*, p. 94; Delachenal, *Charles V* 2: p. 290; Cazelles, "Parti navarrais," pp. 852–853; Coville, review cited above, note 69, pp. 530–535.

[77] Cazelles, "Parti navarrais," pp. 853–854; Avout, *Meurtre*, p. 19.

ing the role of the bourgeoisie. It suggests the existence of a rather coherent bourgeois party, dominated by municipal oligarchs and looking to Marcel for leadership. Marcel, in turn, is credited with deriving much of his inspiration from the example of James van Artevelde in Flanders. He is said to have envisioned a restructuring of French politics in which the towns, armed with much-increased autonomy, would form a sort of federation under Parisian leadership, loyal to the crown but able to wield a significant corporate political influence independent of the nobles and clergy.[78] Some features of such a scheme might well have advanced the aspirations of reform-minded bourgeois, but one finds little convincing evidence that such a plan was really formulated or that Etienne Marcel ever commanded the kind of following that would permit it to be considered seriously.

It seems equally doubtful that the bourgeois reformers ever gave much thought to anything resembling what we should call a parliamentary regime. The Estates General were used, and at times rather aggressively, by the representatives of the towns in their efforts to bring about changes in the government. It was natural that they should make such use of these assemblies, given their experience with regional meetings in the earlier 1350's. Yet there is very little evidence that a permanent role for central assemblies was a major part of the reformers' program. Had these assemblies retained wide support from all three Estates and produced the taxes needed to complement their reforms, it is likely that they would have become too valuable to abandon. Yet in the months before Poitiers, the Estates had failed to meet these conditions, and the absence of the king made it even less likely that they would do so thereafter. In October, 1356, the Estates General were

---

[78]*Ibid.*, pp. 32–37, 45–47, for the changing role of the towns and Marcel's supposed interest in the Flemish example. Avout seems, in general, to follow Luce, "Examen critique," pp. 258–260, 266; and S. Luce, *Histoire de la Jacquerie*, (new edn., Paris, 1894), pp. 46–47, 123–124. As a cloth merchant, Marcel naturally had contact with the Flemings, and some of his correspondence with Flemish towns in the dark days of 1358 appealed to bourgeois solidarity, but I find no evidence that he or other bourgeois leaders envisioned a permanent role for the greater towns as a corporate group. A recent study has shown, moreover, that even in Flanders the towns showed no more than a passing interest in establishing permanent new political structures. They pursued limited, short-range objectives through traditional institutional means. See D. Nicholas. *Town and Countryside: Social, Economic, and Political Tensions in Fourteenth Century Flanders* (Bruges, 1971), concluding section, especially p. 348.

simply the device that lay at hand, the only apparent means through which any party—the government, the reformers, or the ambitious schemers—could pursue their objectives at this critical moment.

5. The Estates of Languedoil, October, 1356

The Estates of Languedoil had already planned to meet at the end of November in order to consider a renewal of the taxes granted a year earlier. En route to Paris from the field of Poitiers, the heir to the throne seems to have sent out orders for the Estates of the entire kingdom to convene at Paris earlier than scheduled.[79] This plan was soon modified, and the Estates of Languedoc were assembled separately by John of Armagnac, the royal lieutenant in the Midi. Those of Languedoil, summoned to Paris for mid-October, began their deliberations on the seventeenth.[80]

At the center of the gathering political storm was Charles of France, the eighteen-year-old duke of Normandy and dauphin of Viennois, eldest son of John II and Bona of Luxembourg. Later acclaimed as Charles the Wise, the future king was frail and inexperienced, and more inclined to intellectual pursuits than to feats of chivalry.[81] Such government as existed in Paris was in the hands of about thirty senior royal advisers, most of them unpopular financial officials.[82] Of the royal princes who survived the battle, the imprisoned Charles of Navarre was probably the most able. Given the absence of proven leadership, the reformers who forgot Charles the Bad's unsavory

---

[79]Avout, *Meurtre*, p. 53; Balas, *Tentative*, p. 12; *Chron. Jean II et Charles V* 1: pp. 74–75, and notes.

[80]*Ibid.*; A. Vuitry, *Etudes sur la régime financier de la France avant la Révolution de 1789, nouv. série* (2 v., Paris, 1878–1883) 2: p. 75.

[81]On the character of Charles, see Perroy, *Hundred Years War*, pp. 132–133, and Lewis, *Later Medieval France*, pp. 111–112. For a laudatory contemporary judgment see S. Solente (ed.), *Le livre des fais et bonnes meurs du sage roy Charles V, par Christine de Pisan* (2 v., Paris, 1936–1940). Christine's testimony is somewhat suspect. She made a good deal of Charles's supposed chivalric qualities (1: p. 116f), but was very discreet about his qualities as a young dauphin, confining herself to general remarks about youth and Christian upbringing (1: pp. 14–36). For the modern revisionist view of Charles and his father see R. Cazelles, "Jean II le Bon: quel homme? quel roi?" *Revue historique* 509 (1974): pp. 5–26.

[82]N. Valois, "Le gouvernement répresentatif en France au XIVe siècle," *Rev. quest. hist.* 37 (1885): p. 65.

past and called for his release may perhaps be excused for what hindsight brands as naiveté.

Of the various contemporary accounts describing the actions of the Estates General, three deserve particular attention, each of them being partisan in character. The official royal account was written by Pierre d'Orgemont, who later became chancellor of France.[83] A journal of unknown authorship is sympathetic to the leaders of the Estates.[84] A third account, clearly polemical in tone, seems to have been drawn up by some of the royal officers whose ouster was demanded by the assembly, and it takes the form of a bill of indictment against the principal spokesman for the Estates.[85]

We do not know how many of those who were present on 17 October had attended the Estates of December, 1355, although it is likely that a large number of them had done so. Nor do we know how many had previous experience in regional assemblies during the 1350's or had become familiar with the royal court by acting as litigants before the *Parlement*. Again, however, it is likely that many of those who were present had some experience of this kind. It would be especially interesting to know how many had been present at the Estates of the late 1347, but again we are uninformed. Because of the passage of time, the impact of the Black Death on the townsmen and clergy, and the impact of the battle of Poitiers on the nobility, it is likely that relatively few of those who were present in 1356 had been in Paris nine years earlier. It should be noted that corporate bodies like towns did not invariably send residents who would incur high travel expenses. Instead, they were inclined to name as deputies some of their citizens who for one

---

[83]Delachenal's edition of *Chron. Jean II et Charles V* is the best version of Orgemont's *Grandes Chroniques*. Avout, *Meurtre*, pp. 93–94, cautions us to use this work with care, since it is so detailed on some matters that each word has some significance and each omission some reason.

[84]R. Delachenal (ed.), *Journal des états généraux réunis à Paris au mois d'octobre 1356* (Paris, 1900).

[85]Douët d'Arcq (ed.), "Acte d'accusation contre Robert le Coq, évêque de Laon," *Bib. Ec. Chartes* 2 (1840–1841): pp. 350–383, with the actual text on pp. 365–383. These three main sources for the Estates, and particularly the "Acte d'accusation," have been analyzed by E. Faral, "Robert le Coq et les états généraux d'Octobre 1356," *Rev. hist. droit fr. et étr.*, sér. 4, 22 (1945): pp. 172–214. Faral believes the "Acte d'accusation" was drawn up late in January, 1357, by Simon de Bucy and Pierre de la Forêt (see below for a discussion of these men). Balas, *Tentative*, calls the "Acte d'accusation" an encounter between "immutable monarchical principles" and "new ideas" (p. 30) and dates it as early as November, 1356 (pp. 80–81).

reason or another already resided in Paris. An example is Robert de Corbie, a faculty member at the university, who represented his native town of Amiens.[86] If this practice was widely followed, it meant that such representatives were relatively more experienced in dealing with the government, were better informed about conditions in the capital, but were less informed of the changing views of their constituents. It also meant that an important nucleus of the urban representatives was still in Paris when the Estates were not in session.

When the Estates first assembled, a formal address by the chancellor, Pierre de la Forêt, was received with evident coldness, and the dauphin felt it necessary to add a brief speech of his own.[87] Following this ceremonial beginning, the assembly, which is said to have numbered some 800 persons, began its deliberations, naming a much smaller group to develop an agenda.[88] The size of this commission has been reported variously by the chroniclers. The estimates run from thirty-six to eighty persons, with modern historians largely disposed to accept the higher figure.[89] Of these persons, thirty-four names are known to us: the eleven prelates, six nobles, and seventeen town representatives whom the royal officers regarded as particularly hostile to the government.[90] A few of these may perhaps be assigned to the category of "true reformers," but most were hard-core supporters of the king of Navarre or, like the representatives from Paris, would soon become so. Paris had three representatives on the commission, while seven other urban deputies were from the Navarrese strongholds of Normandy and Picardy.[91]

---

[86] Cazelles, "Parti navarrais," pp. 858–859.

[87] Delachenal, *Charles V* 1: p. 251.

[88] *Journal des états*, pp. 18–19. Balas, *Tentative*, p. 77, describes the formation of this commission as a first attempt in France at representative government. His position is not convincing, however, because he does not deal with the legal principles of consent and representation as they were known in the fourteenth century.

[89] *Ibid.*, p. 45; Faral, "Robert le Coq," p. 200; Delachenal, *Charles V* 1: pp. 251–252 and notes.

[90] "Acte d'accusation," pp. 382–383.

[91] *Ibid.*; About, *Meurtre,* p. 58; Valois, "Gouvernement," pp. 87–94. The archbishop of Reims and the marshal of Champagne, as well as several other nobles named on this list, became supporters of the dauphin during the next year and may perhaps be called "true reformers" as opposed to Navarrese partisans. According to *Chron. Jean II et Charles V* 1: pp. 76–79, the early deliberations of the commission were attended by royal councillors, but these left after there were objections to their presence.

This commission spent two weeks, an unusually long time for the period, deliberating on the demands to be submitted to the crown by the Estates. In the end, three main proposals emerged. The first of these, dismissal of certain leading financial officers, could be assured of widespread support on various grounds. The second one, the release of Charles of Navarre, was justified on the ground that it would bring an end to the chaos in Normandy and halt the threat that Navarrese companies posed to Paris, but it was hardly calculated to facilitate real reform.[92] The final proposal called for the dauphin to appoint a "great and secret council" from members of the Estates, to consist of four clergy and twelve each from among the nobles and the bourgeoisie, or a total of twenty-eight persons.[93] Since the Estates contained many persons of high rank with experience in the royal government, this scheme was not so much a plan to turn the administration over to popular representatives as an effort to replace discredited royal advisers with persons more dedicated to reforming the government. The proposal had two implications, however, that must be kept in mind. First, it amounted to an attempt by a somewhat hostile assembly to dictate the composition of the royal council. Secondly, it offered the possibility that a new council composed in this way would be packed with supporters of Charles the Bad who would be more anti-Valois than pro-reform.[94]

The dauphin responded to these proposals by asking what subsidy the Estates would furnish in return. He was offered a tax which supposedly would support 30,000 men-at-arms for a year: the annual salary of one man for every hundred non-

---

[92] *Journal des états*, pp. 24–25; Faral, "Robert le Coq," pp. 189–202; Delachenal, *Charles V* 1: pp. 254–257, and notes; Balas, *Tentative*, p. 34 (suggesting that the release of Charles the Bad would not have been demanded if the dauphin had presented strongly the reasons against it); Avout, *Meurtre*, p. 61; Valois, "Gouvernement," pp. 70–74; Cazelles, "Parti navarrais," p. 867 (noting the hope that Charles the Bad would clear the Seine valley of *routiers*); and Fowler, *King's Lieutenant*, p. 157 (who points out that the imprisonment of Charles the Bad was all that kept his brother Philip firmly bound to Edward III).

[93] *Chron. Jean II et Charles V* 1: pp. 78–80; Delachenal, *Charles V* 1: pp. 257–258; Valois, "Gouvernement," pp. 74–76; Balas, *Tentative*, pp. 63–64, 85–86; Avout, *Meurtre*, p. 62.

[94] Luce, "Examen critique," p. 264, suggests that the dauphin was "incensed" by the "insolence" of the bourgeois members of the commission. Balas, *Tentative*, p. 77, seems to exaggerate in saying that the Estates had produced the essential elements of a modern parliamentary regime.

noble hearths and an income tax of 1½ tenths (15 per cent) on nobles and clergy. A number of princes urged Charles to accept this bargain, which was endorsed by the full assembly. The royal councillors, however, naturally opposed it since they would be its victims. They pointed out that the tax would not support 30,000 men, and here they were on strong ground, given the failure of other recent assemblies to deliver promised taxes.[95]

On 31 October the prince told a delegation of the Estates that he wished to defer an answer for several days while he conferred further with his advisers and considered letters which were expected from his father the king and his uncle the emperor. Perhaps he was skillfully buying time, hoping the representatives would weary of their long and costly sojourn in Paris. Perhaps he was merely showing the weakness and confusion of political immaturity in the face of conflicting advice. It seems pointless to speculate on the matter, for the really important fact was that Charles was neither king nor regent, but was merely acting as royal lieutenant, and he had no authority to conclude binding agreements with potential constitutional implications. Herein lay one of the critical obstacles to reform: in the absence of the king it is doubtful that any government at Paris could institute or approve changes that John II would regard as binding, unless they were part of an arrangement to secure his release and pay his ransom.[96]

To analyze some of the motives that were at play in the political maneuvering of late 1356, let us now consider a few specific individuals who were prominently involved: the seven royal officers whose disgrace was demanded by the spokesmen of the Estates on 31 October, and the eight members of the assembly who presented this demand. The seven royal officers included (1) Simon de Bucy, an obscure lawyer from the Paris bourgeoisie who had been ennobled in 1335 and had risen to be the first president of the *Parlement* despite a brief

---

[95]*Chron. Jean II et Charles V* 1: pp. 81–83; Delachenal, *Charles V* 1: pp. 258–259; Valois, "Gouvernement," p. 78.

[96]*Ibid.*; Delachenal, *Charles V* 1: 260–261; *Chron. Jean II et Charles V* 1: pp. 84–85; Avout, *Meurtre*, pp. 64–66; Luce, "Examen critique," p. 265. Viollet, "Etats," pp. 269–271, described a war party and a peace party. Most leaders of the Estates belonged to the former and were not especially anxious to secure the king's return.

disgrace for alleged corruption;[97] (2) Nicholas Braque, the ennobled son of a bourgeois of Paris, who had served two kings in various financial posts and who was, with his brother Amaury, particularly associated with the mint administration;[98] (3) Robert de Lorris, another Parisian who had risen from obscurity to nobility in the royal service, becoming John II's chamberlain, although briefly disgraced in 1354 for supposedly betraying royal interests;[99] (4) Enguerrand du Petit-Celier, bourgeois of Paris and a member of the Chamber of Accounts as early as 1340;[100] (5) Jean Poilevilain, bourgeois of Paris, member of the Chamber of Accounts, and master of mints, who had spent time in prison for "civil and criminal" offenses and had received his pardon by Philip VI just a year before being placed in charge of the royal currency;[101] (6) Jean Chauvel (or Chauveau), bourgeois of Chartres and war treasurer, brother of the treasurer of Normandy and of the late bishop of Chalon who had died at Poitiers;[102] (7) Pierre de la Forêt, scion of a noble family of Maine and long-time royal servant who had been John's chancellor of Normandy before becoming chancellor of France and, in 1351, archbishop of Rouen.[103]

Those who spoke for the Estates had all been members of the commission that formulated the assembly's requests, and all were numbered among the thirty-four who were regarded as most hostile to the government. They included (1) Raymond Saquet, a lawyer of southern origins, long-time royal servant, and now archbishop of Lyon;[104] (2) Jean de Craon, archbishop of Reims, who had not answered the king's

[97] Valois, "Gouvernement," pp. 66–67; Delachenal, *Charles V* 1: p. 254, note 3. On Bucy's career, see also H. Furgeot, *Actes du Parlement de Paris*, 2e sér. (2 v., Paris, 1920–1960) **2**: no. 8478; and Luce, *Jacquerie*, P.J., nos. 1, 54.

[98] N. Valois, "La revanche des frères Braque," *Memoires de la Société de l'Histoire de Paris* **10** (1883): pp. 101–111, and P.J. 3–5; Valois, "Gouvernement," p. 70; Delachenal, *Charles V* 1: p. 255, note 2.

[99] *Ibid.*, pp. 254–255, and note 1; Valois, "Gouvernement," pp. 67–69, 103–104; Fowler, *King's Lieutenant*, pp. 140–141.

[100] Valois, "Gouvernement," p. 69; Delachenal, *Charles V* 1: p. 255, and note 3.

[101] Prest, "Policy and Protest," p. 66; Avout, *Meurtre*, p. 93; Valois, "Gouvernement," p. 69; H. Fremaux. "La famille d'Etienne Marcel, 1250–1397," *Memoires de la Société de l'Histoire de Paris* **30** (1903): p. 195.

[102] Delachenal, *Charles V* 1: p. 255 and note 5.

[103] *Ibid.*, p. 254; *Chron. Jean II et Charles V* 3: P. J. 6 (this text being the announcement, in December, 1356, that La Forêt was being elevated to cardinal).

[104] Delachenal, *Charles V* 1: p. 260.

summons to the Poitiers campaign, and whose family was connected to other noble houses of the north and west;[105] (3) Robert le Coq, bishop of Laon and a Picard by origin, who had succeeded la Forêt as royal advocate in *Parlement* in 1347 but had been frustrated several times in his bid for ecclesiastical preferment;[106] (4) Waleran de Luxembourg, a relative of both the emperor and John II's first wife, who had served in royal armies but was linked to the Navarrese party;[107] (5) Jean de Conflans, marshal of Champagne, a noble with ties to the Evreux family and the late constable, Raoul de Brienne;[108] (6) Jean de Picquigny, a Picard noble whose father had served Philip VI but who was linked to the Evreux faction through marriage connections with the house of Boulogne and Raoul de Brienne;[109] (7) Etienne Marcel, provost of the merchants of Paris, member of a family of wealthy drapers and connected to other prominent families of the Parisian bourgeoisie, yet poorer than many of his relations and in-laws;[110] (8) Charles Toussac, *échevin* of Paris and a close political collaborator of Marcel's.[111]

These men were the principals in the drama that was about to unfold, and while it is unwise to make generalizations from a group of fifteen people, some of their careers deserve closer scrutiny. Nearly half of them had originated from the bourgeoisie of Paris—five of the seven royal officers and both the bourgeois spokesmen for the Estates. The ensuing political struggle was, in a sense, a conflict between elements of the upper bourgeoisie of Paris.[112] Those who had profited from royal favor and governmental service were attacked by those

---

[105]*Ibid.*; Avout, *Meurtre*, p. 60.

[106]On Le Coq, see below, notes 118–119.

[107]Delachenal, *Charles V* 1: p. 160; Cazelles, "Parti navarrais," pp. 843–844, 847.

[108]*Ibid.*, pp. 846–847; Delachenal, *Charles V* 1: p. 260.

[109]S. Honoré-Duvergé, "Des partisans de Charles le Mauvais: les Picquigny," *Bib. Ec. Chartes* 107 (1948): pp. 85–89; 92, note 1.

[110]R. Cazelles, "Etienne Marcel au sein de la Haute Bourgeoisie d'Affaires," *Journal des Savants* 1965: pp. 413–427; Fremaux, "Famille," pp. 179, 181, 185–186; Avout, *Meurtre*, p. 43.

[111]Delachenal, *Charles V* 1: p. 260. *Cf.* Secousse, *Charles le Mauvais* 1: pp. 128–130.

[112]The list of persons prominent in either camp could be enlarged to include the thirty-four opponents of the government named in "Acte d'Accusation," pp. 382–383 and the twenty-two royal officers dismissed in March, 1357 (*Ord.* 3: pp. 124–146, art. 11). This enlarged list includes additional members of important Parisian families. The presence of these Parisians in both camps has led most scholars to dismiss the idea that any significant class conflict was involved in the political struggle at this

who hitherto had been excluded, some of whom hoped, perhaps, to replace the incumbents in their lucrative positions.[113] We must not overlook the strong current of ambition that underlay the many demands for "reform."

On the other hand, it is equally clear that the royal officials who were under attack were not mere scapegoats or innocent victims of demogoguery. They were, for the most part, men of modest origins who had grown suspiciously prosperous in the king's service and had not always served the crown with the loyalty and gratitude that might have been expected of them. They were concerned mostly with the government's finances, which were believed to have been chronically mismanaged. Three of them—Bucy, Lorris, and Poilevilain—had been in trouble previously for serious misdeeds, while Braque and Poilevilain were associated with the coinage policies that reformers found particularly offensive.

Equally important is the fact that these embattled royal advisers had personal enemies among the men who now were attacking them in the name of reform. The celebrated Etienne Marcel was, in a sense, a typical bourgeois reformer, who deplored the failure of the king and nobles to defend the realm adequately, attacked corruption and waste, and supported the demand for a stable currency. Early in 1356 he had cooperated with the king and had sent Parisian troops against the Navarrese, but he felt that John broke a promise when he resumed coinage mutations in the summer. He may even have believed sincerely that the release of Charles the Bad would deliver his city from the menace of Navarrese men-at-arms.[114] The fact remains, however, that Marcel was a jealous and ambitious man who was determined to increase his wealth and power.

Jean Poilevilain, who had married one of Etienne Marcel's cousins and had enjoyed a successful career, was one target of his resentment. Marcel himself had contracted two advantageous marriages; his second wife was the daughter of Pierre

---

stage. See Cazelles, *Soc. politique*, 429; Balas, *Tentative*, p. 31, note 1; Valois, "Gouvernement," p. 73; A. Funk, "Robert le Coq and Etienne Marcel," *Speculum* 19 (1944): pp. 470–487.

[113] Cazelles, *Soc. politique*, pp. 427–429.

[114] Avout, *Meurtre*, pp. 55, 77, 85, 90, 95; Cazelles, "Parti navarrais," pp. 852–853, 867. See also Coville, review cited above, note 72, p. 534.

des Essars, a prosperous royal official. For a time, Essars appeared to be a dubious connection, for after the defeat at Crécy he fell into disgrace and purchased a royal pardon only by paying a large fine.[115] In 1350 he left an estate encumbered with debts, and Marcel and his wife prudently refused their share of the questionable inheritance. Another daughter of Essars had married Robert de Lorris, who already was well placed in the royal entourage. Lorris and his wife accepted their share of the Essars inheritance and later were able to gain the rehabilitation of Essars's memory and the restoration of much of the fine he had paid. His estate, of which the Marcels now had no share, was valuable once again, and Robert de Lorris was all the richer.[116]

Etienne Marcel, in short, presents the picture of a man who was able and yet overly cautious, ambitious, and yet frustrated in his ambitions. Jean Poilevilain, the husband of his cousin, and Robert de Lorris, the husband of his sister-in-law, had risen to wealth and power in the government. Marcel was excluded, whether by bad luck, bad judgment, stronger scruples, or insufficient skill at court politics. His road to power was to become *échevin*, then provost of the merchants, and to employ his position to manipulate the grievances and the expectations of those Parisians who, like himself, were not sharing in the material advantages of royal service.[117]

Marcel's position made him a formidable political figure whether or not the Estates were in session, but during the sessions of the assembly, he was generally eclipsed by the bitter eloquence of Robert le Coq, bishop of Laon and a staunch supporter of the Navarrese party.[118] Even more than Marcel, Le Coq had reason to resent the royal officers whom the Estates now marked for dismissal. Pierre de la Forêt had long been his rival for preferment. Failing at first to unseat him as royal advocate, Le Coq had secured this post at last in

---

[115] Cazelles, "Etienne Marcel," pp. 417–420; Prest, "Policy and Protest," p. 66. See also Avout, *Meurtre*, p. 43; Fremaux, "Famille," p. 205; and S. Luce, "Documents nouveaux sur Etienne Marcel," *Mémoires de la Société de l'Histoire de Paris* 6 (1879): p. 306.

[116] Cazelles, "Etienne Marcel," pp. 421f.

[117] Delachenal, *Charles V* 1: pp. 288–289.

[118] *Ibid.*, p. 253; Funk, "Robert le Coq," *passim*; Cazelles, "Parti navarrais," p. 850; Denifle, *Désolation* 2: p. 136; Luce, *Du Guesclin*, p. 244; Avout, *Meurtre*, pp. 57–59; Faral, "Robert le Coq," pp. 193f.

the personnel shuffle which the Estates had engineered at the end of 1347. Simon de Bucy was another of his enemies, having allegedly spread malicious rumors in an attempt to frustrate his appointment as bishop of Laon. Le Coq also disliked Jean Chauvel, whose late brother Regnaut had been his rival for the post at Laon. Regnaut had been protected by Charles of Spain, thereby adding the late constable to the list of the bishop's enemies.[119]

His hostility to Charles of Spain drew Le Coq into the camp of Charles the Bad, who was responsible for the constable's assassination. Although a prisoner from April, 1356, until the fall of 1357, the king of Navarre has been called, with reason, the "true agitator" against the government during the months of his captivity.[120] Three royal advisers whom he hated were Pierre de la Forêt, Simon de Bucy, and Regnaut Chauvel, all of them enemies of Robert le Coq.[121] Cazelles has associated Le Coq with Charles in the attempt to induce the dauphin, late in 1355, to seek the emperor's aid in a conspiracy against the king.[122] Common enemies and self-interest brought them together, and the bishop of Laon's oratory quickly made him the most visible of the Navarrese partisans in the Estates, the one person whom the dauphin would never agree to pardon.[123]

Although it is hard to disagree with Luce's description of Charles the Bad as "perfidy personified,"[124] the king of Navarre remains a somewhat mysterious and even tragic figure in the tangled French politics of the mid-fourteenth century. His claim to the throne may well have been better than anyone else's, and he seems to have been a young man of ability, charm, and kingly bearing, well marked for success in a world of chivalric tastes. We cannot dismiss him as an insignificant

---

[119] On Le Coq's early career, see *ibid.*, pp. 180–189; and Cazelles, *Soc. politique,* pp. 255f. On his enemies, see also Delachenal, *Charles V* 1: pp. 252–253; "Acte d'accusation," p. 366; and S. Luce (ed.), *Chronique des quatre premiers Valois (1327–1393)* (Paris, 1862), p. 57.

[120] Delachenal, *Charles V* 1: p. 253.

[121] *Ibid.*, note 2, quoting a text from the Vatican archives.

[122] Cazelles, *Soc. politique,* pp. 259–261.

[123] On the refusal to pardon Le Coq, see below, chap. III, at note 25. Cazelles, "Parti navarrais," pp. 854–857, reminds us that Le Coq was not, however, the only clerical supporter of Charles the Bad, or even the earliest one.

[124] Luce, *Du Guesclin,* p. 240.

figure who was trapped between the superior resources of the French and English monarchies. As Cazelles has suggested, his support was so widespread that he ought to have triumphed over the captive king and inexperienced dauphin.[125] Yet Charles the Bad suffered from a fatal defect in character and personality. His celebrated perfidy was only part of it; after all, the skillful use of treachery often proved successful to the princes of the Renaissance. What Charles really lacked was that sense of the greatness and sacred majesty of French kingship which had characterized the most successful and revered Capetian monarchs and formed one of the most basic assumptions of the future Charles V. Little interested in genuine reform, the king of Navarre proved unable to deliver the Ile-de-France from the brigandage of the soldiers who fought in his name.[126] He showed no interest in an Anglo-French peace, but worked to circumvent it for the sake of his own security. He pursued the limited goal of short-term territorial aggrandisement, and felt that John II should be prepared to grant him lands instead of giving them to Edward III, conveniently forgetting that John was Edward's captive. In the end, Charles alienated or ruined those who supported him, and no program of reform could hope to succeed as long as it was associated with him.[127]

It should now be clear that the issues raised at the Estates of October, 1356, involved a complex mixture of personalities and principles. It is doubtful that the dauphin fully understood these factors as he pondered the demands of the assembly. Needing more time, and still uncertain of opinion in the provinces, he rejected the proposals, declared the Estates disbanded, and left Paris.[128] Many representatives obeyed the order to return home, but those who were not prepared to accept dismissal remained in Paris and convened illegally on 3 November.[129] This reduced assembly listened to a long and fiery speech by Robert le Coq, who repeated and sought to justify the earlier demands. He reaffirmed the offer of the

---

[125] Cazelles, "Parti navarrais," p. 862.

[126] *Ibid.*, p. 867.

[127] *Ibid.*, pp. 862–863, 869; *cf.* Valois, "Gouvernement," p. 72; Balas, *Tentative*, p. 67: and citations note 65, above.

[128] *Chron. Jean II et Charles V* 1: pp. 87–88.

[129] *Ibid.*, pp. 88–89; Balas, *Tentative*, pp. 80–81, 85; Avout, *Meurtre*, p. 67.

subsidy and sought to refute the arguments of the king's men against the assembly's program. Above all, he attacked the government and its officers for all the abuses, real or imagined, that Frenchmen found hateful in the aftermath of defeat: excessive taxes and wasted revenues, failure to shore up the kingdom's defenses, constant manipulation of the currency, and dishonesty of officials.[130] These were not extemporaneous comments; Le Coq was summarizing the results of two weeks of discussion. Some of his demands were to be enacted later, but for the present the Estates were powerless, and the initiative had passed to the dauphin.

[130]*Ibid.*, pp. 59, 68, 73–76; *Journal des états*, pp. 28–46; *Chron. Jean II et Charles V* 1: pp. 88–89; Funk, "Robert le Coq"; Balas, *Tentative*, pp. 86–87.

II. The Dauphin and The Estates: Languedoil, 1356–1358

1. *The Estates and Reform: The Final Opportunity*

Having declared the Estates dissolved, the dauphin faced two immediate problems. The most obvious and pressing was the need for money. The second was the need for political support, or what feudal society would describe as "good counsel." In his search for money, the youthful prince took two measures, both of which were hallowed by tradition. He made an effort to negotiate subsidies locally, bypassing the hostile Estates, and he ordered a new alteration of the coinage.[1] To obtain political advice and backing, he turned to the emperor, Charles IV, who had some serious outstanding differences with the French government and with the dauphin himself, but who was in a position to offer valuable moral and material support in return for the resolution of these differences.[2]

A contemporary chronicler charged the dauphin with neglect of duty for leaving to visit Metz in this time of crisis,[3] while the splendor of his entourage seemed only to confirm the impression that the court was needlessly luxurious.[4] Yet the trip to confer with Charles IV proved profitable to France in the long run. Notwithstanding the house of Luxembourg's traditional friendship towards France, Charles had not been a pro-French emperor. In 1347 he had made a treaty of friendship with the future John II and his four sons, but within a year he had reached an agreement with England promising official neutrality in the Anglo-French war while letting

---

[1] Vuitry, *Régime financier* 2: p. 76; Delachenal, *Charles V* 1: p. 291. Balas, *Tentative*, p. 105.
[2] Delachenal, *Charles V* 1: pp. 268–271.
[3] *Venette*, p. 65.
[4] Avout, *Meurtre*, p. 79.

Edward III recruit soldiers in the empire.[5] Thereafter, his
relations with the Valois were strained by a continuing French
encroachment on imperial territory.[6] With full-scale hostilities about to resume with England in the spring of 1355, John
II had sent an embassy to Charles IV. France made enough
concessions to head off a possible Anglo-Imperial alliance,
but the emperor showed no willingness to support the
French,[7] and at the end of the year those who plotted against
John II still hoped to enlist the aid of Charles IV.[8] Late in
1356 Charles planned to convene the imperial diet at Metz and
complete the implementation of his Golden Bull. With the
French king now a captive, Innocent VI launched a strenuous
peace offensive which was based on the hope that the emperor
could act as an arbiter in the Hundred Years' War.[9]

There were, in short, good reasons why the dauphin should
travel to Metz at this time. At best, he could hope to resolve
outstanding Franco-Imperial differences and obtain a revival
of the short-lived alliance of 1347. Failing that, he could at
least participate with the emperor and papal legates in
formulating proposals for a peace that would expedite John
II's release from captivity. So it was that the young Charles left
for Metz with a large entourage on 5 December, 1356, arriving
there on the twenty-second. He quickly confirmed earlier
French promises, performed homage for Dauphiné, acknowledged imperial suzerainty over the county of Burgundy, and
promised the emperor a gift of 50,000 florins. In return, he was
invested with Dauphiné and obtained a new treaty of friendship with the emperor. The agreement did not turn Charles IV
into a French ally, but it assured his benevolent neutrality and
enabled France, rather than England, to recruit mercenary

---

[5] Luce, *Du Guesclin*, p. 233, note 1; Delachenal, *Charles V* 1: p. 269; 3: pp. 208, 230
(on the emperor's continuing coolness towards France); A. Leroux, *Recherches
critiques sur les relations de la France avec l'Allemagne de 1292 à 1378* (Paris, 1882),
pp. 244–246.

[6] *Ibid.*, p. 248.

[7] *Ibid.*, pp. 254–255; Fowler, *King's Lieutenant*, p. 146.

[8] See above, chap. I, notes 61, 122.

[9] Luce, *Du Guesclin*, p. 235; Leroux, *Recherches*, pp. 261–262; Denifle, *Désolation*
2: pp. 140–143, 146, and notes showing considerable papal correspondence. See also
N. Zacour, "Talleyrand: The Cardinal of Périgord (1301–1364)," *Trans. Amer.
Philos. Soc.* **50**, 7 (1960): p. 54 and notes; and Delachenal, *Charles V* 1: p. 274f.

troops in the empire.[10] At the same time, it dealt a blow to the peacemaking efforts of the pontifical court, for Charles IV was no longer in a position to offer his arbitration in the Anglo-French war.[11]

Having achieved success in his first essay at foreign policy, the dauphin left for home before the end of the year, arriving at Paris on 14 January to discover that his domestic measures had failed.[12] Their goal had been to obtain desperately needed revenues in Languedoil without having to grant the three conditions which the Estates General had demanded. There was every reason to try the time-honored technique of local negotiations, since recent experience had shown that individual localities were able to deliver taxes, whereas the Estates General so far had been unable to do so.

The documentation, such as it is, comes almost exclusively from regions identified as strongholds of the anti-government forces: Normandy, Picardy, and the Massif Central.[13] In Normandy the dauphin's own *apanage,* a full-scale war was in progress, as the strong Navarrese faction was assisted by troops who were, or had been, in English employ. Militarily, the French did not fare badly. The duke of Lancaster let himself be immobilized in Brittany by a long and costly siege of Rennes. From the French-held stronghold of Pontorson on the Norman-Breton border, forces led by an anti-English Breton captain, Bertrand du Guesclin, managed to harass Lancaster's army.[14] In lower Normandy, the dauphin's marshal, Robert de Clermont, invaded Anglo-Navarrese territory, and while the campaign did not achieve important military results, Godefroy d'Harcourt was killed in battle.[15]

Even when it favored the Valois cause, however, this military activity was not conducive to the collection of subsidies. Numerous receipts and pay orders indicate taxation in

---

[10]*Ibid.,* pp. 275–276, 279–281; Leroux, *Recherches,* p. 265. Luce, *Du Guesclin,* P.J. 10, has published the treaty, but as Delachenal points out (*op. cit.* 1: p. 280, note 7), he has incorrectly dated it 1357.

[11]Leroux, *Recherches,* p. 265.

[12]Delachenal, *Charles V* 1: p. 282.

[13]See above, chap. I, at note 63.

[14]Luce, *Du Guesclin,* pp. 185–195; Fowler, *King's Lieutenant,* pp. 158–164; Denifle, *Désolation* 2: p. 144.

[15]*Chron. Jean II et Charles V* 1: pp. 90–91; Delisle, *St. Sauveur,* pp. 91–93, 95–99, 142–143; Denifle, *Désolation* 2: p. 144; Luce, *Du Guesclin,* p. 262.

Normandy during 1356, but these diminish sharply in number after the battle of Poitiers and all seem to refer to taxes granted much earlier in the year.[16] The only such document after early November is a receipt dated 3 January, 1357, which refers to the hearth tax of 10 *sols* granted in the duchy more than six months earlier.[17] Although the crown obtained no new subsidies in Normandy, the military struggle still made demands on Norman resources. At Rouen, for instance, a special levy of 2½ *sols* per hearth was needed in order to raise 4000 *moutons* with which to ransom a local fortress captured by the enemy.[18] Other documents from northern France deal with municipal taxes established for local defense,[19] but one finds little evidence of the numerous provincial assemblies which the dauphin is said to have convened towards the end of the year.[20] It is reported that the Estates of Vermandois and Beauvaisis met late in January, 1357, and finally granted a very small tax, but by this time a new central assembly was on the point of meeting.[21]

Our only well-documented example of provincial Estates at work late in 1356 comes from Auvergne. The Auvergnats had paid the taxes authorized by the Estates General in 1355–1356, but only after local ratification and subject to the proviso that the money not be taken outside their region.[22] Frightened by the advance of the Prince of Wales, Auvergne had supple-

---

[16] For documents belonging to the months before the battle of Poitiers, see *RTF 1322–1356*, p. 300, notes 201–203. Those for the later months of 1356 include BN MS. fr. 26001, nos. 663, 672, 674, 688; BN Clairambault 213, nos. 69–71, 74, 75.

[17] BN P.O. 1522, *dossier* 34634, no. 9.

[18] BN NAF 7609, fol. 359.

[19] E. Le Maire (ed.), *Archives anciennes de la ville de Saint-Quentin* (2 v., Saint-Quentin, 1888–1910) 2: no. 668; A. Guesnon (ed.), *Inventaire chronologique de chartes de la ville d' Arras* (Arras, 1862), pp. 119–120.

[20] G. Picot, *Histoire des états-généraux, considerés au point de vue de leur influence sur le gouvernement de la France de 1355 à 1614* (5 v., Paris, 1872) 1: p. 59.

[21] V. de Beauvillé, *Histoire de la ville de Montdidier* (2nd ed., Paris, 1875), p. 109, describes an assembly of the three orders of Vermandois, Beauvaisis, and Corbie, held at Roye to deliberate with the dauphin on the defense of the country. The meeting apparently reached no conclusion, for it was followed by a new assembly at Noyon, where eight of the fourteen towns represented agreed to a small tax of 1 d./1. (less than 1 per cent) on certain products which had not been taxed formerly.

[22] D. F. Secousse, introduction to *Ord.* 3: p. lx. This scholar's discussion of the subsidy in Auvergne is supplemented and modified in some respects by BN MS. lat. 17714, which has been published in part and analysed by E. Ledos, "L'imposition d'Auvergne en janvier, 1357," *Mélanges Julien Havet* (Paris, 1895), pp. 429–450.

mented these taxes with a new grant of men-at-arms in September, 1356.[23] Troops were still being paid from the proceeds of this grant in mid-December,[24] when the government asked a new assembly of towns for a *fouage*. On the thirteenth, the urban representatives agreed to support one man-at-arms per 100 hearths, essentially the same tax already offered by the Estates General of Languedoil.[25]

Having secured this offer from the towns, the dauphin's commissioner convened all three Estates of the region to an assembly which opened at Clermont on 29 December. Like the assembly at Paris two months earlier, this body chose a committee to work out recommendations: six men from each Estate, later increased to seven. The 21-member commission deliberated in the bailiff's presence. Its recommendations were accepted subsequently by the full Estates and the representatives of the dauphin, subject, however, to the latter's ratification. Quite clearly, this assembly was concerned primarily with regional defense, not governmental reform. The Estates authorized a force of 400 *glaives* [26] for the defense of Auvergne and asked that the royal lieutenant in the region, Jean de Boulogne, act as captain of the troops and organize the defense with the aid of six *élus* of the Estates. For non-nobles the principle of one soldier's salary for so many hearths was retained. The nobles and clergy would pay 7½ per cent of their revenues. Aside from the fact that Jean de Boulogne has been linked with the Navarrese party, one finds little trace of political intrigue in the Estates of Auvergne.[27] On the other hand, while they displayed no revolutionary fervor, they were sensitive only to the needs of their own defense and showed no disposition to relieve the central government of its financial embarrassment.

Without documentation, we cannot speculate as to the action of provincial assemblies elsewhere. It is said that

---

[23] *INV AM Montferrand* 1: p. 393 (CC 166).

[24] BN Clairambault 213, no. 73.

[25] *INV AM Montferrand* 1: p. 394 (CC 166).

[26] The *glaive*, actually the metal spearhead of a mounted warrior's lance, came to be one of the synonyms for a mounted man-at-arms. See Fowler, *Plantagenet and Valois*, p. 107.

[27] BN Clairambault 213, nos. 87, 88; BN MS. fr. 22295, no. 2; BN MS. fr. 26001, no. 502; *INV AM Montferrand* 1: p. 394 (CC 166); Secousse, introduction to *Ord.* 3: p. lxi; Vuitry, *Régime financier* 2: pp. 76–79; Ledos, "Imposition," pp. 430–432, 442–450.

Robert le Coq and other leaders of the Estates General had informed the provinces of their demands in the hope of creating some solidarity against any effort on the part of the dauphin to obtain taxes locally and bypass the central assembly.[28] Perhaps such propaganda prevented the government from gaining the taxes it desired; perhaps the local regions were too worried about their own defense to conceive of taxation in national terms. In any case, the dauphin's financial problems were not solved by recourse to regional negotiations.

There remained the coinage, which had served the crown as a source of emergency funds at other times of crisis. On the eve of his departure for Metz, the dauphin had ordered a new currency, this one actually strengthening the alloy by placing the money on the 48th *pied*.[29] The change proved very unpopular, however. It offended those reformers who questioned the royal right to manipulate the coinage at will, and it irritated those who were suspicious of any governmental effort to raise money without recourse to the Estates. The merchants of Paris may have objected to the new money on both these grounds. In any case, they reacted with hostility under the leadership of their provost and with the support of many poorer Parisians. While the dauphin was en route to Metz, John II, a captive at Bordeaux, dispatched a letter to Etienne Marcel on 12 December, thanking him and the Parisians for their support of the dauphin and their efforts to obtain the king's release. Perhaps John was trying to practice some diplomacy which might keep Marcel separate from the Navarrese clique and induce him to work for reform through cooperation with the crown. Whatever the letter's intention, however, it must have reinforced Marcel's self-esteem and sense of mission.[30]

The change in currency was announced several days after the dauphin had left for Metz, in accordance with a decree prepared a fortnight earlier in still another violation of the ordinance of late 1355. An uprising by the Parisians forced the

---

[28] Lot and Fawtier, *Institutions* 2: p. 565.

[29] Bridrey, *Théorie*, pp. 485–488; Prest, "Policy and Protest," pp. 131f; H. Miskimin, *Money, Prices, and Foreign Exchange in Fourteenth Century France* (New Haven, 1963), p. 177.

[30] Avout, *Meurtre*, p. 88.

government to suspend the measure. Soon after the dauphin returned to the capital, Marcel led a massive demonstration which made it clear to Charles that he was beaten. The coinage mutation was now out of the question, and on 22 January, 1357, the dauphin ordered the Estates General to reconvene at Paris in two weeks' time.[31] The royal officers whom the Estates had marked for dismissal now began to slip away from Paris.[32] Twice in two months the Parisians had taken to the streets and forced their will on the government, first obtaining suspension of the new coinage and then compelling the dauphin to recall the Estates. Thus although the young prince had gained some time and experience and had reached a beneficial accord with the emperor, he was in a weaker position than ever in dealing with the Estates.[33]

The Estates, however, were also weaker. When the assembly met on 5 February, several of the great fiefs and *apanages* were unrepresented, and many nobles who had been at Paris four months earlier did not return. Some of the deputies who stayed at home must have done so out of a reluctance to make another costly trip. Localism, conservatism, lack of support from constituents at home, and suspicion of the more vocal opponents of the monarchy were doubtless other factors in the smaller attendance.[34] The new assembly seems to have contained a greater percentage of bourgeois than its predecessor. What is much less clear is the relative strength of the "true reformers" and the hard core Navarrese partisans. From the ordinance that followed this assembly, it would appear that the former had gained appreciably in strength, as if Le Coq and his associates had overplayed their hand in October and had lost support. One finds no further question of releasing

[31]*Chron. Jean II et Charles V* 1: pp. 92–99; Prest, "Policy and Protest," pp. 131–133; Balas, *Tentative*, p. 93; Delachenal, *Charles V* 1: p. 295.

[32]*Ibid.*, p. 297; *Chron. Jean II et Charles V* 1: p. 99. Scarcely had the officials left than sergeants were sent to occupy their houses and inventory their possessions. See Valois, "Gouvernement," pp. 79–80.

[33]Picot, *Etats* 1: pp. 62–63, describing this crisis, called it a "striking example of concessions made too late."

[34]*Ibid.*, p. 63; Delachenal, *Charles V* 1: p. 299. Lot and Fawtier, *Institutions* 2: p. 566, claim that the Estates reassembled after having received the approval of their local constituents. Avout, *Meurtre*, p. 97, whose analysis seems much more satisfactory, suggests that disapproval by constituents was one of the reasons why attendance at this assembly was reduced from that of the preceding fall. See also Balas, *Tentative*, pp. 110–112.

Charles the Bad, and relatively few Navarrese sympathizers admitted to the royal council. Yet the Estates obtained a long and detailed list of reforms aiming at a more stable currency and a more honest and efficient governmental administration. A desire for genuine reform and a hostility to existing officials apparently prevailed, while there was little disposition to advance the cause of the Evreux family at the expense of the Valois.[35]

Avout has suggested an explanation for this behavior of the Estates. He argues that Marcel, who as yet had no great interest in the Navarrese cause, made a deal with the dauphin, whereby the ouster of unpopular officials and reform of the government and coinage would be exchanged for a subsidy, while the other demands of the earlier assembly would be dropped. In support of this thesis, Avout invokes a papal letter to Marcel on 10 February, applauding the accord he had reached with the dauphin and asking him to be tolerant of the prince's youth and work to eliminate their remaining disagreements.[36] Despite the vagueness of the letter, this explanation has some plausibility, but it presupposes that Marcel had a considerable influence over the Estates, or at least the bourgeois majority. It is far from certain that Marcel had such an influence, but the Estates may well have deemed it wise to work closely with the dissident burghers of the capital now that they were losing the backing of the aristocracy.

Assembling as scheduled on 5 February, the Estates remained in Paris for about four weeks and were still in session on 3 March, when they were treated to another oration from Robert le Coq.[37] The bishop of Laon evidently enumerated demands that became the provisions of a "Grand Ordinance" soon to be issued in the dauphin's name.

One of the longest ordinances of reform to be promulgated in France during the fourteenth century, the Grand Ordinance contained sixty-one articles. A third of these repeated provi-

---

[35] Avout, *Meurtre*, pp. 100–104. Delachenal, *Charles V* 1: p. 305, seems to ignore the fact that the assembly of February 1357 made no more mention of Charles the Bad's release.

[36] Avout, *Meurtre*, pp. 95, 104. The text has been published in Denifle, *Désolation* 2: p. 138, note 2; and *Chron. Jean II et Charles V* 3: P.J. 8.

[37] *Chron. Jean II et Charles V* 2: pp. 100–107; Delachenal, *Charles V* 1: pp. 299–301; Denofle, *Désolation* 2: p. 139, note 1; Avout, *Meurtre*, pp. 100–101.

sions of the ordinance of late 1355, and several other articles
were taken directly from the list of demands presented to the
Estates by Le Coq in November.[38] In its emphasis, this
document differed sharply from Philip IV's ordinance of 1303
which was reissued on so many subsequent occasions.[39] The
earlier enactment was aimed primarily at checking the tyranny of the crown and its officers, and protecting seigneurial
rights against their encroachment. The new ordinance reflected entirely different sentiments and represented the culmi-
nation of a trend which had been developing since the defeat
at Crécy. Frenchmen no longer feared the tyranny of a strong
and ruthless government, but rather the incompetence of a
weak one. The Grand Ordinance established rules about
salaries of officers, required them to be at work by sunrise and
deal with public business in the order of urgency, prohibited
the delegation of power to unqualified subordinates, and
generally enacted measures calculated to improve the economy and efficiency of government.[40]

The purge of unpopular officials which had been demanded
in the fall of 1356 was now extended to include twenty-two
names. As before, a significant proportion of these had originated among the bourgeoisie of Paris, and we need not doubt
that personal jealousies and animosities played a role in their
ouster.[41] Yet it is equally certain that these wealthy *parvenus*
were widely blamed, and with reason, for the corruption and
inefficiency which bourgeois reformers found so offensive. At

---

[38]*Ord.* 3: pp. 124–146. For discussion of this document, see Picot, *Etats* 1: p. 87; and
Vuitry, *Régime financier* 2: pp. 79–80. At least twenty provisions (arts. 2–5, 15–17,
22–25, 28, 29, 31, 32, 35, 37, 38, 40, and 50) were taken directly from the ordinance of
late 1355 (*Ord.* 3: p. 19f). At least four (arts. 42, 44, 46, and 49) embodied new
proposals made by Le Coq in November 1356 (*Journal des états*). Several other
provisions were derived less directly from one or both of these two sources. Picot, *loc.
cit.*, attributed too many of the provisions to Le Coq's November speech and gave
insufficient credit to the precedents of 1355, but he seems right in saying that twenty-
three provisions (arts. 1, 6–9, 12, 18, 19, 26, 27, 30, 33, 34, 36, and 52–61) were
attributable to neither of these sources and therefore probably were drawn up by the
Estates in February.

[39]*Ord.* 1: pp. 354–367. For the reissues of this famous ordinance, one of which
occurred in 1357, see R. Cazelles, "Une exigence de l'opinion depuis Saint Louis: La
réformation du royaume," *Ann. Bull. Soc. Hist. Fr.* 1962–1963: p. 92.

[40]*Ord.* 3: pp. 124–146. One may place 70 per cent of the entire ordinance in this
category (arts. 6–10, 12–14, 16–31, 36, 40, 42–49, 53–60).

[41]*Ibid.*, art 11. See above, chap. I, at notes 112–122.

the behest of the Estates, a general review of all royal officers was ordered, and it is symptomatic of the new outlook that the *enquêteur-réformateur* was reinstituted as an agent of genuine reform. Royal use of these commissioners as fiscal agents had so impaired their popularity that by the end of Philip VI's reign people were asking that they not be used.[42] Now, however, a board of nine *généraux-réformateurs* was established for the purpose originally envisioned by St. Louis—the hearing of complaints against royal officers.[43]

This concern with honest, economical, and efficient government rather than the protection of rights against royal tyranny makes it doubtful that the ordinance of 1357 should be regarded as an attempt at constitutional change. To be sure, there were a number of provisions with potential constitutional implications. No alterations of the coinage were to be made without the consent of the Estates. The Estates were to meet again in April and twice more during the year. No truce was to be concluded without the counsel of the three Estates.[44] In addition, a certain number of new councillors, favored by the assembly, were to replace those who had been ousted. Unlike previous assemblies, this one did affirm explicitly the right of consent, but this right was asserted only in connection with changes in the *pied de monnaie*. It was merely a question of taking another principle from Oresme's treatise, enlarging on what had already been said in the ordinance of 1355, when the Estates had first made use of Oresme's ideas.[45] The effect on the royal prerogative as a whole cannot have been great. The stipulation on making truces seems more significant at first glance, but kings had long been expected to take counsel on

---

[42] See Henneman, "Enquêteurs," *passim*.

[43] See Denifle, *Désolation* 2: p. 139 and note 1; BN MS. fr. 25701, no. 134; Avout, *Meurtre*, p. 111; Valois, "Gouvernement," pp. 98–99. A majority of the *généraux-réformateurs* were clerics, and moderate reformers seem to have predominated, despite the presence of a few anti-government zealots. As will be seen below, their subordinates in the field soon gave evidence of being less moderate.

[44] *Ord.* 3: pp. 124–146, arts. 1, 4, 5, 15, and 39, can be called the provisions with constitutional implications. Balas, *Tentative*, p. 117, says that the Estates had become the effective masters of the government, but he neglects the more important fact that they devised no machinery for maintaining such mastery. See also *ibid.*, p. 119, and Delachenal, *Charles V* 1: pp. 302–303.

[45] *Ord.* 3: pp. 124–146, art. 15; Avout, *Meurtre*, p. 105; Bridrey, *Théorie*, pp. 280f and 489f; Prest, "Policy and Protest," pp. 132–134. In effect, Oresme had argued that the currency could be altered only with the consent of the public in time of necessity.

matters of war and peace (consent was not demanded). This provision actually was a concession to the Navarrese party, which would be left in a vulnerable position in the event of an Anglo-French peace. The guaranteed re-convening of the Estates, also of potential constitutional importance, had been tried a year earlier, with the king's approval and without important results. Its significance was tied to the capacity of the Estates to produce the subsidy that was promised.

The dismissal of financial officers and the use of *réformateurs* were certainly not new. The introduction of new councillors chosen by the Estates could have had important implications as originally proposed, for it would have gone far beyond what was done in 1347 and would have replaced the entire council with twenty-eight nominees of the Estates. By March, 1357, however, this earlier plan had been scrapped. Some new men were named to the council, and they included members of the Navarrese party. They replaced those councillors who were on the list of expelled royal officers. Relatively few in number, they were able to exercise a decisive influence as long as Marcel and the Parisians could intimidate the dauphin. Yet their power was merely *de facto*. The former council was not entirely dismissed; no new machinery for selecting the royal council was established; and of course the king was not present to ratify any such scheme if it had been proposed. There were no sanctions, other than short-term political realities, to compel the dauphin to retain the new councillors who had been thrust upon him. In short, the dissidents gained the substance of power without any institutional or constitutional basis for perpetuating it.[46]

These measures of a potential constitutional importance

---

[46]Delachenal, *Charles V* 1: pp. 304–307. Commenting on the earlier view that there was a new, "elected" council after March, 1357, Valois, "Gouvernement," pp. 81–82 re-examined the composition of the council and concluded (*ibid.*, pp. 95–96) that 7–10 new members had appeared on the council by 10 March and that they represented only about one-third of the total membership. Avout, *Meurtre*, pp. 102–105, accepts this conclusion and argues that the Estates were displaying discretion in playing down demands on which the dauphin was sensitive. He suggests that they preferred piecemeal gains to the risk of demanding too much and gaining nothing. The difficulty with this analysis is that it implies that the dauphin had some freedom of choice. In fact, his position was more difficult than it had been in October, and the Estates were able, for the present, to impose their will. What they did with this power was to impose short-term policies of no great novelty, rather than attempting long-term structural changes in the government.

were *ad hoc* actions to please a particular faction or deal with a particular abuse. They were not part of a coherent plan; they did not look beyond the short-term future; and they were a very small part of the changes that the Estates demanded. Some of them had been attempted before, without great success. It seems clear that the issue in March, 1357, was administrative reform, not constitutional change. One finds no real attempt to limit the power of the monarchy and nothing to ensure a permanent role for the Estates. True, it was ordered that the actions of the assembly would be binding on the count of Flanders and the duke of Burgundy, whether or not they attended the next meeting scheduled in April.[47] This requirement was fully in accord with the Romano-canonical principle of procedural consent and it is noteworthy that the Estates embraced the principle, but it was utterly unenforceable. What the crown had never succeeded in doing when the king was present, the Estates could not hope to do in his absence.

When it came to the all-important question of taxation, the Estates of February, 1357, were far from innovative. Having forced the dauphin to recall the men he had sent out to negotiate taxes locally,[48] they finally produced the same basic plan that had been proposed by four successive assemblies in the preceding fifteen months. The ransom of the king, which might have elicited a more favorable public response to taxation, was barely mentioned.[49] Instead, the Estates remained attached to the concept of a nationwide grant of men-at-arms, with its unrealistic goal of an army of 30,000 men. The subsidy to support this force was to prejudice no rights for the future and was conditional upon the cancellation of all other taxes. It was to be administered by *élus* appointed by the Estates General and supervised by *généraux-députés* at Paris. As before, the money was to be paid directly to the troops.[50]

---

[47]*Ord.* 3: pp. 128; Vuitry, *Régime financier* 2: pp. 83–84.

[48] Le Maire, *St. Quentin* 2: no. 669.

[49] On this subject, see J. Henneman, "The French Ransom Aids and Two Legal Traditions," *Studia Gratiana* 15 (1972): pp. 620 and note 26; 622–629. *Ord.* 3: pp. 124–146, mentions the deliverance of the king briefly in the preamble and in art. 5, but art. 2 stressed the diversion of other war subsidies to improper purposes and promised that the subsidy granted at this time, as well as *prouffis, emolumens ou amendes*, would be applied to no purpose whatever except the maintenance of men-at-arms.

[50]*Ord.* 3: pp. 124–146, arts. 3, 4, 51. The first installment of the tax was due, perhaps unrealistically, at the early date of 1 April. See Avout, *Meurtre*, pp. 114–115; Valois,

In short, the assembly not only avoided radical constitutional change, but it stubbornly adhered to the plan which had failed repeatedly to produce the desired results. It offered no counsel on negotiating peace with England or obtaining the king's release, and indeed appeared to avoid this subject rather pointedly. The Estates did continue the recent trend towards placing a heavier fiscal burden on the wealthy, especially nobles. The tax of 15 per cent on revenues meant that a noble whose income was five thousand pounds would have to pay 750, while those with greater revenues would have to pay proportionately more. Just one year earlier, the Estates had abandoned indirect taxes for regressively graduated income taxes which assessed a noble 102 pounds for five thousand pounds of revenue but levied nothing more on higher incomes. Each assembly since late 1355 had increased the taxes on wealthy nobles. It is doubtful that there were many nobles with income exceeding, or even approximating five thousand l. t., so the higher rates were not likely to augment subsidy receipts dramatically. Their importance was largely symbolic, demonstrating that the Estates were determined to exact contributions from the privileged class, but also demonstrating to the nobles that assemblies with heavy bourgeois representation were prepared to tax wealthy nobles more heavily than wealthy bourgeois. This shift in the tax structure may have weakened the Estates by encouraging nobles to boycott future assemblies in Paris. Non-nobles were to support one man-at-arms for every hundred hearths. Even with the payments apportioned according to capacity to pay, wealthy bourgeois must have escaped more lightly than their noble counterparts.[51]

King John, a captive at Bordeaux, was not unaware of events in Paris, but his information largely came from the ousted officials who were most hostile to the Estates. On 23 March, 1357, John concluded a truce with the Prince of Wales. It was to last two years in order to furnish time to negotiate a peace treaty. Presumably the truce would make war subsidies unnecessary and permit the French to marshal their resources

---

"Gouvernement," p. 100; Balas, *Tentative*, p. 116; Vuitry, *Régime financier* 2: pp. 79–82.

[51]*Ibid*. See *RTF 1322–1356*, pp. 291–296, for taxation of the nobles in 1355–1356. See also Avout, *Meurtre*, pp. 100–101.

for the inevitable royal ransom. John was soon to leave for England, where papal legates would join in the peace negotiations.[52] Having concluded the truce, John now sought to checkmate the Estates by invoking what amounted to the old principle of *cessante causa*. He wrote to Paris, announcing that the truce made subsidies unnecessary, and since the Estates were no longer needed, he forbade them to hold their meeting scheduled for 25 April.[53]

When this letter reached Paris on 6 April, it created consternation, since the Estates had not been consulted on the truce. The dauphin was in no position to defy Marcel and his new councillors, and the government was in desperate need of money even if the truce were fully respected and observed. So although he had no authority to oppose the king's order, and may even have wished to obey it, he had no choice but to disregard it. The meeting of the Estates went ahead as scheduled, although postponed a few days to 30 April.[54] Although it was not observed, the letter of the king must have weakened the Estates, since it canceled taxes on the very grounds that royal subjects themselves had invoked so often in the past. Those who did not wish to pay the subsidy now had an excuse to resist it, while those who did not wish to attend the new assembly now had an excuse to stay home.

The truce of Bordeaux was, in fact, a dead letter as far as France was concerned. Captains who had been in English employ now shifted their allegiance to the Navarrese or continued their depredations on a free-lance basis. The duke of Lancaster himself continued his siege of Rennes long after the truce was concluded.[55] Normandy now suffered continually from English, French, and Navarrese garrisons who fought each other and ruined the countryside. Another type of brigandage arose from the growing number of vagabonds,

---

[52] F. Bock, "Some New Documents Illustrating the Early Years of the Hundred Years' War (1353-1356)," *Bull. John Rylands Library* 15 (1931): pp. 77-79; *Foedera* 5: pp. 858-859; 6: pp. 3-10; Denifle, *Désolation* 2: pp. 147-148; Delachenal, *Charles V* 1: p. 307.

[53] Avout, *Meurtre*, pp. 112-113.

[54] *Chron. Jean II et Charles V* 1: pp. 108-109; Balas, *Tentative*, pp. 120-121; Delachenal, *Charles V* 1: p. 314; Vuitry, *Régime financier* 2: p. 85; Lot and Fawtier, *Institutions* 2: p. 566; A. Coville, *Les Etats de Normandie. Leur origine et leur developpement au XIVe siècle* (Paris, 1894), p. 85.

[55] *Chron. Jean II et Charles V* 1: 111; Fowler, *King's Lieutenant*, pp. 162-164.

drifters, and displaced peasants, called *tuchins* or *guetteurs de chemins*—desperate men forced to struggle for survival.[56] Normandy and Brittany were not alone in facing brigandage and local warfare. Philip of Navarre's forces began to ravage the environs of Chartres in the summer of 1357. An English company under James Win penetrated Auvergne and Forez, while Arnaud de Cervole formed a company which threatened the Rhone valley.[57] The scourge of these troops, steadily increasing in the next decade, became the "monster of a thousand arms which devoured France,"[58] a grim fact of life that complicated efforts to raise taxes and reorganize the government.

In the face of these political and military difficulties, the restructured administration at Paris set about trying to collect subsidies. There is scanty documentation with which to measure the progress of this effort. In war-torn Normandy, the tax ordered by the Estates General was being collected by late March, without subsequent ratification by the Norman Estates. Yet the few documents indicating this levy seem to be concerned with the bailiwicks of upper Normandy, and except for Philip of Navarre's county of Longueville, we can probably assume that only those lands controlled by the French crown contributed to this subsidy.[59]

In Auvergne the provincial Estates had already granted, at the beginning of 1357, a tax similar to what the Estates General had offered in October. Collection of this tax was contingent on the approval of the dauphin and a new enumeration of hearths. Every hundred hearths was to support a man-at-arms for a year at a salary of 15 *écus* per month. Letters announcing the dauphin's ratification and ordering collection of the subsidy were not sent to Auvergne until late in February, nearly two months after the tax was granted.[60] Subjects of

---

[56] Luce, *Du Guesclin*, pp. 272–273; Delisle, *St. Sauveur*, p. 111; Secousse, *Charles le Mauvais* 1: p. 191.

[57] G. Guigue, *Les Tard-Venus en Lyonnais, Forez, et Beaujolais*, Lyon, 1886: p. 7.

[58] Luce, *Du Guesclin*, p. 290.

[59] BN Clairambault 213, nos. 77–80; BN MS. fr. 26001, no. 714; BN MS. fr. 26002, no. 723; BN MS. fr., 24120, especially fols 1r-v. A text of 25 February (BN P.O. 2169, *dossier* 48880, no. 3) refers to a subsidy "graciously granted in Normandy," obviously an earlier local grant since the Estates in Paris had not yet acted.

[60] Ledos, "Imposition," pp. 430, 433–435; Secousse, introduction to *Ord.* 3: pp. lxii–lxvi.

the lords, including those of the duke of Bourbon, were required to contribute.[61] By 7 April the hearths had been enumerated, but as late as 25 May the *élus* in Auvergne had received no money. It was August before their accounting was complete, but collections finally totaled over 30,000 pounds for a period of two months.[62] The tax in Auvergne was to have run for a year, but it was limited to two months by the news that the grant of the Estates General had superseded it. Although representatives from Auvergne were in Paris during February securing the dauphin's ratification of their subsidy, it appears that Auvergne was not affected by the actions of the Estates of Languedoïl in that month. Five representatives from Auvergne did attend the next meeting of the Estates General, on 30 April,[63] and it was this assembly's deliberations that were reported to the people of Auvergne in May. The Auvergnat representatives who had been to Paris were named as *élus* in their region, and it seems that Auvergne became subject to the subsidy granted by the central assembly in time for the second installment which was payable in June.[64]

The financial position of the central government was as bad as ever when the Estates General reconvened at the end of April. The dauphin had been forced to suspend payment of royal debts for six months and reiterate earlier orders for the recovery of alienated royal domain.[65] Early in May, we find the bailiff of Vermandois trying to enforce collection of sums owed for the *arrière-ban* of November, 1355, although such earlier taxes had supposedly been canceled by the Grand Ordinance.[66] The Estates, when they convened, reaffirmed the taxes already granted, and their efforts to tax the clergy were now supported by a letter from the Pope.[67] Many nobles, however, balked at paying the high income tax which had

---

[61] BN MS. fr. 22295, no. 1.

[62] Ledos, "Imposition," p. 438; Picot, *Etats* 1: p. 59, note 2. BN Clairambault 213, no. 87, indicates payment of a sum from the receipts of this tax on 1 July.

[63] Secousse, introduction to *Ord.* 3: p. lix.

[64] *Ibid.*, pp. lxvii–lxviii. *Cf.* Ledos, "Imposition," who has published BN MS. fr. 26001, no. 720 on p. 438, but seems to have confused the assemblies of Estates at Paris (p. 437).

[65] *Ord.* 3: pp. 161–162.

[66] P. Varin (ed.), *Archives administratives de la ville de Reims* (5 v., Paris, 1843) 3: p. 94.

[67] Vuitry, *Régime financier* 2: p. 209.

been imposed on them, and we may be sure that the non-nobles of some regions were less willing to pay than they would have been if the subsidy had been approved by the king or levied to obtain his release. It is at this point that Delachenal first noted a reaction setting in against the Estates General.[68] The assembly was smaller than its predecessor in February and had few nobles in attendance. It could do little more than reaffirm the earlier enactments, announce that the next installment of the subsidy was due at the beginning of June, and then disband. The next assembly was scheduled for 22 July.[69]

It is possible that collection of taxes increased during the summer of 1357. There are certainly many more documents relating to collection in Normandy.[70] In mid-June the dauphin was able to send 2000 écus from the Norman receipts to his father in England.[71] The war in Normandy, which must have made subsidies more difficult to collect, may also have made the populace more willing to pay them, because there was no denying that an emergency existed. The situation was very different in the archdiocese of Lyon, which had been largely untouched by the Hundred Years' War up to this time. In Forez and Beaujolais there was violent opposition to the levy of taxes authorized by the Estates General. Men of the local lords reacted with such hostility against the tax collectors that the bailiff of Mâcon was forced to send troops to put down the disorder. Within a year the activities of brigand companies would bring a new sense of crisis to the valley of the Rhone, but in the meantime there was little feeling of "evident necessity."[72]

It appears, in short, that the attitudes which characterized the age of the war subsidy still prevailed in the year following

---

[68] Delachenal, *Charles V* 1: p. 316; Avout, *Meurtre*, pp. 111–112, 115–116 (noting that the government was not strong enough to pursue recalcitrant taxpayers effectively). We have seen (Secousse, introduction to *Ord.* 3: p. lix) that three of Auvergne's representatives to the spring assembly had come from the towns and only two from the other two orders. At Reims, the inhabitants had to be forced to pay the expenses of their emissaries to the Estates (Varin, *Reims* 3: p. 96)

[69] Picot, *Etats* 1: p. 68; Delachenal, *Charles V* 1: p. 315.

[70] BN MS. fr. 26002, nos. 728, 729, 734–736, 739–741, 743, 745.

[71] BN MS. fr. 20402, no. 24.

[72] Guigue, *Tard-Venus*, pp. 5–6, 24–26; E. Perroy, "La fiscalité royale en Beaujolais aux XIVe et XVe siècles," *Le Moyen Age* 39 (1928): p. 10.

the king's captivity. In Normandy, Auvergne, and Mâconnais, the local sense of danger still dominated popular thinking about taxation. The Estates General had pressed for governmental reform, but in the realm of finance they continued to think in terms of war subsidies rather than stressing the king's release. They were still confronted by the apparently insurmountable obstacle which had thwarted a succession of central assemblies since 1355: the inability to produce the subsidy that they had promised. When the Estates reconvened in July, the results throughout Languedoil continued to be disappointing, yet the assembly could not devise any new initiatives to improve the situation.[73] So great was the government's need for money that it was prepared to make extensive concessions to the reformers, as the ordinances of 1355 and 1357 amply demonstrated. The Estates were given excellent, and repeated, opportunities to make themselves indispensable and thereby guarantee the survival of the reforms, but these opportunities hinged on the ability of the Estates to collect the urgently needed taxes. With each failure, the possibility of achieving permanent changes in the government grew more remote.

The dauphin, who doubtless longed for a chance to put aside the tutelage of advisers who were not of his own choosing, now began to realize that he had little to lose by doing so. The forces of opposition began to experience defections during the summer of 1357, with the archbishop of Reims now becoming a partisan and counselor of the dauphin.[74] The prince began to make a cautious bid for provincial support against the Parisians, and some of the dismissed royal advisers began to regain favor.[75]

Ironically, it was the *réformateurs* named by the Estates who gave the dauphin his first great opportunity to reassert authority. As already stated, these *réformateurs* were entrusted with the task of investigating royal officials accused of malfeasance. In this respect they represented a return to the tradition of St. Louis, whose *enquêteurs* had served a similar purpose a

---

[73] A. Coville, "Les Etats de 1332 et de 1357," *Le Moyen Age* 6 (1893): pp. 61–62; Balas, *Tentative*, p. 122. Vuitry, *Régime financier* 2: pp. 85–86, noted that the nobles and clergy were increasingly uncooperative about paying taxes.

[74] Avout, *Meurtre*, p. 116; Balas, *Tentative*, p. 123.

[75] *Ibid.*; Picot, *Etats* 1: pp. 69–70; Delachenal, *Charles V* 1: p. 318.

century before. Yet they differed from the earlier *enquêteurs* in that they were not royal appointees, and among them were Navarrese partisans who were as intent on revenge against individual officers as they were committed to governmental reform. The more recent tradition of using *réformateurs* for fiscal purposes was not eradicated from people's memories. When the new commissioners began their work, they must have been greeted with some suspicion, and the continuing failure to collect sufficient taxes put them under increasing pressure to exploit their positions for the profit of the treasury. They began to exact large fines, impose excessive sentences on officials who were royalist, and dig up old accusations for which pardons had long since been issued. As early as 7 July, 1357, the dauphin jailed Jean d' Arrabloy, a vengeful *réformateur* who had pursued ruthlessly the deposed officers of the monetary administration. By August he declared the powers of the *réformateurs* to have expired, and many of those whom they had punished were released from prison. The harshness of these agents of reform had quickly made them unpopular and had persuaded some people that the régime imposed by the Estates was no great improvement on its predecessor. In moving first against the *réformateurs*, Charles found himself on relatively strong ground politically.[76]

Towards mid-August the dauphin announced to Marcel and the *échevins* of Paris that henceforth he would govern in person and without their help. While probably not unexpected, this action apparently marked the end of whatever understanding he had reached with the provost of the merchants in January.[77] Thereafter, Marcel was gradually drawn into the ranks of the Navarrese partisans. The party of "true reformers" soon disintegrated and the members of this group were forced to choose between the Valois and Evreux factions or withdraw from the increasingly polarized political arena.

The dauphin now left Paris and went to Rouen, the capital

---

[76]Avout, *Meurtre*, pp. 112, 116; Valois, "Gouvernement," pp. 101–104. On the tactics of *réformateurs* earlier in the century, see Henneman, "Enquêteurs," *passim*. Some of their transactions during the period of John II's captivity are descirbed in AN JJ 89, nos. 319, 638; and BN MS. fr. 26002, no. 732. In connection with his effort to restore the disgraced royal officers to their positions, the dauphin changed the recent enactment revoking alienations of royal domain and exempted those properties acquired by royal officials. See *Ord.* 3: p. 175.

[77]*Chron. Jean II et Charles V* 1: p. 112; Avout, *Meurtre*, p. 117.

of his Norman *apanage*.[78] The documents indicating collection of taxes in Normandy are fairly numerous for 1357, but the duchy still faced a difficult military situation. With English assistance, the Navarrese finally succeeded in their strenuous effort to capture Pont Audemer, while other enemy forces at Honfleur were able to blockade the lower Seine.[79] To raise money with which to ransom Pont Audemer, the dauphin ordered the commissioners for the subsidy in Normandy to use receipts from fines and forfeitures as well as tax revenues.[80] Arriving at Rouen, Charles convened an assembly of nobles and clergy which granted a supplementary tax for the defense of the duchy. It was to take the form of a 10 s. *fouage* and to run for a year, apparently being payable in three installments, for the dauphin's commissioners were ordered to collect the money for the first four months as quickly as possible.[81] The documents touching on Norman taxation during the last four months of 1357 are, for the most part, receipts and pay orders like those from earlier in the year. They do not distinguish between this new tax and the subsidy already granted by the Estates General, but it does appear that the new *fouage* had still not been collected by late October.[82]

Surviving pay orders indicate the levy of war subsidies at Chartres and in the bailiwicks of Troyes and Meaux during 1357, evidently the tax granted by the Estates at Paris.[83] It is not clear whether it was being levied in Burgundy, as the Estates General intended, but assemblies at the bailiwick level were convened in the duchy to prepare for a meeting of the Burgundian Estates scheduled for Dijon. Burgundians did participate in the assemblies at Paris, but the tradition of independence in the duchy may have necessitated these local meetings.[84] Local assemblies also continued to meet frequently in Auvergne, as the brigandage of armed companies

---

[78] Coville, *Etats Norm*, p. 85.

[79] *Chron. Valois*, p. 62; Secousse, *Charles le Mauvais* 1: pp. 62–63, 481.

[80] BN NAF 1433, no. 7.

[81] Coville, *Etats Norm.*, pp. 86, 361–364; BN Clairambault 213, no. 85; BN MS. fr. 26002, no. 778. It appears that the *fouage* was supposed to be renewed explicitly before the next two four-month installments could be collected. See below, note 107.

[82] Collections in Normandy during the later fall are indicated in BN Clairambault 213, nos. 82, 84; BN MS. fr. 26002, nos. 763, 766–769; BN P.O. 1082 *dossier* 24901, nos. 5, 6; P.O. 1280 *dossier* 28818, nos. 17, 18.

[83] BN MS. fr. 20684, p. 899; 25701, no. 121.

[84] J. Billioud, *Les états de Bourgogne aux XIVe et XVe siècles* (Dijon, 1922), pp. 21, 154.

made it continually necessary to raise troops and ransom castles. Such a meeting was held late in October, and it was probably on this occasion that the Estates of Auvergne granted a new special tax that was to last for four months. Our earliest reference to this levy is dated 6 November, 1357,[85] and it continued to be collected through the end of the year before being superseded by the action of still another provincial assembly.[86] Like Normandy, therefore, Auvergne had to supplement the subsidy granted in Paris with a special tax for local defense. Other regions may well have had to do the same. It is also likely that the needs of local defense diverted much of the money collected by the *élus* of the Estates General and further reduced the tax receipts reaching Paris.

Nowhere, perhaps, were the central Estates more unsuccessful than in their effort to manage the mints. At their behest the coinage had been returned to the 28th *pied*, and this reform had been extended to Languedoc, which was otherwise little affected by the political events at Paris. It appears, however, that the revaluation was too severe for the conditions prevailing in 1357. Bullion could not be attracted to the mints unless a competitive price was offered for it. A monarchy well financed by tax revenues might find it desirable to operate the mints at a loss in order to preserve a strong and stable currency. In 1357, however, the mints could not be subsidized from the empty treasury. If anything, they were needed as a source of revenue. For the mints to attract bullion and operate at a profit, the 28th *pied* was unrealistically low. Consequently, the reform of the coinage failed, as it had in 1356. There is evidence that one mint began to strike coins on the 45th *pied* as early as 29 July, 1357, while others followed suit in the fall. It is not clear on whose authority they were acting, but presumably they did so on orders from the dauphin. In any case, the new *pied* was not rescinded, and early in 1358 the Estates were forced to give it their blessing, thereby admitting defeat in this attempt at reform.[87]

---

[85] BN P.O. 1675 *dossier* 38869, no. 10; Secousse, introduction to *Ord.* **3**: pp. lxxvi–lxxvii. The government's willingness to leave considerable initiative to the local Estates is revealed in a document published by H. Rivière, *Institutions historiques de l'Auvergne* (2 v., Paris, 1874) **2**: P.J. XXVII.

[86] BN MS. fr 22295, nos. 6, 8, 9; 26002, no. 764.

[87] Prest, "Policy and Protest," pp. 135–138; Avout, *Meurtre*, p. 111; Balas, *Tentative*. p. 141; Picot, *Etats* **1**: p. 74.

During his brief stay in Normandy (August-September, 1357), the dauphin had the number of the general masters of the mints reduced to four, presumably in order to reduce government expenses.[88] This measure has been regarded as an effort to mollify those critics of the crown who demanded more economical government,[89] but it may be nothing more than further evidence of the monarchy's lack of funds. This penury made it essential that Charles reach some new *modus vivendi* with Etienne Marcel when he returned to Paris in September, but we need not doubt that his recent show of independence had made Marcel more suspicious of him than ever. At the beginning of October, the dauphin and the provost agreed on the necessity of convening some representatives of the towns in order to obtain a subsidy.[90] What they had in mind may well have been a supplementary tax for purposes of defense, such as had been adopted already in certain regions, but the suspension of the *réformateurs* and the new mutation of the coinage may have been regarded as an abrogation of the arrangements of the preceding March, under which circumstances a new agreement on taxes would have to be negotiated.

In any case, the dauphin called to Paris the representatives of some seventy towns, many more, apparently, than had been envisioned by Marcel. The latter may have suspected Charles of ulterior motives, and perhaps with good reason, for there was the possibility that a large assembly of burghers from the lesser towns might dilute the influence of the Parisians and show some support for the dauphin. If the latter hoped to capitalize on latent anti-Parisian sentiments in the other towns, he was disappointed, however. The assembly was not well attended, and those who came expressed unwillingness to act unless the three Estates were represented. Charles therefore had to summon the Estates General of Languedoil, who were

---

[88]*Ord.* **3:** p. 182. In another economy measure, the dauphin imposed a tax on royal officers on 4 September (AN P 2292, pp. 729-732).

[89]Avout, *Meurtre*, p. 119.

[90]*Ibid.; Chron. Jean II et Charles V* 1: p. 114; Coville, *Etats Norm*, p. 87; Delachenal, *Charles V* 1: pp. 321-322; Picot, *Etats* 1: p. 72. Among the modern writers there are some differences as to when the dauphin actually returned to Paris and how he reached agreement with Marcel.

ordered to assemble in Paris on 7 November.[91] To back up this official summons, the provost of the merchants dispatched personal letters of his own. This assertion of independent authority by Marcel may have been thought necessary to ensure a well-attended meeting, but it was a slap at royal authority nonetheless. Avout regards it as the first indication that Marcel was contemplating a more revolutionary policy.[92]

Whether or not Avout is right, everything points to a serious deterioration of the reforming movement between July and November, 1357. The success of the "true reformers" depended on the faithful implementation of the Grand Ordinance in all its particulars. Above all, this meant the collection of an adequate subsidy, the maintenance of a stable currency, and the punishment and replacement of corrupt royal officials. It also implied the continued incarceration of Charles the Bad, the continued adherence of Marcel to the party of reform (as opposed to the Navarrese clique), and the ability of the dauphin to maintain a sound working relationship with the reformist leaders. By November, none of these conditions prevailed any longer. An adequate tax had not been collected; stable currency had been abandoned; the réformateurs had abused their powers and given the dauphin an excuse to restore ousted officers; a growing distrust had developed between dauphin and provost; the latter was drawing closer to the Navarrese party while other reformers were moving into the dauphin's camp.

As we have seen, the institutional development of central assemblies in France had been retarded by various factors; yet since the disaster at Crécy the political and financial troubles of the monarchy had given the Estates repeated opportunities to assume an indispensable role in providing stable finances and administrative reform. By 1357 the last of these opportunities was at hand, and the Estates, by reason of their frequent meetings, had overcome one of their most serious early handicaps, their lack of experience and continuity. This final opportunity for the fourteenth-century Estates was in grave

---

[91]Chron. Jean II et Charles V 1: p. 115; Delachenal, Charles V 1: p. 322; Avout, Meurtre, p. 120; Lot and Fawtier, Institutions 2: p. 567. A copy of the summons to the Estates has been published in Arch. hist. Poit. 46: pp. 182–183.

[92]Avout, Meurtre, p. 120.

jeopardy, however, when they assembled on 7 November for their eighth meeting in two years. If any hope remained for the advocates of genuine reform, it was utterly demolished on the second day of the assembly, when Charles the Bad was released from prison.

2. The Navarrese Party and the Parisian Revolution

The chronicler Jean de Venette wrote that the king of Navarre was "freed from prison through the industry and diligence of certain Picard nobles, among them Jean de Picquigny."[93] The latter, a long-time Navarrese partisan, was governor of Artois and was well placed to engineer the release of his hero, but most chroniclers believed that Etienne Marcel and Robert le Coq actually put him up to it.[94] Whether by previous design or by force of circumstances, Etienne Marcel was now linked to Charles the Bad, and this alliance would bring about his destruction in less than nine months. To wield effective power, Marcel had to retain some control over the dauphin, but his various agreements with that prince had not yielded satisfactory results and there remained no basis for mutual trust. Not yet ready to employ direct violence in order to intimidate the dauphin, the provost may have hoped to capitalize on his rivalry with a liberated Charles the Bad.[95] He even may have clung to the view, expressed by Le Coq a year earlier, that the release of the Navarrese king would convert into allies the troops who fought under his banner, thus ending the grave military threat to Normandy and the Ile-de-France.[96] These are the most charitable interpretations of his actions which are possible.

---

[93]Venette, p. 69

[94]Chron. Jean II et Charles V 1: pp. 115–119; Chron. Valois, p. 61. For evidence of a plot to release Charles, see Secousse, Charles le Mauvais 1: p. 322. The Navarrese archives reveal a continuing effort to secure his release, including the raising of funds and troops to be sent to Normandy and the rewarding of those who had participated in the project. See J. R. Castro, Diputacion foral de Navara, Catalogo del Archivo General. Seccion de comptos. Documentos (46 v., Pamplona, 1952–1967) 2: nos. 966, 1048, 1062, 1067; 3: nos. 292, 923; 4: no. 630.

[95]Avout, Meurtre, p. 124. Without mentioning Marcel's possible motives, Denifle, Désolation 2: p. 151, argued that Innocent VI worked for the release of Charles the Bad purely through blindness, while Le Coq did so deliberately for motives of his own.

[96]Journal des états, p. 32. On various reasons advanced for the release of Charles, see also Guesnon, Inv. Arras, pp. 120–121; Delachenal, Charles V 1: pp. 335, 372.

Charles the Bad was joyfully acclaimed by his many partisans at Amiens, and his Parisian supporters forced the dauphin to issue him a safe conduct. When this document was brought to him by the *échevin* Charles Toussac and a member of the Picquigny family, the king of Navarre proceeded to Paris, which he entered in triumph on 29 November. He soon recaptured the favor of the populace.[97] Despite some difference of opinion among contemporaries, it is very doubtful that the Estates had advised Marcel and Le Coq to bring about Charles the Bad's release. The assembly had been in session for no more than a day when the event occurred. Moreover, the Estates were thrown into complete disarray by the news that he had been released. Despite the efforts to ensure a representative gathering this time, there again were many absentees, especially among the nobility.[98] If the assembly was somewhat small to begin with, it suffered a further reduction when the representatives from Champagne and Burgundy departed as soon as they learned of Charles the Bad's release.[99] Although the Estates did not immediately disband, it was clear that the political situation had undergone a radical change and that no major decisions on taxes or reforms could be made at this time. These were deferred until a new assembly, scheduled for early in the new year, when it was hoped, once again, that more regions would be willing to send representatives.[100] The dauphin's government, still without adequate funds, was left to confront a dangerous new coalition between the partisans of Charles the Bad and the bourgeoisie of Paris who still followed Marcel.

It took some pressure to make the dauphin give in to the new political realities, but Navarrese partisans regained their positions in the council and Robert le Coq now enjoyed his period of greatest political influence. Early in December the prince had to agree that the king of Navarre would receive back his lands and get an indemnity as well. He and his

---

[97]*Chron. Valois*, p. 61; *Chron. Jean II et Charles V* 1: pp. 117-121; Delachenal, *Charles V* 1: pp. 325-326; Denifle, *Désolation* 2: p. 152; Avout, *Meurtre*, pp. 123-125; Balas, *Tentative*, p. 128.

[98]Vuitry, *Régime financier* 2: p. 86; Delachenal, *Charles V* 1: p. 323.

[99]*Ibid.*, pp. 325-326; Coville, *Etats Norm.*, p. 88.

[100]Vuitry, *Régime financier* 2: p. 86; Delachenal, *Charles V* 1: pp. 331-332. It was at this point that Viollet, "Etats," pp. 261-262, would have us believe that the "revolution resumed" its "irresistible march."

partisans, including those who had helped him escape, would be granted amnesty, while four supporters who had been executed at Rouen in April, 1356, were to receive honorable burial. These promises were embodied in a treaty which was dated 12 December. It provided that certain outstanding differences were to be resolved by the Estates General at the next meeting, now scheduled for 14 January, 1358. Both princes agreed to abide by the decisions of this assembly.[101]

Charles the Bad was in some haste to conclude this agreement because there were rumors that an Anglo-French treaty for the release of John II would soon be arranged in London. It was necessary for him to establish the strongest possible position before his father-in-law returned. On 13 December, the day after the formal agreement, he departed for Mantes to solidify his gains. He had Anglo-Navarrese companies from Brittany and lower Normandy moved into the vicinity of Paris to strengthen his military position. Then, early in January, he went to Rouen to stage an elaborate rehabilitation of his executed followers.[102]

The dauphin, meanwhile, was all but a prisoner. Everything he did was carried out under the watchful eye of Robert le Coq. Before Charles the Bad left Paris, he and the dauphin made a number of public appearances together, always accompanied by the bishop of Laon. Under pressure from the Navarrese, the government had to release most persons who were confined in the prisons of Paris.[103] As life in the surrounding countryside became ever more precarious, a chronicler who still considered Marcel "very solicitous for the commonweal," said that the Parisians wondered why the dauphin was not acting.[104] Charles did, in fact, appoint a trustworthy captain, Pierre de Villiers, as commander of the garrison at Paris,[105] but beyond this step he could do little, being without money and under the continuing domination of le Coq and Marcel.

---

[101] Secousse, *Charles le Mauvais* 1: pp. 65–68, 70, 76–77, has published a series of documents relating to the new treaty, based on manuscripts in AN JJ 89. See also Avout, *Meurtre*, pp. 126–128; Delachenal, *Charles V* 1: pp. 331–332.

[102] *Ibid.*, p. 333; Denifle, *Désolation* 2: p. 154; Avout, *Meurtre*, pp. 128–129.

[103] *Ibid.*, pp. 128–130; Secousse, *Charles le Mauvais* 1: pp. 68–70.

[104] *Venette*, pp. 67–68.

[105] Luce, *Du Guesclin*, p. 248.

Judging from the continuing activity of *élus* and *généraux*, it appears that the subsidy granted in March, 1357, was still being collected, albeit in a slow and piecemeal fashion.[106] The Norman representatives to the Estates at Paris in November seem to have granted a subsidy, but the account which mentions this action is too cryptic to furnish other information. The Normans were already subject to the subsidy for men-at-arms which the Estates General had authorized, and the special *fouage* for defense of the duchy, granted to the dauphin at the end of August. The action of the Normans in November was probably related to this second tax, either replacing or superseding it or else authorizing the collection of a second four-month installment. Whatever tax was authorized, it was to be collected by *élus* chosen by the Normans and was levied during the first four months of 1358. Since documents relating to Norman taxation drop off sharply after April, 1358, it is likely that the 10 s. *fouage* granted in August, 1357, had been subject to the requirement that it be explicitly renewed every four months.[107] This would explain the action taken in November, and the absence of documents after April permits us to conclude that the Normans did not authorize a third installment.

In Auvergne, the practice of recurrent local assemblies continued. The three Estates of the region met at the beginning of January, 1358, doubtless to name those who would represent them in Paris on the 14th. This region, perhaps more than any other part of France, was plagued by the brigandage of men-at-arms, and the assembly also had to consider local defensive needs. It granted, or renewed, a subsidy to pay for forces needed to protect the district from these enemies.[108] The Lyonnais region faced similar problems and had been forced to take measures for defense during the year after the battle of Poitiers. Towards the end of 1357, the

---

[106]*Ibid.*, P.J., nos. 9, 12; BN MS. fr. 25701, nos. 122–125, 127, 128, 133, 135; 20582, nos. 24, 75; BN P.O. 2886, *dossier* 64120, no. 8; BN NAF 20026, no. 62.

[107]Coville, *Etats Norm.*, pp. 364–365; BN MS. fr. 26002, no. 800; BN MS. fr. 25701, no. 120. The military situation in lower Normandy was particularly difficult in this period, and the inhabitants of two dioceses refused to pay the tax for men-at-arms granted by the Estates General. See Luce, *Du Guesclin*, pp. 267–268, 276–277, and P.J. 14; Secousse, introduction to *Ord.* 3: p. lxxii.

[108]BN MS. fr. 26001, no. 697; 22295, nos. 3–4; Picot, *Etats* 1: p. 75; BN P.O. 524, *dossier* 11785, no. 2.

archbishop of Lyon held an assembly which agreed to support these measures with a tax of 2 d./l., despite the opposition of certain privileged bodies.[109]

As the time approached for a new assembly of the Estates of Languedoil, the dauphin decided to try a political technique which Etienne Marcel and Charles the Bad had both employed successfully. On 11 January he addressed a large crowd of Parisians and sought to persuade them that he would serve their interests and effectively defend the realm if provided with adequate resources. The prince appears to have made a favorable impression, for Marcel thought it wise to stage a counter-demonstration the following day. The dauphin appeared at this meeting and took turns with Marcel and Toussac in addressing the citizens.[110]

The Estates who convened in mid-January cannot be called "General," since they consisted mainly of urban representatives, with a sprinkling of pro-Navarrese clergy. Uncertain what action to take, they adjourned until 11 February,[111] after taking a step that revealed the impotence of the reforming movement by this date. The Estates authorized the coinage to be minted on the 45th *pied,* thereby ratifying what had been done some months earlier without their authorization.[112] This action amounted to an admission of what the crown had long since learned: that reform of the coinage and adequate revenues from taxation were inextricably tied together. The former could not occur without the latter.

During the interval between meetings of the Estates, the atmosphere in Paris grew increasingly tense, as violent incidents exacerbated relations between the partisans of the dauphin and those of the provost of the merchants. On 24 January the dauphin's treasurer was murdered and the suspected assassin sought ecclesiastical sanctuary. A force of troops loyal to the dauphin, led by his marshal, Robert de Clermont, apprehended the culprit and put him to death. In the process they violated sacred ground, and the bishop of

---

[109]Guigue, *Tard-Venus,* pp. 3, 27–29.

[110]*Chron. Jean II et Charles V* 1: 134–139; Avout, *Meurtre,* pp. 133–134; Delachenal, *Charles V* 1: pp. 337–340.

[111]*Ibid.,* p. 341.

[112]*Ord.* 3: pp. 193, 195; Prest, "Policy and Protest," pp. 137–138; Balas, *Tentative,* pp. 142–143; Picot, *Etats* 1: p. 74; *Chron. Jean II et Charles V* 1: p. 140.

Paris excommunicated the marshal. Feeling ran high and each side now had a martyr.[113]

When the Estates General reconvened on 11 February they were scarcely more numerous than their immediate predecessors. Again they were dominated by bourgeois supporters of Etienne Marcel and Charles the Bad, and most of the sources state that no nobles at all were in attendance.[114] With respect to taxation, this assembly abandoned the idea that absent nobles could be bound by its actions. It ordered a 15 per cent income tax on clergy and non-nobles only, perhaps the first tax up to this time which would impose a great burden on wealthy bourgeois. The money was to be payable by 24 June and was supposed to support one man-at-arms for every 75 hearths. Another step in the direction of practicality was the decision that each *pays,* and the mayor and *échevins* of each town, could determine the form of tax if they wished to raise the desired troops by some other means. This concession to local sentiment was balanced by another one which aimed to ensure a monopoly of tax-granting power for central assemblies—provincial Estates were forbidden to meet. In addition, the *généraux* named by the Estates General were to appoint the *élus* who would collect the tax in each district.[115] Thus the Estates of Languedoil, or the restricted group which has been given this name, belatedly gave some recognition to local sentiments. The gestures, however, came too late, and the prohibition of local assemblies was bound to be ignored by regions concerned for their own defense. Moreover, while the decision not to tax the nobility may have been realistic, an assembly truly concerned with the common welfare might have found a way of taxing the aristocracy by declaring that the tax was for the king's ransom rather than for troops.[116]

---

[113] Delachenal, *Charles V* 1: pp. 345–347.

[114] Secousse, introduction to *Ord.* 3: pp. lxxi; BN NAF 20075, no. 20; Viollet, "Etats," p. 268; *Chron. Jean II et Charles V* 1: p. 147.

[115] *Ibid.;* Viollet, "Etats," pp. 268, 272. Viollet has published the ordinance enacted after this assembly (*ibid.,* pp. 273–292). See also Vuitry, *Régime financier* 2: pp. 86–87; Delachenal, *Charles V* 1: p. 353.

[116] Delachenal (*ibid.,* p. 354) argued that this ordinance demonstrated that the representatives had not given up on the reforms they had been seeking for two years. It would be more proper to say, however, that most of the reformers were no longer attending the Estates. The return of the king, which would have facilitated the cause of genuine reform while compromising the political adventurers, was not stressed at

The ordinance which the dauphin issued on behalf of this assembly was much shorter than that of 1357, but it was by no means limited to fiscal enactments. It reaffirmed the Grand Ordinance, ordered changes in governmental personnel, reinstated the *réformateurs*, and again revoked alienations of royal domain. It also ordered the destruction of indefensible fortresses and required that unpaid arrears from the subsidy of the preceding year be used to buy back those strongholds which had been occupied by hostile troops.[117]

This small assembly of February, 1358, showed some awareness of the mistakes of preceding meetings. Some of the provisions of the new ordinance might have proven very effective if enacted earlier when the Estates were more representative, Marcel less alienated, and Charles the Bad still in captivity. Coming in 1358, however, these measures were too late to revive the Estates as a forum for a reforming party. One may doubt, moreover, that reform was any longer a serious consideration among those who now were dominating the government. Having gained effective power, they found no clear course of action to follow next. Charles the Bad might threaten Paris and seek the throne of France; Le Coq might still yearn for a cardinal's hat; he and Marcel might enjoy the satisfaction of ruining their enemies in John II's government. Neither Le Coq nor Marcel, however, could seriously hope now for advancement in the service of the Valois monarchy, nor could any amount of governmental reform guarantee them permanent security against the vengeance of John II and the dauphin. Their interests as individuals would seem to demand the replacement of the dynasty by Charles the Bad, yet they shrank from advocating this step in public, perhaps because they knew that it would not have much support. The Estates had scarcely disbanded when Marcel took part in a violent act which damned him permanently in the eyes of the dauphin and the bulk of the French nobility.

During the preceding year, the nobility had increasingly disassociated itself from the deliberations of the Estates. Some lords no doubt were weary of repetitive assemblies in which

---

the Estates of February, 1358, yet there were various reasons why the ransom would have elicited broader support than taxes merely for war. See Henneman, "Ransom Aids," pp. 622–629.

[117] Viollet, "Etats," pp. 266–269, 276–278, 281, 284–286; Delachenal, *Charles V* 1: pp. 350–351.

bourgeois played a dominant role. Others must have resented the increasing tax burden which the assemblies assigned to nobles. Others probably were alienated by the apparent lack of interest in obtaining the king's release. We have no way of assessing the relative importance of these and other motives, but it is clear that the nobles were not anxious to support the Estates. The aristocracy, which could have been a force for reform, now remained on the sidelines. Most nobles were not yet ready to make common cause with any party, since they were torn between loyalty to the dauphin and the monarchy, and attachment to Charles the Bad. Cazelles states that the first nobles to rally to the dauphin were the military commanders.[118] They quickly became the object of the Parisians' ire. The capital was filled with refugees from the countryside who fled from the depredations of men-at-arms. Most of these troops were supporting Charles of Navarre, but the latter's alliance with the Parisians placed him above criticism, and resentment at brigandage was quickly translated into anti-noble sentiments. So it was that the dauphin's military supporters quickly became the targets for popular wrath. On 22 February, 1358, Etienne Marcel held a large public meeting which focused on the menace of brigandage and the dauphin's alleged inertia in resisting it.[119] The mob grew angry, stormed the palace, and in the dauphin's bedchamber slew the marshals of Normandy and Champagne before the prince's eyes. Robert de Clermont, marshal of Normandy, had long supported the Valois party against the Navarrese and had but recently antagonized the Parisians,[120] but Jean de Conflans, marshal of Champagne, had been a member of the reforming party. His murder effectively destroyed the Navarrese party in Champagne, while the two assassinations pushed the aristocracy of Languedoil into the dauphin's camp and permanently compromised Etienne Marcel. All historians agree that a new turning point in the political situation had occurred.[121]

---

[118] Cazelles, "Parti navarrais," p. 867.

[119] Avout, *Meurtre*, pp. 148–149.

[120] *Chron. Jean II et Charles V* 1: 148–155; Delachenal, *Charles V* 1: pp. 356–363; S. Luce, "Pièces inédites relatives à Etienne Marcel et à quelques-uns de ses principaux adhérents," *Bib. Ec. Chartes* 21 (1860): pp. 73–92, no. 11; Denifle, *Désolation* 2: p. 156 and notes.

[121] *Ibid.*, p. 157, charged Charles the Bad with instigating the murders because Jean de Conflans had led the defections of the Champenois from the Navarrese party. It was

The king of Navarre returned to Paris on the twenty-sixth and extorted new concessions from the dauphin, including lands in southwestern France, a residence in Paris, and a monthly allowance from royal subsidy receipts sufficient to pay the salaries of 1000 troops.[122] In effect, Charles the Bad was now looting the treasury on a scale even greater than those royal officials who were so often accused of embezzling money. Although masquerading as defenders of Paris, his troops were the enemies of the crown and the cause of much of the brigandage which the Parisians resented. Now they were to be paid from the laboriously collected subsidies. Again we are reminded of the destructive effects of the Valois-Evreux contest, not merely on royal finances, but on the reforming movement and the public peace as well. Meanwhile, the various agreements made between the dauphin and Charles the Bad could not be fully implemented because the royalist captains of certain fortresses refused to abandon them to the Navarrese without express orders from John II.[123] Friction continued, therefore, and none of the "reconciliations" removed the threat of the Navarrese hirelings who threatened the Paris basin.

After his humiliations in Paris, it is not surprising that the dauphin sought to throw off the tutelage of adversaries who were following the path of violence and extortion far more than that of reform. He therefore resolved to leave Paris and make an effort to recruit support elsewhere by convening an assembly of nobles from Picardy, Beauvaisis, Artois, and upper Normandy which was to meet at Senlis on 25 March. It was on the twelfth that this assembly was summoned.[124] Some historians, mindful of the fact that Marcel could no longer control the prince when he was once out of Paris, have

---

Marcel, however, who actually directed the murders and was widely blamed. See Valois, "Gouvernement," p. 106; Luce, "Examen critique," p. 265; Luce, *Jacquerie,* p. 48, note 1; Funk, "Robert le Coq."

[122] Delachenal, *Charles V* 1: pp 363–370 (where Charles the Bad is described as being the "arbiter of the situation"); *ibid.* 2: p. 399 (P.J. XXI); Secousse, *Charles le Mauvais* 1: pp. 71–76; Castro, *Catalogo* 2: no. 1003 (indication that Charles received 10,000 pounds in revenues from the seneschalsies of Toulouse and Bigorre). See also Avout, *Meurtre,* p. 158.

[123]*Ibid.,* pp. 157–158. Avout thinks that Marcel now worked for a new accord between the two princes, but only until a new rupture would suit his purposes.

[124] See the documents published by Coville, *Etats Norm.,* pp. 365–367.

implied that his departure for this assembly amounted to an "escape," carried out against the wishes of the provost of the merchants.[125] Such was not the case, however, for the royal council, which now contained a strong contingent of Navarrese partisans, acquiesced in the plan. For one thing, Charles the Bad was to join the dauphin at this assembly. More important, perhaps, was the perennial lack of money. Marcel and Le Coq might control the government, but this control meant little if the government remained nearly bankrupt. To obtain adequate funds and to make their power effective, they had to obtain the participation of the nobility in the next session of the Estates of Languedoil, scheduled for May.[126] It was risky to let the dauphin leave Paris, but the risk seemed unavoidable, and it was doubtless thought that the eloquence and charisma of Charles the Bad would re-establish the old rapport between the king of Navarre and the nobles of the North.

Marcel and the Navarrese party had reason to believe that their control of the government was greater than ever. The dauphin had reached the age of twenty in January, and on 14 March he assumed the title of regent, thereby acquiring a greater legal authority than he had formerly possessed. In the short run, his new powers were less valuable to Charles than to those who controlled him, and he doubtless assumed the title of regent at the urging of Marcel and Le Coq. Among other things, the action undercut the position of those commanders who insisted on orders from the king before surrendering their fortresses to Charles the Bad, and the latter could applaud any change which would weaken the authority of the absent John II.[127] It is perhaps noteworthy that the regency

---

[125] The notion of an escape has been presented, implicitly or explicitly, by Vuitry, *Régime financier* 2: p. 91; Lot and Fawtier, *Institutions* 2: p. 568; Picot, *Etats* 1: p. 77; Delachenal, *Charles V* 1: p. 371f; and Denifle, *Désolation* 2: p. 158. In his review of Denifle's work (*cit. supra,* chap. I, note 69), Coville attacked the view that the dauphin had escaped, and pointed out that Secousse had realized this as early as the mid-eighteenth century. See Secousse, *Charles le Mauvais* 2: p. 106f, and introduction to *Ord.* 3: p. lxxii.

[126] Viollet, "Etats," p. 268; Avout, *Meurtre,* pp. 163–165.

[127] BN NAF 7376, fol. 316, announcing the assumption of the title of regent. Picot, *Etats* 1: pp. 75–76, thought that Charles took the title during the time that the Estates were in session, several weeks earlier. On the reasons for the assumption of the title, see Valois, "Gouvernement," pp. 108–109; Delachenal, *Charles V* 1: pp. 371–375; and Avout, *Meurtre,* pp. 159–162.

was not assumed by the king of Navarre himself. Such a step
would have entailed serious political risks, but it might have
been considered if the pro-Navarrese council had not felt
confident of being able to control the dauphin.

As it happened, this control was lost soon after the new
regent left Paris for Senlis. Charles did not immediately
declare his independence, but proceeded cautiously and was
able to recover the essence of authority within two months.
His position was strengthened greatly by a development
which his enemies had not anticipated. Charles the Bad failed
to attend the meeting at Senlis, apparently because of illness.
Like many recent assemblies, this one was not well attended,
but it may have given some provisional endorsement to a tax
on the nobles. The dauphin proceeded to Compiègne, where
he received messages from his father. Then he directed his
attention to Champagne, where the aristocracy nursed a
strong resentment at the murder of their marshal, Jean de
Conflans. The three Estates of Champagne were summoned to
meet at Provins on 9 April.[128] En route to this assembly,
Charles stopped at Meaux, a strategic city on the Marne where
he had previously installed his wife and sister in the fortified
stronghold called the Market.[129]

At Provins, as at Senlis, Charles the Bad was expected to
attend but did not do so. Two representatives from Paris were
present, but the regent skillfully introduced the topic of the
murdered marshals in such a way as to place these delegates in
an embarrassing position. In the end, the Champenois gave
Charles a sympathetic response but declined to make any
financial commitment until a new assembly should meet at
Vertus in three weeks' time.[130] Pending this gathering, the
regent moved quickly to secure the allegiance of those who
garrisoned the fortresses commanding the upper Seine and its
tributaries. The Market of Meaux was reinforced, and there
was now little doubt of his hostile intentions towards Paris.
Realizing what was afoot, Marcel seized the artillery stored in
the Louvre and began to fortify the capital. He wrote to the
dauphin on 18 April, reproaching him for his hostile attitude

[128] Coville, review of Denifle *cit. supra;* Delachenal, *Charles V* 1: p. 377f; Coville,
Etats Norm., p. 89; *Chron. Jean II et Charles V* 1: pp. 163–164.

[129] Avout, *Meurtre,* pp. 166–167.

[130] *Ibid.,* pp. 167–169; *Chron. Jean II et Charles V* 1: pp. 164–167; Delachenal,
Charles V 1: pp. 379–381; Vuitry, *Régime financier* 2: p. 91.

and using pseudo-deferential language which the regent regarded as "rude, ugly, and ungracious."[131]

When the Estates of Champagne reconvened at Vertus on 29 April, they responded with the grant of an aid, still in the familiar form of a war subsidy based on men-at-arms, but with a higher burden on the bourgeoisie and a lower one on the nobles than had been common at the Parisian assemblies of 1357. Urban non-nobles were to support one man-at-arms for every 70 hearths, while rural non-nobles were to support one for every hundred hearths. The clergy would pay a tenth and the nobles a twentieth (5 per cent). The return of the nobility to the assemblies was thus clearly recorded in the tax structure.[132]

The Estates General of Languedoil were to have assembled at Paris on the first of May, and indeed the dauphin's activity in the five preceding weeks had been intended, ostensibly, to drum up support for this assembly among the nobles. Both the dauphin and Etienne Marcel desired the attendance of the nobles, for in their absence the Estates had been unable to grant subsidies that were truly collectable. The real issue was who would control the assembly. Without any guile at all, the regent was now in a position to argue that the nobles would come to assemblies if he called them but that they would not come to Paris to be intimidated or insulted by the provost of the merchants. Charles therefore rescheduled the meeting for 4 May and summoned it to Compiègne, a town under his control.[133] Two days before the assembly, he conferred with the king of Navarre in the Beauvaisis. Charles the Bad sought his promise to reach an accord with the Parisians; the dauphin declared his affection for them but insisted on his right to punish those who had inflicted indignities upon him. Unable to obtain specific concessions, Charles of Navarre returned to Paris and avoided the forthcoming assembly.[134]

---

[131]Chron. Jean II et Charles V 1: pp. 170–171; Avout, Meurtre, pp. 170–176; Denifle, Désolation 2: p. 159; Luce, Jacquerie, p. 49; Secousse, Charles le Mauvais 1: pp. 100–101. Marcel's letter to the dauphin has been published by H. Kervyn de Lettenhove, Œuvres de Froissart (18 v., Brussels, 1876–1877) 6: pp. 462–464, and also by Avout, Meurtre, pp. 301–303.

[132]Chron. Jean II et Charles V 1: pp. 172–173; Vuitry, Régime financier 2: p. 92.

[133]Chron. Jean II et Charles V 1: p. 173; Delachenal, Charles V 1: p. 389f; Vuitry, Régime financier 2: p. 92.

[134]Chron. Jean II et Charles V 1: pp. 174–175; Denifle, Désolation 2: p. 160.

The Estates who met at Compiègne were as poorly attended as the recent meetings at Paris, but their composition was very different. There were more nobles and fewer bourgeois, and the latter were mainly from towns no longer supporting Etienne Marcel or Charles the Bad. Those remaining steadfast to the pro-Navarrese insurgents were largely unrepresented. Robert le Coq did attend, but he was greeted by the nobles with such hostility that he was obliged to flee.[135] Historians have stated that the Estates intended their action to be binding on those who were absent,[136] but this conclusion is derived from later documents and it is more likely that the crown decided subsequently to apply the tax more broadly.[137]

The Estates of Compiègne are considered to mark a general reaction against the anti-Valois coalition in Paris, but they by no means abandoned the movement for reform. Following the meeting, on 14 May, the dauphin published an ordinance of twenty-eight articles which included a number of familiar items: the use of *élus* rather than royal officers to collect the tax; the use of *réformateurs* to investigate and punish the misdeeds of royal officers; an end to the pursuit of debtors to the Lombards. In addition, the assembly not only refused to countenance a weakening of the currency for fiscal reasons, but actually required that the coinage be returned to the 28th *pied*.[138]

Delachenal stated that this ordinance was the first to mention the king's ransom,[139] and it is likely that this subject was given more emphasis than at recent meetings in Paris. Not only was a treaty being concluded in London, but the nobles, who often resented paying war subsidies, were entirely willing to help ransom their suzerain. Since this assembly had present an important number of nobles, and few of the party that might desire to prolong the king's absence, the dauphin may

---

[135]*Ibid.*; Vuitry, *Régime financier* 2: p. 92; Luce, *Jacquerie*, pp. 50, 98; Delachenal, *Charles V* 1: pp. 392–393.

[136]Picot, *Etats* 1: p. 78; Vuitry, *Régime financier* 2: p. 96.

[137]*Ibid.*, citing *Ord.* 3: p. 692, a letter of 15 June (also BN MS. lat. 9146, fol. 161r-v; and BN NAF 7610, fols. 42–44) from John II, who was at this time interested in raising money for his ransom. See below, chap. III. It does appear, however, that the inhabitants of Auvergne were contributing to the taxes granted at Compiègne: *INV AM Riom*, pp. 57–58 (CC 1); BN Clairambault 213, no. 89.

[138]*Ord.* 3: p. 219f. *Cf.* Vuitry, *Régime financier* 2: p. 95.

[139]See Henneman, "Ransom Aids," p. 620, and note 26; see also above, at note 49.

have found it politic to place some emphasis on the ransom. Nevertheless, Delachenal is misleading, for the ransom *had* been mentioned at earlier assemblies and it was not the central consideration in this one.

When the Estates granted a tax, it was just another war subsidy based on men-at-arms, modeled on the recent grant at Vertus and thus reflecting the increased political strength of the nobles. The latter would pay an income tax of 5 per cent, based on their own statements of their income. The amount normally paid as *tailles* by their serfs would not be counted as taxable income on this occasion because rural serfs were being taxed directly at the rate of one man-at-arms for every 200 hearths. Non-servile peasants would support one man for every hundred hearths. Non-servile peasants would support one man for every hundred hearths, while the towns were to pay at the rate of one man for every seventy. At a daily wage of ½ *écu* for each soldier, the average bourgeois family would pay slightly more than 2½ pounds, but taxes were to be apportioned according to wealth.[140] Clerics in general were assessed a tenth, but bishops and most abbots were to pay at a flat rate (15 and 12 *écus* respectively).[141] The tax on everybody was payable in two installments—24 June and 1 November.[142]

When the Estates disbanded and the new ordinance became known, Marcel and the Navarrese were seriously alarmed for the safety of Paris. In hopes of reaching a last-minute settlement, a distinguished delegation from the university called upon the regent, urging him not to attack the capital. Once again Charles declared that his feelings towards the Parisians were generous, but he demanded that they deliver him a few of the leaders of the opposition whom he regarded with the greatest suspicion. An accord based on this condition was tantamount to a death sentence for men like Marcel and Toussac, so no settlement was possible. The dauphin prepared for open war and began to assemble an army which included mercenaries recruited in the lands of the emperor.[143]

---

[140]*Ord.* **3**: p. 219f; Vuitry, *Régime financier* **2**: pp. 93–94.

[141]BN NAF 7610, fols. 39–41.

[142]Vuitry, *Régime financier* **2**: p. 94. According to Picot, *Etats* **1**: p. 144, this tax was the most justly apportioned one of the period 1356–1358, but it is not clear what criteria he had in mind.

[143]*Venette*, p. 72; Luce, *Jacquerie*, p. 98: Luce, *Du Guesclin*, p. 234.

The desire to subdue Paris was but one of the regent's military concerns. He also had to face the Navarrese and other companies who continued to ravage the land. In recognition of this growing brigand menace, the Estates of Compiègne had expanded on a measure adopted earlier by the assembly at Paris in February. The ordinance of 14 May required that indefensible castles were to be torn down, while those that still were useful were to be stocked with provisions, garrisoned, and placed in good repair.[144] Although this order was an essential step in organizing an attack on brigandage, it was viewed by the peasants of Languedoil in a very different light.

The worst years of brigandage still lay ahead, but the people of the countryside had already suffered grievously. They began to fortify village churches, hoping for some protection.[145] Yet there was little they could do against armed bands which roamed at will through the open country during 1358.[146] Most of these troops were nobles or at least made some effort to abide by the law of arms when dealing with other members of the military class. Their relations with the nobility were sometimes cordial and always correct.[147] They saw no reason to use similar consideration towards the peasants, who were left unprotected by the impotence of the dauphin's government. Forced to pay blackmail to the companies, they then were fined by the crown for having dealings with brigands.[148] The lords who lived off their labor could not or would not protect them. To the peasant, the nobles were the cause of all misery; and the castle was the symbol of the nobles' power, whether it was the stronghold of a group of brigands or the place to which manorial exactions had to be paid. Immediately following the Estates of Compiègne, the repair and restocking of castles began, especially in those regions which controlled the supplying of Paris. Thus the symbols of oppression were to be made stronger, and at the expense of the peasants themselves. Just one week after the ordinance of Compiègne, the horror of the *Jacquerie* began.[149]

---

[144]*Ord.* **3**: p. 219f; Timbal, *Guerre*, pp. 106–107.

[145]*Venette*, p. 85: Luce, *Jacquerie*, p. 27.

[146]*Ibid.*, p. 9; Luce, *Du Guesclin*, pp. 278–281; *Venette*, p. 73.

[147]Luce, *Jacquerie*, pp. 38–39. See Keen, *Laws of War*, pp. 190–191.

[148]Luce, *Jacquerie*, p. 15.

[149]*Ibid.*, pp. 50–53, 77. Luce pointed out, *ibid.*, pp. 161–163, that the use of violence by peasants against lords accused of brigandage could have been construed as nothing

In Champagne, Picardy, and Beauvaisis, the peasants rose in fury against the nobles, and inflicted death and destruction on a scale worthy of the brigand companies themselves.[150] The uprisings lasted no more than three weeks, but they must have rendered impossible the collection of taxes in the very regions which had so recently granted subsidies. More important from the political standpoint was the bitter cleavage between social classes which now disrupted all pre-existing political alignments. An early victim of the peasants was a member of the Picquigny family, those close allies of Charles the Bad. Although he might have advanced his interests by encouraging the Jacques, the king of Navarre was too much a noble to desert his class, and he now became the implacable foe of the insurgent peasants.[151]

Etienne Marcel, on the other hand, became their sympathizer. Among the nobles were some of the more hated royal officers. Some of their castles were in a position to threaten Paris in the event of a siege. The destruction of castles near Paris and the death or discomfiture of the royalist nobles were not merely manifestations of revenge; they also were actions which might be desirable on military grounds. The provost of the merchants therefore dispatched a contingent of armed Parisians to conduct a *Jacquerie* of its own against the castles and noble houses outside the city. Only once, and then briefly, did these burghers actually collaborate with the rebellious peasants; yet there is no doubt that Marcel welcomed the diversion which the *Jacquerie* afforded, even as he publicly (and perhaps sincerely) deplored the excesses of violence and brutality.[152]

The dauphin, who opposed both Marcel and the king of Navarre, also opposed the *Jacquerie,* but he did not play a great role in its suppression. As the representative of royal power, he profited from it in the long run because the violence helped to crystallize the growing demand for law and order and the conviction that only a strong monarchy could provide such order. In the short run, the *Jacquerie* appeared disastrous

---

more than an obedience of royal orders. The Grand Ordinance of March, 1357, authorized such forcible resistance. See *Ord.* 3: pp. 124–146, arts. 17 and 35.

[150] Delachenal, *Charles V* 1: pp. 395–416; *Chron. Jean II et Charles V* 1: pp. 177–178, 180–185; Luce, *Jacquerie,* pp. 77f.

[151] *Ibid.,* pp. 72–74; Cazelles, "Parti navarrais," pp. 867–868.

[152] Luce, *Jacquerie,* pp. 96, 99–111, 116–117.

for the dauphin because it prevented collection of the all-important subsidy, diverted the military class from the business of recapturing Paris, and gave Charles the Bad a valuable opportunity to regain favor with the frightened aristocracy.[153]

The decisive events in the brief history of the uprising took place on 9 and 10 June, 1358. The dauphin's family, and the families of other princes and nobles, were installed in the fortified Market of Meaux. It was a strategic stronghold, for it dominated a town which controlled one of the essential supply routes to Paris. The mayor and citizens of Meaux were sympathetic to Marcel, and when the latter sent his Parisian forces to attack the Market, the inhabitants of Meaux and other non-nobles enthusiastically joined in the enterprise. This fortress at Meaux became a symbol of the great conflicts of 1358: noble vs. non-noble, Marcel vs. the regent, and the Parisians vs. their potential besiegers. Relatively few men-at-arms protected the place, for most of those inside the stronghold were women and children.[154]

At the moment when the decisive confrontation at Meaux was coming about, the king of Navarre was proceeding into Beauvaisis with an army composed of outraged nobles, Navarrese partisans, and English mercenaries. The fate of the *Jacquerie,* and perhaps the monarchy as well, hinged on two battles. There was little doubt about the outcome of Charles the Bad's venture. By a strategem he seized the person of Guillaume Cale, the leader of the peasants, and his troops quickly annihilated the Jacques and began the brutal suppression of the rebellion in Beauvaisis and Picardy.[155] At Meaux, however, the outcome was much less certain, for the defenders of the fortress were badly outnumbered. At a critical moment, however, reinforcements arrived in the persons of two Gascon lords who were related by marriage to Charles the Bad—Gaston Phoebus, count of Foix, and Jean de Grailly, captal of Buch. Seeking adventure during the Anglo-French truce, they had spent a year crusading in Prussia and now were on their way home. Finding some of the illustrious families of French chivalry besieged by non-nobles at Meaux, they plunged into the fight and attacked the besiegers, who soon were put to rout

---

[153]*Ibid.,* pp. 147–148; Cazelles, "Parti navarrais," pp. 867–868.

[154]Denifle, *Désolation* 2: p. 161; Luce, *Jacquerie,* pp. 96, 132–134.

[155]*Ibid.,* pp. 149f; *Venette,* pp. 76–78; Denifle, *Désolation* 2: p. 162.

with great slaughter.[156] At Meaux and in the countryside of Picardy, the rising of non-noble against noble was decisively crushed, and the major role was played by the king of Navarre and his supporters. For a moment, at least, the interests and loyalties of class had superseded other considerations. The nobles were still a decisive force in France, rescuing the dauphin with their support against the *Jacquerie* as surely as they had ruined the Estates General by their non-support.

It is sometimes said that Etienne Marcel's support for the *Jacquerie* was a blunder which permanently compromised his cause,[157] yet this contention does not stand up under close scrutiny. The excesses of the *Jacquerie* and Marcel's willingness to support the peasants *did* compromise the provost of the merchants in the eyes of modern historians who believed he was fighting for a great ideal, but if one takes a more realistic view of his goals, it becomes apparent that his actions with regard to the *Jacquerie* were not of decisive importance. It is merely calling attention to the obvious to point out that Marcel, the supporter of the peasants, and Charles of Navarre, their destroyer, very quickly resumed their alliance. More important, perhaps, is the fact that the documents generally describe the *Jacquerie* as an uprising of non-nobles against nobles.[158] The fact that the *bourgeoisie* had little in common with the peasants did not prevent the nobles and the regent from lumping them together under the single heading of nonnobles. The uprising aroused the hatred of the nobles against non-nobles generally, and it is most unlikely that the Parisians could have won the confidence of the nobles by standing aloof from the *Jacquerie* or condemning it. By declining to attend the assemblies in Paris, the nobility had already shown a disinclination to support the militant leadership of the upper bourgeoisie; yet the assembly at Compiègne had shown the nobles to be as interested as ever in genuine reforms. No longer identifying Marcel with reform, the nobles were hostile to him well before the *Jacquerie* began. The provost of the

---

[156] Luce, *Jacquerie*, pp. 135-136. Many letters of remission in AN JJ 86 document the history of the *Jacquerie*. Among those relating to the attack on the Market of Meaux, see those published by Luce, *loc. cit.*, P.J. 3, 4, 6-14, 22, 27.

[157] See *ibid.*, pp. 122-123. For the discussion of Marcel's motives and his involvement in the *Jacquerie*, see above, note 152.

[158] Among the many examples in AN JJ 86, one may cite no. 241, which has been published by Secousse, *Charles le Mauvais* 1: pp. 81-83, and Luce, *Jacquerie*, P.J. 23.

merchants had been a marked man since the murder of the two marshals in February. The *Jacquerie* merely intensified antagonisms which already existed; Marcel had nothing to lose by supporting the peasants and nothing to gain by opposing them. His one important ally, Charles the Bad, was not alienated by Marcel's support for the Jacques.

In short, Marcel was no longer fighting for reform, but for his very survival. This survival depended on keeping the regent from retaking Paris. If he could use the *Jacquerie* to weaken the already hostile nobility, encourage anti-noble sentiment in other towns, and destroy the fortresses which threatened Paris, he had everything to gain. The *Jacquerie* was an unexpected blessing, offering him some possibility of escaping from an increasingly desperate situation. He had no choice but to exploit the opportunity which was presented to him.

For a time, at least, Charles the Bad appeared to be the principal beneficiary of the *Jacquerie*. He swift response to the appeal of the nobles of Beauvaisis and his victory over the peasants enabled him to regain some standing with the nobles, but he ignored Marcel's support for the peasants and extended his protection to Paris. He thus had hopes of driving a wedge into the principal source of the regent's support, while retaining his favored position at the capital.[159] The Navarrese alliance still offered some hope to the Parisians that their supply routes could be cleared of the dauphin's troops, and it gave Marcel some force to exert against the growing number of critics in the city who had lost enthusiasm for his policies. So it was that Charles the Bad returned to Paris on 14 June and was acclaimed captain of the town at the urging of Charles Toussac, his strongest supporter among the *échevins*. Marcel promised to write to other towns proposing that he be chosen captain of the whole kingdom. Charles was more powerful than ever, and perhaps he felt that his claim to the French throne would soon become a reality.[160]

In the final week of June, 1358, Charles the Bad left Paris with his troops, intending to gain unbroken communications

---

[159] Avout, *Meurtre*, p. 215.
[160] *Ibid.*, pp. 216–218; *Chron. Jean II et Charles V* 2: 185–186; Denifle, *Désolation* 2: pp. 158, 162.

with his supporters in Picardy by securing the Oise valley. Representatives of the university tried to bring about negotiations with the dauphin, whose troops laid siege to Paris at the end of the month. On the twenty-eighth, Marcel wrote to the towns of Flanders, calling for them to provide aid against the "nobles" who were besieging Paris. Reacting to the aroused class-consciousness of the aristocracy in the only way possible, he sought to impress the Flemish burghers with a duty to collaborate against the lords.[161]

The regent, for his part, wished to avoid a direct assault on Paris. His insufficient resources made the venture risky from a military point of view, and his political sense made him desirous of avoiding a bloody encounter. He therefore acceded to the pressures of papal representatives and the dowager queen, Joan of Evreux, and agreed to new negotiations with Charles of Navarre on 8 July. The two princes reached a settlement whereby Charles the Bad would swear loyalty to the crown in return for a large sum of money, some of it in revenues, and some to be paid from receipts of war subsidies. The dauphin promised a general amnesty and the Navarrese king undertook to persuade the Parisians to accept the agreement and contribute to the ransom of John II. This tentative agreement was not well received in Paris, although men like Robert le Coq and Jean de Picquigny supported Charles the Bad against his critics. Soon thereafter, a Parisian sortie was repulsed by the dauphin, who summoned Charles the Bad to his aid, only to be accused of breaking the treaty by starting the skirmish. Amid general distrust and recriminations, the agreement collapsed, and on 11 July, Marcel sent a new, and considerably more desperate, appeal for support to the towns of Flanders.[162]

New negotiations took place on the nineteenth, with Parisian representatives participating, and the dauphin, who could no longer pay his troops, used the new discussions as an excuse to raise the siege. This action gave new confidence to the Parisians and restored some of their faith in Marcel, but it

---

[161] Avout, *Meurtre*, pp. 219-221.

[162] *Ibid.*, pp. 222-225; *Venette*, pp. 74-75, and editor's notes, p. 239, note 36; Denifle, *Désolation* 2: 165-166. Marcel's letter is published in *Froissart* (ed. Kervyn de Lettenhove) 6: pp. 466-472.

also led them to revive some of their old hostility to the English and Navarrese *routiers* whom Charles the Bad had brought into the city.[163]

The friction between the bourgeois of Paris and their increasingly unwelcome protectors grew steadily greater. Marcel and Le Coq could not prevent angry demonstrations against the Anglo-Navarrese troops in the capital. These forces were withdrawn, but tension increased when a contingent of Parisians outside the walls was ambushed and massacred by the *routiers*. At Saint-Denis, Charles the Bad awaited reinforcements from his brother before attempting to re-enter Paris. While Marcel continued to work on his behalf, numerous influential Parisians began to distrust their leader and long for the dauphin's return. Some of Marcel's strongest supporters during his period as an advocate of reform began to abandon him at the last minute, preferring any alternative to the deliverance of Paris into the hands of the hated Anglo-Navarrese soldiers. Etienne Marcel, increasingly worried about his own safety, seems to have contemplated just such a step, and on the night of 31 July, his erstwhile supporter, Jean Maillart, forcibly prevented him from opening the gate of the city at the road to Saint-Denis. Marcel was killed, and in the ensuing uproar some of his staunchest followers were put to death while others were imprisoned.[164]

The day following Marcel's death, a delegation from Paris approached the dauphin at Meaux. Charles readily agreed to demand no new concessions, and on 2 August he entered Paris. Royalist officers quickly took over the functions of government from those who had acted at Marcel's bidding, but no repressive reaction followed. A handful of captives were executed in the next few days, and certain royalists were permitted to pursue their private revenge, but most of Marcel's

---

[163] Avout, *Meurtre*, pp. 229–231; Denifle, *Désolation* 2: p. 163. Luce, *Du Guesclin*, pp. 319–320, noted the brigandage of the Italian mercenaries of the dauphin who had not been paid.

[164] Avout, *Meurtre*, pp. 231–245; Denifle, *Désolation* 2: pp. 167–172; Luce, "Examen critique," pp. 255–257, 278–279; S. Luce, "Du rôle politique de Jean Maillart en 1358," *Bib. Ec. Chartes* 18 (1857): pp. 417–418, 422; L. Lacabane, "Mémoire sur la mort d'Etienne Marcel (1358)," *Bib. Ec. Chartes* 1 (1839–1840): p. 96; Delachenal, *Charles V* 1: p. 417f; Castelnau, "Etienne Marcel," pp. 303–304; *Venette*, pp. 79–81. The six major contemporary accounts of the incident have been reprinted in an appendix by Avout, *Meurtre*, pp. 312–318.

former supporters were accepted as loyal subjects.[165] The pardon granted to the populace excluded the crime of treason, but this offense was not broadly interpreted. It included those accused of trying to make Charles the Bad king of France or of thwarting the ransom of King John, but no mention was made of fomenting or supporting the *Jacquerie*. On 10 August the regent issued a general pardon to all who had supported the war of non-nobles against nobles.[166] Navarrese sympathizers naturally lost their places on the royal council, but the new councillors included certain Parisians who, although responsible for Marcel's overthrow, had nevertheless been strongly committed to the reforming party.[167]

Robert le Coq, who had fled secretly to Laon, could not remain there long, for he was branded as a rebel and his property was confiscated.[168] No longer having to fear Marcel, the dauphin made few allusions to the rebellion of the Parisians and now sought to blame Charles the Bad for everything. In a famous letter to the count of Savoy on 31 August, which may duplicate letters sent to other European princes, the French regent accused Charles of Navarre of trying to seize the throne and linked him with the murder of the two marshals six months before.[169] It is understandable that he now used every weapon of propaganda against his brother-in-law, for the Navarrese were all around Paris, ravaging Saint-Denis, cutting royal communications on the Oise, and on 4 August, occupying the stronghold of Melun which belonged to Blanche of Evreux.[170] Charles the Bad also maintained communications with a few remaining partisans in Paris.[171]

---

[165]*Ibid.*, pp. 245–248; Luce, "Examen critique," p. 270; Fremaux, "Famille," p. 203; *Chron. Jean II et Charles V* 1: pp. 210–212.

[166]AN JJ 86, no. 240; BN NAF 7376, fols. 358–362v; 7610, fols. 56–66, 72r–79v; Avout, *Meurtre*, p. 250. See also Secousse, *Charles le Mauvais* 1: pp. 87–88.

[167]Avout, *Meurtre*, pp. 257–258.

[168]Secousse, *Charles le Mauvais* 1: pp. 85–86; Denifle, *Désolation* 2: pp. 223–224.

[169]S. Luce, "Negociations des Anglais avec le roi de Navarre pendant la révolution parisienne de 1358," *Mem. Soc. Hist. Paris* 1 (1875): p. 118, note 1; Avout, *Meurtre*, pp. 259–262; Froissart (ed. K. de Lettenhove) 6: pp. 473–479.

[170]Documents on the occupation of Melun and other campaigns of Charles the Bad in this period have been published by Secousse, *Charles le Mauvais* 1: pp. 88–89, 99–100, 102–103, 123–125. As always, his aunt and sister, the dowager queens Joan and Blanche, cooperated with him. See also Avout, *Meurtre*, pp. 251–253, 255–257; . Luce, *Du Guesclin*, p. 297; Venette, pp. 82–83.

[171]Avout, *Meurtre*, p. 254.

No sooner had he regained Paris than the regent began to concern himself once again with matters of finance. He briefly ordered a new coinage on the 80th *pied,* which stimulated profitable activity at the mints; then, on 22 August, he catered to reformist sentiments by restoring the 32nd *pied.*[172] He was also quick to seek financial advantage from the recent disorders, naming commissioners to negotiate *finances* with those accused of fomenting the recent civil disturbances in and around Paris. His many subsequent letters of remission were undoubtedly granted for a price.[173]

More important from the government's point of view was the need to obtain taxes which could actually be collected. On 10 August, the day he issued the general pardon, the regent obtained taxes in Paris which were to support troops at the rate proposed by the last meeting of the Estates—one man for every 70 urban hearths and every 100 rural hearths. The Parisians were to pay a sales tax of 8 d./l., a *gabelle* on salt, and a levy on wine for this purpose. They also were to contribute a tax of 10 per cent on houses and incomes for the ransom of John II.[174] Once this grant was obtained, Charles wrote to his Norman duchy, where the warfare seems to have brought taxation to a standstill. The Norman Estates were convened at Rouen and asked for the same subsidy that Paris had agreed to pay.[175] The king of Navarre, meanwhile, was taxing his own Norman lands.[176] At the same time, the Estates of Auvergne convened to consider a tax for the ransom of John II[177] and the bailiff of Mâcon was ordered to seek a war subsidy from his district.[178] Late in August, 1358, the crown received a

[172]*Ibid.,* pp. 255-259.

[173]Secousse, *Charles le Mauvais* 1: pp. 80-81; Luce, *Jacquerie,* pp. 157-159.

[174]AN P 2292, p. 705; AN PP 117, pp. 747-748; BN NAF 7610, fols. 68r-v; Balas, *Tentative,* pp. 183-184; Coville, *Etats Norm.,* pp. 367-369.

[175]*Ibid.;* BN MS. fr. 26002, no. 782; BN NAF 20026, no. 66; Secousse, introduction to *Ord.* 3: pp. lxxxiii-lxxxiv.

[176]S. Honoré-Duvergé, "Un Fragment de Compte de Charles le Mauvais," *Bib. Ec. Chartes* 102 (1941): pp. 294-297. The Navarrese had mounted a strenuous military effort in Normandy during the six months following Charles the Bad's release from prison, and it is not surprising that there is so little evidence of royal taxation in this period. Evidence of the Navarrese military build-up is found in Castro, *Catalogo* 2: nos. 968, 971, 974; 3: nos. 24, 36, 38-40, 151.

[177]BN P.O. 1675, *dossier* 38869, no. 15; AM Riom, AA 16, no. 1401; Secousse, introduction to *Ord.* 3: pp. lxxxv-lxxxvi, and notes; M. Boudet, *Thomas de la Marche, bâtard de France, et ses aventures (1318-1361)* (Riom, 1900), P.J. 21.

[178]Guigue, *Tard-Venus,* pp. 6-7, 208.

payment from Lyon which was earmarked for the royal ransom.[179] In Forez, violent opposition to royal taxation provoked an investigation by royal commissioners, who sentenced the offenders to pay heavy fines before agreeing, early in November, to pardon them in return for a contribution to the ransom.[180]

Thus the ransom of the captive king, which had received so little attention from the Estates General in 1357 and early 1358, had become a matter of great concern now that the dauphin had regained the initiative and the nobles resumed attendance at assemblies. Strenuous negotiations in Bordeaux and London had, moreover, finally produced a treaty intended to bring about the king's release.

---

[179]*Ibid.*, pp. 254-256, 267-268 (P.J. XVI, XXIV).
[180] AN JJ 90, no. 40; Secousse, introduction to *Ord.* 3: pp. lxxiii-lxxiv.

III. Negotiating the King's Release: Languedoil, 1358–1360

1. The Ransom Treaties of 1358 and 1359

THE papacy had made a continuing effort to secure a peace, beginning long before the battle of Poitiers.[1] Throughout 1357 and 1358, this campaign was intensified, especially after the Anglo-French truce was concluded in March, 1357. Following the news of the truce, Innocent VI made a familiar plea to Edward III, urging that the Christian kingdoms settle their differences and cooperate against the Muslims.[2] He informed John II that he considered the time appropriate for a conclusive treaty and was therefore sending a peace mission to England.[3] The papal legates, Cardinals Talleyrand and Capocci, were experienced diplomats, having conducted the futile truce negotiations on the eve of Poitiers, when their efforts left them subject to criticism from both sides.[4] For the present task they may have been unfortunate choices, having had some difficulty getting along with each other. Their mission, moreover, was complicated by the fact that the pope also wished them to obtain a settlement of certain Anglo-papal disputes which had arisen from a growing English suspicion of Avignon's policies. Talleyrand, a Frenchman, had incurred English wrath as the recipient of English benefices conferred by a French pope. In seeking the simultaneous resolution of Anglo-French and Anglo-papal discord, the cardinals were pursuing two objectives which were not entirely compatible and were in a poor bargaining position.[5]

Notwithstanding these difficulties, the negotiations proceeded once the cardinals reached London in the summer of 1357.[6] Edward III's claim to the French throne delayed prog-

---

[1] *RTF 1322–1356*, pp. 167, 228, 276, 302.
[2] Denifle, *Désolation* 2: pp. 147–148, text published in note 7.
[3] *Ibid.*, p. 148, notes 1, 2.
[4] *RTF 1322–1356*, p. 302.
[5] Zacour, *Talleyrand*, p. 58.
[6] *Ibid.*, p. 57. Documents relating to the peace mission are in *Foedera* 6: pp. 20, 21, 46.

ress, for the French would not accept a permanent settlement unless he abandoned this claim. Further delay, however, merely strengthened Edward's hand, since the dauphin's position in France deteriorated badly after Charles the Bad was released.

By the end of 1357, however, the two kings had reached agreement on the draft of a treaty, and a copy was sent to Paris for the dauphin's approval. According to Zacour, this draft contained a renunciation of Edward's claim to the throne.[7] In Paris, a royal officer in possession of the draft, Regnaut d'Acy, was killed early in 1358, and the Navarrese partisans learned of the contents of the document. They were not at all pleased by what they discovered. For one thing, the treaty proposed to cede to Edward much more territory than John had ever been willing to give to Charles the Bad. For another, it provided for a list of hostages to go to England while the ransom of John II was being paid. Because it would take some years to pay the proposed ransom of four million *écus*, the hostages could anticipate an extended exile, and the list of persons named in the treaty (particularly those who were noble) contained a disproportionately large number of Navarrese partisans. Advised by the embittered councillors whom the reformers had driven from Paris, John II had hit upon the expedient of using the treaty as a means of removing from France his most strenuous critics. Cazelles has argued that John had drawn up the list of hostages very early in his captivity, when he was still at Bordeaux, for some of those who were included had deserted the opposition party later in 1357.[8]

Already anathema to the anti-royalist forces in Paris, the treaty also encountered obstacles in England, where hostility to the papacy became manifest soon after Parliament convened on 5 February, 1358. The assembly sought to bargain over the treaty in order to gain concessions on the question of papal reservations and benefices, the very practices which Talleyrand and Capocci had been instructed to protect.[9] Despite the obstacles, however, this "First Treaty of London" was formally concluded by John II and Edward III at Westminster on 8 May. Described by Delachenal as a moderate

---

[7] Zacour, *Talleyrand*, p. 57.

[8] Cazelles, "Parti navarrais," pp. 863–866.

[9] Zacour, *Talleyrand*, p. 58.

settlement, this treaty bore some resemblance to that concluded at Brétigny exactly two years later. The territorial provisions were similar, and so was the initial payment on John II's ransom: 600,000 *écus* before the first of November in order to secure the king's release.[10]

As formally concluded, this treaty seems not to have contained an explicit renunciation of the French crown by Edward III. John le Patourel, the scholar who has argued most forcefully that Edward really desired the French throne, claims that he made no real concessions at all in this treaty. Instead, it was nothing more than a "ransom treaty," comparable to those which Edward had already made with the duke of Brittany and king of Scotland. No issues were resolved other than the release of John II, and a general settlement was deferred to a later date. The French had to concur because the weak bargaining position of the dauphin left little room for further negotiation.[11] The sudden upsurge in references to the ransom during the spring and summer of 1358 shows that the French government hoped to execute the treaty. At the same time, the continued emphasis on subsidies for men-at-arms would seem to support Le Patourel's conclusion, for the French do not seem to have associated the king's release with a peace settlement, as they were to do in 1360. Perhaps the pope thought otherwise, for he authorized two tenths on the French clergy, the first of which was to be payable by 1 November, when the first ransom payment was due.[12]

John II was eager for his release, and he soon learned of the meeting of Estates at Compiègne early in May, when the assembly had shown more sympathy for the crown than had any of its recent predecessors. Learning of the small size of this assembly, he began in June to send letters to the continent, urging the clergy and nobles who had been absent to contribute a tax comparable to that granted at Compiègne. He ordered commissioners in all bailiwicks and seneschalsies to apply this tax throughout Languedoil.[13]

[10]*Ibid.;* Denifle, *Désolation* 2: p. 149; Delachenal, *Charles V* 1: p. 394; 2: pp. 72–75.

[11]*Ibid.;* J. le Patourel, "The Treaty of Brétigny, 1360," *Trans. Royal Hist. Soc.*, 5th ser., 10 (1960): pp. 25–27.

[12]AN PP 117, p. 747; Denifle, *Désolation* 2: p. 150, note 2; Delachenal, *Charles V* 2: pp. 72–73.

[13]*Ibid.*, pp. 69–70, and notes; *Ord.* 3: p. 692; BN MS. lat. 9146, fols. 161r-v; BN NAF 7610, fols. 42–44; Varin, *Reims* 3: p. 105. See above, chap. II, note 137.

The summer of 1358, however, was no time to elicit a great fiscal effort from the embattled French population. For two years, taxes had repeatedly been ordered but not collected. Not until August did the dauphin regain Paris, and, as we have seen, the Navarrese forces remained a powerful threat well after Marcel's death. Little money must have been collected for the ransom, and the failure to produce the required sum by 1 November ensured the treaty's failure.[14] Well before this date, however, it was virtually a dead letter, thanks to the diplomacy of Charles the Bad.

As soon as the contents of the draft treaty had become known, the king of Navarre had opposed it. The release of John II would put him in danger; surrender of lands to Edward III offended the prince who believed his claim to the throne was better than Edward's; and the list of hostages betrayed King John's intention to break up the Navarrese party. More to the point, perhaps, was the possibility that Charles could hope to supplant the Valois on the throne as long as his friends held Paris. Had Marcel lived a few days more, the Navarrese might have gained a firm grip on the capital. To protect himself, however, Charles had been carrying on negotiations with the English, and many English troops were enrolled under his banner during 1358 when the Anglo-French truce prevented Edward III from conducting overt military operations.[15]

When the murder of Marcel prevented him from securing Paris, the king of Navarre quickly concluded a treaty of his own with England. Luce has seen this treaty as a last resort, whereby Charles hoped to salvage something from his unsuccessful bid to take over Paris. Déprez, on the other hand, argued that the treaty was the product of long negotiations

---

[14]Zacour, *Talleyrand*, pp. 58–59; Le Patourel, "Treaty of Brétigny," p. 20; Delachenal, *Charles V* 2: p. 72.

[15]Denifle, *Désolation* 2: pp. 150–151, 174–175, 177–179; Luce, "Negociations," p. 119. On Charles the Bad's claim to the French throne there is some uncertainty. If women could transmit a claim to a son, Charles (the grandson of Louis X) had a better claim than Edward (the grandson of Philip IV), and such French scholars as Cazelles and Perroy consider that Charles had a better claim on this basis. Donald Sutherland, however, has expressed to me some doubts on this score. Charles was born in 1332, and it was four years earlier that the right of a woman to transmit a claim was being debated. Sutherland suggests that Charles was disqualified as a valid claimant because he was not *in rerum natura* in 1328.

and was not precipitated by the fall of Marcel.[16] Undoubtedly
Déprez is right about the Anglo-Navarrese negotiations, but
Luce still seems convincing on the point that the treaty was a
retreat for Charles the Bad from his high hopes of early July.
Two questions may never be fully resolved—whether Marcel
knew about the treaty, and whether Charles the Bad actually
waited until hearing of Marcel's death before concluding it.[17]
The treaty called for a partition of France. Charles the Bad
would recognize Edward as king and would be given Champagne and Brie. His earlier demands for Normandy and
Picardy the English had rejected, but final resolution of this
question would await a meeting between the two kings.[18]

The new Anglo-Navarrese accord, as much as anything else,
ruined the prospects for the first London treaty. Once he
possessed Melun, Charles the Bad waged full-scale war against
the dauphin. Royal taxes must have been all but impossible to
collect in large parts of Languedoil, and such money as was
received had to be applied to the war. Even if it was only a
ransom treaty to arrange for John's release, the agreement
reached in London could not be implemented, and the
negotiations with Navarre may have caused Edward to lose
interest in it. In September, 1358, the papal nuncios left
England, despairing of a settlement.[19]

As long as there was some hope for the release of John II,
every possible revenue was set aside for the ransom. Payment
of royal debts and salaries of officials were suspended; profits
from the mints, fines, and forfeitures were to be devoted to the
ransom.[20] When the deadline for the first ransom payment
passed and the treaty appeared to be a dead letter, the dauphin,
on 30 November, reassigned the revenues from fines and

[16] Luce, "Negociations," pp. 113–114, 117–118; E. Déprez, "Une conférence anglo-
navarraise en 1358." *Revue historique* **99** (1908): pp. 34–39. Coville, in his review of
Denifle (*op. cit.* above, chap. 1. note 69) sided with Luce, arguing that the treaty was a
hastily drawn expedient, and criticized Denifle, whose position was somewhat similar
to the one taken by Déprez in 1908.

[17] Luce, "Negociations," pp. 117–118, was certain that Charles the Bad knew of
Marcel's death before signing the treaty. He thought it possible that Marcel never
knew of the treaty, but insisted that his plan to admit Charles to Paris would have
meant the dismemberment of France in any case.

[18] The treaty is published *ibid.*, pp. 128–131.

[19] Zacour, *Talleyrand*, pp. 58–60.

[20] BN NAF 7610, fol. 96; AN P 2293, pp. 143–144.

forfeitures to rebuilding the royal palace and paying salaries.[21] Later, they were reassigned once more, this time to meet the cost of John II's household, which now faced an indefinite sojourn in England.[22] In still another stop-gap fiscal measure, the dauphin used his "joyous accession" to the government as an excuse to issue a new coinage in December, 1358.[23]

All this juggling and manipulating of domainal revenues suggests very strongly that tax receipts still were proving woefully inadequate to meet the needs imposed by the royal ransom and the war. The continued hostility of the Navarrese and the activities of unemployed companies that operated for their own profit combined to frustrate orderly administrative practice in much of the kingdom.[24] Although some rebels were punished, and others, like Robert le Coq, could never hope for royal pardon,[25] the dauphin did pardon many of his former foes and sought to restore order and encourage loyalty.[26] Even Amiens, a long-time center of Navarrese sympathizers, was pardoned in September, 1358, and a Navarrese army was repulsed when it tried to take the city.[27]

These efforts at pacification and the restoration of order did not, however, achieve enough success to permit a notable increase in tax collections. We have seen that Normandy was approached for new taxes almost as soon as the dauphin had secured Paris and obtained a subsidy from the capital. Yet receipts and pay orders attesting to collections, which are plentiful for much of this period, are practically non-existent after April, 1358, and there are few traces of royal taxation in the duchy during the last two-thirds of the year. The dauphin's commissioners did consult some nobles of the bailiwick of Caux early in October at Caudebec. These agreed to a hearth tax of one *écu* for a year, to be apportioned according to ability to pay. Although collection was scheduled to begin

---

[21] BN NAF 7610, fol. 102; AN P 2293, pp. 165–167.

[22] *Ibid.*, pp. 179–184, 947–952.

[23] BN Moreau 234, fols. 51r–52r.

[24] Guigue, *Tard-Venus*, pp. 256–257 (P.J. XVII); Secousse, *Charles le Mauvais* 1: pp. 110–112; Denifle, *Désolation* 2: p. 240.

[25] On Le Coq, see Secousse, *Charles le Mauvais* 1: pp. 103–104, 119–120.

[26] Avout, *Meurtre*, p. 250; numerous letters of remission in AN JJ 86.

[27] Secousse, *Charles le Mauvais* 1: pp. 97–99; BN NAF 7376, fols. 366–371v; Avout, *Meurtre*, pp. 269–270; A. Thierry (ed.), *Recueil des monuments inédits de l'histoire du tiers état, première série* (4 v., Paris, 1850–1859) 1: pp. 586–589, 599–601.

in November, the dauphin did not ratify the agreement until
January, 1359, and no documents indicate collection before
that time.[28] Lower Normandy also made a grant in October
and followed more closely the dauphin's request that the
example of Paris be followed. These Normans offered a sales
tax of 6 d./l. and a levy of 1 s./l. on houses, with a special tax
on beverages. Collection was to run for six months, beginning
early in November. It encountered opposition at both Caen
and Falaise because the hard-pressed inhabitants wished to
save their resources for local defense.[29] The crown had already
authorized Caen to raise and maintain a force of fifty crossbowmen to protect the town.[30]

Other evidence of royal taxation in Languedoil during the
final weeks of 1358 is very limited. We know of levies at
Poitiers, Vitry, and Montferrand.[31] The first two of these were
probably the taxes ordered in the assembly at Compiègne the
preceding May. At Montferrand the tax in question was a
contribution to the ransom; the dauphin's officers were ordered to levy a sales tax of 6 d./l. or else collect the 300 l. t.
which the town had traditionally paid for feudal aids. Possibly a contribution to the ransom had been agreed to at the
assembly held by the duke of Bourbon in August, when the
treaty with England was still alive.[32] For the rest of the winter
of 1358–1359 the evidence of taxation remains scattered and
fragmentary, thereby reinforcing the impression of warfare,
disorder, and disrupted administration which one obtains
from the chroniclers. The merchants who transported goods
along the Seine river were assessed a special tax for the
purpose of financing an effort to drive the Navarrese from
Melun.[33] In February, 1359, Saint-Quentin was authorized to

---

[28]Coville, *Etats Norm.*, pp. 91, 371–372, 373–374. On the effort to tax Normandy at
the end of the summer of 1358, and the Navarrese military effort in the duchy, see
above, chap. II, notes 175–176.

[29]Coville, *Etats Norm.*, pp. 91–92, 372–373.

[30]*Ord.* **3**: p. 297.

[31]*Arch. hist. Poit.* **46**: p. 184; AN P 2293, pp. 953–954; *INV AM Montferrand* 1: p. 3
(AA 7).

[32]*Ibid.;* F. Lehoux, *Jean de France, duc de Berri: sa vie, son action politique* (3 v.,
Paris, 1966–1968) 1: pp. 120–121, and notes. Montferrand and Riom did escape from
paying part of an assessment owed to the captain of *routiers*, Thomas de la Marche
(Boudet, *Thomas de la Marche*, P. J. 20). On the assembly convened in August, 1358,
by Bourbon, see above, chap. II, note 177.

[33]*Ord.* **3**: p. 298. For references to the Navarrese occupations of Melun, see Secousse,
Charles le Mauvais 1: pp. 117, 122.

raise a municipal tax on condition that it not interfere with the royal subsidy.[34] On 11 March a letter from the dauphin referred to taxes at Reims which had been granted at Paris and Compiègne.[35] It appears from these texts that an effort was being made to collect in Vermandois the royal subsidy obtained from the Estates in May, 1358.

At the same time, the *gabelle* on salt was revived in Vermandois, being levied with the approval of lords with high justice.[36] We have seen that different regions had chosen different ways of financing the men-at-arms granted by the Estates at Compiègne. The two parts of Normandy had chosen an apportioned hearth tax and an *ad valorem* sales tax respectively, while Paris had chosen the latter plus a *gabelle*.[37] Besides being levied in Vermandois, this tax on salt was also revived in the bailiwick of Chartres.[38] Following its first five-year trial, the *gabelle* had been suppressed in one region after another in 1346–1347, and it had met great resistance when revived at the beginning of 1356.[39] Now, in 1358–1359 its revival in some localities marked its third appearance during the fourteenth century. It would soon be reintroduced on a broader scale in Languedoc and the needs of John II's ransom would make it a permanent part of the French fiscal system.

Another district which was paying taxes in the early months of 1359 was Auvergne, where the subsidy for men-at-arms authorized at Compiègne was being collected under the watchful eye of the regional Estates, who continued to meet periodically.[40] Riom's share of the subsidy was 400 *écus*, but the town asked to be excused from paying it so that the money could be used instead to pay for defensive preparations against an impending enemy attack.[41] An assembly of the three Estates of the bailiwick of the Mountains (*Haut-pays*) also granted a war subsidy in this period, and Aurillac was allowed to levy

---

[34] Le Maire, *St. Quentin* 2: no. 671. Arras also was levying a municipal tax and trying to drive the enemy from an important castle: Guesnon, *Inv. Arras,* pp. 121–125.
[35] AN P 2293, pp. 157, 217, 221; Varin *Reims* 3: pp. 130–132.
[36] *Ibid.,* pp. 132–136, 139.
[37] See above, chap. II, note 174.
[38] AN P 2293, p. 173.
[39] *RTF 1322–1356,* pp. 196, 293–294.
[40] BN Clairambault 12, no. 137; Clairambault 213, no. 93; BN P.O. 1675, *dossier* 38869, no. 10; AD Lot F 35; Boudet, *Thomas de la Marche,* P.J. 24; Lehoux, *Jean de France* 1: pp. 121–123.
[41] AM Riom CC 13, no. 1323.

an additional local tax on wine for the next ten years in order to pay for repairs to its fortifications.[42] In Auvergne, as elsewhere, the recent trend towards local assumption of military responsibility continued, as the central government remained weak. Local defense was an urgent matter for the people of Auvergne, for as the Anglo-French truce continued, more and more *routier* captains were finding that the Massif Central offered many bases and refuges from which to conduct brigandage. The dreaded English captain, Robert Knolles, abandoned his former haunts in the Breton marches and took Chateauneuf-sur-Loire in October, 1358. By March he had advanced to Auxerre, where he exacted from the population a ransom of 40,000 *moutons*. Berry and Auvergne were soon to feel his wrath.[43]

In Normandy, the Franco-Navarrese war continued, and in October, 1358, Charles the Bad ordered all persons living in his lands to serve with his forces or risk confiscation of their property.[44] We may assume, of course, that most of these people were to pay a subsidy in lieu of actually serving. Faced with continuing military danger, Norman towns, like those in Auvergne, were allowed, and perhaps encouraged, to assume more responsibility for their own defense. Rouen was permitted to levy a "subsidy" on merchandise, for fortifications.[45] A subsequent document reveals that the citizens of Rouen were actually paying more (8 d./l.) for the town's defense than the tax of 6 d./l. they were paying to the crown. The combined sales tax, nearly 6 per cent, must have been a hardship for many consumers during this period of economic difficulty, and it evidently caused violent opposition.[46] Hoping to improve the fiscal, political, and military situation in Normandy the dauphin named a new lieutenant in the bailiwicks of Rouen, Caux, Caen, and Cotentin—Louis d'Harcourt, viscount of Chastelleraut, one of the few loyal members of the Harcourt family, who had been assigned some of the confiscated lands of his pro-Navarrese relations. He was empowered to hold assemblies, impose and collect subsidies, arrange

---

[42] AN JJ 90, no. 33; *INV AM Aurillac* 1: p. 397 (CC 1).
[43] Luce, *Du Guesclin*, p. 291; Guigue, *Tard-Venus*, p. 33.
[44] Secousse, *Charles le Mauvais* 1: p. 141.
[45] AN JJ 87, no. 143.
[46] AN JJ 87, no. 267.

ransoms, and assemble men-at-arms.[47] Acting on this authority, Harcourt did summon the three Estates of the bailiwicks of Rouen and Caux, to meet at Rouen on 31 March, 1359. There is no evidence, however, of any new Norman subsidy at this time; if the assembly did meet, it must have concerned itself with matters other than taxation.[48]

Individual localities in Normandy continued to raise money for their own defense. Caen employed taxes—8 d./l. inside the town and 6 d./l. on goods leaving the town—to pay the salary of forty men-at-arms employed for local military operations.[49] Other texts refer to a subsidy at Caen imposed for the purpose of forcing the enemy to evacuate local fortresses.[50] It is not clear whether this was the same tax or a separate one imposed by the crown, but such local taxes, being employed to wage war on enemies of the king and kingdom, must be included in any assessment of royal taxation in these years. Fragmentation and localization of fiscal and military responsibility were an obvious response to the crown's weakness during the king's captivity. Curiously reminiscent of an earlier fragmentation of authority during the raids of the ninth century, they were to have some constitutional importance.

While efforts to restore public order thus proceeded on a very makeshift basis, the dauphin received extremely disturbing news from the diplomatic front. With the first treaty of London having been subverted by the intrigues of Charles the Bad and the hostility of England towards the papal representatives, John II had to resume negotiations with Edward III on his own. Extremely eager for his release from captivity, and perhaps also anxious to relieve his kingdom of the continuing war, John was in a poor bargaining position.[51] The two-year truce with England was scheduled to expire on 9 April, 1359, and some months earlier Edward III began preparations for the invasion of France that was supposed to bring him a decisive victory. In Paris, of course, the dauphin was stronger

---

[47] Secousse, *Charles le Mauvais* 1: pp. 134–136, 171; BN MS. fr. 25701, no. 146; Secousse, introduction to *Ord.* 3: pp. lxxxiv–lxxxv.

[48] Coville, *Etats Norm.*, pp. 96, 373–374.

[49] *Ibid.*, pp. 374–375; BN NAF 3645, nos. 37, 38.

[50] BN MS. fr. 26002, nos. 816, 818, 819; Coville, *Etats Norm.*, pp. 373–374.

[51] Denifle, *Désolation* 2: p. 324.

than he had been a year earlier, but his revenue and military strength had not kept pace with his political progress. There was little to deter Edward from demanding much harsher terms than in 1358. The result was the second Treaty of London, far more unfavorable to France than its predecessor, which was signed on 24 March, 1359. The earlier agreement had proposed to cede to England the territory comprised in the twelfth-century duchy of Aquitaine; the new treaty added Normandy and Anjou, virtually restoring the "Angevin empire" of Henry II while retaining the feature of an extremely high ransom. The truce was extended until 24 June, doubtless because the French needed time to ratify the treaty.[52]

English historians have wondered why Edward III should have negotiated such an agreement. His preparations for invading France were well underway, and yet he agreed to prolong the truce and abandon his claim to the French throne. In all probability, he needed more time to prepare his expeditionary force and felt that he had little to lose. Even if his real objective was the crown of France, there was small risk in abandoning his claim in return for a settlement which would give him so much of the kingdom without a fight. Even if the French ratified the treaty, the Valois monarchy would face a struggle to survive in the territory left to it, particularly in view of the enormous ransom that John would have to raise.[53]

In fact, Edward probably knew that the second London Treaty imposed a price which the dauphin and his advisers were unwilling to pay. With the Valois government again in possession of Paris, the king's return must have seemed less urgent than it did a year before. Moreover, recent experiences with the *routiers* had shown that an Anglo-French peace would not necessarily relieve the kingdom from war and disorder. There was, in any case, little prospect that the realm could deliver the ransom if deprived of so much territory.

Having received power from the king to complete negotiations with the English,[54] the regent now issued a summons, late in April, for the three Estates of the kingdom to assemble

---

[52] Zacour, *Talleyrand*, p. 61; Delachenal, *Charles V* 2: p. 79f.
[53] Le Patourel, "Treaty of Brétigny," pp. 29–30; Fowler, *King's Lieutenant*, p. 198; *Foedera* 6: pp. 121–122, 126.
[54] BN NAF 7376, fols. 420–421.

at Paris on 19 May.[55] It was the first time in more than eleven years that the entire realm was to be represented at a single assembly. Perhaps because of the lack of recent precedent, the summons did not leave enough time for communities in lower Languedoc to have properly instructed proctors in Paris on the appointed day. Issued on 24 April, the summons to Montpellier allowed a time of only twenty-five days. A generation earlier, it required this much time to make a round trip between Montpellier and Paris. Under the best conditions of travel, there remained no leeway, so that Montpellier had no time in which to select and instruct its proctors. A more distant town such as Carcassonne would have needed ten days more in order to have a properly empowered representative in Paris by 19 May. As it happened, the hazardous state of the roads in 1359 slowed down communications even more, so that the summons itself did not reach Montpellier until 16 May. This town could not have been represented when the first session of the Estates finally convened on the twenty-fifth.[56] Since Poitiers, a town much nearer Paris, received a summons dated 22 April, it is possible that the letter to Montpellier was delayed by unknown circumstances.[57] If lack of time prevented some regions from being represented on the appointed day, there were other factors that tended to keep the assembly small in size. The continuing Anglo-Navarrese occupation of so much of Normandy, for instance, prevented much Norman representation at the Estates.[58] We are told that only twenty-five persons were present when the first session was finally held, and that these were the ones who denounced the treaty of London as neither *passable ni faisable*.[59]

It is curious that the regent did not wait for more arrivals, but as it was, the assembly convened nearly a week late, and the government may have felt that a decision was urgently

---

[55]*HL* 10: cols. 1155–1156; Luce, *Du Guesclin*, p. 293; Delachenal, *Charles V* 2: pp. 84–85.

[56]*Ibid.; HL* 9: p. 704, note 2. According to J. Petit, M. Gavrilovitch, *et al., Essai de restitution des plus anciens memoriaux de la chambre des comptes de Paris* (Paris, 1899), p. 188, a round trip between Montpellier and Paris in the 1320's required twenty-four days, while a round trip between Carcassonne and Paris required thirty days.

[57]*Arch. hist. Poit.* 46: p. 187.

[58]Coville, *Etats Norm.*, p. 96.

[59]*Chron. Jean II et Charles V* 1: p. 232f.; Vuitry, *Régime financier* 2: p. 97.

needed. There being no clear evidence of attendance from Languedoc, it is possible that the summons of people from the Midi was canceled. The rejection of the treaty was evidently the dauphin's main objective, and a sweeping mandate from a large assembly did not seem necessary. The truce having ended, this rejection automatically made it necessary to obtain substantial war subsidies, and for this purpose a more representative body was desirable. As a result, the Estates were kept in session another week, until 2 June, during which time there must have been more new arrivals. Even so, the townsmen deferred an answer on a subsidy until further consultation with their constituents.[60] Although the resultant delay may have been frustrating to the dauphin, he could not realistically have expected a better result. Representatives who had learned of the treaty's provisions would make effective ambassadors to the provinces, explaining why the continuation of the struggle was essential. A grant without such reference back, however, would risk the fate of other subsidies granted by the Estates General in this period: uncollectable taxes. Still another reason why reference back to local constituents was particularly appropriate in 1359 was that the localities had borne the main responsibility for organizing the war effort.

The clergy agreed to pay whatever tax should be decided on by the towns. Significantly, the nobles did the same, showing a willingness to follow the lead of the bourgeoisie, in sharp contrast to their stance of earlier years. They also offered to render military service for a month at their own expense. The first of the towns to make a definite commitment was Paris, which needed little time to refer back to constituents. The capital promised to pay the cost of 2,000 footsoldiers, while the rest of the towns were supposed to have a reply ready by Trinity Sunday.[61] Since this feast fell on 16 June, there was little time for the towns to deliberate, and those farthest from Paris could not have met the deadline. Coville, noting that a Norman assembly was held in the fall of 1359, concluded that

---

[60] Delachenal, *Charles V* 2: p. 89. While the Estates were in session, the dauphin rehabilitated a long list of royal officers who had been disgraced by earlier assemblies. This action underscored the change in the character of the Estates since early 1358. BN MS. fr. 20413, fols. 4–8; AN P 2294, pp. 153–164.

[61] BN Clairambault 34, no. 101; Clairambault 108, nos. 23, 24; BN NAF 7610, fols. 165–185; Vuitry, *Régime financier* 2: pp. 96–97; Delachenal, *Charles V* 2: pp. 92–93, 108.

the response of the towns was disappointing and that the dauphin finally appealed to the Normans as a last resort.[62] What is more likely is that the continuing obstacles to effective collection caused the actual receipts to fall behind.

The towns seem to have agreed in principle that each district would support "a certain number" of men-at-arms, and in effect this meant a one-year extension of the grant made by the Estates at Compiègne in May of 1358.[63] What was left to local negotiation was the form of tax to be used in raising these troops. Citing the cryptic remarks of different chroniclers, Delachenal concluded that all of Languedoil had promised a force equal to 12,000 *glaives* and that a sales tax of 4 d./l. was to be levied for this purpose.[64] The sales tax must only have been employed in a particular region, for Normandy and Auvergne seem to have avoided it. Auvergne's quota of armed men was five hundred *glaives*, and when the local Estates delayed in granting the necessary tax the dauphin grew impatient. In July, however, they adopted a *fouage* of one *écu*.[65]

While awaiting the slowly collected subsidy receipts, the crown took additional financial measures in anticipation of an early renewal of major hostilities with England. The *gabelle* on salt, which had been collected at Reims for three months, was extended to the outlying countryside on 4 June.[66] Two months later, on 9 August, a royal ordinance extended the tax over a much larger area, and after a second ordinance on 15 October the *gabelle* was in force over almost the entire area north and east of the Loire.[67] By this time most of the kingdom was paying it, since Languedoc had already renewed a general *gabelle*.[68]

In general, royal subsidies remained less popular and more difficult to collect than taxes levied by towns and local districts to finance specific measures of defense. A long tradition of localism had been reinforced by the growing fear that the

---

[62] Coville, *Etats Norm.*, p. 97.
[63] Vuitry, *Régime financier* 2: pp. 97–98.
[64] Delachenal, *Charles V* 2: p. 93 and notes.
[65] BN Clairambault 213, no. 97; BN MS. fr. 26002, no. 886.
[66] Varin, *Reims* 3: pp. 139–140.
[67] AN P 2293, pp. 205–206, 945–946; AN PP 117, p. 765; *Ord.* 3: pp. 358–359.
[68] See below, chap. IV, at note 83.

central government was too weak to guarantee effective defense to all regions. In some areas, moreover, the preoccupation with local defense was gradually becoming almost an obsession because of the ever-increasing brigandage of men-at-arms left unemployed by the Anglo-French truce. Although this scourge had not yet reached its peak, it was already a serious problem in 1359.

Robert Knolles had led his company from Auxerre into Berry and Auvergne by the late spring. Anglo-Navarrese forces were threatening Beaujolais at the same time.[69] Eustache d'Auberchicourt, another prominent captain, served English interests but maintained a pretense of legality by calling himself lieutenant of the king of Navarre as long as the Anglo-French truce lasted. He occupied Nogent-sur-Seine and generally ravaged the regions between the Seine and the Loire.[70] French commanders in Picardy were criticized for failing to pursue more aggressively the Anglo-Navarrese forces, who enjoyed some support from the local population.[71] In Beauvaisis, a band of peasants won acclaim as heroes when they successfully repulsed the English at Longueuil.[72] The inhabitants of Reims had to buy back the castle of Roucy from enemy forces who had occupied it. The burghers of Paris, Senlis, and other towns of the Ile-de-France similarly paid dearly to restore the fortress of Creil to friendly hands.[73] In Beaujolais and Forez, the ravages of the *routiers* culminated in the burning of Montbrison in July, 1359.[74]

Faced by this kind of continuing military danger, and unable to count on the royal government for aid, each region was forced to take military measures of its own, thereby becoming all the more accustomed to local management of taxes for war. The metropolitan chapter of Lyon had to keep a small army in the field in order to check brigandage.[75] The

---

[69] Guigue, *Tard-Venus*, p. 33.

[70] Luce, *Du Guesclin*, p. 292.

[71] *Venette*, pp. 87–88.

[72] *Ibid.*, pp. 90–92; Delachenal, *Charles V* 2: p. 132f; S. Luce, *La France pendant la guerre de Cent Ans* (Paris, 1890), pp. 149–156.

[73] *Venette*, p. 95; *Chron. Jean II et Charles V* 1: pp. 247–248; Secousse, *Charles le Mauvais* 1: pp. 143–147, 158.

[74] Guigue, *Tard-Venus*, pp. 35–37.

[75] *Ibid.*, pp. 261–262 (P.J. XIX). A similar local effort was underway at Chartres: BN Clairambault 29, no. 88.

town of Saint-Quentin, with the cooperation of local royal officers, employed a detachment of twelve men-at-arms who would serve under the captain of the town and defend the surrounding country.[76] In Auvergne, where the *routiers* repeatedly tried to capture Saint-Flour, the royal lieutenant employed another captain, Thomas de la Marche, to resist them. He successfully defended Saint-Pourçain but the consuls of Riom and Montferrand feared his troops as much as the enemy. Thomas sought to recruit troops in Auvergne and asked the commissioners of the local Estates to provide him with money to support four hundred men-at-arms.[77]

All these local efforts required taxes, and because the money was used for defense we must continue to treat these levies as an extension of royal taxation or, more accurately, a temporary substitute for royal action. The struggle to oppose brigands and ransom fortresses went on everywhere with local financing. Perhaps the best documented case is provided by Normandy, where military conditions were so bad as to prevent the attendance of Norman representatives when the Estates General met at Paris late in May. In the Navarrese stronghold of lower Normandy, the city of Caen was the main bastion of the Valois monarchy. This town had outfitted troops who were paid from the proceeds of a municipal sales tax.[78] Although entirely local in character, the tax was called a war subsidy, and throughout the summer and early autumn it was collected and paid to the French forces operating in the district.[79] This tenacious local effort led to the recapture of many strongholds,[80] a vindication of the decentralized administration of military financing which was practiced in these years.

Almost without exception, the financial documents from Normandy during the spring and summer of 1359 specify the bailiwick of Caen as the region being taxed.[81] In order to tap

---

[76] Le Maire, *St. Quentin* **2**: no. 672.

[77] Boudet, *Thomas de la Marche*, P.J. 22, 26, 27, 33 pt. 2.

[78] Delisle, *St. Sauveur*, pp. 116–117; Coville, *Etats Norm.*, p. 93.

[79] BN MS. fr. 26002, nos. 835–838, 842–844, 848, 852, 867, 870, 874, 876, BN MS. fr. 22468, nos. 9, 84, 85, 90; BN P.O. 2886, *dossier* 64120, no. 12; BN Clairambault 213, nos. 95, 96.

[80] Delisle, *St. Sauveur*, pp. 114–115; Coville, *Etats Norm.*, p. 95.

[81] See above, note 79. One text which does not so specify is BN P.O. 1522, *dossier* 34634, no. 14.

the resources of the rest of Normandy, the regent had to convene an assembly in September at Rouen, where the three Estates of the bailiwicks of Rouen, Caux, and Cotentin granted sales taxes on numerous commodities.[82] Farmed for one year, these taxes amounted to over 53,000 l. t.[83] Intended exclusively for the payment of troops, the subsidy would run through September, 1360.[84] Despite the existence of various documents indicating its collection during the following months,[85] we are told that the process was difficult,[86] and certain privileges of exemption were honored.[87]

Now that a major renewal of the English war was certain to be added to the dauphin's burdens, it became imperative to neutralize the threat of Charles the Bad. In one sense, chances for a peace with the Evreux were now improved, for the French rejection of the new treaty had again postponed the Anglo-French peace that Charles dreaded. Before talking peace with the king of Navarre, the dauphin was determined to eject his forces from the vital stronghold of Melun. A possession of Charles the Bad's sister Blanche (Philip VI's widow), Melun had been occupied by Navarrese forces in August of 1358. Since that time, Paris had been in a most vulnerable position, ringed by enemy fortresses that threatened the capital's sources of supply and communication with the rest of the realm. The force of troops which the Parisians offered to support at the Estates of May, 1359, was largely intended to break this dangerous encirclement.[88]

Without waiting for the additional resources he hoped to receive from the towns, the regent began a siege of Melun towards the middle of June. The ensuing struggle gave him his first opportunity to observe at first hand the skills of a military commander whose subsequent career would be bound closely to his own as ruler of France. Bertrand du Guesclin, the Breton *routier* captain who had spent five years of intermittent campaigning in Brittany and lower Normandy, was a leading participant in the siege of Melun. The

---

[82] Coville, *Etats Norm.*, p. 97.
[83] BN MS. fr. 26002, no. 856.
[84] Coville, *Etats Norm.*, p. 98; Delachenal, *Charles V* 2: pp. 128–129.
[85] BN MS. fr. 26002, nos. 873, 875, 879, 883, 884, 897, AN K 47, no. 59.
[86] Coville, *Etats Norm.*, p. 97.
[87] AN JJ 87, no. 239.
[88] Delachenal, *Charles V* 2: p. 109.

French did not take the city, but Queen Blanche agreed to abandon it to the dauphin as part of a new settlement between the Valois and Evreux families. The result was the treaty of Pontoise, concluded on 21 August. Promised large sums of money and the return of certain of his possessions which the French had captured, Charles the Bad finally made peace with his brother-in-law, rendering homage to the dauphin and acquiescing in the installation of a royal garrison at Melun.[89] The treaty ended three years of destructive Franco-Navarrese hostilities at a critical moment when a new English invasion was expected. Du Guesclin, meanwhile, returned to the still-unpacified Norman-Breton border region, where his capture of an important English captain led the duke of Lancaster to recall Robert Knolles from his escapades in central France.[90]

It is likely that both the settlement with Navarre and the withdrawal of Knolles from Auvergne greatly improved the prospects for royal taxation. Certainly, the documents relating to collection of subsidies in Normandy show a sharp increase after July of 1359, after fifteen months for which the surviving texts are few in number.[91] Improved collection of taxes did not, of course, imply a rapid improvement in the dauphin's financial situation, since most of the money was still ear-marked for local defensive operations.

The dauphin, moreover, does not appear to have been entirely realistic about the state of his finances and the mood of the taxpaying subjects. Scarcely had the second treaty of London been rejected than he began to pursue a line of diplomacy that would have cost as much as the first ransom payment which the treaty had proposed. The plan was for an alliance with the king of Denmark, who had grievances of his own against the English. If supplied with 600,000 *ecus* by the French, the Danes proposed to invade England. The towns of Languedoil are said to have promised one-third of this sum, with the rest to be obtained from Languedoc. If the northern towns really endorsed the plan, they must have done so when the Estates met in Paris late in May.[92] It is doubtful that they

---

[89]*Chron. Jean II et Charles V* 1: 238–240; Secousse, *Charles le Mauvais* 1: pp. 155–156; Luce, *Du Guesclin*, p. 303.

[90]*Ibid.*, pp. 310–311.

[91]See above, notes 28, 79, 85.

[92]Delachenal, *Charles V* 2: pp. 97–98.

did so with much enthusiasm. Already burdened with the need to finance local defense, the towns of Languedoil had steadily resisted efforts to use their taxes in other parts of the realm. A proposal to send so large a sum outside the kingdom must have seemed even more repugnant to them, particularly since there was no certainty that it would guarantee the king's deliverance and the end of warfare. The government did pursue the scheme in Languedoc,[93] but the documents from northern France pass over it in silence. Even if the project was discussed at the Estates, it came to nothing.

2. The Treaty of Brétigny and the First Ransom Payment

Whether or not the dauphin took the Danish project seriously, its failure cannot be called a real setback; if anything, it spared France a new financial burden at an unpropitious time. Far more important to the Valois cause was the failure of Edward III to mobilize his forces with sufficient speed to deliver the decisive blow against France that he had contemplated. When the first treaty of London could not be executed, Edward had several months of truce remaining in which to organize a resumption of hostilities. Had he been ready to invade France when the truce expired in April, 1359, he would have found the dauphin stronger than in 1358 but still very vulnerable, and still at war with Charles the Bad. Unable to attack by this date, Edward had agreed to the second treaty and the accompanying prolongation of the truce until June. He could hardly have been surprised at the rejection of this treaty, but he may have miscalculated its effects upon the French. Although we know rather little of the Estates of May, 1359, it seems certain that the dauphin made use of the occasion to exploit the anti-English sentiments that the *routiers* had inspired, and to arouse the French on behalf of the Valois dynasty. Even so, an English attack when the truce again expired late in June could have proven successful, but Edward still was not ready. Given a valuable respite, the dauphin's forces made their strong showing at Melun and made possible the vitally important treaty with the Evreux

---

[93] See chap. IV, part 2.

princes in August. By this date the English were almost ready to attack, but the king of Navarre could not afford to wait for their arrival. He therefore reached his accord with the dauphin and remained neutral during the crucial months that followed.[94]

As early as 10 July the dauphin was able to warn the city of Reims that Edward III had chosen it for his objective. Knowing that the archbishop had once been hostile to the Valois government, the king of England seems to have hoped for a coronation as king of France. Announcing his resumption of hostilities in mid-August, he did not arrive with his forces at Calais until October. Although prepared for a battle, he hoped for an unopposed march to Reims. When he arrived at the city, however, he did not gain an easy entry, and he had to inaugurate a costly siege, far from his bases, with winter coming on.[95]

The wretched financial state of the regent's government, if nothing else, prevented the French from giving battle to the large invading army, and there was little alternative but to pursue a scorched-earth policy in a land already laid waste by the *routiers* and the *Jacquerie*. Almost by accident, the French were forced to adopt the policy that would bring them victory in the end. The siege of Reims got underway in mid-November, despite an ineffectual papal letter urging Edward III to make peace.[96] Supplying his troops proved far from easy, and Edward also had to worry about the *routier* captains in his army, lest they ravage unmercifully the kingdom which he hoped to claim as his own. To find employment for men like Eustache d'Auberchicourt, Edward allowed their brigandage a free rein along the borders of the kingdom, well to the east of Reims. They occupied various fortresses which they could profitably hold for ransom, but they had little impact on the siege itself. Finally, on 11 January, 1360, the king decided to raise the siege.[97]

As already mentioned, the French knew well in advance that

---

[94] Fowler, *King's Lieutenant*, p. 200.

[95] *Ibid.*, pp. 200–201; *Foedera* **6**: pp. 134–135; H. Moranvillé, "Le siège de Reims, 1359–1360," *Bib. Ec. Chartes* **56** (1895): p. 92.

[96] *Ibid.*, p. 93; *Chron. Jean II et Charles V* **1**: p. 251f; *Foedera* **6**: pp. 145–146.

[97] Fowler, *King's Lieutenant*, pp. 203–204; Varin, *Reims* **3**: p. 152; Moranvillé, "Siège," pp. 94–98.

Edward III would advance from Calais towards Reims, but
Picardy was an unfavorable place in which to resist him.
Long a stronghold of Navarrese sympathizers, it had been very
imperfectly pacified. The constable, Robert de Fiennes, served
as the dauphin's lieutenant there. As early as 11 July, 1359, he
seems to have convened a local assembly at Béthune, presumably to discuss military preparations and the taxes to pay for
them.[98] Doubtless dissatisfied by the response of this assembly,
he announced on 16 July that Lancaster and the Black Prince
had already sailed for Calais, and ordered his subordinates to
have all nobles and non-nobles report in arms to Picquigny a
week later under pain of being called traitors.[99] A new
assembly of towns from Vermandois was held at Noyon on 19
August to discuss ways of reducing brigandage in the region.[100] Three days later a group of twenty-four towns from
Artois and Picardy wrote to those of Vermandois and called
for a new assembly to meet at Compiègne and draft a list of
grievances to be sent to the dauphin at Paris.[101]

All these events took place before the dauphin's treaty with
Charles the Bad, and it must be remembered that the northern
districts of the kingdom were among the least friendly to the
house of Valois. Edward III doubtless realized that his march
to Reims would be through such a country. Artois belonged to
the dowager countess of Flanders, whose son was trying to
maintain a delicate neutrality between France and England.
Picardy had been a center of pro-Evreux sympathies. The
opposition to Fiennes and to the dauphin's government was
therefore understandable, but again the delay that occurred
before the English attack worked to the advantage of the
Valois. After the Franco-Navarrese treaty and the actual
arrival of a formidable invading force from England, the
Picards showed a more sympathetic attitude towards the
dauphin, for their own immediate security was threatened.
Saint-Quentin had already been authorized to levy municipal
taxes provided that these did not interfere with royal aids and
subsidies.[102] When the towns were called upon to raise contin-

---

[98] Secousse, introduction to *Ord.* 3: p. lxxxviii.
[99] Le Maire, *St. Quentin* 2: no. 673.
[100] *Ibid.*, p. 248, note 1.
[101] Varin, *Reims* 3: pp. 142–144.
[102] Le Maire, *St. Quentin* 2: no. 675.

gents of troops and have them join the nobles at Arras in November, they showed a willingness to respond. Noyon, unable to find enough money to pay its forces, had to borrow from the cathedral chapter for this purpose.[103] By the early part of 1360, the Picard towns on the left bank of the Somme were contributing money to a proposed offensive operation against England which apparently was intended to rescue John II while the bulk of the English army was floundering about in the heart of France. Parisians under Jean de Neuville were to carry out this venture, while the mayor and *échevins* of Abbeville undertook to assemble the money collected from the towns of the Somme valley.[104] There is no evidence, however, that this ambitious scheme was actually set in motion.

Unable to take Reims, Edward III abandoned his effort in January and advanced on Burgundy. As yet relatively untouched by brigandage, this duchy was vulnerable to the English army and the seasoned captains of *routiers* who accompanied it. Philip, the young duke, was not only King John's stepson, but also a peer of France whose mother was a member of the generally pro-Navarrese house of Boulogne. His support would be valuable to Edward's effort to be crowned as king of France. For six weeks the English army campaigned in Burgundy. Then on 10 March an agreement with the duke was concluded. This was the treaty of Guillon, by which the duchy and county of Burgundy promised Edward III 200,000 *moutons* in return for a three-year cessation of hostilities in the two Burgundies and the English surrender of the castle of Flavigny. It was stipulated that, if a majority of the peers of France should support Edward as French king, the duke of Burgundy must do the same or face the immediate termination of the truce.[105]

The agreement of Guillon was advantageous for Edward's treasury and also for his claim to the French throne. To make his claim irresistible, however, he would have to capture Paris or, at least, defeat the dauphin in a pitched battle. He may

[103] BN Moreau 234, fols. 114r-v.

[104] BN Moreau 234, fols. 128-129; Le Maire, *St. Quentin* 2: no. 676; Luce, *Du Guesclin*, P.J. 22.

[105] *Foedera* 6: pp. 161-166; BN NAF 7610, fols. 231r-242v; E. Martène and U. Durand, *Thesaurus novus anecdotorum* (5 v., Paris, 1717) 1: cols. 1415-1422; Fowler, *King's Lieutenant*, pp. 205-206.

have hoped for aid from the Parisians; rumor had it that Charles the Bad was plotting to kill the regent.[106] The latter, whether by inclination or necessity, was already earning his future sobriquet of "the Wise" by declining battle with the English army, but the French fleet raided Winchelsea in a bid to bring the ravages of war to England.[107] Edward's army now engaged in systematic burning and looting of the countryside as it approached Paris. Brief negotiations took place early in April, but the regent was unwilling to consider the exorbitant English demands. In Easter week the English thoroughly pillaged the suburbs of the capital.[108]

Other regions also felt the ravages of enemy attack, either from the English or from *routiers* operating more or less autonomously. Lyonnais was one region that had to take energetic measures for its own defense.[109] Like Lyonnais, the Mountains of Auvergne continued to be beset by hostile soldiery, who made the abbey of Jussac the base from which they pillaged the environs of Aurillac.[110] As on previous occasions during the fourteenth century, Auvergne occupied an ambiguous position between the separate fiscal/military administrations at Paris and Toulouse. Traditionally regarded as part of Languedoil, the Auvergnats generally found that military danger came from the Southwest. Now they were cut off from Paris by the English army, and their lord, John of France, count of Poitiers, was the royal lieutenant in Languedoc. Because of these facts, some of the subsidy in Auvergne in 1359 was levied by the count of Poitiers, rather than officials from Paris.[111] It was also the count who allotted Riom certain funds for local defense in the spring of 1360, by which time Auvergne appears to have granted a new *fouage* for the war.[112]

---

[106]*Ibid.;* Delachenal, *Charles V* 2: pp. 174–176.

[107]*Ibid.,* pp. 176–184.

[108]*Ibid.,* pp. 186f.; Fowler, *King's Lieutenant*, p. 207. On 1 April, John II empowered the dauphin to negotiate with the Prince of Wales and arrange a peace. See Martène, *Thesaurus* 1: cols. 1422–1423.

[109]Guigue, *Tard-Venus*, pp. 44–46; 180, note 6; 258–260 (P.J. XVIII); *INV AM Mâcon*, CC 1; A Cherest, *L'Archiprêtre: episodes de la guerre de Cent Ans au XIVe siècle* (Paris, 1879), P.J. 6.

[110]*INV AM Aurillac* 2: p. 8 (EE 1).

[111]Boudet, *Thomas de la Marche*, P.J. 24. In fact, of course, most of these taxes were employed for local defense, so there was little practical difference between a grant to commissioners sent from Paris and a tax levied by the lieutenant in Languedoc.

[112]AM Riom CC 13, no. 414; BN MS. fr. 26003, no. 1010; Boudet, *Thomas de la Marche*, P.J. 25.

Most of the fiscal documents for the winter of 1359-1360 deal with Normandy, which was still in some disorder but was probably better able to deliver taxes than at any time since 1355, now that peace had been made with Charles the Bad and the English campaign farther east had attracted many troops. The bailiwick of Caen still acted as a separate unit. Having employed local resources so successfully in clearing the district of hostile garrisons, Caen raised its local sales tax to 12 d./l. (5 per cent) in October, 1359. This rate was still in force in May of 1360.[113] Between these two dates, the money continued to be collected and turned over to troops under the direction of the dauphin's Norman lieutenant.[114] Although Caen seems to have exercised unusual local control over military activity, other communities also levied municipal taxes to deal with specific local military needs.[115] The other parts of Normandy had granted the dauphin a subsidy in the fall of 1359, and numerous documents record its collection and distribution in subsequent months.[116] There is a striking contrast between the abundance of Norman fiscal documents for the fall and winter of 1359-1360 and the dearth of such texts in the preceding year and a half. The cessation of formal hostilities with Navarre and the gradual recovery of occupied castles obviously permitted the crown to collect far more in taxes from this valuable duchy than had been possible in the terrible year of 1358.

Such signs of progress can have been of small comfort to the regent in April of 1360, for the English were investing Paris and ravaging its environs. On the twenty-eighth, Charles appealed to the great lords of the kingdom for aid against the invader.[117] To provide emergency funds, he manipulated the currency in drastic fashion. Coins minted at Rouen early in April attained the 500th *pied* at a time when another mint was issuing money on the 12th *pied*.[118] In Poitou and Saintonge

[113] BN MS. fr. 26002, no. 970.

[114] BN MS. fr. 22468, no. 89; 26002, nos. 865-867, 871, 878, 898, 928, 951, 972; BN NAF 3645, no. 41; BN Clairambault 213, nos. 99-100, 214, no. 3.

[115] Coville, *Etats Norm.*, pp. 375-376; AN K 48, no. 5.

[116] BN MS. fr. 20413, no. 9; 25701, nos. 168, 175; 26002, nos. 896, 903, 904, 909, 912-914, 918, 919, 921, 923, 925, 926, 932-934, 937, 938, 940, 941, 947, 959, 962, 966, 969, 973, 978, 985, 986, 988, 990, 992, 996; BN P.O. 1522, *dossier* 34634, no 16; 650, *dossier* 15320, no. 5.

[117] BN NAF 7610, fols. 259-260.

[118] Prest, "Policy and Protest," pp. 151-152. Earlier, when the Estates had met during May and June of 1359, the dauphin had expressed a desire to reform the

the royal currency was so discredited that Marshal Boucicaut, the local French commander, actually found it necessary to strike counterfeit money, resembling the coinage of Tours and Angers, in order to pay his soldiers.[119]

Time, however, was on the dauphin's side. The English king could not entice him to leave Paris and fight a pitched battle, nor could he force his own way into Paris. Dwindling supplies and a loss of momentum hindered the English campaign, and a torrential rain added to the misery of the besiegers. By the beginning of May, Edward was forced to negotiate. Discussions at Brétigny, near Chartres, led to a truce on 7 May,[120] and the celebrated treaty of Brétigny was concluded a day later. Encouraged by papal legates, the negotiators were mainly clerks and lawyers who were able to save a good deal of time by building on the earlier treaty negotiations in London. The treaty finally adopted the territorial provisions of the first London treaty of 1358, granting to England, Poitou, Limousin, Périgord, Quercy, and Rouergue, and thereby re-creating the twelfth-century duchy of Aquitaine. This territory was to be held by Edward III in full sovereignty, subject to the renunciation of his claim to the throne of France. King John was to be released in return for a ransom of 3,000,000 écus, of which a down payment of 600,000 was to be made within four months of John's arrival at Calais, or towards the end of September. Upon receipt of this first payment, Edward would release John and the formalities of implementing the treaty would be completed. The whole settlement was to be ratified by the two kings in England.[121]

Because the treaty of Brétigny formalized the losses which France suffered as a result of John's capture, it is sometimes seen as a serious defeat for France, eventually averted only because the treaty was not fully implemented. In fact, how-

---

currency but expressed fear about the economic dislocations which might follow from a sudden reinforcement of the alloy. He did briefly reduce the *pied de monnaie* from the 72nd to the 60th, but his straitened finances soon forced him to undertake frequent new mutations, steadily raising the *pied* (*ibid.*, pp. 147–149, and *Ord.* 3: pp. 344, 357, 369, 401).

[119]*Arch. hist. Poit.* 17: pp. 279–284.

[120]On the negotiations, see *Chron. Jean II et Charles V* 1: 259–267; *Foedera* 6: pp. 175–177; BN NAF 7610, fol. 272; Martène, *Thesaurus* 1: cols. 1423–1425.

[121]*Foedera*, VI, 178–196; *Chron. Jean II et Charles V* 1: 267–300; Zacour, *Talleyrand*, p. 61; Delachenal, *Charles V* 2: pp. 196–202.

ever, we must concur with the English scholars who have called the treaty a defeat for Edward III. All the English gains in Brittany, Normandy, Flanders, and elsewhere outside of Aquitaine, were to be abandoned, along with Edward's claim to the French throne. His one substantial gain was an end to the feudal status of Aquitaine. The degree to which the treaty was a reverse for Edward depends, of course, on how seriously one thinks he desired the French throne; but the fact remains that the treaty was concluded at a time when the French were stronger and the English weaker than at any time in the preceding four years.[122] Since 1358 the dauphin had broken the Parisian revolution, neutralized Charles the Bad, regained some control over Normandy and its finances, and shown the English that there was more to winning a war than winning pitched battles. The French may also have been strengthened by the fact that the treaty was not negotiated by John II himself, and therefore not influenced strongly by the king's desire to obtain his liberty.

The treaty of Brétigny proved to be one of the most important documents of French medieval history, not because of the territorial provisions, or the reciprocal renunciations which never were executed, but because the royal ransom was to mark a turning point in the history of French taxation. The initial payment of 600,000 *écus* was to be followed by annual installments of 400,000 *écus* for the next six years. To raise this sum, substantial annual taxes would be required, to be payable in peacetime and levied by a special administration for extraordinary revenues, and yet not subject to the traditional sort of negotiation between the crown and the populace. The significance of this ransom, from the fiscal point of view, will become apparent in the later chapters of this study. The legal basis for the resultant taxes is a question of no small

---

[122] Le Patourel, "Treaty of Brétigny," pp. 21, 31–33, 39; Le Patourel, "Edward III and France," pp. 177–178; Fowler, *King's Lieutenant*, pp. 210–213; Fowler, *Plantagenet and Valois*, pp. 62, 66. These scholars, who see the treaty as an English defeat, oppose the earlier view set forth by C. Petit-Dutaillis and P. Collier, "La diplomatie française et le traité de Brétigny," *Le Moyen Age*, 2e sér., 1 (1897): pp. 1–35. They saw the treaty as an unavoidable, but temporary acceptance of defeat on the part of the French. Coville, in the review cited above, chap. I, note 72, supported Petit-Dutaillis and Collier's view that the subsequent failure to implement fully the ratified treaty of 1360 was the result of a conscious policy of Charles V, who wished to evade the treaty where possible. As will be seen below, however (chaps. VI-VII), this view no longer seems tenable.

importance. A lord's ransom, of course, was one of those cases which justified a feudal aid, and the feudal aspect of the ransom did provide a basis for taxing nobles and clergy without obstructive claims of privilege. The nobles and clergy, however, were but a small part of the population, and many bourgeois controlled considerable wealth. Earlier efforts to extend feudal aids to persons other than direct royal vassals had met with bitter resistance.[123] The ransom, however, was more than just a feudal aid; it offered the only hope of ending the agony of war, and as such it presented a case of "evident necessity." To the vast non-noble population, the necessity was so evident and urgent as to preclude debate, and in such cases rights, privileges, and precedents lost much of their relevance. This time the common profit was not linked to a clash of armies, but to the prevention of such conflict, and a large financial sacrifice seemed not only reasonable but necessary. Thus every class of Frenchman could find compelling reasons for contributing to the ransom, and with the usual grounds for opposition removed, the crown was able to establish at last the regular system of taxation which had eluded it for generations. The ransom, therefore, involved two legal traditions—the feudal obligations of royal vassals and the Romano-canonical principle that taxes for the common profit were justified in time of evident necessity.[124]

The first order of business, of course, was not the establishment of regular taxes but the execution of the treaty, and this depended on the collection of the down payment of 600,000 écus by the appointed time. A massive organizational effort was required for this purpose, especially since the country still was infested with *routiers* who made the roads unsafe. Soon after the treaty, the dauphin sent messengers to the pope, king, emperor, lord of Milan, and inhabitants of Dauphiné, all to discuss the ransom.[125] He also ordered that domainal revenues no longer be applied to warfare. They were to be collected by

[123] See the summary treatment in Henneman, "Ransom Aids," pp. 618–619. For a detailed examination of the effort to levy feudal aids in the 1330's, see *RTF 1322–1356*, pp. 90–107.

[124] For a discussion of the aids as a case of "evident necessity," see Henneman, "Ransom Aids," pp. 622–629. For more on the ransom, see Vuitry, *Régime financier* 2: p. 104; A. Callery, "Histoire du pouvoir royal d'imposer depuis la féodalité jusqu'au règne de Charles V," *Rev. quest. hist.* 26 (1874): p. 483; and G. Mouradian, "La Rançon de Jean II le Bon," *Posit. Thèses, Ec. Chartes* 1970: p. 152.

[125] AN P 2294, p. 41.

non-military officials and used to meet the costs of the regent's household.[126] On 22 May, Charles granted a sweeping amnesty to all rebels and persons who had committed crimes during the war.[127] On the same day he issued a series of enactments aimed at collecting the down payment on the ransom. He announced that Paris had agreed to contribute 100,000 *écus*, one-sixth of the required sum,[128] and he established quotas for the other towns. Villeneuve-le-Roy, for instance, was to pay 6,000 florins in the form of a loan.[129] Lille was to pay 12,000 *écus*; Douai, 10,000; and Lens, 1,000.[130]

From the historian's point of view, however, the most important document of 22 May, 1360, is a set of instructions to commissioners who were to collect these funds.[131] The instructions reveal an efficient and well-thought-out scheme which had been evolved for the purpose of tapping all available sources of wealth. The dauphin stressed that the government was proceeding on the principle "that all people subject to the king are obliged . . . by the general custom of the kingdom" to contribute to traditional aids, with the ransom of St. Louis being carefully singled out as a precedent. It was not a tax as such which was being sought, but a kind of forced loan (although "gifts" would be welcomed). The loan was to be repaid from the receipts of a forthcoming subsidy, the form of which could be negotiated locally, although the taxes already adopted by Paris were suggested as a model. In Paris there was to be a general sales tax of 5 per cent, a substantial special tax on wine, a 10 per cent tax on annuities, a *gabelle* on salt, and a special imposition of 4 d./l. on goods sent out of the city. The commissioners were to use all methods, including force, to obtain money, and all were expected to pay, regardless of status. On the other hand, there were assurances as to the use of the funds collected: receivers chosen by local inhabitants were to handle collections and prevent the receipts from being diverted to any other use, even if the king or dauphin tried to

---

[126] Vuitry, *Régime financier* 2: p. 104

[127] *Ord.* 3: pp. 407–408.

[128] BN NAF 7376, fols. 328r-430v.

[129] *Ibid.;* BN NAF 7610, fol. 297.

[130] Text published by Delachenal, *Charles V* 2: pp. 440–443. These quotas for the first ransom payment are all discussed *ibid.*, pp. 222f.

[131] See the comments *ibid.*, p. 224f. The instructions, located in AD Pas-de-Calais A 691, have been published by J. Richard, "Instructions données aux commissaires chargés de lever le rançon du roi Jean," *Bib. Ec. Chartes* 36 (1875): pp. 81–90.

order it. Once collected, the money was to be transported promptly to Saint-Omer in Artois, where the abbot of the monastery of Saint-Bertin and a member of the royal household were in charge of the down payment.[132] The commissioners were to issue periodic progress reports to the Chamber of Accounts and investigate and tap any reserves of cash on hand in the towns. They were especially instructed to put pressure on wealthy men of whatever status. The clergy now were excused from the double tenth previously granted by the pope to finance the royal ransom, and were instead to be solicited for loans like other persons.[133] Systematic efforts were made to collect from the countryside as well as towns.

Although in some instances the clergy were assessed separately for the loan, these instructions clearly suspended all traditional privileges in order to speed up collection.[134] As sometimes used in the past, but now on a much more extensive scale, the forced loan was here a vitally important supplement to taxation as such. It seemed to be the one device by which the crown could overcome what had traditionally been one of its most formidable obstacles—the problem of delay. If influential members of the community now depended upon taxation for all hope of repayment of their loan, tax grants might perhaps be more readily forthcoming. The instructions indicate that the commissioners had considerable latitude in negotiating the taxes by which lenders would be repaid. The taxes raised in each community were to repay the lenders from that locality. Paris had already decided on its tax; other places would levy municipal *tailles* much as many had long been doing for military purposes. Reims, on the other hand, delayed four years in adopting its municipal tax and Rouen had to levy special taxes and retain part of royal ones to complete repayment.[135]

Thus the procedure for raising money which was set in motion by the enactments of 22 May made the towns responsible for paying designated sums of money and made the royal commissioners responsible for collecting these sums quickly

---

[132]*Ibid.*, arts. 1, 3–5, 7, 9, 11, 19–21. See also Timbal, *Guerre,* p. 395; Mouradian, "Rançon," p. 152; Delachenal, *Charles V 2*: p. 226.
[133]Richard, "Instructions," arts. 16–18, 21.
[134]Timbal, *Guerre,* p. 383.
[135]*Ibid.*, p. 379.

by whatever means were necessary. In effect, the government was condoning and utilizing that pattern of local financing that had been so widespread in recent years.

These measures were followed by feverish activity on both sides of the Channel, especially after the two kings ratified the treaty on 14 June in the Tower of London.[136] Anticipating his early release, John II dispatched letters to practically every person or group in France who might facilitate collection of the money. He wrote to Reims on 8 June and again on 11 July, and in the meantime sent Arnoul d'Audrehem to the city to hurry up collection.[137] On 5 July he wrote to the Chamber of Accounts reporting his departure for Canterbury and thence to Calais, and urging speedy accumulation of the money. He sent a second letter, similar in content, a few days later.[138] On 27 June he acknowledged receipt of a sum sent to him in England by the town of Saint-Quentin.[139] He confirmed the appointment of the abbot of Saint-Bertin as the person in charge of receiving the money at Saint-Omer.[140] At about the same time, the pope gave his blessing to whatever contributions the clergy wished to make.[141]

The actual collection of this crucial first payment on the royal ransom encountered widely varying conditions and was often attended by difficulties and abuses. In the ensuing years the repayment of forced loans obtained in 1360 would be a cause of litigation and dispute.[142] Besides the large sum promised by the city of Paris, the clergy and nobles of the viscounty of Paris agreed to a loan of 100,000 *royaux* (125,000 *écus*),[143] with the abbot of Saint-Denis supplying 1,000 *royaux*.[144] At Saint-Quentin an assessment of 6,000 *écus* had to be raised almost entirely from the town itself, because the surrounding *plat pays* was destitute.[145] Reims continued to be

---

[136] BN NAF 7376, fols. 432–434; Martène, *Thesaurus* 1: cols. 1426–1427.

[137] Varin, *Reims* 3: pp. 163–166.

[138] AN P 2294, pp. 47–49, 53–55; BN NAF 7610, fols. 313–314, 321–322; BN NAF 7376, fols. 437r-v.

[139] BN Moreau 234, fols. 151r-v; Le Maire, *St. Quentin* 2: no. 678.

[140] BN MS. fr. 20412, no. 12; BN P.O. 2477, *dossier* 55737, no. 2.

[141] AN P 2294, pp. 51, 63–67, 69–75. Cf. Delachenal, *Charles V* 2: p. 231.

[142] Timbal, *Guerre*, p. 381.

[143] Vuitry, *Régime financier* 2: p. 107.

[144] AN K 48, no. 8.

[145] BN Moreau 234, fols. 161–162; Le Maire, *St. Quentin* 2: no. 680.

deluged with royal letters before finally borrowing enough for a contribution of 20,000 *écus* in the fall.[146] By early August, Lille and Tournai had made partial payments of 2,000 and 5,500 *écus* respectively.[147] Efforts to collect at Soissons gave rise to charges of corruption. Citizens who assisted the commissioners in apportioning the tax there were accused of seeking to collect more than the town's quota of 8,000 *royaux*.[148] At Vervins in Thiérache, there were similar complaints. The commissioners had levied the quota of 200 *royaux*, but then had provoked an uprising by trying to extort more money.[149] Commissioners at Abbeville had to be ordered not to take more than 2000 florins.[150]

In the case of Normandy, the documents clearly differentiate between the "aid for the deliverance" of the king and the "subsidy for men-at-arms." There are many indications that the Normans continued to pay a war subsidy in the months after the announcement of the truce and the treaty in May.[151] An army had to be kept in the field to limit or prevent violations of the peace by Charles the Bad's Norman followers.[152] An assembly in the bailiwick of Gisors and the two Vexins met in May to grant a new subsidy in the form of a sales tax.[153] The money was needed in order to speed the pacification of the region around Paris, so recently infested with English troops. On 13 May, the earl of Warwick, marshal of England, promised immediate evacuation of some fortresses near Paris, but demanded in return a ransom of 12,000 florins, payable by 24 June and guaranteed by hostages, including the provost of the merchants of Paris.[154]

Despite some early references to the ransom aid in Normandy,[155] the principal effort to raise money in the duchy for

---

[146] Varin, *Reims* 3: pp. 166–168, and notes.

[147] Delachenal, *Charles V* 2: p. 230.

[148] An JJ 88, no. 21.

[149] AN JJ 89, no. 474.

[150] BN Moreau 234, fols. 159r-v.

[151] BN MS. fr. 26003, nos. 1000, 1006; BN NAF 20026, no. 86; BN P.O. 358, *dossier* 7761, nos. 9, 10; 493, *dossier* 11104, no. 15; 1603, *dossier* 36925, no. 2; AD Lot F 36.

[152] The French lieutenant in Normandy, Louis d'Harcourt, had been captured by the enemy, and the roads in Normandy were not safe to travel. See *Chron. Valois*, p. 110; Luce, *Du Guesclin*, P.J. 21; Secousse, *Charles le Mauvais* 1: p. 170; Castro, *Catalogo* 3: nos. 441, 445; Coville, *Etats Norm.*, pp. 98–99.

[153] *Ibid.*, p. 99; BN Clairambault 213, no. 101.

[154] Luce, *Du Guesclin*, P.J., nos. 20, 51.

[155] BN MS. fr. 26002, no. 958; BN Clairambault 214, no. 2.

this purpose did not get underway until 8 July, 1360,[156] and several more months had passed before the documents indicate collection of taxes specifically imposed for the ransom.[157] As with other regions, Normandy doubtless began by advancing money in the form of loans. The one well-documented case is that of Rouen, which borrowed 20,000 *moutons* from the count of Namur to pay its share of the down payment. An assembly of the inhabitants on 15 August set up a schedule of municipal taxes to help repay this loan. On 2 September the dauphin ratified these, and the count received his first repayments late in December.[158]

The foregoing discussion has been based on documents from a limited part of France—Normandy, the Ile-de-France, and the bailiwicks of the far North. They indicate a total of 315,750 *écus*, paid or promised.[159] The documentation from these regions is probably incomplete, and we know that Languedoc promised to pay more than 200,000 *écus*, bringing us close to the total sum required.[160] No documents relating to this first ransom payment have been found for the other parts of Languedoil, and it seems possible to conclude that the government collected no money at all for this installment of the ransom from a broad belt of territory including Champagne, Burgundy, Auvergne, and the entire Loire valley. The surviving documents from this vast region make no mention of the royal ransom; they reveal only the depredations of the *routiers* and the desperate local efforts to cope with the danger and regain lost fortresses.[161] It thus appears that the brigand companies still prevented effective royal taxation in a very large part of the kingdom, and that the entire burden of financing the initial payment to obtain the king's release was borne by the population of the extreme north and extreme

---

[156] BN MS. fr. 25701, no. 179.

[157] BN MS. fr. 20402, no. 28; 25700, no. 122. Both texts belong to November.

[158] AN JJ 87, no. 325; BN Clairambault 214, nos. 6, 11.

[159] For the individual figures, see above, notes 128–158. Reckoned in *écus*, the contributions were as follows: Paris (town), 100,000; Paris (nobles and clergy of viscounty), 125,000; Reims, 20,000; Rouen, 20,000; Lille, 12,000; Douai, 10,000; Soissons, 10,000; Villeneuve, 6,000; Saint-Quentin, 6,000; Tournai, 5,500; Lens, 1,000; Vervins, 250. Even without mentioning central France, there are many gaps in our documentation from Normandy, Artois, Vermandois, and the Ile-de-France.

[160] See below, chap. IV, part 3.

[161] See, for instance, AN JJ 89, no. 390; Boudet, *Thomas de la Marche*, P.J. 31–38; Cherest, *L'Archiprêtre*, P.J. 8–10; *Chron. Jean II et Charles V* 1: pp. 327–328.

south of the realm. Their achievement was all the more remarkable on this account.

Despite the strenuous effort just described, the French were unable to assemble more than 400,000 *écus* at the abbey of Saint-Bertin by October. The failure to pay the full amount on time was probably due to the difficulties of raising money in Languedoc and shipping it northward.[162] In any case, Edward III agreed to release John II as promised and collect the rest of the down payment in two separate installments payable at Christmas and Candlemas.[163] In the last week of October, 1360, the two kings at Calais formally ratified the treaty, making certain changes in the original provisions. Extensive guarantees on both sides accompanied the ceremony, as princes, prelates, and great nobles swore to uphold the treaty, and the major towns of France lent their support by supplying hostages who would go to England pending full payment of the ransom. Elaborate efforts were made to commit both sides fully and eliminate all likelihood of fraud or bad faith. The important mutual renunciations of rights, claims, and territories were deferred to a new meeting between the two kings, planned for Bruges on 30 November.[164]

After four years and one month, John II was finally free. His defeat and captivity had inflicted misery on France, costing the kingdom substantial amounts of territory and a very large ransom, as well as creating the circumstances which permitted brigandage by unemployed troops, rebellion in Paris, and the discrediting of the Estates General by political adventurers. Now his return was conditional upon payment of a ransom which enabled the monarchy to levy regular taxes in peacetime without further consultation. The amount so laboriously collected in 1360 was only a fraction of the total amount needed, and the king had incurred debts in England amounting to 200,000 *écus*. To improve his finances further, John II arranged a treaty of marriage with Milan, where the ruling Visconti family was prepared to pay 600,000 *écus* to win a

---

[162] See *HL* 10: col. 1238; Delachenal, *Charles V* 2: p. 225.

[163] *Ibid.*, pp. 444–445; D. Broome, "The Ransom of John II, King of France, 1360–70," *The Camden Miscellany* 15 (1926): p. viii.

[164] Delachenal, *Charles V* 2: pp. 250–259. The numerous documents implementing the treaty have been published in *Foedera* 6: pp. 219–301; Martène, *Thesaurus* 1: beginning at col. 1429. Manuscripts include AN JJ 89, no. 399; BN NAF 7611, fols. 112f; BN NAF 7376, fols. 462f; and others.

prestigious marriage to a French princess.[165] John confirmed all actions taken by the dauphin in his absence, but he soon modified this act by revoking all assignments on royal revenues.[166] The most pressing business after his release was the need to put royal finances on a sound footing and provide the vast sums which would be required to meet the six annual installments of the ransom which would be owed by France commencing in 1361. This task was accomplished by an ordinance issued at Compiègne on 5 December, 1360.[167]

Called by Delachenal one of the most important and best executed ordinances of John II's reign,[168] the enactment of 5 December was more than that. It was probably the most important fiscal document issued in France during the fourteenth century. It established the basic system of *aides* and *gabelles* which would survive with minor interruptions for four centuries. With some accuracy, Vuitry has observed that the payments required by the new ordinance had the duration and general application to qualify as the first true royal tax, in the modern sense of the term.[169] For all their importance, the taxes occupied but a small part of the ordinance, most of which was devoted to a subject which had been of great concern to Frenchmen of all classes during the preceding decade, namely the royal currency. The ransom made it necessary to establish a stable coinage that was easily convertible to pounds sterling, and the taxes imposed for the ransom gave the crown sufficient resources to avoid operating the mints for profit. The result was a long-overdue and ardently desired monetary reform.

The French silver coinage now was stabilized on the 24th *pied*, which became the new symbol of "strong money." A new gold coin, the franc, was established, with a value of one *livre tournois* in money of account. The reform not only terminated the monetary anarchy of the past four years but also achieved in substance one of the major objectives of the reforming party of the 1350's. It conformed to the thinking of Nicole Oresme, who by this date had become a member of the

[165] Delachenal, *Charles V* 2: p. 231; Vuitry, *Régime financier* 2: p. 107; Luce, *Jacquerie*, p. 133, note 1.

[166] BN NAF 7611, fol. 83r; 7612, fols. 38r–41r; AN P 2294, pp. 95–96.

[167] *Ord.* 3: pp. 433–442; AN P 2294, pp. 237–249.

[168] Delachenal, *Charles V* 2: p. 264.

[169] Vuitry, *Régime financier* 2: pp. 112–113.

dauphin's circle. Delachenal viewed the new currency as evidence of Charles's continuing influence on royal policy, whereas Cazelles gives the king major credit for the reform and its duration.[170]

Just as insufficient revenues from taxation had led the crown to the worst excesses of monetary mutation, so the establishment of sound money was made possible by regular taxes. The new taxes were three in number: a general sales tax of 12 d./l. (5 per cent), a levy of one d./s. on wine (usually called the "thirteenth"), and a *gabelle* on salt. They became more or less permanent and were applied with uniformity throughout Languedoil.[171] They were not, however, new in form, for indirect taxes had enjoyed widespread use in Languedoil between 1340 and the middle 1350's, and they had reappeared at Paris in 1358. Only in 1356-1358 had these traditional indirect taxes been abandoned, in an effort to shift a greater burden to the wealthy. The experiments of those years, which would have some importance for the future, had arisen from the government's dire need for money and the increasing bourgeois influence in the assemblies that granted the taxes.[172]

The decision to return to traditional indirect taxation in levying the new aids requires some explanation. Since large sums were needed each year for the ransom, why did the government not establish hearth taxes or income taxes? Aside from the weight of tradition and precedent, the regressive nature of the aids undoubtedly reflected the conservative reaction that had been growing in Languedoil since 1358. Direct taxation had been part of the recent effort of the Estates to shift a greater fiscal burden onto the nobles. Now the cleavage between nobles and wealthy burghers seemed to be closing, and it is significant that the new indirect taxes, which

---

[170]Delachenal, *Charles V* 2: pp. 264-265; Bridrey, *Théorie*, pp. 511-512. With the first ransom payment well underway, the dauphin in August had convened some magnates and coinage experts, and at their urging had strengthened the currency by placing it on the 32nd *pied*. This action prepared the way for the final reform and minimized the economic dislocation. See Prest, "Policy and Protest," pp. 154-155, and *Ord.* 3: p. 424. I can find no basis for believing that the Estates met in November to consider taxes for the ransom. See also L. Dessales, "Aide payé par les habitants du diocèse de Paris pour le rançon du roi Jean," *Société des Bibliophiles Français: Mélanges de litterature et d'histoire* (Paris, 1850), p. 164.

[171]Vuitry, *Régime financier* 2: pp. 109-111; Timbal, *Guerre*, pp. 377, 395; Delachenal, *Charles V* 2: pp. 329-330; Mouradian, "Rançon," pp. 151-152.

[172]See *RTF 1322-1356*, p. 291f, and above, chap. II.

weighed upon the consumer, helped to end the royal reliance on *monnayage,* which bore mainly on the rich. Direct taxation of the wealthy was not merely politically dangerous; it also had failed to produce adequate revenues. Taxes on the poor consumer had proven collectable; those on the wealthy had been resisted so effectively that they may have yielded less than the old-fashioned sales taxes. Recently, still another reason has been suggested for the return to indirect taxation: since war subsidies and local levies for military defense were now commonly taking the form of apportioned hearth taxes, the ransom aids were set up as sales taxes in order to emphasize their distinct and special purpose.[173] Whatever the reason for employing this form for the aids, the fact remains that the *aides pour la délivrance* were indirect taxes, and the term *aide* gradually came to mean this type of tax. It was never very popular in the towns, which made periodic efforts in the ensuing century to replace it with a substitute or equivalent that could be paid by means of direct taxation.

The *gabelle,* long a term for salt taxes only in Languedoil, came to acquire this restricted meaning throughout the country. It too was no innovation, of course, having spread gradually throughout Languedoil after its third introduction, in mid-1358. Since both were generalized for the same purpose in December, 1360, the terms *aides et gabelles* are often mentioned together in fiscal documents. Another institution which had appeared sporadically in the past became permanent after the ordinance of December, 1360—the *élu.* After appearing in the 1340's and again after 1355 as appointees of assemblies which granted taxes for men-at-arms, the *élus* had been adopted by the crown in 1358 and they now became the basis of a permanent administration for the collection of "extraordinary" revenues.[174] Normally assigned to a diocese, the *élu* supervised the farming and collection of taxes and was accountable to superiors in Paris who usually were called *trésoriers généraux* in the 1360's.[175] As important as the regular taxes themselves was the emergence of this administration to deal with them, but the innovation could not have

---

[173] Mouradian, "Rançon," p. 152.
[174] On the early history of *élus,* see *RTF 1322–1356,* pp. 151, 185, 225, 229f.
[175] Vuitry, *Régime financier* 2: pp. 110–111.

seemed striking in 1360 because *élus* had become common in much of France since 1356.

From the first, the *gabelle* was administered separately from the other two impositions, probably as a result of precedent, since this tax had originated as a generalized seigneurial right and had been administered separately in the 1340's. The government issued brief instructions on the *gabelle* administration on 23 December, 1360.[176] Five days earlier, the procedures for dealing with the other two taxes had been outlined. In terms of later parlance, these were the *aides*, properly speaking. Like indirect taxes in the past, they were to be farmed, and the *élus* were to collect from the farmers in regular monthly installments.[177]

For the preceding six years, the monarchy's relations with Charles the Bad had been a major factor in royal taxation. The king of Navarre and his partisans had been able to disrupt Normandy, forcing the diversion of valuable resources to military activities and seriously threatening Paris itself. Throughout these years since the murder of Charles of Spain, his security had required a prolongation of hostilities between England and France. Now that a treaty had been ratified and John II had returned, it was imperative for Charles the Bad that he secure his position by reaching a new accommodation with the king of France. The latter also had reason to seek an agreement, since Charles could jeopardize the treaty by disrupting collections of the aid for the ransom. The principal point at issue no longer seems to have been personal animosity between John II and his son-in-law, but rather the names of the Navarrese partisans who were to be pardoned. There are two extant lists of about 300 persons who were to receive royal letters of remission. Each list is headed by the count of Harcourt, and they are generally similar except for the one important omission of Robert le Coq's name from one of them.[178] The dauphin was utterly unwilling to agree to a pardon for the bishop of Laon, and it is likely that Charles the Bad was so anxious for an agreement with the crown that he was willing to sacrifice le Coq, whose devotion to the Navar-

---

[176] AN P 2294, pp. 119–120.

[177] BN MS. fr. 25701, no. 189; AN P 2294, pp. 113–117; Timbal, *Guerre*, p. 383; Guigue, *Tard-Venus*, pp. 264–265.

[178] Secousse, *Charles le Mauvais* 1: pp. 176–185.

rese cause had largely been dictated by self-interest. The eventual Franco-Navarrese treaty arranged for his translation to a bishopric outside the kingdom. The treaty also contained Charles the Bad's ratification of the treaties of Brétigny and Calais,[179] and thus presumably his acquiescence in the ransom aids now being levied throughout the French realm. A final agreement, on 29 January, 1361, involved the king of Navarre's acceptance of certain royal demands on matters of jurisdiction.[180]

At last the French monarchy was at peace, juridically speaking, and soon its subjects would learn that treaties did not always guarantee peace. The peace with Charles the Bad would not last out the reign of John II, while the treaty with England would be a dead letter before the terrible decade of the 1360's was ended. Even before the resumption of formal hostilities, the problem of the *routiers,* now greatly magnified, would defy solution. Yet these problems were not perceived clearly in January of 1361. The monarchy had survived a great ordeal and had emerged with many advantages from a situation of apparent defeat. Unable to produce the taxes they promised, the Estates had been equally unable to bring about significant reforms. The ransom promised regular taxes without the need for assemblies, and the dauphin adopted the goals of many of the reformers. Consequently, the monarchy, not the Estates, emerged as the institution which levied taxes and carried out reforms. The crown also emerged as the symbol of law and order, while the Estates were tarnished by public recollection of the Parisian rebellion and the *Jacquerie.* The English had finally shown the limitations of their ability to campaign in France, and the inconclusive expedition of 1360 marked the end of fifteen years of English military success on the continent. Both Charles the Bad and Edward III had recognized anew the Valois title, while the dauphin had acquired valuable political experience and had learned what tactics were most effective against invading armies. The king's subjects had suffered terribly, but they too had reason to be hopeful, for they had been offered the promise of peace and a long-desired monetary stability.

---

[179]*Ibid.,* pp. 172–176; Martène, *Thesaurus* 1: cols. 1480–1483; *Chron. Jean II et Charles V* 1: pp. 329–330; BN NAF 7612, fols. 28r–37r; 7376, fols. 608–613.
[180]Secousse, *Charles le Mauvais* 1: p. 186.

Yet the unity of the French kingdom was less certain than ever. The treaty of Brétigny had granted England territories, supposedly to be held in full sovereignty, which all but severed lower Languedoc from the rest of the realm. Even before 1360, however, this separation was well advanced, for the problems of communications, the weakness of the government at Paris, the *routiers* in the Massif Central, and the difference in political and financial traditions had forced the Midi to confront its own problems in its own way. Throughout the reign of John II, the history of Languedoc was generally different from that of the North. After the battle of Poitiers, this difference became pronounced.

IV. Taxation for the Defense of Languedoc, 1356–1361

1. The Conservatism of the Estates of Languedoc

LANGUEDOC had always differed from the rest of France in cultural and legal traditions, and after the English offensive of 1345, the Midi began to diverge significantly from Languedoil in terms of political administration and fiscal history. In 1346, when the Estates General met in two separate sessions, those of Languedoc proved their usefulness by granting modest taxes. Although Languedoc seems to have been represented at the Estates General of late 1347, it was treated differently from the north in the crown's efforts to repair finances after the Black Death, and by 1351–1352 the region was following a pattern of its own in taxation and representation.[1] After the battle of Poitiers, the Midi followed a markedly separate course, for the king's captivity left doubts as to where the responsible government of the kingdom was located. Communications with both the king and dauphin were difficult, but as the news from Paris in 1356–1358 was hardly reassuring, the inhabitants of the Midi generally preferred to maintain communications with John II in captivity.[2]

Administrative documents define Languedoc as the region south of Dordogne river—the three great seneschalsies of Beaucaire, Carcassonne, and Toulouse, and the adjacent districts of Bigorre, Rouergue, Périgord, and Quercy.[3] Governed by a royal lieutenant with vice-regal powers, Languedoc had acquired the habit of paying taxes that were granted by assemblies and apportioned first among the seneschalsies and

---

[1] On these developments, see *RTF 1322–1356*, pp. 185f, 202f, 244f, 255f, 272f, and notes.

[2] Vuitry, *Régime financier* 2: p. 98.

[3] On the Dordogne as boundary, see BN MS. fr. 20412, no. 37; AD Hérault A 4, fol. 326r.

then among the towns and *vigueries* according to the number of taxable hearths they had possessed before 1348. Some large towns often escaped with reduced payments, but because of the effects of plague, these reductions may well have been equitable.

In 1355 Languedoc had suffered a disaster that northern France had escaped: a destructive raid by the Prince of Wales from his base at Bordeaux.[4] After this sobering experience, the towns of the southern seneschalsies had sent representatives to an assembly that granted a hearth tax of one *agnel* and a sales tax on 6 d./l. in March of 1356. The representatives displayed anxiety about the willingness and ability of the monarchy to act energetically in their defense, and they asked the king to send the dauphin to the Midi as royal lieutenant.[5] His presence would offer proof of John II's concern for his southern subjects, and when the struggle with the Navarrese in Normandy prevented Charles from coming, John quickly designated his third son, the count of Poitiers, in the dauphin's place.[6] The crisis of the king's capture delayed the arrival of this prince for nearly two years, but the towns did not press the matter.

The southern Estates had met with enough frequency since 1346 to acquire some continuity and institutional form. In fact, these "Estates" usually consisted only of representatives from the towns. In most situations, they could speak for all, since many nobles and clergy lived in the towns and paid taxes on their urban property. The battle of Poitiers accentuated the administrative autonomy of Languedoc and aggravated the sense of crisis, but it did not alter the political leadership of the Midi and did not disturb the tradition of periodic assemblies. Pending the arrival of a royal prince, the king's lieutenant in Languedoc was John I, count of Armagnac and Rodez, who summoned the barons, prelates, and towns to

---

[4]*RTF 1322–1356*, pp. 278–279.

[5]P. Dognon, *Les institutions politiques et administratives du pays de Languedoc, du XIIIe siècle aux guerres de religion* (Toulouse, 1895), p. 604; *HL 9*: pp. 656–657. Subsequently, late in May, the Estates of the Carcassonne district seem to have granted an aditional tax (*ibid.*, p. 658).

[6]See *RTF 1322–1356*, pp. 280–281, on the desire to have a royal prince in the South. John of France, count of Poitiers, was already designated as lieutenant in Languedoc by 18 June 1356: BN Clairambault 213, no. 58.

meet at Toulouse as soon as he heard of the king's capture.[7] Some confusion was created by a simultaneous summons from the dauphin to an assembly at Paris, but as we have seen, the idea of a single assembly for the whole realm was soon abandoned.[8]

The meeting at Toulouse was to have begun on 8 October, but it was delayed by slow communications. Nîmes did not name and instruct its proctors until the tenth.[9] Although all the seneschalsies of Languedoc were represented, local military action reduced attendance from places near the Gascon frontier.[10] The assembly finally began on 13 October and its decisions were embodied in an ordinance issued by Armagnac on the twenty-first. The Estates took note of the need to ransom the king, but the continued presence of the Black Prince at Bordeaux made it necessary to think first of military preparations.[11] They agreed to finance a force of mounted *glaives*, horse sergeants, and bowmen for one year. The hearth tax of one *agnel* was retained, but other levies were canceled and replaced with a *capage* (head tax or poll tax), payable at the rate of three *deniers* per week by everyone over the age of twelve. In addition, the Estates granted a property tax of two *deniers* per week for every hundred pounds of movable property and half that much for every hundred pounds of immovables. Only individual nobles who were exempt from war subsidies were excused from paying, and while property in excess of 20,000 l. t. in value was generally exempt, the movable wealth of merchants was taxable at the rate of one

---

[7] BN MS. fr. 20413, fols. 2r–3v; Secousse, introduction to *Ord.* 3: p. liv; BN Coll. Languedoc 85, fol. 149r (misdated 1358, but clearly referring to 1356).

[8] C. Compayré, *Etudes historiques et documents inédits sur l'Albigeois, le Castrais, et l'ancien diocèse de Lavaur* (Albi, 1841), pp 259–260; *INV AM Narbonne*, p. 358 (AA 173); BN Doat 8, fols. 260–263; *HL* 9: p. 666; and BN Baluze 87, fol. 83, where it is indicated that Albi did not even receive the earlier summons to Paris until late in October. See also E. Albe, "Cahors: Inventaire raisonné et analytique des archives municipales," *Bulletin de la Société des Etudes Litteraires, Scientifiques et Artistiques du Lot* 41 (1930); 43 (1922); 45 (1924): no. 441.

[9] L. Ménard, *Histoire civile, ecclésiastique, et litteraire de la ville de Nismes, avec des notes et des preuves* (7 vs., Paris, 1744–1758) 2: *preuves*, pp. 182–183.

[10] G. Lacoste, *Histoire générale de la province de Quercy* (4 v., Cahors, 1873–1876) 3: p. 155.

[11] A. Breuils, "Jean Ier, comte d'Armagnac, et le mouvement national dans le Midi au temps du prince Noir," *Rev. quest. hist.* 59 (1896): pp. 60–61; *HL* 9: pp. 667–668.

obole for every hundred pounds of value between 20,000 and 250,000 l. t.[12]

It is not clear whether the *capage* affected all adults or males only; nor do we know how many persons per household were subject to it, so it is difficult to compare the taxes proposed by the respective Estates of Languedoil and Languedoc. If the average southern hearth contained as many as three people subject to the *capage*, this tax alone would yield 195 l. t. per hundred hearths if levied for a full year, thus rather more than the salary of a man-at-arms at fifteen *écus* per month. Yet these taxes in Languedoc were not as heavy as they seem, for they were payable on a week-by-week basis and were to be canceled in the likely event that a truce were concluded. Above all, they were considerably more favorable to nobles and less favorable to wealthy burghers than the taxes proposed at Paris. The conservative southern Estates did not antagonize the nobles and therefore did not succumb to factionalism.[13] They did, however, insist on appointing their own treasurers-general to supervise collection of the money, and they named four men from each Estate to inspect accounts. The count of Armagnac had to promise to redress grievances and maintain a stable coinage, and the entire agreement had to be ratified by the dauphin.[14]

The Estates also required that net domainal revenues be retained in Languedoc to help support the war effort, rather than being sent to Paris as usual. Thus regional particular-

---

[12]*Ord.* **3**: pp. 99–109; AM Millau ee 32, no. 25; BN Coll. Languedoc 85, fols. 76r–79v, 87r–90v, 99r–v; *INV AM Toulouse*, p. 97 (AA 5, no. 332); *INV AM Lunel* **2**: no. 2224 *bis* (CC 60); *Gr. Chartrier*, no. 2387; Breuils, "Jean d'Armagnac," p. 61; Dognon, *Institutions*, p. 604; Vuitry, *Régime financier* **2**: pp. 87–88; A. Bardon, *Histoire de la ville d'Alais* (2 v., Nîmes, 1891–1896) **2**: p. 41; M. de Gaujal, *Etudes historique sur le Rouergue* (4 v., Paris, 1858–1859) **2**: pp. 190–191.

[13]The main distinction, of course, lay in the fact that the northern nobles and clergy were taxed on income, while in the Midi the tax was on property. Whether every hundred hearths in Languedoc contained three hundred people subject to the *capage* is, of course, pure speculation. If many poor families were excused altogether (as usually was the case with direct taxation), then the *capage* receipts would have been much lower. Languedoc's tax was, in any case, an emergency measure, payable by the week, in case the Black Prince should make a new attack. Only if it had been collected for the better part of a year would it have exceeded the amount of tax that the government hoped to collect in Languedoil.

[14]Sources cited above, note 12. *Cf.* Picot, *Etats* **1**: p. 59; Vuitry, *Régime financier* **2**: pp. 89–90; BN Coll. Languedoc 85, fols. 84–86; *Ord.* **3**: pp. 111–113 (giving the dauphin's confirmation and response to certain grievances).

ism, which had long been evident in the employment of subsidy receipts, was now extended into an area long reserved to the royal prerogative—the revenues of the royal domain.[15] This action might be seen as yet another way of interpreting the principle of "evident necessity." The Estates may have felt that if the emergency justified overriding traditional rights and taxing their property for the common profit, then it also justified the application of the same rule to the king, whose domain and its emoluments could be requisitioned to help finance urgent local military operations.

However justified, this appropriation of domainal profits in Languedoc can only have aggravated the financial plight of the hard-pressed dauphin during the winter of 1356–1357. Indeed, the loyalty and royalism of the southern Estates in this period have probably been exaggerated by historians.[16] The military threat posed by the Prince of Wales had led them to agree to substantial taxes, but these were to end immediately in the event of a truce, and such a truce must surely have been anticipated. The Estates of Languedoc produced no Marcel or le Coq; nor were they distracted by Navarrese companies or by rivalries such as divided the leading families of Paris. Otherwise, they were far from docile. They insisted on managing directly the taxes they granted, and they undertook to regulate the coinage and the employment of domainal revenues. There were important political and military differences between north and south, but the main difference between the northern and southern Estates lay in the fact that the latter were more conservative and less affected by factional strife.

The enactments that emerged from the assembly at Toulouse ran into various obstacles. Officials continued to collect the taxes of the preceding spring until formally notified of the new arrangements; in some places the delay was a matter of weeks.[17] By mid-November the clergy were refusing payment because they said the pope had not given his consent.[18] Before the end of the year, however, the taxes were being collected at

---

[15] Vuitry, *Régime financier* 2: pp. 88–89.

[16] See for example, *ibid.*, p. 89; Avout, *Meurtre*, p. 75.

[17] *INV AM Pézenas*, p. 249, no. 1664; AM Alès I S-13, no. 2; Bardon, *Alais* 2: p. 41, and P.J., pp. ix–xii.

[18] *Ord.* 3: pp. 109–110.

Nîmes and Lunel,[19] while Najac seems to have begun paying in November.[20] Throughout the autumn, there remained some fear that the Prince of Wales might launch a new raid, and this possibility may have helped to speed collections.[21]

The prince, of course, did not attempt any new expedition, having been fortunate to escape from his recent campaign with so impressive and unexpected a success. The taxes in Languedoc, like those elsewhere, appear to have produced disappointing results, and the Estates reconvened at Béziers on 1 March, 1357, to review the problem of raising and maintaining an adequate army. This new meeting decided to retain the existing taxes and obtained from the count of Armagnac new guarantees with respect to the coinage.[22] By now, however, the military danger was clearly receding and there was less enthusiasm about continuing taxation. The town of Alès eventually went so far as to disavow the representative it had sent to Béziers.[23] Nîmes preferred to replace the taxes with a lump sum *finance* of 1300 gold florins, while Montpellier fined for 1000 florins.[24]

Some weeks after this assembly, John II and the Prince of Wales concluded the truce at Bordeaux which was supposed to make war subsidies unnecessary,[25] and which should have terminated the taxes in Languedoc if the agreement of October, 1356, were carried out. As always, however, it seemed essential to the count of Armagnac to maintain a royal army of some sort along the rarely quiet Gascon border. He therefore summoned the nobles and towns of Languedoc to a new assembly which was to meet at Toulouse on 1 May. He persuaded this meeting to endorse a continuation of the taxes, notwithstanding the truce. Immediately, the citizens of Toulouse rose in rebellion.[26] This uprising contrasted sharply

---

[19] AM Nîmes NN 1, no. 41; Ménard, *Nismes* 2: *preuves*, p. 183; T. Millerot, *Histoire de la ville de Lunel depuis son origine jusqu'en 1789* (Montpellier, 1879), p. 146; Bardon, *Alais* 2: p. 44.

[20] AD Aveyron 2E 178, no. 8, pt. 3

[21] Ménard, *Nismes* 2: *preuves*, p. 173.

[22] BN Coll. Languedoc 85, fols. 105r–106r, 109–110; AM Alès I S–3, no. 7; Dognon, *Institutions*, p. 604; Vuitry, *Régime financier* 2: pp. 90–91; *Ord.* 3: pp. 152–153

[23] The text, in AM Alès I S–3, no. 8, has been published by Bardon, *Alais* 2: P.J. VIII.

[24] Ménard, *Nismes* 2: *preuves*, p. 174; AM Castres CC 1; *Gr. Chartrier*, no. 492.

[25] See above, chap. II, note 52.

[26] J. Regné, "La levée du capage et l'emuete Toulousaine de 9 Mai 1357," *Annales du Midi* 30 (1918): p. 421f; J. Roquette, *Le Rouergue sous les Anglais* (Millau, 1887),

with what transpired at Paris in this period. At the capital, the citizens were supporting the Estates against the royal lieutenant, while at Toulouse they were rebelling against a decision of the Estates taken at the behest of the royal lieutenant. Again we are reminded of the fact that conservative interests continued to predominate in southern assemblies.

The insurrection at Toulouse appears to have left the rioters in control of the city through the month of May. On the ninth, Armagnac was forced to order cancelation of the *capage* and other subsidies and grant pardons to the rebels. Once safely out of the city, he reached Verdun early in June and took a more repressive stance, ordering the seneschals of Languedoc to arrest fugitives from Toulouse. The *capitouls* and assessors, however, were not included in this order, and Armagnac did not think it wise to reimpose the taxes.[27] During the rebellion, the king's son and lieutenant-designate for Languedoc, Count John of Poitiers, issued an ordinance of reform to placate the discontented.[28]

The unwillingness of Languedoc to pay taxes during the truce posed serious problems for the royal government, and to obtain money its local officials tried, where possible, to ignore the revocation of the taxes. At Lunel, a commissioner trying to levy the *capage* as late as June claimed that he knew nothing of the truce.[29] To make matters worse, the English in Gascony seemed to be displaying a similar ignorance, and after various incidents which the French regarded as truce violations, the Estates of Languedoc were reconvened at Albi in July. Meeting for the fifth time in sixteen months, these Estates may have served a useful purpose in restoring public order by endorsing Armagnac's measures of punishment and pacification. They also had to review the accounts of the treasurers they had named the preceding fall, but they showed no inclination to grant new taxes.[30] Besides the old resistance to peacetime

p. 12; J. Artières, *Documents sur la ville de Millau* (*Archives historiques du Rouergue* 7) (Millau, 1930); no. 207; Breuils, "Jean d'Armagnac," p. 63; Vuitry, *Régime financier* 2: pp. 90–91; *HL* 9: p. 672.

[27] Regné, "Levée," pp. 423–424, 426–428; *INV AM Toulouse*, p. 535 (AA 45, nos. 42–46).

[28] *Ibid.*, p. 536 (AA 45, no. 49); AD Hérault A 4, fols. 315r–320v.

[29] *INV AM Lunel* 2: no. 2225.

[30] Dognon, *Institutions*, p. 604; Roquette, *Rouergue*, pp. 12–13; *Arch. hist. Rouergue* 7: no. 224; *INV AM Toulouse*, p. 535 (AA 45, no. 47); Vuitry, *Régime financier* 2: p. 91.

taxes, there may have been a growing disenchantment with the regime of John of Armagnac. His long lieutenancy in the region had been notable for military reverses and increasing taxes.[31]

Left without taxes, Armagnac turned to the traditional fiscal expedients, a necessary step, no doubt, but hardly one to revive his sagging popularity. He ordered commissioners to exact more money from those who had farmed the sales tax of 1356.[32] He sought money from notaries, investigated acquisitions of fiefs by non-nobles, sent out commissioners to investigate usury, and pressed the collection of regular taxes on Italian merchants.[33]

Meanwhile, Languedoc had encountered the scourge of the *routiers* for the first time. It was in July, 1357, that Arnaud de Cervole's company descended the Rhone. By the end of the year the towns of the Beaucaire district were thoroughly alarmed, and Armagnac led a large force into Provence to attack the castles that Cervole had taken. The dauphin's government authorized the destruction of any fortresses in the seneschalsy of Beaucaire which seemed indefensible.[34] The towns busied themselves with repairing fortifications, and levied local taxes for this purpose.[35]

Towards the end of 1357, John of Armagnac was finally able to step down as royal lieutenant in Languedoc. The seventeen-year-old John of France, count of Poitiers, was finally en route to the Midi, ready to assume the lieutenancy which had been intended for him since the spring of 1356. Both John II and the dauphin reappointed him to this post in the winter of 1357-1358.[36] On his way south, the new lieutenant sent

---

[31] Breuils, "Jean d'Armagnac," p. 65.

[32] AD Hérault A 4, fols. 287r-288r.

[33] *Ibid* fols. 332v-335v; BN MS. lat. 9174, fols. 282-288v; A. Mahul (ed.), *Cartulaire et archives des communes de l'ancien diocèse et de l'arrondisement administratif de Carcassonne* (7 v. in 6, Paris, 1857-1882) 1: p. 240.

[34] *Petit Thalamus*, p. 352; Secousse, introduction to *Ord.* 3: p. lxxv; Bardon, *Alais* 2: p. 45.

[35] *INV AM Beaucaire*, fol. 34v (AA 9); Bardon, *Alais* 2: p. 44. A subsidy or "gracious gift" of one florin per hearth was levied in Dauphiné in this period. See A. Dussert, *Les états du Dauphiné aux XIVe et XVe siécles* (Grenoble, 1915), p. 44f. This tax may also have been a response to the brigand threat of 1357, although its precise date is not clear.

[36] Roquette, *Rouergue*, pp. 13-14; Vuitry, *Régime financier* 2: p. 91; Breuils, "Jean d'Armagnac," p. 65.

advance word indicating his intention of holding assemblies. Despite a lukewarm response from the consuls of Nîmes, who said they were not well enough informed to offer useful advice, the count asked representatives of the southern towns to meet him at Lyon on 8 January, 1358. This assembly probably did not meet, for towns appeared to prefer sending individual embassies to the count instead of convening together in an assembly.[37] One infers that the townsmen wished to make an assessment of the new lieutenant and to express their grievances, but that they did not want to be confronted with demands for a subsidy in time of truce.

As he headed south, however, the count of Poitiers exchanged an increasing amount of correspondence with the seneschal of Beaucaire and other officials who kept him informed of the danger posed by Anglo-Gascon *routiers* and the company of Arnaud de Cervole.[38] Money was sorely needed if Languedoc was to field enough troops to resist these enemies, and royal officers sought to levy the arrears (some 13,000 *écus*) of the earlier *capage* and imposition granted in 1356 for the maintenance of troops. This effort encountered predictable resistance and was suspended towards mid-January.[39] The count of Poitiers called another assembly of the southern towns, this one to meet him at Pont-Saint-Esprit on the Rhone on 30 January.[40] Once again, the assembly probably did not meet, but a preliminary meeting of the towns of the Beaucaire district, scheduled for 11 January, may have been held, since it was about this time that the effort to collect the *capage* was halted.

Finally reaching Nîmes early in February, John of France reissued a fourteen-year-old directive on fines payable by new acquirers of noble fiefs, thus indicating his determination to raise money by exploiting this traditional expedient.[41] At Montpellier, he met an assembly representing nearly seventy towns of the Beaucaire district and obtained a two-month

---

[37] Lehoux, *Jean de France* 1: pp. 94–95; Dognon, *Institutions*, p. 605.

[38] Lehoux, *Jean de France* 1: p. 108, note 5.

[39] *HL* 9: p. 679, note 5; and 10: cols. 1141–1142; Ménard, *Nismes* 2: *preuves*, pp. 197–199.

[40] AD Hérault A 4, fols. 293r–v; *HL* 10: cols. 1140–1141.

[41] AD Hérault A 4, fols. 344r–350v; Lehoux, *Jean de France* 1: p. 103. Subsequently, the inhabitants of Cahors were excused from paying for *franc-fief* because of the costs incurred for local defense. See Lacoste, *Quercy* 3: p. 158.

grant of funds—a combined *capage* and tax on property like the grant of October, 1356. The levy of this money was made subject to various conditions, including the assessment of all temporalities of bishops and the *roturier* property of nobles. The resumed collection of unpaid arrears from the previous year seems to have been accepted.[42] Towns could buy off these taxes with lump-sum payments; Nîmes paid 800 florins and Montpellier 2000 *moutons*.[43]

Other parts of Languedoc seem to have made comparable short-term grants to the count of Poitiers soon after his arrival in the South.[44] Rouergue was faced with a serious military threat because the companies in Quercy had taken Calvignac. The seneschal convened the Estates of the district twice, once at Rodez and once at Villefranche. They agreed to contribute 2100 florins to pay fifty men-at-arms for operations against the companies, and it appears that Quercy also contributed to this effort.[45] In many parts of Languedoc the requirements of local defense forced towns to emulate their northern counterparts and levy taxes for fortifications, often in the face of opposition from some inhabitants.[46] In Quercy, a land particularly hard-pressed by enemy forces, the crown remitted some subsidies because of the sacrifices which had been made for local defense.[47] Meanwhile, the needs of the captive king made additional demands on the southern towns, some of which sent him money to help defray the costs of his household.[48]

Arriving at Toulouse in March, Count John of Poitiers granted a general amnesty to those involved in the uprising of the preceding spring, and received a large monthly allowance to be used for the maintenance of his household and other

---

[42] AD Hérault A 4, fols. 297-298, 305r-308v, 309v-312v; Dognon, *Institutions*, p. 605; A. Le Sourd, *Essai sur les Etats de Vivarais depuis leurs origines* (Paris, 1926), pp. 29-30 (showing that it was still debated whether tallageable dependents should be subject to the *capage*). See also BN Coll. Languedoc 85, fols. 122r-123v; *Ord.* 3: pp. 689-691; *HL* 9: p. 679; 10: cols. 1141-1142.

[43] *Gr. Chartrier*, nos. 1791-1792, 2406; Ménard, *Nismes* 2: *preuves*, pp. 188, 201.

[44] *HL* 9: p. 679, 10: cols. 1142-1143; Lehoux, *Jean de France* 1: p. 102 and notes.

[45] *Ibid.*, p. 108, note 5; Roquette, *Rouergue*, p. 14. According to Lacoste, *Quercy* 3: p. 161, the town of Cahors owed 120 florins, but paid less because it sent troops to the successful campaign to recover Calvingnac in June.

[46] C. Portal, *Histoire de la ville de Cordes, 1222-1799* (Albi, 1902), pp. 52-53; AN JJ 90, no. 141; *INV AM Toulouse*, p. 82 (AA 5, no. 170); Bardon, *Alais* 2: p. 46.

[47] Lacoste, *Quercy* 3: p. 161; AM Gourdon CC 1, nos. 17, 19 AD Lot F 114.

[48] *Gr. Chartrier*, no. 3898; Vuitry, *Régime financier* 2: p. 98.

expenses.[49] During this period the dauphin in Paris assumed the title of regent, and by 9 April, 1358, one of his advisers, Philippe de Troismons, was in Languedoc.[50] His errand was probably to raise money in coordination with the dauphin's simultaneous negotiations with regional assemblies in the North. He called an assembly of the Estates of Languedoc to meet at Toulouse in mid-April, but this meeting soon was canceled, probably when Troismons learned of the different conditions that prevailed in the Midi. Instead, the count of Poitiers ordered an assembly of townsmen to meet at Toulouse on 1 May.[51]

2. Taxation and the Struggle Against Brigandage

The assembly of May, 1358, had one major purpose: to consider how to deal with brigandage, but this in turn raised the always distasteful question of taxation in time of truce. Reluctantly, the representatives of five seneschalsies agreed to support a force of two thousand troops (*glaives* and foot sergeants) for two months. They required the subjects of nobles to contribute, and they insisted that the grant was an emergency measure, and not to be construed as a peacetime subsidy.[52] As in the north, the government undertook to demolish useless fortresses and strengthen the others.[53]

It was also in May that the dauphin was rebuilding his support in Languedoil and the king was concluding the first treaty of London. John's letter announcing the treaty only reached Nîmes on 9 July,[54] but the southern towns already knew of the impending agreement. Gilles Aycelin, bishop of Thérouanne, had been sent to the Midi to enlist support for the first installment of the ransom, and had reached Nîmes on 17 June. As early as the sixth, the count of Poitiers had ordered

---

[49] BN Coll. Languedoc 159, fols. 89v–90r; *HL* 9: p. 681; Lehoux, *Jean de France* 1: pp. 103–104.

[50] BN Coll. Languedoc 159, fol. 86v.

[51] *Ibid.*, fols. 85v–86v; Lehoux, *Jean de France* 1: p. 106; *HL* 9: p. 680. Roquette, *Rouergue*, pp. 15–16, seems incorrect in saying that the two assemblies met at Toulouse.

[52] Dognon, *Institutions*, p. 605; *HL* 9: pp. 680–681; *Gr Chartrier*, nos. 498, 3897; Lacoste *Quercy* 3: p. 160; Lehoux, *Jean de France* 1: p. 107, note 1.

[53] *Ibid.*, p. 107. An altercation arose when some of the demolished structures proved to have been under royal safeguard: BN Doat 60, fols. 115–117v.

[54] Ménard, *Nismes* 2: *preuves*, p. 204. See above, chap. III, 1, for the treaty.

the Estates of Languedoc to meet at Toulouse on 1 July to consider the necessary taxes,[55] and on the same date he demanded a forced loan from royal officers.[56] He soon re-scheduled the assembly for Béziers on 27 June, only to postpone it until 3 July, when all but the towns of the Carcassonne district were to meet at Montpellier.[57]

The crown intended that Languedoc pay 260,000 florins or *moutons* as its share of the 600,000 needed for the first ransom payment. Most of the money could be obtained by assessing the *roturier* population one *mouton* per hearth, while the nobles and clergy who were royal vassals would also con-tribute to the ransom of their lord.[58] After Aycelin visited the leading towns to explain the situation, their assembled repre-sentatives agreed to apportion the tax among the seneschalsies as the crown desired: Rouergue, 6000 florins; Beaucaire, 70,000; Toulouse, 50,000. Lands occupied by the English could not be assessed. Consent to this tax was largely proce-dural in nature, and the acrimonious bargaining that had attended previous royal attempts to levy taxes in time of truce was strikingly absent on this occasion.[59] Such debate as did occur arose over additional taxes for regional defense and support of the king's household in England. The assembly adopted a 2 d./l. imposition for defense, which was replaced in some towns by a *capage*.[60] The government agreed to halt the activities of commissioners and *réformateurs* and to levy no other taxes before the first ransom payment fell due on

---

[55] BN Coll. Languedoc 159, fol. 87; Ménard, *Nismes* 2: *preuves*, p. 203. Lehoux, *Jean de France* 1: p. 111, following Ménard's text, states that Aycelin requested 6000 florins from Nîmes for the ransom. The amount is much more than Nîmes should have paid if the assessment was based on pre-plague hearths (below, note 58). It is likely that the 6000 florins, mentioned in Ménard's text is an error for 600,000 florins, the total down payment on the ransom, to which Nîmes, like other towns, was expected to con-tribute.

[56] AD Hérault A 4, fols. 327v–328v.

[57] BN Coll. Languedoc 159, fol. 86; AD Hérault A 4, fols. 325r–v; *HL* 9: pp. 682–683; 10: col. 1144, no. 6.

[58] Ménard, *Nismes* 2: preuves, p. 203 where it is made clear that the assessment is to be based on pre-plague hearth figures (*juxta antiquum numerum focorum*); BN Coll. Languedoc 85, fols. 139r–142v.

[59] For evidence of consent at the local level, see AM Alès I S–13, no. 3; AD Hérault A 4, fols. 351v–355r. On the generosity of Languedoc, see Delachenal, *Charles V* 2: p. 71; Lehoux, *Jean de France* 1: p. 113. *Cf.* Henneman, "Ransom Aids," p. 620. I now believe that the element of consent was more important in Languedoc in 1358 than suggested in that article, although it remains uncertain whether consent was given as a matter of right (i.e., *quod omnes tangit*) or for reasons of practical administration.

[60] *Arch. hist. Rouergue* 7: no. 228.

1 November. The towns of the Beaucaire district sent a delegation to England with a gift of 10,000 florins for the king's maintenance. The sources differ as to when and where this twice-rescheduled meeting actually convened,[61] but the towns of the seneschalsy of Carcassonne certainly met separately, at Béziers. They agreed to pay their share of the ransom payment (90,000 *moutons*) but obtained the promise of a renumeration of taxable hearths in the near future.[62]

Although letters from the king and dauphin thanked the southern towns for their loyalty and prompt grants of money,[63] it proved difficult to collect the ransom payment of 1358. Rouergue's share was apportioned among the towns of the district on 20 August at Saint-Affrique, but only 1400 *moutons*, less than a quarter of the total, actually were paid, and the count of Poitiers had to order force used against reluctant contributors.[64] By the end of the summer, of course, the treaty with England was about to collapse, but now the companies of *routiers* posed a growing danger.[65] It was necessary to call to arms the nobles of the Carcassonne district as early as late July,[66] and the government turned to the traditional expedients that produced modest revenues when subsidies were not available.[67] To complicate matters further, the dauphin, who had just recovered Paris, sent *réformateurs*

---

[61]*Ord.* 4: pp. 187–190; AM Rodez (Cité) CC 361, no. 13; AM Alés I S-3, no. 9; Ménard, *Nismes* 2: *preuves*, p. 206; Lehoux, *Jean de France* 1: pp. 112–113; Vuitry, *Régime financier* 2: p. 99; *HL* 9: p. 84; Bardon, *Alais* 2: p. 47; Dognon, *Institutions*, p. 605. The last two of these sources seem to believe that the assembly met at Toulouse, rather than Montpellier.

[62]Vuitry, *Régime financier* 2: p. 99; *HL* 9: p. 684; Lehoux, *Jean de France* 1: p. 113; BN Coll. Languedoc 85, fols. 144–145; *Ord.* 3: pp. 337–338.

[63]Delachenal, *Charles V* 2: p. 70; Ménard, *Nismes* 2: *preuves*, pp. 188–189.

[64]On slow collection in some areas, see *ibid.*, pp. 205–206. See also Delachenal, *Charles V* 2: pp. 71, 414; *HL* 9: pp. 686, 715 (the latter page dealing with 1360 but in fact referring to 1358); Roquette, *Rouergue*, pp. 24–5. For Millau's share of the ransom payment in 1358, see *Arch. hist. Rouergue* 7: no. 228. on coercive measures needed for collection in Rouergue, see Lehoux, *Jean de France* 1: p. 114, note 2.

[65]A. Jacotin (ed.), *Preuves de la Maison de Polignac* (5 v., Paris, 1898–1906) 2: p. 24; *Petit Thalamus*, pp. 352–355; Lehoux, *Jean de France* 1: pp. 116–117. See also T. de Loray, "Les Grandes Compagnies et l'Archiprêtre en Bourgogne, 1360–1361," *Rev. quest. hist.* 29 (1881): p. 266, where it is pointed out that the companies did not become a serious problem until after Charles the Bad began to wage war openly against the Valois in mid-1358. From this time onwards, people like Knolles could and did claim to be fighting for the king of Navarre when England and France were nominally at peace.

[66]*HL* 9: p. 685; Lehoux, *Jean de France* 1: p. 115.

[67]AD Hérault A 4, fols. 358r–360v, 365r–366v, 392–394v. These revenues included fines for acquisition of fiefs, collection of silver marks from privileged groups which

to Languedoc to obtain subsidies, although his brother had recently promised not to do so.[68]

A number of documents reveal the concern with repairing fortifications during the second half of 1358 and the levy of municipal taxes for this purpose.[69] The subsidy authorized in July to finance local military operations seems to have been intended to equal half the amount promised for the ransom— 3000 florins from the seneschalsy of Rouergue and a like amount from Montpellier alone.[70] By November the town of Rodez was contributing to Rouergue's subsidy, but the government had to seize the temporalities of the bishop to force collection.[71] In Vivarais and Velay, the chronic opposition of the nobles to war subsidies appears to have prevented the levy of a *capage*.[72]

When the deadline for the first ransom payment passed (1 November), so also did the moratorium on other taxes which the count of Poitiers had promised in July. To obtain new funds for defense, John of France scheduled an assembly of the Estates for 4 November at Carcassonne, only to cancel the order when he was unable to be there. There is no further trace of an assembly in the fall of 1358, but since an embassy from the towns was sent to John II at the end of the year, it appears that regional meetings or mutual consultations of some sort must have taken place.[73] Scattered documents make mention of taxes. In Rouergue, the government was collecting money

---

owed them periodically, taxes on exports, and the so-called *boite aux Lombards* owed by Italians. All of these were more or less regular in theory, but throughout the century the documentary evidence of these revenues sharply increased in periods when receipts from subsidies or aids were insufficient or unavailable.

[68] BN Coll. Languedoc 159, fol. 85; *HL* 9: p. 690, note 3. Perhaps as a result of these investigations, the inhabitants of Nîmes secured from the dauphin a confirmation of privileges in fiscal matters which had been granted originally by Louis X (AD Hérault A 6, fols. 4v–7v).

[69] *Gr. Chartrier*, no. 688; *INV AM Lunel* 2: nos. 2226–2227; BN Doat 60, fols. 109–113; Ménard, *Nismes* 2: *preuves*, pp. 207, 213.

[70] *Arch. hist. Rouergue* 7: no. 228; *Gr. Chartrier*, no. 499.

[71] *Arch. hist. Rouergue* 17: p. 7; De Gaujal, *Rouergue* 2: p. 192; AD Aveyron G 31 (Un-numbered document).

[72] E. Delcambre, *Les états du Velay des origines à 1642* (Saint-Etienne, 1938), p. 59.

[73] On the canceled assembly, see BN Coll. Languedoc 159, fol. 94; *HL* 9: p. 687; Dognon, *Institutions*, p. 605. A reference to an assembly in BN Coll. Languedoc 85, fol. 149r, surely should be dated 1356. On the sending of representatives to the king in England, see *HL* 9: p. 688, and Lehoux, *Jean de France* 1: p. 128, note 3. Subsequently, the king acknowledged receipt of some money and confirmed certain privileges: *HL* 10: cols. 1153–1154; AD Hérault A 4, fols. 370r–372v.

for the support of sergeants from late 1358 until April of 1359, and a *gabelle* may also have been in effect there.[74] These were probably not new subsidies, however, for there is evidence that taxes granted in 1358 were far behind schedule and were still being collected in the early months of 1359.[75]

In early 1359, brigandage claimed the attention of all France, and the count of Poitiers was in Auvergne, where the problem was especially critical.[76] The Anglo-French truce was to expire in the spring, but well before then the peace in the Midi was rudely shattered by the outbreak of war between John of Armagnac and Gaston Phoebus, count of Foix. During his long career, Gaston III was to become the most powerful and wealthy lord in Languedoc. He claimed to hold the viscounty of Béarn in full sovereignty although both English and French wished to enforce their suzerainty there. He also coveted Bigorre, over which Foix and Armagnac had been feuding for generations. Connected by marriage to Charles the Bad, he had been imprisoned by the king in 1356 and had formed an anti-French alliance with Aragon, but his brief involvement in the *Jacquerie* had served the royalist cause.[77] His enemy, John of Armagnac, had marriage connections with the royal family and soon betrothed his daughter to the count of Poitiers. The latter appeared to support Armagnac's claims when he told the seneschal of Bigorre, in 1358, that the crown would not abandon this district without Armagnac's approval. The government's pro-Armagnac bias provoked Gaston Phoebus, who attacked Armagnac with Navarrese and Anglo-Gascon aid.[78]

Although this struggle began in 1359, its major impact may not have come until 1360. A letter from John of France to the consuls of Montpellier, dated 1359 by most scholars, describes a major offensive by Gaston in the upper Garonne valley and refers to a large tax recently granted for the defense of Languedoc. John is described as count of Poitiers and Mâcon, but he was not yet count of Mâcon in early 1359, and his

---

[74]*Arch. hist. Rouergue* 17: pp. 8–10, 13. Because a *gabelle* in this region could mean any sales tax, we cannot assert that it was a tax on salt only.

[75]*HL* 9: p. 697; AD Hérault A 4, fols. 428r–429v; BN NAF 7389, fols. 253r–v.

[76]Lehoux, *Jean de France* 1: p. 120f.

[77]*Ibid.*, pp. 12–125; P. Tucoo-Chala, *Gaston Fébus et la vicomté de Béarn, 1343–1391* (Bordeaux, 1960), pp. 71, 72, 81.

[78]*Ibid.*, p. 82.

biographer has assigned the document to a later date. Since Languedoc had not granted a large tax for defense in early 1359, it is likely that the text describing Gaston's major campaign belongs to 1360.[79] Nevertheless, his hostility in 1359 did complicate a situation that the *routiers* and the impending resumption of Anglo-French hostilities had already made dangerous.

Faced with these threats, the council of the count of Poitiers, acting in his absence, assembled the towns of the Beaucaire district at Alès on 25 February, ostensibly to consider English violations of the truce.[80] Apparently this meeting diverted to local defense the money collected in the preceding year for the king's ransom.[81] The full Estates of Languedoc (representing seven seneschalsies) convened at Montpellier late in March. The proctors of Rodez received their powers on the fifteenth of that month and they had returned home by 9 April.[82] This assembly decided to finance military forces by re-introducing throughout Languedoc the *gabelle* on salt and salted meat. It was to be levied until Christmas, under the supervision of specially appointed *conservateurs* who were empowered to make final decisions on all complaints and disputes.[83] Henceforth the *gabelle* would be renewed until it became a permanent tax, but it continued to be controlled carefully by the Estates. During these years, it was sometimes farmed and sometimes collected by paid *gabelliers*. It was levied when the salt was taken from the *salins* to the warehouses *(greniers)*. Thereafter, the commerce in salt was not taxed except insofar as it involved salted

---

[79] Originally in AM Montpellier D 19, no. 6, the text was copied in BN MS. lat. 9174, fol. 290, and published in *HL* 10: cols. 1152-1153. According to Louvet's inventory (*Gr. Chartrier*), the text at Montpellier was dated 20 March. That in BN MS. lat. 9174 is dated 20 January. Lehoux, *Jean de France* 1: p. 149, argues that the text cannot belong to 1359, but the historiography of the struggle between Foix and Armagnac remains confused here because so many sources have accepted the dating of January 1359: *Arch. hist. Rouergue* 17: p. 11, note 3; Tucoo-Chala, *Gaston*, pp. 82-83; Bardon, *Alais* 2: p. 48; Breuils, "Jean d'Armagnac," p. 66.

[80] Dognon, *Institutions*, p. 605; Bardon, *Alais* 2: p. 48; Lehoux, *Jean de France* 1: p. 126; *HL* 9: p. 691, note 4. The extension of the truce, as a result of the second London treaty, was not yet known in Languedoc.

[81] Ménard, *Nismes* 2: *preuves*, pp. 214-215.

[82] *Arch. hist. Rouergue* 17: p. 13, and notes; *HL* 9: pp. 690-691; Lehoux, *Jean de France* 1: pp. 126-127. An assembly summoned to Lavaur on 24 February apparently did not meet.

[83] *Ibid.*, p. 127; *HL* 9: p. 692; 10: cols. 1161-1162; Ménard, *Nismes* 2: *preuves*, p. 216; Bardon, *Alais* 2: p. 49; Dognon, *Institutions*, p. 605.

meat.[84] As yet, no mandatory minimum purchases were required.

When enacted in March of 1359, the *gabelle* was granted reluctantly as a temporary measure for defense, and the consuls of Nîmes debated at length over possible ways of substituting another form of payment.[85] Albi had to borrow money to pay its share of the subsidy, and one infers that the burghers substituted a lump sum payment for the *gabelle*.[86] There were delays and difficulties in implementing the tax on salt, some of them caused by the count of Foix.[87] It was 25 April before John of France confirmed the appointment of *conservateurs* for the Beaucaire district[88] and still another month before the collectors arrived at Cahors. Their arrival in Quercy created great hostility, for the region had suffered seriously from the English campaigning. In April, John of Poitiers asked the bailiff of the Mountains and the seneschal of Rouergue to come to the aid of the Cahorsins, who had been unable to till their fields and were running short of grain. The effort to avoid the *gabelle* failed, however; John refused to make Quercy an exception to the general levy.[89]

While the Estates were meeting at Montpellier, the truce was extended, to expire on 14 June instead of 9 April.[90] The companies were making the truce irrelevant in some parts of France, and the count of Foix kept the southwest in turmoil. Innocent VI failed to make peace between Foix and Armagnac, and the count of Poitiers finally proclaimed Gaston III a rebel, ordering the confiscation of his property and that of his subjects.[91] In May, Gaston's forces burned the suburbs of Toulouse.[92] At the same time, *routiers* in Auvergne, led by Robert Knolles and Bertucat d'Albret, were beginning to threaten northern Languedoc.[93]

There is reason to think that John of France convened a

---

[84] G. Peroùsse, "Etude sur les origines de la gabelle et sur son organisation jusqu'en 1380," *Posit. Thèses, Ec. Chartes* 1898: p. 96.

[85] Ménard, *Nismes* 2: *preuves*, pp. 217–219.

[86] AM Albi CC 69, first pc.

[87] Lehoux, *Jean de France* 1: p. 127.

[88] *HL* 10: cols. 1158–1160.

[89] Albe, "Cahors Inv.," nos. 447–449.

[90] *Foedera* 6: pp. 121–122; BN MS. lat. 9174, fols. 297–300.

[91] *HL* 10: cols. 1157–1158; Breuils, "Jean d'Armagnac," p. 67; Lehoux, *Jean de France* 1: p. 132.

[92] Tucco-Chala, *Gaston*, p. 388, no. 177 (from AM Toulouse, AA 46).

[93] *Petit Thalamus*, p. 356; Lehoux, *Jean de France* 1: pp. 134–135.

new assembly to deal with the military danger. After proclaiming the *arrière-ban* on 8 May,[94] he made an announcement the following day concerning taxes granted at Carcassonne. These were to be paid earlier than originally
scheduled, and John ordered the seneschal of Beaucaire to
enforce the same early collections.[95] On the twelfth he ordered
a new coinage,[96] and four days later he regulated the administration of taxes at Le Vigan.[97] About the same time, Montpellier arranged to farm various municipal taxes for 24,500 l. t.[98]
All these developments suggest strongly that the count of
Poitiers had consulted an assembly early in May, probable at
Carcassonne. A document of 20 September proves that the
Estates did meet at Carcassonne and agreed to advance 100,000
florins on the *gabelle* promised earlier at Montpellier.[99] Although Dognon cited this text as proof of an assembly at the
end of May, and Vaissete associated it with a meeting in
September, it seems probable, from the evidence just dis-
cussed, that this action occurred at the beginning of May.[100]

This assembly would have heard that the truce was extended, and it is noteworthy that the Estates were willing to
speed up tax collections in order to be prepared for renewed
hostilities. Before 1358, Languedoc had shown unwillingness
to pay taxes during a truce, even when its early termination
was expected. After their reluctant peacetime grant of May,
1358, the southern Estates at Montpellier and Carcassonne,
confronted by the hostile count of Foix, had to continue
raising money for defense. Gradually, they were compelled to
realize that "evident necessity" did not have to be synonomous
with outright war.

The extension of the Anglo-French truce was, as we know,
associated with the second treaty of London. When he summoned the Estates General to discuss this treaty, the dauphin
invited the southern towns to send representatives to Paris,

---

[94] AD Hérault A 5, fols. 54v–55r.

[95] *Ibid.*, fols. 53–54; *HL* **9**: p. 697.

[96] *Ibid.* **10:** cols. 1161–1162.

[97] AD Hérault A 5, fols. 58v–60r.

[98] *INV AM Montpellier* **11:** pp. 15–16.

[99] *HL* **10:** cols. 1162–1163.

[100] Dognon, *Institutions*, p. 606; *HL* **9**: p. 702. For evidence of collection of the
gabelle for men-at-arms in Rodez in July, see *Arch. hist. Rouergue* **17:** pp. 12–13.

although Montpellier's proctor could not have reached the capital by the appointed day.[101] It is still not certain whether representatives from Languedoc ever reached that assembly, but the ensuing rejection of the treaty affected Languedoc as well as Languedoil. For one thing, John II now required more money for his household in England, and on 16 June, 1359, the ordinary and extraordinary revenues of the seneschalsy of Beaucaire were set aside for this prupose.[102] In addition, the crown vigorously pursued in Languedoc the plan to finance a Danish attack on England.

It would cost France 600,000 florins to induce Waldemar III of Denmark to invade England with 12,000 men. The plan met with little enthusiasm in Languedoil, and commissioners were sent to the Midi in the extravagant hope of obtaining 400,000 écus, a sum which exceeded by more than 50 per cent the figure discussed previously as Languedoc's share of the first payment on John II's ransom.[103] Because the southern Estates had not rebelled against the crown and had been willing to send aid to King John in England, the dauphin may have had a distorted impression of them, thinking them more generous and docile than in fact they were. In any case, his commissioners were sent to Languedoc in June and soon began to visit the important towns individually. Perhaps they wished to influence the larger communities and test public opinion before convening any assemblies.

The royal agents received replies from Toulouse (24 June), Carcassonne (4 July), and Montpellier (10 August), and are known to have been at Nîmes, whose consuls were deliberating on 6 August. These towns all gave non-committal responses, indicating a willingness to help but wishing to hear what other communities would do when consulted in an assembly.[104] Whether or not such an assembly had originally been planned, it had become clear that one was necessary and

---

[101] Delachenal, *Charles V* 2: p. 94 and notes: *HL* 10: cols. 1155-1156. See above, chap. III, note 56.

[102] AD Hérault A 4, fols. 383v-386v; A 5, fols. 72v-73v; *Petit Thalamus*, p. 355; *HL* 9: p. 699.

[103] Delachenal, Charles V 2: pp. 94, 98f; AD Lot F 35. See above, chap. III.

[104] A Germain, "Projet de descente en Angletere concerté entre le gouvernement. français et le roi de Danemark Valdemar III, pour la délivrance du roi Jean," *Mémoires de la Société archéologique de Montpellier* 4 (1855): pp. 25-28; Ménard, *Nismes* 2: pp. 201-211.

it was scheduled for 16 August at Béziers.[105] In the meantime, preparatory assemblies were held at the seneschalsy level. One of these was at Millau on 3 August, where the towns of the *Haute Marche* of Rouergue met the commissioners of the dauphin.[106] Late in July, the towns of the seneschalsies of Beaucaire and Carcassonne met respectively at Nîmes and Carcassonne, but if these meetings considered the Danish alliance they also were preoccupied with the financing of local defense.[107]

In any case, it is clear that considerable effort was expended in an attempt to induce the towns of Languedoc to send representatives to Béziers who were ready to make a firm commitment on behalf of the treaty with Denmark. This effort, however, was in vain, for when they convened at Béziers the burghers would do no more than postpone a decision until a new assembly which was scheduled for 8 September at Toulouse. Prior to this new meeting, townsmen of several districts convened at Nîmes (1 September) where they expressed discontent with the salt tax, discussed the need for more troops for local defense, and requested a new delay in making their response on the Danish treaty.[108] The representatives of Millau left home for Toulouse on 6 September and did not return until eighteen days later.[109] It seems that the assembly planned for Toulouse was delayed for a week or so and possibly transferred to another site.[110]

At this meeting the towns of Languedoc finally agreed to pay 200,000 florins for the Danish treaty (half of what had been requested) and send a seven-man embassy to Waldemar III. The communities of Rouergue met on 28 September to apportion their share and name their envoy.[111] The southern towns may also have discussed a new contribution for the war against brigandage, pending further action by a new assembly, of all three Estates, to be held later.[112] It seems clear that

---

[105] AM Alès I S-3, no. 10, published in Bardon, *Alais* 2: P.J. X, and discussed *ibid.*, p. 50: full powers given to those who will represent Alès at Béziers.

[106] Roquette, *Rouergue*, p. 132.

[107] Dognon, *Institutions*, p. 606; *HL* 10: col. 1162.

[108] See the note of Molinier in *HL* 9: p. 703, note 4; and Dognon, *Institutions*, p. 606.

[109] *Arch. hist. Rouergue* 7: no. 231.

[110] *HL* 9: pp. 702–703; Dognon, *Institutions*, p. 606.

[111] *Ibid.*; Delachenal, *Charles V* 2: pp. 101–102.

[112] *HL* 9: p. 703, note 4; *Arch. hist. Rouergue* 17: pp. 16–17, note 2.

there was far more interest in local defense than in the Danish treaty. Except for Rouergue, one finds no evidence of any further effort to pursue the alliance with Waldemar III, and Languedoc's grant for this purpose had been too little and too late. By the time the dauphin could have learned of it, he was already occupied with the imminent new invasion of France by Edward III, and the project seems to have been dropped.[113]

Throughout France, regional defense was the urgent consideration, and the southern towns, which had already advanced 100,000 florins on the *gabelle*, were being drawn increasingly into that peacetime taxation they had struggled so long to avoid. For the moment, the resumption of Anglo-French hostilities spared them further embarrassment on this matter of principle, for while Edward III posed no direct threat to the Midi, they could raise taxes to fight brigands without setting a distasteful precedent. The actual danger came from two sources—the count of Foix in the Garonne valley and the *routiers* in Auvergne. Of the latter, Robert Knolles inspired the greatest fear during the first half of 1359, threatening the inhabitants of Rouergue in June.[114] The seneschal of Beaucaire, late in June, led troops to Le Puy for a campaign against brigands, and on 1 July he named a local seigneur to act as his lieutenant in the seneschalsy while he was occupied with military affairs.[115] When the towns of the district met at Nîmes late in July to discuss the Danish project, they also had to raise 30,000 florins for defense, apparently their share of the promised advance on the *gabelle*.[116] At Carcassonne, the towns of that seneschalsy granted a small hearth tax in July, either for defense or for the captive king's household.[117] Otherwise, indirect taxes prevailed in Languedoc, and the government busily pursued the collection of the *gabelle* and the 4 d./l/ levied on exports.[118] Where the clergy objected to paying municipal taxes for defense, the royal

---

[113] Delachenal, *Charles V* 2: p. 438 (P.J.); Breuils, "Jean d'Armagnac," p. 67.

[114] *Arch. hist. Rouergue* 17: pp. 16–17 note 2. Later in the summer of 1359, the king made a gift to the town of Gourdon in Quercy because of the sufferings caused by the war (BN MS. fr. 20581, no. 48). The *routiers* may well have been a factor.

[115] AD Hérault A 4, fols 274r–375r; Lehoux *Jean de France* 1: p. 136, note 6.

[116] *Ibid.*, p. 137, citing Ménard, *Nismes* 2: *preuves*, p. 235; Dognon, *Institutions*, p. 606.

[117] *Ibid.*

[118] AD Hérault A 4, fols. 375v–377r, 382r–v, 394v–395v; BN NAF 7389, fol. 254r; *Arch. hist. Rouergue* 17: pp. 15–17.

lieutenant showed little sympathy.[119] He took new measures against usury, probably hoping to augment revenues through fines.[120]

When the southern towns, in September, 1359, made their grant for the Danish alliance, they do not seem to have specified how the funds would be raised. Even when this project was abandoned, the problem of brigandage and the unpopularity of the *gabelle* dictated a new meeting, and all three Estates assembled at Carcassonne on 18 October. Lengthy discussions must have taken place, for the decisions were not announced until four weeks later.[121] It was finally decided to extend the *gabelle* until Christmas, 1360. The money was to be used exclusively for the war, but repayment of the 100,000 florins previously advanced by the towns would have priority over new expenditures. The assembly also granted a hearth tax of one *mouton,* to be payable in quarterly installments beginning in January and to be levied by the towns themselves. The conditions surrounding these taxes were carefully set forth. All persons of whatever status were to pay them, and no other taxes were to be levied except in case of "eminent necessity or evident utility," such as an invasion of Languedoc by the Prince of Wales. If a new truce or treaty of peace were concluded, the taxes would cease and all royal commissioners would be recalled. Finally, all the towns were permitted to levy a sales tax of 2 d./l. for six months in order to meet their own budgetary needs.[122] The count of Poitiers augmented and clarified these arrangements with further enactments during late November and early December. They included instructions for the farming and collection of the customs on exports;[123] the constraint of persons who had resisted payment of taxes;[124] and the appointment of those who were to supervise collection of the *gabelle.*[125]

---

[119] AD Hérault A 4, fols. 389v-390r; A 5, fols. 74v-76v; *HL* 9: pp. 695-696.

[120] RN NAF 7389, fol. 280r; *Arch. hist. Rouergue* 7: no. 232.

[121] On the length of the assembly, see *ibid.*, no. 233.

[122] Dognon, *Institutions,* p. 606; Lacoste, *Quercy* 3: p. 167; BN MS. lat. 9174, fols. 327-344; *HL* 9: pp. 705-706, and note 4; 10: cols. 1163-1176; *INV AM Pézenas,* nos. 1666-1667; *Gr. Chartrier,* nos. 1793, 2415. On the subsequent levy of 2 d./l. in towns of the Beaucaire district, see AD Hérault A 5, fols. 60v-64v; *INV AM Montpellier* 11: p. 17.

[123] *Gr. Chartrier,* nos. 2416, 3785.

[124] AD Hérault A 4, fols. 390r-v, 396v-398v.

[125] *HL* 10: cols. 1164-1165.

Although the Estates were careful to insist on many conditions and royal guarantees, most of the representatives at the
assembly faced a substantially smaller personal sacrifice than
those who had convened at Toulouse three years earlier, in the
aftermath of the battle of Poitiers. The taxes of November,
1359, were sharply regressive in nature, bearing mainly on the
consumer and not affecting property. The fact that the English invasion of 1359 was taking place in the North, while the
main attack in 1356 had been launched from Bordeaux, clearly
affected the thinking of the assembly. The return of Robert
Knolles to the Breton marches from Auvergne may also have
influenced Languedoc's sense of necessity.

Gaston of Foix now posed the greatest danger to the Midi.
His feud with John of Armagnac became a royal affair in
October, 1359, when the count of Poitiers married Armagnac's
daughter. The prince still relied heavily on the advice of his
new father-in-law, who accompanied him everywhere,[126] and
Foix had few qualms about aligning himself with the Anglo-
Gascons against the French régime in Languedoc.

Late in December, the count of Poitiers proclaimed the
arrière-ban, calling for a general muster of armed men on 10
January, 1360, at Toulouse.[127] Most evidence suggests that this
action was directed against the count of Foix, particularly if
Françoise Lehoux is right in assigning to 1360 the document
of 20 January which describes Gaston's incursion into the
Garonne valley.[128] It is possible, however, that this *arrière-ban*
had another purpose. The town of Millau sent an emissary to
Toulouse who left on 9 January. His errand was *la prevezia de
trametre gens d'armes en Fransa,* and he did not return to
Millau until the twenty-fifth. This trip has been regarded as
evidence of an assembly aimed at aiding the dauphin against
the invasion of Edward III.[129] Charles had appealed for troops
from Languedoc in October,[130] and it is conceivable that his

---

[126] Breuils, "Jean d'Armagnac," p. 67; Lehoux, *Jean de France* 1: p. 141. Brigandage, meanwhile, did not cease completely with the withdrawal of Knolles, for
companies in the mountains of Auvergne remained menacing. See Boudet, *Thomas
de la Marche,* P.J. 33 pt. 5.

[127] AD Hérault A 4, fols. 407r–v; BN NAF 7389, fols. 253r, 254r; Lehoux, *Jean de
France* 1: p. 147, notes 5, 6.

[128] See above, at notes 78 and 79.

[129] *Arch. hist. Rouergue* 7: no. 235.

[130] Delachenal, *Charles V* 2: p. 438 (P.J.).

brother now sought to interest the southern towns in the fate of Languedoil.

There is no indication, however, that Languedoc responded to the dauphin's appeal. In this period no part of France showed much enthusiasm for coming to the aid of another region. The Midi, beset by troubles of its own, could never count on any assistance from Paris. The count of Poitiers, moreover, may not have pressed very hard for the diversion of resources from Languedoc to the north. The count of Foix had challenged him personally, for Gaston III now demanded the lieutenantcy of Languedoc for himself. Apparently estimating that the subsidies granted in November would produce 500,000 florins, he proposed that John of France accept one-fifth of this sum and withdraw from Languedoc, leaving the rest of the money for Foix.[131] No doubt John was determined to reject this proposition, but Gaston's incursion up the Garonne made it desirable for John to make sure of the support of the southern towns. The assembly at Toulouse, while it may have discussed the possibility of aiding the dauphin, probably devoted its major attention to the challenge of the count of Foix.

No new taxes were levied at this time, but the documents of the next few months reveal payment of subsidy receipts to commanders and war treasurers;[132] squabbling over claims of privilege;[133] and efforts to improve the collection of the gabelle.[134] On 16 March, the arrière-ban was again proclaimed,[135] and it seems clear that the government was waging a losing struggle against Gaston Phoebus. The count of Foix cut communications between Toulouse and Albi, and his forces occupied much of the lower Tarn and upper Garonne valleys.[136] The lord of Mirepoix now attempted to desert the French crown and cast his lot with the victorious Gaston, but John of France assembled forces early in April, 1360, and

---

[131] HL 10: cols. 1152–1153. Cf. Tucoo-Chala, Gaston, pp. 82–83.

[132] BN Coll. Languedoc 85, fol. 154: BN MS. fr. 26002, nos. 907, 915; BN NAF 20026, no. 83.

[133] HL 9: pp. 707–708, 10: cols. 1166–1167.

[134] AD Hérault A 5, fols, 50v–53r; BN NAF 7389, fol. 253v.

[135] AD Hérault A 4, fols. 430v–431v.

[136] Tucoo-Chala, Gaston, p. 83. See also HL 10: cols. 1259–1261, a document which almost certainly should be dated 1360.

occupied the lands of Mirepoix.[137] Following this triumph, the count of Poitiers returned to Carcassonne where an assembly of town representatives was to review the difficult military situation. Although this assembly seems to have remained in session for some time, there is no evidence of new taxation.[138] Late in May, Albi was making payments on the hearth tax of one *mouton* granted by the seneschalsy of Carcassonne in November, 1359,[139] and it is likely that this assembly concerned itself with the existing taxes in order to hasten collection and perhaps accelerate the timetable for paying the installments originally scheduled for January, April, July, and October. The consuls of Montpellier, who had had trouble meeting their payments to date, resisted efforts to collect the July installment several weeks early.[140] There is some evidence that Alès also sought to hold the government to the original schedule.[141]

3. The High Cost of Peace, 1360

About the time that the assembly at Carcassonne was breaking up, the dauphin concluded his truce with England and then the treaty of Brétigny.[142] When Gaston Phoebus learned that the treaty would assign Bigorre to England, he decided to move quickly and assert his claim to the territory, hoping that the new English overlord would accept the *fait accompli* and give his rights precedence over those claimed by John of Armagnac. He sent troops into Bigorre and Armagnac, raising grave doubts as to whether the Anglo-French treaty could be enforced in the Southwest.[143] Persons from the county of Foix who lived in the seneschalsy of Toulouse were suspected of disloyalty and were ordered expelled from the district unless they had lived there ten years or more.[144]

---

[137]*Ibid.*, cols. 1178–1179. For evidence that Charles the Bad was supporting Gaston of Foix, see Castro, *Catalogo* 3: no. 496.

[138]Dognon, *Institutions*, p. 607; *Arch. hist. Rouergue* 7: no. 236; Lehoux, *Jean de France* 1: p. 152.

[139]A. Vidal, *Douze comptes consulaires d'Albi du XIVe siècle* (Albi, 1906), pp. 4–5.

[140]*Gr. Chartrier*, no. 1794.

[141]AM Alès I S-13, no. 4: the town obtained a *vidimus* of the earlier promises regarding the schedule at which the *gabelle* was to be paid.

[142]AD Hérault A 5, fols. 56r–v; and above, chap. III (7–8 May, 1360).

[143]Tucoo-Chala, *Gaston*, p. 83.

[144]*INV AM Toulouse*, pp. 536–537 (AA 45, no. 53).

Despite the dangers inherent in the Foix-Armagnac struggle, the attack on Bigorre had given Languedoc a respite by diverting the energies of Gaston Phoebus in a westerly direction. For the moment, therefore, most of the southern seneschalsies could concern themselves with the ransom of John II. Just as the king and dauphin issued numerous letters and instructions to the taxpayers and tax collectors of northern France, so they also urged the towns of the Midi to act quickly on the down payment.[145] Quick action, however, was not really possible, for Languedoc was separated by long distances, not only from London and Paris, but also from Saint-Omer, where the ransom funds were being stored. Communications were slow; collection was slow; and the need to transport the money all the way to Saint-Omer made for further delays. It is likely that most of the 200,000 écus still unpaid by late October were owing from Languedoc.

Two months after the treaty of Brétigny, the Foix-Armagnac struggle was temporarily halted. Somewhat like Charles the Bad in Normandy, Gaston III had used Anglo-French hostilities as a means of taking action, with relative impunity, to satisfy personal ambitions and grievances. Unsuccessful in gaining the royal lieutenantcy in Languedoc, he had tried to secure control over Bigorre, but he soon realized that the seizure of this territory was not necessarily the best policy to pursue. Peace between England and France would leave him in an exposed position if he continued to fight the French authorities in Languedoc. He therefore decided to accept the dauphin's offer of mediation, deferring the question of Bigorre until he could deal with his new English overlord. Representatives of the dauphin and the pope assisted in the ensuing negotiations, which led to a series of treaties early in July.[146]

On 7 July, at the Dominican cloister in Pamiers, the count of Foix concluded peace with the counts of Armagnac and Poitiers. Gaston agreed to evacuate the towns and fortresses he had occupied.[147] The next day, John of France authorized the

---

[145]*Gr. Chartrier*, no 3899; Delachenal, *Charles V* 2: pp. 443–444 (P.J.).

[146]*HL* 9: pp. 709–711; Tucoo-Chala, *Gaston*, p. 83.

[147]*Ibid.*, pp. 83–84, 389; AD Basses-Pyrenéés E 408, no. 77; *HL* 10: cols. 1180–1186; Breuils, "Jean d'Armagnac," p. 68.

towns of the Midi to assemble when they wished, to deal with
Gaston.[148] Obviously, the count of Foix was prepared to make
peace only at an advantageous price, and the agreement at
Pamiers doubtless depended on whatever settlement the hap-
less southern towns could make with him. It was on 9 July
that representatives of important southern towns met with the
count and agreed to a costly peace. They were to pay Gaston
10,000 gold florins immediately, 90,000 more in several weeks'
time, and a second 100,000 in two later installments (Christmas, 1360, and 24 June, 1361). In return, the count of Foix
promised to execute the peace treaty and to aid and defend
Languedoc against its enemies.[149]

Just who those enemies would be is not made clear, but
John of Armagnac must have viewed with great suspicion the
promise of large sums to his bitter enemy. With his son-in-law
John of France about to leave for England as a hostage under
the terms of the treaty of Bretigny, Armagnac was ready to
resume his prominent role in Languedoc. Scarcely had the
southern towns purchased the withdrawal of Gaston Phoebus
than they were again assembled, this time by Armagnac, at
Sommières on 23 July. There they had to grant a large sum to
Armagnac and a sizable "gift" to the departing count of
Poitiers. Although amounts are not specified, the king authorized Armagnac to collect as much as Gaston, so he probably
obtained a grant of 200,000 florins.[150] The *gabelle*, which
should have been halted by the treaty of Brétigny, now had to
be continued.[151]

Even before considering the ransom, therefore, the communities of a diminished Languedoc had agreed to pay sums
which probably exceeded 400,000 florins in order to end what
amounted to a private feudal war in their region. The two
counts promised, of course, to live in perpetual peace and to
defend Languedoc, so there may have been hope that Foix and
Armagnac might together deal a decisive blow against the

---

[148]*Gr. Chartrier*, no. 1025.

[149]*Ibid.*, nos. 3413; D-19, no. 1; AD Hérault A 5, fols 102r–109v; *HL* 10: cols.
1186–1191, 1197–1198; Dognon, *Institutions*, p. 607.

[150]*Ibid.*; BN Doat 193, fols. 1–24v; Lehoux, *Jean de France* 1: p. 174. AD Hérault
A 5, fols. 155r–156v.

[151]*Ord.* 4: pp. 199–202. Meanwhile, Montpellier was allowed to continue levying
certain municipal taxes in order to repay the town's debts: *Gr. Chartrier*, no. 2421.

companies. Nevertheless, practical men must have doubted that these two longtime enemies could bury their differences permanently. Were the towns of Languedoc, in trying to buy peace, actually raising the money to finance a new Foix-Armagnac encounter?

In the light of this staggering new financial burden, it is not surprising that there was even less enthusiasm for royal taxation than there had been in 1358. The consuls of Le Puy drew up a document for circulation among the other southern towns, urging them to resist any new subsidy requests because of local impoverishment. Le Puy had faced serious attacks from the companies during the two preceding years.[152]

In spite of the understandable reluctance to undergo new financial burdens, Languedoc was committed to paying a large part of the down payment owed for the king's ransom. It is difficult to determine when the money for this purpose began to be collected, for the crown simply reimposed the same assessment originally agreed to in 1358. On 9 July, the constable, Robert de Fiennes, ordered the levy of sums required for the ransom, but it is likely that the first 100,000 florins owed to the count of Foix had to be paid before the royal ransom.[153] Assemblies met at Rodez late in August and at Lunel in mid-September, and these meetings, about which little is known, probably discussed the means of raising the funds for the king's deliverance.[154]

As in 1358, the quotas for the ransom were based on the principle of one florin or *mouton* for each taxable hearth. The seneschalsy of Carcassonne therefore owed 90,000, and that of Beaucaire 70,000, with an additional thousand *moutons* to be contributed by a seigneurial enclave within the district. From the Toulousain, the share was 50,000 *moutons*, with the town and *viguerie* of Toulouse owing slightly more than one-third and the *jugeries* paying sums ranging from 3,800 to 10,500 *moutons* to complete the total.[155] The earlier assessment of six thousand *moutons* was imposed on Rouergue, although this

[152] BN MS. lat. 9175, fols. 5r–7v, partially published by E. Molinier, "Etudes sur la vie d'Arnoul d'Audrehem, marechal de France (1302–1370)," *Mémoires présentées par divers savants à l'Académie des Insciptions et Belles Lettres, 2e sér.*, 6, 1 (1883): P.J. 87.

[153] AD Hérault A 5, fols. 65r–v. Molinier, "Audrehem," p. 123, concluded that Gaston received the first payment of 100,000 florins rather promptly.

[154] Dognon, *Institutions*, p. 607.

[155] *HL* 10: cols. 1213, 1228, 1237. Hearths were still reckoned by pre-plague totals.

district was now scheduled for cession to England.[156] The nobles of the seneschalsy of Beaucaire offered 15,000 florins, to which the count of Beaufort added another 695.[157] The nobles of Carcassonne agreed to pay 10 per cent of their revenues, but it is not known how much money this tax was expected to produce.[158] Overall, the laymen of Languedoc seem to have undertaken to supply nearly 40 per cent of the 600,000 *écus* needed at Calais in October,[159] and the Church supplied additional resources. The Order of St. John of Jerusalem promised 3000 florins but could raise less than two-thirds of that total. The clerical tenth of 1360 also was applied to the ransom.[160]

Tax collections in France always were slow, and the great distance separating Languedoc from Saint-Omer further complicated the task of meeting the deadline for John II's release. As late as October, 1365, the crown was still collecting from the nobles of Carcassonne for this first installment, and the towns of that district did not complete their first payment until 1362.[161] The delays are really less surprising than the fact that so much money did reach Saint-Omer by 24 October. From the seneschalsy of Beaucaire, 50,000 *moutons* arrived on time, including 4,750 from Montpellier.[162] Prompt collections were reported at Pézenas,[163] but as always the nobles of the Velay-Vivarais-Gévaudan region resisted taxation of their men and tried to limit contributions to a minimum. They could not oppose the feudal aid for the ransom, but they tried to declare themselves exempt from any future taxation other than for the ransom.[164] The count of Armagnac, now scheduled to receive a large grant from the towns of Languedoc,

---

[156]*Ibid.*, cols. 1240, 1243. These references indicate that 1400 florins had been collected. Since this was the same amount actually collected in 1358, it would appear that Rouergue was credited with what it had paid in the former year.

[157]*HL* 9: pp. 713–714; 10: col. 1239; Secousse, introduction to *Ord.* 3: p. xcv.

[158]*HL* 10: cols. 1211–1212; Mahul, *Cartulaire* 1: p. 208; 5: p. 210.

[159]Delachenal, *Charles V* 2: pp. 224–225, seems to have added up the figures incorrectly. Vaissete is also somewhat unclear (*HL* 9: p. 714).

[160]*HL* 10: col. 1239. For receipts of the tenth, see *ibid.*, cols. 1249–1252. This tenth was granted by the pope in August, 1360, for two years.

[161]*Ibid.*, cols. 1219, 1244.

[162]*Ibid.*, col. 1238; *Gr. Chartrier*, no. 4027; BN MS. lat. 9175, fols. 10r–12v. For its share, Alès had to borrow 1850 florins: Bardon, *Alais* 2: pp. 56–57.

[163]*INV AM Pézenas*, no. 10.

[164]Delcambre, *Velay*, p. 59.

was supposed to contribute the first installment of this sum to the royal ransom.[165] His rival, Gaston of Foix, promised 20,000 florins for the ransom, but not for the down payment, apparently. This money later was deducted from unpaid arrears of the sum that the towns still owed him in 1362.[166]

Although the brigand threat, the ransom, and the sums promised to the Gascon lords seemed to require substantial taxation, people still resisted collection when they found an excuse for doing so. The hearth tax of one *mouton*, granted in November, 1359, was to have been halted in the event of truce or treaty. Since formal hostilities were now at an end, Alès and other towns objected to paying the uncollected portions of this tax.[167] Yet at this time, Languedoc's promised payments to the counts of Armagnac, Foix, and Poitiers, as well as the first ransom installment, may have exceeded 700,000 florins.[168] It was evident that a new assembly was required in order to arrange a satisfactory way of financing these heavy obligations.

It was in November, at Pézenas, that the new assembly convened, in the presence of the chancellor of John of France. Since his Poitevin *apanage* was scheduled for cession to England, John had now been named duke of Berry. He was no longer in Languedoc, having left for England to be one of the hostages provided for in the treaty of Brétigny. Until the arrival of John's successor, his chancellor and council exercised the authority of lieutenant in Languedoc. The assembly at Pézenas was not large, and we may infer that many communities hoped to cut costs by sending joint representatives. Proctors from nineteen towns in the Beaucaire district were understood to represent the other communities as well as their own. The seneschalsy of Carcassonne was represented by proctors from sixteen towns, none of whom were from the four main centers of Béziers, Carcassonne, Limoux, and Narbonne. Only three *jugeries* of the Toulouse district had

---

[165] BN Coll. Languedoc 85, fols. 178r–179v.

[166] *HL* **10**, col. 1242; Vidal, *Douze Comptes*, p. 33.

[167] AM Alès I S-16, no. 21; *Gr. Chartrier*, no. 442.

[168] The Beaucaire district owed John of France 20,000 florins (chap. V at note 20), so the whole of Languedoc may have owed more than 60,000. Added to 200,000 florins each for Foix and Armagnac and 260,000 for the first ransom payment, this obligation amounted to a total of more than 700,000 florins.

deputies at Pézenas. In an ordinance of thirty-four articles, dated 27 November, 1360, this assembly took measures intended to supersede the provisional action of two earlier meetings—that at Sommières in July (which had granted 200,000 florins to Armagnac) and that at Lunel in September.[169] The *gabelle* on salt was retained, with an installment payable on Ash Wednesday, 1361, being assigned to the duke of Berry, and another installment, payable at Pentecost, to be applied to the cost of troops. Berry and the municipal governments would divide any surplus between them. The *gabelle* was not to cause higher prices for consumers, and the receivers-general of taxes were to submit their accounts to appointees of the Estates in each seneschalsy. To meet the other heavy financial obligations they had incurred during the summer, the towns were empowered to levy municipal taxes of their choice. Royal sergeants could be sent to force payment when collections lagged, but their methods were circumscribed and all past seizures of property were nullified. The ordinance reaffirmed the provisions of those enacted at the assemblies in 1359 and forbade towns to apply to the king for tax reductions. Those not represented at Pézenas, however, could make separate arrangements with the royal lieutenant as to the payment of their share of taxes.[170] In a separate letter of the same date, Pézenas was excused from paying the remainder of the one-*mouton* hearth tax granted the year before.[171]

The towns of Languedoc thus hoped to discharge their many financial obligations by continuing the distasteful tax on salt and arranging additional municipal levies of their own. Only a few days later, the king's ordinance of 5 December, 1360, imposed on the entire kingdom a higher *gabelle* and the other taxes known as the *aides pour la délivrance*.[172] This ordinance proved to be unsuitable to Languedoc, first because the *gabelle* was already in force and was committed to other uses, and secondly because the Midi had always preferred apportioned *fouages* to sales taxes. In due course, Languedoc

---

[169] Dognon, *Institutions*, p. 607.
[170] BN MS. lat. 9175, fols. 14r–23v; *Gr. Chartrier*, no. 3449.
[171] *INV AM Pézenas*, no. 1670.
[172] AM Toulouse AA 6, no. 209. Vuitry, *Régime financier* 2: p. 111, thought that the ordinance for Languedoc had been lost.

proposed equivalent taxes to replace the aids, and the difference between the two parts of France in fiscal matters became more pronounced than ever.

4. Peace Denied: The Campaign at Pont-Saint-Esprit, 1360–1361

The principal purpose of taxation in Languedoc late in 1360 was to raise the large sums of money that were supposed to buy peace—the royal ransom and the funds promised to the counts of Foix and Armagnac. Repeatedly, however, it was necessary to divert money to military needs, and documents indicate contributions for the repair of fortifications and the salaries of troops.[173] Military measures were dictated by the renewed menace of the companies. Left unemployed again by the Anglo-French treaty, they soon proved capable of more widespread destruction than during the earlier truce of 1357–1359.[174] Late in October, Berry ordered persons with goods or movable property in non-fortified places to remove them to fortresses for storage so that the *routiers* could not supply themselves.[175]

At this very moment, a dangerous force of brigands began to descend on the Rhone valley. Led by the Englishman, John Hawkwood, and a captain from Périgord named Seguin de Badefol, these troops converged on Pont-Saint-Esprit, a fortress on the right bank of the river above Avignon. In hostile hands, this stronghold would threaten the pontifical city, and it was a particularly lucrative prize for brigands at this time because tax receipts from Languedoc for the king's ransom were being collected there for re-shipment to Saint Omer. Badefol and his men captured the place on 28 December, 1360.[176]

Perhaps because it threatened the papacy, the capture of Pont-Saint-Esprit was one of the few exploits of the companies in Languedoc that attracted the attention of chroniclers

[173] BN Doat 192, fols. 238–239; *HL* 9: p. 718, note 1; BN NAF 3654, no. 45.

[174] Denifle, *Désolation* 2: p. 376, mentioning the geographical spread of brigandage.

[175] AD Hérault A 5, fols. 114r–115r; *cf.* L. H. Labande, "L'occupation du Pont-Saint-Esprit par les Grandes Compagnies (1360–1361)," *Revue historique de Provence* 1901: p. 81.

[176] Denifle, *Désolation* 2: 387–390; *HL* 9: p. 719, note 4; Guigue, *Tard-Venus*, p. 48.

in the Ile-de-France.[177] Although the attack had been expected, the royal administration in the Midi was undergoing an interregnum between the departure of the duke of Berry and the arrival of the constable, Robert de Fiennes, his replacement as royal lieutenant. The senior official on the scene, Jean Souvain, seneschal of Beaucaire, hastened to the defense, and the *routiers*, who thought a shipment of money would accompany him, delayed their attack until his arrival. As it happened, however, the officials charged with transporting the funds took fright at the report that the brigands were near, and diverted their cargo to Avignon on 26 December.[178]

The arrival of the seneschal may have encouraged the defenders of Pont-Saint-Esprit, but in the ensuing battle he was seriously wounded (apparently in a fall from the battlements)[179] and captured by the attackers. The citadel, defended by mercenaries from Lucca, capitulated, and the remaining defenders took refuge in a fortified church. They finally surrendered after promising the brigands 6000 florins to guarantee their safety.[180] The fall of Pont-Saint-Esprit caused great fear at Avignon, where the ramparts begun in 1358 were far from complete. Wooden barricades were used to block access to the city.[181] The situation quickly grew more dangerous. New bands of *routiers*, passing through Lyonnais and Forez, reinforced those at Pont-Saint-Esprit, while Seguin de Badefol led his forces on pillaging expeditions westward, past Nîmes and Montpellier.[182] Until late February, the royal lieutenantcy was administered by the duke of Berry's council, based at Toulouse, and in the seneschalsy of Beaucaire there was a serious lack of authority.[183]

In this extremity the initiative passed to the pope. Innocent VI preached a crusade against the brigands on 8 January,

---

[177]*Venette*, pp. 106–107.

[178]Labande, "Occupation," p. 82.

[179]*Petit Thalamus*, p. 357; Luce, *Du Guesclin*, pp. 362–363; Bardon, *Alais* 2: p. 54.

[180]Labande, "Occupation," p. 82. Those who were accused of dealings with the brigands later received a royal pardon: *HL* 10: cols. 1294–1295.

[181]R. Michel, "La défense d'Avignon sous Urbain V et Grégoire XI," *Mélanges d'archéologie et d'histoire de l'Ecole française de Rome* (Jan.-June 1910): p. 131; Martène, *Thesaurus* 2: cols. 1050–1051; Labande, "Occupation," p. 84. According to Luce, *du Guesclin*, p. 364, the brigands resented the papal peacemaking effort, since the Anglo-French treaty deprived them of employment.

[182]*Petit Thalamus*, p. 357; Guigue, *Tard-Venus*, p. 55.

[183]*HL* 9: p. 720.

1361. He wrote to the bishop of Valentinois, asking to be kept informed of their movements. He urged the governor of Dauphiné to prevent them from entering his jurisdiction, and he begged the duke of Burgundy to halt the transit of *routiers* across his duchy. Those who opposed them were to be rewarded with crusading indulgences.[184] On the thirteenth, John II informed the seneschal of Carcassonne that Jean Souvain had been captured and ordered him to have indefensible fortresses torn down. Other forts were to receive garrisons and provisions.[185] During the second half of January, the pope kept up his correspondence, exhorting numerous towns to take up arms against the *iniquas societates malignantium*,[186] begging Fiennes to hasten to act against them,[187] and informing various foreign powers of the menace.[188]

All this activity produced responses from various quarters. Those parts of France which were most seriously affected responded with a significant amount of local initiative on their own behalf. The archbishop of Lyon, whose own district had lately been menaced, sent 200 men-at-arms at his own expense, while the frequently reticent nobles of Gévaudan, Velay, and Vivarais contributed money to the cause.[189] Towns and nobles of the seneschalsy of Beaucaire assembled at Nîmes in mid-January, 1361 and decided to attack Pont-Saint-Esprit. The consuls of Nîmes and Montpellier borrowed money to pay troops and named captains who would lead the contingents to the mustering point of Bagnols.[190]

The clergy offered moral and material support to the effort to oust the brigands who threatened the papal city, contributing 3.3 per cent of their revenues to the campaign and promising crusading indulgences to those who fought the companies for six months.[191] Once again we find miscellaneous local efforts and stopgap taxes being employed to fill the

---

[184]*Petit Thalamus*, p. 357; Martène, *Thesaurus* 2: cols. 846, 848–850; Labande, "Occupation," p. 146; Guigue, *Tard-Venus*, p. 56.

[185]AD Hérault A 5, fols. 115v–116v.

[186]Martène, *Thesaurus* 2: cols. 852–854.

[187]*Ibid.*, col. 867.

[188]*Ibid.*, cols. 858–860, 862–864, 867–870.

[189]Guigue, *Tard-Venus*, p. 56.

[190]*Gr. Chartrier*, no. 491; D-viii, no. 39. The viscount of Narbonne contributed 900 *moutons*. AN Nîmes NN 1, nos. 42, 43.

[191]*HL* 9: pp. 720–721.

void left by ineffective royal government. They were to become a familiar part of the long struggle against brigandage and would form an important chapter in the evolution of royal taxation, even though they were "royal" only in the sense that they contributed to the defense of the realm.

The campaign against Pont-Saint-Esprit cannot be called very successful. The brigands who held the stronghold were besieged, but others ravaged the Beaucaire district, particularly the environs of Lunel, and the seneschal of Carcassonne rushed east with reinforcements.[192] On 13 February, negotiations began at Pont-Saint-Esprit under papal auspices, and after some weeks, the brigands agreed to accept a bribe of 14,500 florins, abandon the fortress, and go to Italy. In April, 1361, Hawkwood and his men finally left.[193] To recover what he had paid for the evacuation, Innocent VI taxed the inhabitants of the Comtat Venaissin six thousand florins and levied a tenth on the revenues of the Church in England.[194]

Another response to the papal appeals for help seems to have come from Aragon, whose king is reported to have sent 600 men-at-arms and 1000 foot-soldiers to the Pont-Saint-Esprit campaign.[195] It is not entirely clear, however, what role Peter IV of Aragon actually did play in this affair. During the latter part of 1360, France and Aragon had been engaged in extensive negotiations over a number of unresolved differences between the two kingdoms.[196] Since Aragon was at war with Castile and was at a military disadvantage, it is understandable that Peter IV desired an accommodation with France, but it is a good deal less credible that he was in a position to send to the pope the troops he is said to have supplied. He may have sent money or, more likely, some *routiers* who were troubling his own lands, and he may have had reasons for seeking the pope's good will. Writing to the king of Aragon early in January, Innocent VI asked him to send to Avignon one of his most trusted diplomats, Juan Fernandez de Heredia. For several years, this man had served

---

[192]*Ibid.*

[193]*Ibid.*, pp. 723–724; Labande, "Occupation," pp. 148–149.

[194]*Ibid.*, p. 150: Martène, *Thesaurus* 2: cols. 938–940; Denifle, *Désolation* 2: pp. 396–399

[195]AD Hérault A 5, fols. 115r–v; Molinier, "Audrehem," p. 89.

[196]*HL* 10: cols. 1198–1208.

both Innocent and Peter IV, and he had been involved in the latter's plan to employ an exiled Castilian prince, Henry of Trastamara, against the king of Castile. Fernandez de Heredia was the agent whom the pope entrusted with the money to pay the *routiers* for evacuating Pont-Saint-Esprit. He later played an important role in Aragonese diplomacy, and it is entirely possible that he and the pope discussed the idea of sending the *routiers* to Spain instead of Italy. If so, the idea was abandoned, but Fernandez de Heredia made contacts with the *routier* captains which would prove useful at a later date.[197]

Soon after the evacuation of Pont-Saint-Esprit, Robert de Fiennes arrived in Languedoc to take up the post of royal lieutenant. Badefol and his men had not followed Hawkwood across the Rhone, and the northern half of the seneschalsy of Beaucaire was still beset by brigands. They sacked an abbey near Le Puy,[198] and Fiennes ordered the *viguiers* of Uzès, Anduze, and Alès to drive them out of the district.[199] Despite the continuing danger, the heavily taxed towns were most reluctant to pay the additional sums needed to pay the troops assembled for the Pont-Saint-Esprit campaign. Perhaps they felt that the evacuation of the fortress should have brought the tax to an end: *cessante causa cessat effectus.* To obtain money from Montpellier and Pézenas, royal officials had to seize the property of the consuls.[200] Some weeks later, on 28 March, Fiennes ordered the levy of another six hundred florins from the towns of the seneschalsy of Beaucaire, in order to pay troops.[201]

To impose some organization on the haphazard fiscal and military measures which the brigands had made necessary, the constable assembled the three Estates of the Beaucaire district, who convened at Lunel early in April, 1361. On the fourteenth, this assembly authorized a special levy of 19,000 florins

[197] For the foregoing, I am indebted to my student, A. Arriaza, "Henry Trastamara, the *Routiers*, and Iberian Politics (1356–1363)," unpublished seminar paper (Iowa City, 1971). For continuing correspondence between the Pope and Trastamara in 1361, see Martène, *Thesaurus* 2: col. 1043.

[198] J. Monicat, *Les Grandes Compagnies en Velay* (Paris, 1928), p. 19.

[199] AD Hérault A 5, fols. 116v–117r. On Fiennes and the Pont-Saint-Esprit campaign, see also E. Garnier, "Biographie de Robert de Fiennes, connétable de France (1320–1384)," *Bib. Ec. Chartes* 13 (1852): pp. 41–42.

[200] *INV AM Pézenas*, nos. 1668–1669; *Gr. Chartrier*, no. 452.

[201] AD Hérault A 5, fols. 117v–118r.

that would not prejudice any rights for the future. Of this total, 6000 florins would be used to pay for the campaign just concluded. The rest would finance local fortifications and the raising of troops to resist the remaining brigands, as well as defraying the expenses of those who attended the assembly.[202] All clergy, nobles, and holders of fiefs were to contribute to this tax, without any exceptions, and while the assembly was still in session Fiennes ordered these people to contribute also to the king's ransom.[203] One infers that the townsmen suspected them of trying to avoid taxes. The Estates at Lunel described their grant of 19,000 florins as a 20 per cent surtax on the aid for the ransom. It is not clear how they arrived at this figure, but if the seneschalsy was obliged to pay 70,000 florins in both 1360 and 1361, the total due by mid-April, 1361, would have attained about 95,000.

The assembly at Lunel met in an atmosphere of danger, for Seguin de Badefol was in the vicinity with *grans gens darmes a caval et a pe.* After a bloody fight on 13 April near Agde, where several hundred men were killed, Fiennes took the field and engaged the *routiers* near Le Vigan.[204] The constable's exertions against the companies on the field of battle were hardly more strenuous than the effort required to collect the 19,000 florins granted by the assembly. The tax itself was light, but it came on top of the heavy financial burdens assumed the summer before. Characteristically, the nobles of Velay led the resistance to paying, and they were still holding out in 1364. In June, 1361, Fiennes had to order force used against recalcitrant communities and demand that the consuls of Le Puy account for the 330 florins they were required to pay.[205] Montpellier, perhaps intimidated by Badefol's proximity, made an immediate payment of 800 florins and soon completed its total assessment of 1345 florins. Both installments were paid to *élus* of the assembly which had made the grant.[206]

The entire history of the Pont-Saint-Esprit campaign sug-

---

[202] BN MS. lat. 9175, fols. 24–26; *Gr. Chartrier*, no. 3960; *HL* 9: p. 722; Dognon, *Institutions*, p. 607.

[203] AD Hérault A 5, fols. 118r–119r; BN MS. lat. 9175, fols. 24–26.

[204] *Petit Thalamus*, pp. 357–358.

[205] *HL* 9: p. 722; AD Hérault A 5, fols. 121r–v, 130r–131r, 131v–132r. Not until 1370 did Pézenas receive a receipt for the final paymet it owed: *INV AM Pézenas*, no. 1676. See *ibid.*, no. 1671 for an earlier payment.

[206] *Gr. Chartrier*, nos. 556; D viii, no. 67.

gests that the people of this district were more willing to raise local taxes during the crisis than to pay royal ones after the immediate threat was over. This attitude was in keeping with tradition, in Languedoc and elsewhere, and it was all the more explainable when one recalls the heavy burden imposed by the unpopular indirect taxes being levied for the ransom. Yet the campaign at Pont-Saint-Esprit, and the cost of paying for it, turned out to be insignificant compared to the military and fiscal burden which the *routiers* would impose in subsequent years. The ordeal of Languedoc was only beginning.

V. Peace without Safety: The Ordeal of Languedoc, 1361–1368

1. Replacement of the Aids with an Equivalent Tax

THE AIDS imposed in December, 1360, for the royal ransom created a situation reminiscent of 1346, when the king had tried to apply to the whole kingdom a financial policy based on his knowledge of Languedoil only.[1] In establishing taxes compatible with tradition in the north, the government was ignoring tradition in the Midi. It may not even have been realized in Paris that the *gabelle*, already in force in Languedoc, was earmarked for financial commitments unique to the Midi. The southern towns soon began to seek an alternative means of meeting the ransom payments. Once they gained this objective, the royal government had to face the administrative problem of an internal fiscal frontier separating lands that paid heavy indirect taxes from lands that did not.

It is not certain when the aids were actually levied in Languedoc. As early as 23 January, 1361, Montpellier submitted a brief to the royal *élus,* contending that the town's ruined condition left it unable to support the indirect taxes.[2] At this time, however, most of Languedoc was still struggling to meet the down payment on the ransom. The Beaucaire district, which was nearest to the collecting point at Saint-Omer, paid 70 per cent of its share on schedule, but other regions cannot have matched this record. The seneschalsy of Carcassonne not only was farthest from Saint-Omer but also had suffered most at the hands of the count of Foix. Some communities, such as the *bourg* of Carcassonne, received remission of two-thirds of their assessment, and even the payments of this reduced obligation trickled in slowly, from January to June, 1361, and even thereafter. Money promised by the nobles of this region was still not entirely paid as late as 1365, and the first

---

[1] See *RTF 1322–1356*, p. 202f.
[2] *Gr. Chartrier,* no. 3450.

collections were not recorded until 2 December, 1360.[3] On the other hand, the crown did collect 6896 *moutons* from the inhabitants of Narbonne.[4]

On 12 February, 1361, John II responded to the consuls of Montpellier, acknowledging the unpopularity of indirect taxes in Languedoc and saying that he had decided to let the Midi adopt a separate subsidy to meet its ransom obligations. The existing taxes were to remain in force for the present, but Montpellier was to send two representatives to Paris to discuss an alternative method of financing.[5] This royal decision settled the matter for some months, but by May the crisis of Pont-Saint-Esprit was past, and relatively few sums were still outstanding on the down payment. The time was ripe for making new arrangements to deal with subsequent installments. Montpellier was evidently not alone in sending representatives to Paris, for it is clear that the settlement ultimately negotiated there concerned the entire seneschalsy of Beaucaire.[6]

The new arrangements, ratified by the king on 7 June, provided that the communities of the Beaucaire district would make an annual contribution of 70,000 *moutons* for the next six years in return for the abolition of the indirect taxes for the ransom. The towns received permission to meet and negotiate among themselves as to how to apportion this amount, but the actual assessments were to be made in the presence of the seneschal. The first 35,000 *moutons* were to be paid on 1 October, 1361. A similar installment was payable early in 1362, and thereafter the full payment would be due each year on 1 October.[7]

The districts of Carcassonne and Toulouse, where collection of the initial ransom payment was lagging, did not pursue the matter of replacing the aids until later in the year, by which time Languedoc had suffered a new catastrophe— the second visit of the Black Death. The new epidemic

---

[3]*HL* 10: cols. 1213, 1217–1220.

[4]BN Doat 53, fols. 297v–298v.

[5]*Gr. Chartrier*, D-19, no. 40. The towns were also becoming discontented with the tactics of royal financial officers (*ibid.*, no. 17).

[6]*HL* 10: cols. 1237–1238.

[7]*Ibid.*, col. 1244; *Gr. Chartrier*, nos. 1795, 3900, 3901, 3913; AD Hérault A 5, fols. 121v–122r, 123v–128r; *Ord.* 3: pp. 496–499; BN Coll. Languedoc 85, fols. 196–199, 201–204v; BN MS. lat. 9175, fols. 28r–29. See also *HL* 9: p. 730, and notes.

apparently struck mountainous areas that had escaped with minor damage in 1348.[8] The accounts of Millau record the deaths of five of the six consuls between May and August.[9] As always, however, the more populous centers of the coasts and valleys were not spared. Montpellier, hard hit already in 1348, is said to have suffered five hundred deaths daily at the height of the plague.[10] A report of 17,000 deaths at Avignon over a four-month period may, however, be an exaggeration.[11] On 30 June, Innocent VI granted a plenary indulgence to the citizens of Alès where the plague was also taking a heavy toll.[12] Less publicized than the great epidemic of 1348, this newest visitation of the Black Death may well have been less serious, particularly in places where some immunity had developed from the former plague. Nevertheless, the sources just cited leave no doubt that it was a real tragedy in some areas. Since the disastrous effect of the earlier plague upon taxation is beyond dispute, particularly with respect to Languedoc,[13] it follows that the epidemic of 1361 must have placed still another strain upon the resources of southern France at a time when the brigand problem was growing acute.[14] This new economic blow may have hastened the determination of the Toulouse and Carcassonne districts to emulate Beaucaire in seeking some way of financing the ransom other than through taxes that bore on trade.

The resources available to the crown in Languedoc were already scheduled to be diminished when the territorial provisions of the treaty of Brétigny were implemented. Not until 27 July, 1361, did John II formally announce to the inhabitants of Rouergue and Quercy their impending transfer to English control,[15] and the actual cession did not take place until several months later, but these districts were not accessi-

---

[8] Vuitry, *Régime financier* 2: p. 111.

[9] *Arch. hist. Rouergue* 7: no. 241.

[10] *Petit Thalamus*, p. 359. The plague was at its height there between May and July. On 6 July, the pope established special rules regarding confessors and indulgences at Montpellier: *Gr. Chartrier*, no. 2255. For the plague in Quercy, see Lacoste, *Quercy* 3: p. 173.

[11] *HL* 9: p. 726.

[12] AM Alès I S-18, no. 32.

[13] See Henneman, "Black Death," pp. 414–418.

[14] See Molinier, "Audrehem," p. 93.

[15] J. Artières, *Annales de Millau* (Millau, 1894–1899), pp. 120–121; BN Doat 192, fols. 286–293.

ble to royal taxation in 1361. For all their past opposition to royal tax collectors and *réformateurs,* the inhabitants of Rouergue and Quercy had strenuously resisted Anglo-Gascon attacks on their strongholds, and it was not easy for them to accept the new allegiance to their longtime foe. In Rouergue, a group of lawyers prepared a lengthy brief to show that they still might recognize legally the king of France after becoming subjects of the newly enlarged duchy of Guyenne.[16] The residue of loyalty to the Valois in upper Languedoc would be valuable to the French a few years later, but for most of the 1360's the three seneschalsies of lower Languedoc would have to contend with a heavier fiscal burden, geographic separation from Paris, and a long frontier with English territory.

During the terrible summer of 1361, the menace of the unemployed soldiers continued to hold center stage in the eastern parts of Languedoc,[17] notwithstanding the plague, the treaty, and the continuing burden of ransom payments. The constable, Robert de Fiennes, held a new meeting of the Estates of the Beaucaire district at Lunel towards the beginning of July. On the eighth of that month he authorized the towns to hold assemblies and form such leagues as they deemed necessary to resist the brigands. This permission was valid only until the end of 1361, and it may have been granted in response to a refusal of the towns to establish more taxes.[18] Nevertheless, it amounted to an official sanction, by the royal lieutenant, of the sort of local initiative which had become common in other parts of France and had been tried in Languedoc at the time of the campaign of Pont-Saint-Esprit. The difficulty of collecting the tax granted in April may have persuaded Fiennes to adopt a policy of *laissez faire* towards the brigand menace for the time being. The towns would act together as their own sense of "evident necessity" dictated. This method might produce more effective opposition to the companies, but if it failed, it might persuade the municipali-

---

16 AD Aveyron C 1520, no. 12. *Cf.* M. Calvet, "Prise de possession par le roi d'Angleterre de la ville de Cahors et du Quercy en 1361," *Rec. Soc. Agen* 5 (1850): p. 167f.

17 Artières, *Annales de Millau,* pp. 119–120.

18 AD Hérault A 5, fols. 128r-129r; *HL* 9: p. 725; Monicat, *Grandes Compagnies,* p. 20; Delcambre, *Velay,* p. 62f.

ties that their self-interest dictated a more cooperative spirit towards requests for royal subsidies.

If the Beaucaire district preferred *ad hoc* arrangements to a formal grant of money for dealing with the companies, it was doubtless because existing taxes were proving to be so much of a burden. Montpellier continued to pay its share of the money owed to the count of Foix,[19] but not until the end of 1362 would it complete the payments promised to the duke of Berry.[20] On 7 June, 1361, the king had approved the offer of 70,000 florins as the equivalent of the ransom aids in the seneschalsy of Beaucaire, and on 9 July, Fiennes ordered the collection of this money from people of all classes.[21] Although they objected to royally imposed indirect taxes, some towns now chose this method of raising their ransom assessments. Alès taxed wine and cereals consumed in the town, a decision which may reflect the power of a wealthy oligarchy or may simply indicate that interior communities did not fear the sales taxes as much as large coastal trading centers like Montpellier.[22]

Robert de Fiennes was recalled by the king late in the summer, to be replaced in Languedoc by Arnoul d'Audrehem, marshal of France.[23] During the transition, the count of Vendôme acted as the principal royal representative in the southwest, and he convened an assembly of town representatives from the seneschalsies of Carcassonne and Toulouse. The meeting began at Béziers but then was moved to Carcassonne. Its purpose was not only to arrange a substitute for the ransom aids, but also to take measures for military defense. Because military needs had to be financed, Audrehem ordered the towns of the Beaucaire district to join the assembly, but they did not wish to do so until first consulting among themselves. By the time Audrehem agreed, the assembly was

---

[19]*Gr. Chartrier*, no. 548.

[20]*Ibid.*, nos. 3035, 3370, 3903, 4080–4081; Lehoux, *Jean de France* 1: p. 174. Berry's treasurer issued a receipt for the last part of 20,000 *moutons* owed to him by the Beaucaire district on 28 May, 1362, but a slightly later document indicates that Montpellier had owed him a much larger sum. Perhaps the town had borrowed from the duke to meet some of its debts.

[21]AD Hérault A 5, fols. 65r–v.

[22]AM Alès I S-13, no. 5.

[23]*HL* 9: p. 731.

nearly over, and it is doubtful that any representatives of the seneschalsy of Beaucaire reached Carcassonne. The assembly agreed to support 1500 *glaives* and three thousand infantry, however, and all three seneschalsies were to contribute.[24]

In seeking an alternative to the ransom aids, the two western districts had before them the model of the down payment of 1360, when each seneschalsy had been assessed at the rate of one florin or *mouton* per hearth. Regions desiring to avoid the aids generally replaced them with a direct tax,[25] and we have seen that the Beaucaire district had promised an annual equivalent tax that was identical to its assessment in 1360. The seneschalsies of Toulouse and Carcassonne were not prepared to be this generous, perhaps because they had experienced such difficulty in meeting the down payment. There were other good reasons why they might insist on paying a lesser sum as their equivalent to the aids. The initial ransom payment of 1360 had been for 600,000 florins, and thus 50 per cent larger than the subsequent annual installments. A large part of France seems not to have been asked to contribute to the down payment but was surely expected to pay its share of subsequent installments. Finally, of course, the hearth figures used for assessing Languedoc were a generation old, and the Black Death had devastated the region twice since the last enumeration. The seneschalsy of Beaucaire had offered 70,000 *moutons* as an equivalent tax before the second epidemic of plague. The *aides pour la délivrance* established in 1360 were essentially regressive taxes which bore especially on the urban population and were not likely to produce as much revenue from the kingdom as a whole as would direct taxes apportioned according to wealth. With the country ravaged by brigands, however, the crown may have felt that it could raise as much as 400,000 florins annually only by placing heavy taxes on the urban consumers.

The foregoing analysis suggests why the seneschalsies of Carcassonne and Toulouse may have been justified in seeking a lower direct tax as a replacement for the aids, but the surviving documents are discreet on this matter and there is no certainty that they advanced arguments any more sophisti-

---

[24] Molinier, "Audrehem," pp. 235–237; *HL* 10: cols. 1263–1273; Dognon, *Institutions*, p. 607.

[25] Mouradian, "Rançon," p. 155.

cated than the usual complaints of local improverishment and devastation by war. In any case, they offered the crown an annual payment of roughly 100,000 francs—64,000 from the Carcassonne district and 35,715 from the Toulousain, due each year on 2 February. In return for this sum, the three indirect taxes for the ransom would be canceled, no new subsidies, *gabelles*, or loans would be sought by the crown during the next six years, and pardons would be issued for past disobediences. The equivalent tax would be raised by a levy of one florin per hearth, but this would not begin until Christmas, 1361, and the whole transaction was subject to the king's ratification. This agreement was concluded on 16 October, 1361.[26]

The franc was a new gold coin, first issued in 1361 and supposed to circulate at a value of one *livre tournois* in money of account. The official who collected the aids for the ransom in Languedoc during the 1360's kept records which show that a franc was equal to fifteen *gros* while a florin was equal to twelve. The offer of 100,000 francs per year by the seneschalsies of Carcassonne and Toulouse amounted, therefore, to 125,000 florins, as opposed to the 140,000 (90,000 and 50,000 respectively) which they had paid for the down payment in 1360.[27] Whereas the Beaucaire district had promised the same amount for an equivalent tax that it had paid earlier for the installment of 1360, the seneschalsy of Carcassonne's offer was 11 per cent lower and that of Toulouse was 6.7 per cent lower. In the meantime, of course, the second epidemic of plague had further reduced the population, but since his ransom obligations were the same as before, the king felt unable to ratify the agreement. The indirect taxes were restored, and John II

---

[26]*HL* 10: cols. 1230–1231, 1264–1268; Dognon, *Institutions*, p. 607; Vuitry, *Régime financier* 2: pp. 111–112.

[27]The important document recording collections for the ransom in Languedoc is found in BN MS. lat. 5957 and is published in *HL* 10: cols. 1211–1255. It has already been cited here a number of times. Sums are expressed, for the most part, in real currency rather than money of account, and a number of equivalents are given: 25,000 florins = 20,000 francs (col. 1231); 4000 florins = 3200 francs (col. 1232). Specifically, it is stated (col. 1231) that a tax of four *gros tournois* per hearth in the seneschalsy of Toulouse, based on 50,000 hearths (pre-1348), produced 16,666 ⅔ florins, the equivalent of 13,333 ⅓ francs. Evidently a florin at this time contained 12 *gros* and a franc 15 *gros*. Computation of receipts in real coins rather than money of account poses problems for the historian which only a coinage expert can resolve with confidence. See appendix I for some remarks on the problem.

adopted the well-established tactic of sending to the Midi a trio of *réformateurs:* Pierre Scatisse (royal treasurer), the bishop of Meaux, and Jean de Bourbon. They were empowered to negotiate taxes.[28]

When Audrehem and Vendôme convened a new assembly of the southern Estates late in May of 1362, the danger from brigandage had become more acute and the effects of plague, perhaps, more evident. In any case, the two royal representatives had to settle for an offer very similar to what the crown had rejected. After hearing a recital of the various calamities which had befallen the land, they agreed to let the seneschalsy of Carcassonne pay 64,000 francs for the first year and 70,000 for each of the next five. The Toulousain would owe 35,715 francs each year. The indirect taxes would cease immediately (1 June, 1362). Carcassonne's initial payment of 64,000 francs was for the installment of the ransom which had been due in 1361. Only 6672 francs of this total were still outstanding, and these were to be paid by Pentecost, 1362. Thereafter, the annual payments were to be made in two installments, half on 29 September and the other half on 2 February each year. The *réformateurs* agreed to the offer on 10 June.[29]

Although the reduced annual payments were probably realistic in terms of economic and demographic conditions, they represented a defeat for the crown, which not only had to accept essentially what it had rejected six months earlier, but also had to levy a proportionately greater share of the ransom from the other parts of France. The reduction, moreover, provoked an immediate reaction from the seneschalsy of Beaucaire, which had offered its equivalent tax of 70,000 florins before the plague of 1361. Now that the western seneschalsies had obtained some relief, the towns of the Beaucaire district felt entitled to demand that their own obligation be reduced. After holding an assembly at the Pont d'Avignon on 13 June, the *réformateurs* agreed to reduce their annual obligation to 50,000 *moutons,* of which Montpellier "graciously and liberally" agreed to furnish 5000 *moutons,* or 10 per cent.[30]

---

[28] BN Coll. Languedoc 85, fols. 214r–v; *Ord.* 4: pp. 214–216.
[29] *HL* 9: p. 732; 10: cols. 1220–1223, 1264–1273; BN Doat 8, fols. 299–316v; Dognon, *Institutions,* p. 607.
[30] *Ibid.,* p. 608; *Gr. Chartrier,* no. 3995; BN MS. lat. 9175, fols. 37r–40v.

Thus the Beaucaire district obtained a reduction of nearly 29 per cent, substantially more than that obtained by either of the other two seneschalsies, and the government in Paris was more reluctant to accept it. Some royal officers preferred to treat as binding the agreement in 1361 to pay 70,000 *moutons* annually, and they tried to ignore the reduction. Consequently, the documents on the subject remain ambiguous and confusing. Bernard François, receiver of the aids for the ransom in Languedoc, noted in 1362 that 70,000 *moutons* were owed *pro isto anno,* but in 1366 Charles V understood the annual finance to be only 50,000.[31] These texts suggest that the crown may have accepted the reduced annual payment beginning in 1363, but in another place François stated explicitly that the Beaucaire district owed 70,000 *moutons* for the years 1363–1365 notwithstanding the arrangement made with Scatisse and the bishop of Meaux, and he continued to resist all reductions in the annual assessment.[32] If 70,000 *moutons* were owed for 1362 and Montpellier owed 10 per cent of the total, that town's share would be 7000, but in September, Audrehem allowed the consuls a reduction to 6000 *moutons.* This transaction seems to have particularly irritated François, whose accounts state in two places that Audrehem had no authority to reach such an agreement and that it was not valid.[33] In fact, however, Audrehem may only have recognized economic realities if the plague of 1361 had been as severe at Montpellier as is believed, for in the years 1363–1365 this town could pay no more than 5117 *moutons* in all.[34]

Assorted documents reveal the arrangements made by other localities in paying their shares of the ransom. In mid-June, 1362, the consuls of Alès were debating how to raise their share,[35] and by the end of the month those of Nîmes had adopted an indirect tax of 6 d./l.[36] The same sales tax was

---

[31]*HL* **10:** cols. 1240–1241, 1245; BN Coll. Languedoc 85, fols. 250r–251r (placing the figure at 70,000 *moutons,* 1362); *Gr. Chartrier,* no. 3923 (50,000 moutons, 1366).

[32]*HL* **10:** col. 1245.

[33]*Ibid.: licet ad hoc potestatem non haberet de aliqua financia facienda nec remittendo aliquid ex redemptione regis.*

[34]*Ibid.,* col. 1246. See *Gr. Chartrier,* no. 458, for Montpellier's payment of 6000 florins for 1362. See *HL* **10:** cols. 1279–1282, for evidence that a merchant transporting ransom money was robbed on the road by brigands.

[35]AM Alès I S-13, no. 6.

[36]Ménard, *Nismes* **2:** p. 233, and *preuves,* p. 244.

employed in the *viguerie* of Anduze.[37] In some places, royal receivers of the money were accused of embezzlement.[38] In July, the king allowed the count of Pézenas to retain half the 2500 francs owed by his county.[39] At Toulouse, amounts in excess of 6000 francs were collected for the equivalent tax during 1362.[40] In Castrais, Albigeois, and Lautrec, subjects of the count of Foix, assessed at 2648 hearths, owed an annual payment of one franc per hearth through 1364.[41] The count of Foix himself owed 20,000 florins for the ransom, and John II directed that this sum be deducted from the amount still owed to Gaston by the towns of the Beaucaire district since 1360.[42]

Substitution of an equivalent tax for the aids in Languedoc aggravated the existing problem of evasion of these sales taxes in border areas. Goods were taxed at 5 per cent in Languedoil, but not in Aquitaine or imperial territory, and now this tax had been abolished in Languedoc as well. The only way to avoid both tax fraud and the dislocation of trade was to levy the 12 d./l. sales tax on all products shipped from regions where the aids were levied to territories where they were not in force. This extension of the aids was called the *imposition foraine*. It differed from the aids only in that the aids were collected inside Languedoil at the place where a transaction occurred, while the *imposition foraine* was collected at the place from which goods were shipped outside Languedoil. Originating as an *ad hoc* measure needed to enforce the aids, the *imposition foraine* was refined and formalized in ordinances of 1369 and 1376. It began to be collected separately, and it eventually became a new customs duty, levied without reference to the aids at all. In the case of goods shipped outside the realm, it was levied in addition to existing export duties. The decision of Languedoc to replace the aids with other taxes created an internal customs barrier, the first of many that would plague the "mercantilist" statesmen of the future.[43]

---

[37] AD Hérault A 5, fols. 173r–v.

[38] Molinier, "Audrehem," p. 106.

[39] *HL* 10: col. 1225.

[40] AM Toulouse CC 1847, pp. 5–6.

[41] *HL* 10: col. 1226.

[42] BN MS. lat. 9175, fols. 41–43.

[43] Vuitry, *Régime financier* 2: p. 157; Picot, *Etats* 1: p. 212; Dupont-Ferrier, *Inst. financières* 2: pp. 151–154. The *imposition foraine* has been studied recently by R. Gore, "The French Customs System: The Impact of Royal Policy," unpublished

2. The Grand Company, 1362

The continuing effort to collect Languedoc's share of the heavy royal ransom was repeatedly disrupted by pressing military dangers, as the brigandage of *routiers* intensified. For one period beginning in 1362, sums totaling 20,820 francs were deducted from the ransom payments of just one district— Carcassonne. These diversions of funds were ordered by Audrehem in a series of seven letters, and the reason given was always the same: *pro necessitate guerre.*[44]

Late in 1361 there was some hope that progress would be made in restoring public order. In November, Fiennes and Audrehem concluded an agreement with Seguin de Badefol, who promised not to molest Languedoc any longer.[45] The Estates of Rouergue bought off other *routiers* with a payment of 5200 florins, to which Millau, hard hit by the plague, was able to contribute only two hundred florins. Audrehem visited the district towards the end of the year, not long before the English representative, John Chandos, formally took possession in February, 1362.[46]

The settlements with the brigands offered some hope that Languedoc might finally enjoy the peace for which it was paying such a high price. The towns were badly in debt, if Montpellier is a typical example,[47] and in October, 1361, Audrehem had promised that *gabelle* receipts above what was needed for the ransom could be turned over to localities to help discharge their debts.[48] Since only the Beaucaire district had received royal approval for an equivalent tax by this date, it is likely that the salt tax elsewhere in Languedoc continued to be applied to the ransom until May of 1362. In any case, the

---

M.A. essay (Iowa City, 1973), pp. 24–33. Contrary to what was implied by Henneman, "Italians," p. 20, the new tax was in addition to earlier, lower customs duties that remained in force. In Charles V's reign, the tax affected goods *leaving* Languedoc only in periods when Languedoc actually paid the aids. Basic documents on the tax are *Ord.* 6: pp. 206–210; *Gr. Chartrier* D-19, no. 41; BN MS. lat. 9175, fols. 119r–120v; AM Toulouse AA 45, nos. 56–57.

[44]*HL* 10: col. 1225.

[45]Monicat, *Grandes Compagnies*, p. 21; Lehoux, *Jean de France* 1: p. 182; Delachenal, *Charles V* 2: pp. 318–319. At the same time, John II ordered the seneschal of Beaucaire not to let any pillagers enter the realm from across the Rhone: AD Hérault A 5, fols. 132v–133r.

[46]Artières, *Annales de Millau*, pp. 122–125; *Arch. hist. Rouergue* 7: no. 253.

[47]*INV AM Montpellier* 11: p. 20.

[48]*HL* 9: pp. 730–731; 10: cols. 1273–1274.

depleted finances of the towns forced them to retain the *gabelle* as a regional tax after the aids for the ransom were replaced. On 18 January, 1362, the towns of Languedoc convened at Béziers and agreed to extend it for two more years. The collectors were unpopular, however, and Audrehem warned them against abusive or unwarranted exactions.[49] More enactments on the *gabelle* followed in March, when there was debate over who should receive the accounts of collectors.[50]

When the *routiers* were persuaded to withdraw from Languedoc, they merely shifted their operations to other parts of the kingdom. Badefol's men began to merge with the troops of another captain, Le Petit Meschin, who held fortresses along the border of Auvergne and Forez. As other groups began to join them, the brigands became concentrated into what soon was called the Grand Company. Another captain of *routiers*, Arnaud de Cervole, had rejoined the royal service, serving as lieutenant in Nivernais, but in 1361 John II replaced him with the count of Tancarville, who was probably regarded as more trustworthy. In an effort to deal decisively with the brigand problem, the king augmented Tancarville's powers in January, 1362, giving him a vast command as royal lieutenant in Berry, Bourbonnais, and Auvergne.[51]

Tancarville's task was made a great deal more difficult, ironically, by the success of other regions in buying off the *routiers*. As they withdrew from lower Languedoc and Rouergue, they merely increased the number of men-at-arms in Tancarville's lieutenantcy. Towards the end of March, another chieftain, Perrin Boias, was paid a ransom to evacuate the town of Saugues near the border of Auvergne and Velay. Joining the swelling ranks of the Grand Company, his troops may have given the brigands a clear military advantage.[52] In any case, the *routiers* congregated around Brignais in Lyonnais, where they were cornered early in April by a royal army led by Tancarville and Jean de Bourbon, count of La Marche. Accustomed to pillage, extortion, and hit-and-run military

---

[49]*Ibid.* **9**: p. 731; **10**: cols. 1274–1275; Vuitry, *Régime financier* 2: p. 112. Dognon, *Institutions,* p. 607.

[50]AD Hérault A 5, fols. 178r–v, 188v–189r.

[51]Guigue, *Tard-Venus,* pp. 59–60; Cherest, *Archiprêtre,* pp. 159–160. See also below, chap. VI.

[52]Monicat, *Grandes Compagnies,* pp. 21–23.

tactics, the Grand Company now was forced unwillingly into a pitched battle against the army of the king of France. For the third time in sixteen years, a royal army joined battle with a cornered and reluctant foe, and once again the French suffered a disastrous defeat. At Brignais on 6 April, 1362, the royal commanders were killed or captured and their troops took flight.[53] The *routiers*, who tried whenever possible to observe the law of arms, were embarrassed by their victory in a battle they would rather have avoided. Many of them sought pardons for having fought against the king of France. Nevertheless, the disaster at Brignais, occurring almost at the gates of Lyon, left the southern half of France in grave danger, and Audrehem hurried to take defensive measures.[54]

Given the repeated military failures of French chivalry, the government began to consider a new policy for coping with the brigand problem—the employment of the *routiers* themselves. Such a policy involved two possible approaches. Some mercenaries might be hired to fight against the others; or all of them might be paid to engage in a campaign outside the kingdom. Either scheme would cost a great deal and would involve an alliance of sorts with professional soldiers of doubtful scruples and brutal habits. It was at this juncture that the complex politics of the Iberian peninsula began to be a major factor in the Hundred Years' War, drawing Castile and Aragon into a conflict that had already involved Navarre, the Netherlands, and the papacy at one time or another. The fiscal and military conditions in Languedoc were particularly affected, beginning perhaps with the uncertain Aragonese role in the campaign at Pont-Saint-Esprit. Peter IV of Aragon had a number of grievances against France,[55] but his principal enemy was the neighboring kingdom of Castile. Seeking allies where he could find them, Peter had negotiated with Charles the Bad and Gaston Phoebus, but he had found a more promising ally who would draw Aragon and France into an uneasy partnership. This was Henry, count of Trastamara, an

---

[53]*Ibid.;* Cherest, *Archiprêtre,* pp. 158–186; Guigue, *Tards-venus,* pp. 59–78, 314–317; *Petit Thalamus,* p. 360; Molinier, "Audrehem," p. 102; Denifle, *Désolation* 2: pp. 406–407.

[54]Loray, *Grandes Compagnies,* p. 274; Guigue, *Tard-Venus,* p. 85; Cherest, *Archiprêtre,* p. 188; Molinier, "Audrehem," p. 102.

[55]On these matters see *HL* 10: cols. 1208–1211.

older but illegitimate brother of the Castilian king. Peter I ("the Cruel") of Castile was strongly disliked by the French royal family, but Castile's powerful fleet of galleys was capable of playing a decisive role in any Anglo-French war. Both France and Aragon began to support Henry's effort to overthrow his brother, and Peter the Cruel allied himself with England in 1362.[56] The francophile party at the Aragonese court pressed for common action against Castile and may have considered using *routiers* for this purpose as early as the beginning of 1361.[57]

The count of Trastamara, however, had been unsuccessful up to 1362; his followers were prone to brigandage, and his presence embarrassed the Aragonese. In February, 1362, he led his men into France, hoping to enlist military and financial support for a new venture against his brother, in return for making Castile an ally of France.[58] After their triumph at Brignais, the *routiers* were in a position to drive too hard a bargain, but Audrehem liked the idea of sending them to Spain and merely awaited the propitious moment to implement the scheme.[59] Meanwhile, Trastamara's Spanish troops were feared by the towns of Languedoc, and a local assembly at Nîmes in the spring agreed to give Audrehem 10,000 florins to pay them for one month. The money was raised by a *fouage* of two *gros tournois* in the seneschalsy of Beaucaire.[60] Collection was supervised by Jean de Croix, the *élu* of the assembly (*receptori generali presentis senescallie per communitates electo pro subsidis*).[61]

In the same period, other assemblies were raising funds to cope with brigandage. In April, communities of the Toulousain raised 7140 florins to drive out local brigands,[62] and later

---

[56]P. Russell, *The English Intervention in Spain and Portugal in the Time of Edward III and Richard II* (Oxford, 1955), pp. xxi, 1–6, 24. Whereas Aragon sought the aid of Foix, Castile made an agreement with the count of Armagnac (*ibid.*, pp. 26–27). Charles the Bad, after flirting with Aragon, now joined his sometime English allies in reaching an accommodation with Castile in June of 1362: Castro, *Catalogo* 4: no. 221.

[57]See above, chap. IV, at note 197. *Cf.* Molinier, "Audrehem," pp. 93–94, note 5.

[58]*Petit Thalamus*, p. 360; Monicat, *Grandes Compagnies*, p. 22. According to Russell, *English Intervention*, p. 4, Anglo-Gascon *routiers* were forbidden to engage in hostile acts against Castile, according to the terms of the Anglo-Castilian treaty.

[59]Molinier, "Audrehem," p. 102.

[60]Ménard, *Nismes* 2: p. 231, and *preuves*, pp. 242–243.

[61]*HL* 10: col. 1238.

[62]AM Toulouse CC 1847, p. 13.

in the month Audrehem held new assemblies at Lunel and Pézenas. By 23 April, the consuls of Nîmes were considering a payment of two thousand florins towards a larger amount being collected to buy off the victors of Brignais.[63] Towns engaged in feverish defensive preparations,[64] adding new burdens to the exactions that were beginning to create friction over hearth counts and privileges.[65] On 3 May, the nobles met at Pézenas, and at the end of the month, when the two western seneschalsies were concluding their arrangement of an equivalent tax to replace the aids, the representatives of the towns reorganized the administration of the *gabelle*.[66] It was necessary to keep supplying money to Trastamara's Spaniards.[67]

At the head of the Spanish mercenaries, Audrehem and Trastamara now advanced into Auvergne and on 3 June severely defeated the brigands near Montpensier.[68] This triumph restored the crown's bargaining position which had been so seriously impaired by the defeat of Brignais, and it permitted implementation of Trastamara's plan for the removal of the companies intact to Spain. A treaty now was signed at Clermont whereby the companies agreed to leave the kingdom within six weeks, make no stops en route longer than six days, and take nothing from anyone but provisions for their men and their horses. They were never to return to the territory of the king of France and would swear an oath of loyalty to Henry of Trastamara, promising not to leave his service without permission. The companies were not to get involved in Anglo-French hostilities, and should they participate in the Foix-Armagnac conflict they would confine their activities strictly to the lands of those two counts. Thirty-four captains would remain as hostages to guarantee the good faith of their companies. They would receive a general pardon for offenses against the French crown, and Audrehem promised to

---

[63] Molinier, "Audrehem," p. 103; Ménard, *Nismes* 2: *preuves*, p. 243.

[64] *Gr. Chartrier*, no. 3908; BN MS. lat. 9175, fols. 34r-v; Molinier, "Audrehem," pp. 103–105, and notes; P.J. 35, pp. 241–242.

[65] BN NAF 7389, fol. 255r; AN JJ 98, no. 65; *Ord.* 3: p. 565.

[66] *HL* 9: pp. 735–736; 10: cols. 1275–1277; Mahul, *Cartulaire* 1: p. 140; 3: pp. 257–258; Molinier, "Audrehem," pp. 103–104.

[67] *Ibid., pp. 106–107.*

[68] *Petit Thalamus*, pp. 360–361; Monicat, *Grandes Compagnies*, p. 23; *HL* 9: pp. 735–736. During his absence, Audrehem was briefly replaced by Tancarville as lieutenant general in Languedoc, but was reappointed in August: *ibid.,* pp. 742–743; AD Hérault A 5, fols. 175r–176v.

help them collect any ransom payments which were owing to them as a result of their earlier depredations. Above all, and crucial to the execution of the treaty, it was provided that the companies would receive 100,000 gold florins from the towns of Auvergne, Mâconnais, and Languedoc.[69] This treaty was followed by other agreements during August, and John II promised Henry of Trastamara an income of 10,000 florins if he would lead the companies out of France.[70]

The way was now open for the people of southern France to be rid of the brigands who had created such havoc since the capture of John II and the ensuing truce. The high cost, however, would have been unthinkable in the more prosperous and peaceful France of a generation earlier. Those who had rejected any sort of peacetime subsidy and had even complained about some light taxes in wartime could not have imagined the burden that their children now assumed in time of nominal peace—an enormous ransom for the king and a large payment to support an expedition to Spain that could hardly be described as defending the realm. The burden of this latter tax, moreover, fell upon the regions south of the Loire that were reduced in territory by cessions to England as well as reduced in population by two epidemics of the plague.

The towns had difficulty raising on short notice the large sum needed to fulfill the treaty with the brigands.[71] The latter showed an initial willingness to act in good faith, and during August and September they passed peacefully through the seneschalsy of Beaucaire en route to the Pyrenees.[72] Their passage was a reminder to the alarmed residents that the money had to be raised on time. A tax of one-half florin per hearth was imposed for the purpose, but it still was being collected as late as 1365, and only the diversion of funds collected for the king's ransom made possible the payment of the brigands.[73] Even as receipts fell behind schedule, the

---

[69]*Petit Thalamus*, p. 361; *Gr. Chartrier*, no. 3904; AN P 2294, pp. 367–374; Guigue, *Tard-Venus*, p. 86; Molinier, "Audrehem," pp. 107–109.

[70]*Ibid.*, p. 110; AN P 2294, pp. 375–386; Cherest, *Archiprêtre*, pp. 190–191.

[71]Molinier, "Audrehem," p. 112, and note 10.

[72]*Petit Thalamus*, p. 361; Molinier, "Audrehem," pp. 113–114.

[73]On the diversion of the ransom, see *HL* 9: pp. 741–742, note 6, and 738. The clerical tenth may also have been used for this purpose (*ibid.* 10: col. 1252. On the assessment and collection of the half florin per hearth, see *ibid.*, cols. 1223, 1224, 1231, 1241, 1246–1248. Dognon, *Institutions*, p. 608, thinks there was an assembly, but his sources do not prove that there was one.

ransom aids or their equivalent provided a steady and undisputed source of revenue that could be used for meeting local emergencies.

The six weeks provided for the execution of the agreement with the companies was nearly over when Audrehem and Trastamara reached Nîmes early in September and found that collection of the half-florin *fouage* was lagging. The marshal urged haste in raising the money, and on 12 September he allowed the consuls of Nîmes to borrow five hundred florins to pay their share.[74] The towns of Anduze and Le Puy had to draw on sums collected for the current installment of the ransom.[75] Montpellier paid two thousand florins for the brigands in addition to its reduced share of the tax for the ransom.[76] The nobles of the Beaucaire district were also expected to contribute to the *fouage* of half a florin, but some managed to escape payment by reason of privileges.[77] Shortly before his death, Innocent VI also made a contribution, and there is some evidence that the French government also tried to tap the resources of the Jews.[78]

The money required by the treaty of Clermont finally was raised, but not until November. When Audrehem and Trastamara moved on to Carcassonne in mid-September, the latter's Spanish mercenaries stayed behind, living off the country around Nîmes, where the citizens lived under conditions approaching a state of siege.[79] As for the *routiers*, on whose account the strenuous financial effort was being made, they awaited with growing impatience the money that would send them off to seek wealth and glory in Castile. The Grand

---

[74] Molinier, "Audrehem," pp. 114–115; AD Hérault A 5, fols. 172v–173r; Ménard, *Nismes* 2: pp. 241–242; *preuves*, p. 247. On the outmoded figures for taxable hearths, see *HL* 9: p. 739, and Molinier's note 4 (*ibid.*, pp. 739–741). *Cf.* Molinier, "Audrehem," p. 125.

[75] AD Hérault A 5, fols. 173v, 174r.

[76] *Gr. Chartrier*, nos. 3905–3906.

[77] *Ibid.*, no. 2571; AD Hérault A 5, fols. 20v–21v, 174v; BN Coll. Languedoc 85, fol. 55r; Jacotin, *Preuves Polignac* 2: pp. 31–32; Delcambre, *Velay*, pp. 61, 65–66.

[78] M. Prou, *Relations politiques du Pape Urbain V avec les Rois de France Jean II et Charles V, 1362–1370* (Paris, 1888), pp. 1–2, and notes. The government ordered an inquiry into usury by Jews (AD Hérault A 5, fols. 185r–186r) and soon thereafter reaffirmed requirements regarding their distinctive dress (*Gr. Chartrier*, no. 1949). These orders were issued in September and October, 1362, when money was needed to pay off the *routiers*, and it is likely that they were connected with an extortion of money from the Jews.

[79] Ménard, *Nismes* 2: pp. 238–239; *Petit Thalamus*, p. 361; Molinier, "Audrehem," pp. 115–116.

Company began to break up late in October, and some brigands who were tired of waiting began to straggle northward again into the seneschalsy of Beaucaire.[80] These early defections were not in themselves disastrous; the remaining *routiers* received 90,000 florins early in November and the rest by mid-month.[81] The count of Foix collected a special payment of four thousand florins for using his good offices to prevent further defections on the part of other brigands who contemplated going back on the treaty.[82] It appeared that southern France had finally purchased relief from the mercenary bands, and after overseeing the delivery of the money, Audrehem departed for Avignon, where John II had arrived to confer with the new pope, Urban V.[83]

Unhappily for the hard-pressed southern towns, the optimism of November, 1362, proved extremely short-lived. A curious loophole in the treaty of Clermont with the brigands was the provision that they might return to France for one purpose, namely to engage in a war between the counts of Foix and Armagnac.[84] This provision must have been included at the insistence of *routier* captains who had reason to expect an early resumption of the struggle between the two Gascon lords and preferred employment nearer home if it became available. The peace between Foix and Armagnac had been extremely fragile. As early as January, 1361, Innocent VI had been trying to prevent a new outbreak of hostilities,[85] while in the fall he was forced to deal with a rupture between Gaston Phoebus and another neighbor, the lord of Albret.[86] Gaston was unwilling to renew the truce which expired at the beginning of 1362, and both sides began employing bands of *routiers* in a sort of guerrilla warfare. The count of Armagnac made alliances with Albret and Comminges.[87] Finally, late in March, 1362, the papal legate engineered a fourteen-month

---

[80]*Ibid.*, pp. 119–120.

[81]*Ibid.*, pp. 115, 118; *HL* 10: cols. 1232, 1298–1300; *INV AM Toulouse*, p. 467 (AA 35, no. 121).

[82]AD Hérault A 5, fol. 99r; *HL* 10: cols. 1231–1232.

[83]Molinier, "Audrehem," pp. 117, 119; *HL* 9: p. 746; Prou, *Relations politiques*, pp. 8–10.

[84]See citations above, note 69.

[85]Martène, *Thesaurus* 2: cols. 856–857.

[86]*Ibid.*, cols. 1056–1057.

[87]Tucoo-Chala, *Gaston*, p. 84, and notes.

truce, but it was very badly observed.[88] Under prodding from John II, the new pope, Urban V, asked Charles the Bad to help make peace between the two counts, and he sent a new nuncio to Gaston on 3 December.[89]

This papal effort was too late, for once they had collected their 100,000 florins the *routiers* began to join the Gascon conflict in large numbers. Some entered the service of John of Armagnac, who apparently reopened hostilities.[90] It was Foix, however, who won the war, with a crushing victory on 5 December at Launac. Among Gaston's nine hundred prisoners were such lords as Armagnac, Albret, Comminges, and Pardiac. It was another dramatic triumph for archers over heavy cavalry, and it left the count of Foix arbiter of Gascony.[91] The peace still sought by the pope now depended on the negotiation of ransom treaties between Gaston Phoebus and his captives.[92] It brought no relief to Languedoc, for the *routiers* were unemployed again, and some now owed ransoms that made them all the more eager to enrich themselves at the expense of the defenseless. The situation was as dangerous as it had been eight months before, after the disaster at Brignais.[93]

Equally serious was the continued presence of the Spanish troops of Henry of Trastamara. They too lived off the land and would have to be paid to leave the country. Early in 1363, assemblies of southern towns began to confront the problem. Those of the Carcassonne district met before 19 January,[94] while those of the Beaucaire district convened at Villeneuve-lès-Avignon in the last week of the month.[95] They agreed to raise four *gros tournois* per hearth in order to pay 53,000 florins to make the Spaniards leave. The collector's accounts show that Languedoc was still assessed on the basis of 200,000

---

[88]*Ibid.*, pp. 84–85 and notes; p. 390, no. 196; *HL* **10**: cols. 1283–1285; Prou, *Relations politiques*, pp. 15–16.

[89]*Ibid.*, pp. 15–17, and P.J. 5–7 (documents from Vatican Register 245).

[90]Guigue, *Tard-Venus*, p. 86; Tucoo-Chala, *Gaston*, p. 85.

[91]*Ibid.*, pp. 86–89; *Petit Thalamus*, p. 362; *Chron. Jean II et Charles V* **1**: p. 338; Breuils, "Jean d'Armagnac," pp. 72–74; *HL* **9**: pp. 747–748; Molinier, "Audrehem," p. 120.

[92]Prou, *Relations politiques*, P.J. 8–10; *HL* **10**: cols. 1281–1283.

[93]*Ibid.*; *HL* **9**: pp. 741–742, note 6.

[94]AM Albi CC 72, no. 4.

[95]Ménard, *Nismes* **2**: *preuves*, p. 251.

hearths, for the tax was expected to yield 66,666⅔ florins.[96] The excess was to be used for other defensive needs, as in the seneschalsy of Beaucaire, where 8000 florins were to finance an expedition against the brigand captain Perrin Boias.[97] The use of some receipts for such local projects merely delayed the departure of the Spaniards and made it necessary to draw again upon the funds being collected for the royal ransom. In March, Henry of Trastamara received the first 39,000 florins, and the rest was paid by 25 April.[98] Henry had also been promised an annuity of 10,000 pounds when he was expected to lead the *routiers* to Spain, and over a third of this sum was also paid to him from ransom funds.[99]

It seems clear that the population of Languedoc was adjusting with reluctance and difficulty to the rising financial burden. Taxes for the expulsion of *routiers*, especially when based on obsolete hearth figures, were collected very slowly. Only the existence of regular taxes for the royal ransom made it possible to meet the financial commitments which the towns assumed. Despite the efforts to reduce or change in form the taxes for the ransom, nobody challenged their justification. As they were diverted to other purposes, the payments for the ransom itself fell steadily farther behind. The town of Toulouse collected slightly more money for the ransom in 1363 than in 1362,[100] but as money was diverted, the seneschalsy fell increasingly short of its quota. Payments were short by 8525 francs in 1362, 12,108 in 1363, 14,903 in 1364, and 27,704 in 1365.[101] Taxes other than for the ransom still encountered opposition. When the *gabelle* on salt had been extended, reluctantly, in the spring of 1362, other indirect taxes had been canceled, but as always it was uncertain whether municipal

---

[96] See last two notes. The 53,000 florins appear to have been promised much earlier, but only now was a tax established to raise the money. See *HL* 10: cols. 1226–1227, 1231, 1242, 1248; BN *Coll. Languedoc* 159, fol. 107r; *Gr. Chartrier*, nos. 3998–4001; Molinier, "Audrehem," pp. 120–121. The lands of the count of Foix refused to contribute to this tax (*ibid.*, p. 123). On the problem caused by the presence of the Spaniards, see also *HL* 10: cols. 1317–1319.

[97] *Gr. Chartrier*, nos. 3998–3999.

[98] *HL* 10: cols. 1224, 1233; BN Coll. Languedoc 159, fol. 105; Molinier, "Audrehem," p. 122. Montpellier did not complete its payment of the 4 *gros* per hearth until September, 1364 (*Gr. Chartrier*, no. 3625).

[99] *HL* 10: col. 1224.

[100] AM Toulouse CC 1847, p. 6.

[101] *HL* 10: col. 1236.

taxes and unpaid arrears from the *gabelle* were included. During the fall of 1362, when every effort was being made to raise the money needed to buy off the Grand Company, Audrehem responded to complaints and ordered that no tax on salt was to be levied except for the *gabelle* which the Estates had granted.[102]

3. The Struggle with Seguin de Badefol, 1363–1365

For all their troubles during 1362, the inhabitants of Languedoc were in for greater difficulties, if we are to accept Denifle's conclusion that the years 1363–1365 were the worst ones from the standpoint of brigandage in the Midi.[103] The seneschalsy of Beaucaire was quick to feel the wrath of the enemy, for the company of Perrin Boias occupied the abbey of Saint-Chaffre in the Velay region and used it as a base for further depredations. King John and Arnoul d'Audrehem were at Villeneuve-lès-Avignon and there they met the assembly which authorized a *fouage* of four *gros*. Although most of the proceeds were intended for Trastamara's Spaniards, some of the money was reserved for a campaign against Boias, and on this occasion the Velay nobility joined in contributing.[104] The brigands were finally expelled from Saint-Chaffre in March, 1363.[105]

It has been pointed out, however, that the companies sacked several places for every one that was taken from them, and they grew so active in the Beaucaire district that the development of another Grand Company was feared.[106] Castilian envoys en route to Avignon were intercepted and detained.[107] Avignon faced a new danger, while the inhabitants of the Comtat Venaissin were still repaying the pope for money spent for the earlier evacuation of Pont-Saint-Esprit.[108] Ur-

[102]*Ibid.*, cols. 1277–1278; AD Hérault A 5, fols. 178v–179v.

[103]Denifle, *Désolation* 2: p. 441.

[104]See above, note 97. *Cf.* Bardon, *Alais* 2: pp. 60, 63; Monicat, *Grandes Compagnies*, pp. 24–25; Jacotin, *Preuves Polignac* 2: pp. 32–33.

[105]Molinier, "Audrehem," p. 125. *Cf. HL* 10: cols. 1306–1308.

[106]Molinier, "Audrehem," pp. 127–128; Michel, "Défense," p. 129; *Petit Thalamus*, p. 362.

[107]*Ibid.*

[108]Michel, "Défense," p. 129; Labande, "Occupation," p. 150. See also Dussert, *Etats Dauphiné*, pp. 49–50.

ban V had to reduce the clerical tenth in much of France because of brigandage.[109]

For much of his long southern tour, John II resided at Villeneuve-lès-Avignon, where a series of foreign adventures dominated his negotiations with the papacy. He wanted Urban V to authorize the marriage of his youngest son to the queen of Naples, and he proposed to make Bernabo Visconti stop harassing papal lands if Urban would supply another 400,000 florins for his ransom.[110] Above all, John and Urban discussed a new crusade to the Levant, and on 31 March, 1363, the kings of France and Denmark took the cross at Avignon, following the arrival there of Peter I of Cyprus. Urban V authorized a tenth on the clergy for six years and made available to John all the funds contributed for crusading purposes during the past twelve years.[111]

However visionary this scheme may have been, the pope undoubtedly saw it as a way of simultaneously ridding Europe of the *routiers* and enhancing the prestige of the Church.[112] Centuries earlier, his namesake, Urban II, had contributed greatly both to papal prestige and to the pacification of France by launching the first crusade. What is still debated is whether John II also viewed the project mainly as a solution to the problem of brigandage, or whether he was indulging in an irresponsible chivalric fantasy.[113] In any case, John was not prepared to leave his kingdom while it faced so much disorder, and he particularly distrusted Charles of Navarre, who had created so much disruption during the king's absence in England. Papal efforts to arrange a definitive Franco-Navarrese peace, however, produced no result.[114]

Another peacemaking effort proved more successful. Under prodding from a papal representative, the count of Foix concluded a treaty with his defeated foes on 14 April, 1363. It brought him over 500,000 florins in ransoms, including

---

[109] Prou, *Relations politiques*, p. 27.

[110] *Ibid.*, pp. 11–15. See *HL* 9: pp. 751–753, note 10, for John's itinerary.

[111] *Petit Thalamus*, pp. 362–363; Prou, *Relations politiques*, pp. 26–28, and P.J. 14–15; Molinier, "Audrehem," pp. 128–129.

[112] *Gr. Chartrier*, no. 2261; Prou, *Relations politiques*, p. 25. On the growing danger from the companies in the Beaucaire district, see *ibid.*, p. 31.

[113] For the latter view, see Perroy, *Hundred Years War*, pp. 140–142. The more favorable view of the king is presented by Cazelles, "Jean II."

[114] Prou, *Relations politiques*, p. 30, and P.J. 16.

300,000 from John of Armagnac. Collection of these sums made Foix the richest lord in Gascony and left his rivals in straitened circumstances.[115] The financial troubles of these Gascon lords would have important consequences for Anglo-French relations and royal taxation before the end of the 1360's.[116] In the short run, Languedoc was put under more financial pressure, for some of the money granted to Armagnac in 1360 had not been paid, and now he was forced to demand it.[117]

Late in March, meanwhile, John II convened an assembly of the three Estates of the seneschalsy of Beaucaire, who met at Villeneuve-lès-Avignon, perhaps for as long as a month.[118] The king must have been present only intermittently, for discussions of the crusade periodically drew him to Avignon. A royal ordinance dated 20 April embodied the decisions of this assembly. It contained forty-three articles, including a two-year extension of the *gabelle* on salt. If it proved inadequate for financing the expulsion of the brigands, the Estates would raise other taxes, but the crown's officers were not to be involved in their collection. The seneschal of Beaucaire, who had successfully driven the brigands from Saint-Chaffre, would be the royal captain of the district's military forces.[119]

Historians have attributed uncommon importance to this assembly. Vuitry called it a kind of southern counterpart to one that was to meet at Amiens in December and grant a long-term tax to deal with brigandage in Languedoil.[120] Cazelles regards it as a successful royal attempt to detach the seneschalsy of Beaucaire from a dangerously independent league of southern towns who were setting up something on the order of what Marcel is supposed to have attempted in the north.[121] Neither of these explanations is convincing. The king merely met with the Estates of a single seneschalsy,

---

[115]*Ibid.*, p. 18 and P.J. 13; Tucoo-Chala, *Gaston*, pp. 89-92, and notes; Molinier, "Audrehem," p. 120; *HL* 10: cols. 1285-1291.

[116]See below, chap. VII, part 1.

[117]*HL* 10: cols. 1308-1310; AD Hérault A 5, fols. 155r-156v.

[118]*HL* 9: p. 754, note 1 (Molinier), citing Ménard, *Nismes* 2: *preuves*, p. 253.

[119]*Ord.* 3: pp. 618-627; *HL* 9: pp. 752-754; BN Coll. Languedoc 85, fols. 262r-270r; BN NAF 7430, fol. 281r; Molinier, "Audrehem," pp. 129-130; Dognon, *Institutions*, p. 609.

[120]Vuitry, *Régime financier* 2: pp. 118-119. See chap. VI, at notes 134-136.

[121]Cazelles, "Jean II," p. 25. See also Dognon, *Institutions*, p. 235; and H. Gilles, *Les Etats de Languedoc au XVe siècle* (Toulouse, 1965), p. 26. Admittedly, the nobles

redressed their grievances, and ratified the measures they authorized to finance their own defense. The *gabelle* was not an innovation; the Estates of Languedoc, both before and after 1363, often consisted only of town representatives; and regional assemblies, throughout the 1360's, acted in their own defense when royal leadership was lacking. Even if one accepts an exaggerated notion of Marcel's idea of a federation of towns, one must concede the essential conservatism of the southern assemblies, which never displayed the hostility towards nobles or the royal government that one finds at Paris in the first half of 1358.

Local problems of defense and claims of privilege continued to affect taxation in the seneschalsy of Beaucaire. Montpellier was paying its own contingents of troops and seeking royal relief for suburban property owners whose buildings had been destroyed.[122] The consuls of Aigues Mortes complained that wealthy and powerful citizens were trying to evade royal taxes and the levy on exports. At this very time, the vicinity was infested with brigands, and those thought to be evading taxes must have been objects of particular bitterness.[123] Audrehem corresponded with Montpellier several times over the lagging payment of taxes owed for 1362 and finally obtained two final installments.[124] While the Estates of Beaucaire were meeting with the king, those of the two western seneschalsies convened and granted a *fouage* of a half-florin for local defense.[125] Although the king and dauphin both issued ordinances aimed at alleviating abuses,[126] these did not prevent Audrehem from inaugurating a strenuous new investigation of acquisitions of noble fiefs.[127]

Taxation in Languedoc continued to be dominated by the activities of the *routier* captains, particularly Seguin de Badefol. In July the representatives of the towns of the Toulousain

---

and prelates condemned the "perpetual union" proclaimed by the southern towns, but the league in question was no more than a desperate attempt to collaborate against the endless danger of brigandage.

[122]*Gr. Chartrier,* nos. 511, 1248.

[123]BN MS. lat. 9175, fols. 47–52; *cf. HL* 10: col. 1312.

[124]*Gr. Chartrier,* nos. 461, 496, 564, 566, 567.

[125]Dognon, *Institutions,* p. 609; AM Toulouse CC 1847, p. 14.

[126]*Gr. Chartrier,* D-19, nos. 3, 22; *HL* 10: col. 1316; AD Hérault A 1, fols. 15r–39v.

[127]*Ibid.,* A 5, fols, 137r–139v; Molinier, "Audrehem," P.J. 43.

brought 2385 florins to Badefol at Caraman.[128] Another brigand, Louis Roubaut, occupied a castle near Béziers, which he evacuated in the fall of 1363 only after he was paid ten thousand francs.[129] Audrehem issued, and then canceled, a general military summons for the inhabitants of the seneschalsy of Beaucaire. An assembly at Carcassonne in August granted a new *fouage* for defense,[130] and early in September, Audrehem launched a brief campaign against brigands at Mirepoix.[131] Soon, however, he had to return to Nîmes to face what appeared to be a more serious *routier* threat.

Hardly had one group of brigands been pardoned for its ravages in the Beaucaire district,[132] than another group replaced it. The formidable Seguin de Badefol, having left the Toulousain, led his forces northeastward, arriving at the town of Brioude, which he occupied on 13 September. From this stronghold, he ravaged Auvergne and also the Velay region of the seneschalsy of Beaucaire.[133] Claiming that inhabitants of Velay owed him money, Badefol had not included this area in his agreement of 1361 not to invade Languedoc.[134] The rest of the Beaucaire district, however, could not afford to assume that Badefol's men would venture no farther south than Velay. Even before the seizure of Brioude, the papal captain of Avignon was prevented from making a trip to Paris because the defense of the Venaissin required his presence.[135] On 30 September and again in mid-October, the consuls of Alès warned those of Nîmes that men-at-arms who had left Brioude were in the vicinity.[136] Montpellier hastened work on fortifica-

---

[128] P. Wolff, *Commerces et marchands de Toulouse (vers 1350-vers 1450)* (Paris, 1954), p. 42. Badefol had not been a party to the treaty of Clermont or the Spanish project of 1362, and he was placed in Lyonnais early in 1363 by Froissart. See Guigue, *Tard-Venus*, p. 88; Cherest, *Archiprêtre*, p. 183. Molinier's long note in *HL* 9: pp. 756-757, note 1, adds other information on the activities of the brigands in Languedoc in 1362 and 1363.

[129] *Petit Thalamus*, p. 363.

[130] AM Nîmes NN 1, no. 44; Molinier, "Audrehem," p. 131; AM Albi CC 73, no. 1.

[131] BN Doat 63, fols. 325-326; Molinier, "Audrehem," p. 133.

[132] AD Hérault A 5, fols. 21v-23v.

[133] A. Chassaing, *Spicilegium Brivatense. Recueil de documents historiques relatifs au Brivadois et à l'Auvergne* (Paris, 1886), p. 359; Guigue, *Tard-Venus*, pp. 95-96; Luce, *Du Guesclin*, p. 242; *Petit Thalamus*, p. 363.

[134] Delcambre, *Velay*, p. 63, notes 24, 25; Molinier, "Audrehem," p. 139. On Badefol's activities, see also Molinier's note in *HL* 9: p. 735, note 1.

[135] Prou, *Relations politiques*, P.J. 18.

[136] Bardon, *Alais* 2: pp. 64-65.

tions and equipped a force of men to defend the city. These troops helped the seneschal of Beaucaire drive off an attack by the company of Bertucat d'Albret late in October.[137] It was feared, however, that more *routiers* were on their way from Catalonia.[138]

The inhabitants on both sides of the Rhone now had to consider again the difficult choice between buying off the companies or raising a sufficient force to drive them out. The towns were unwilling to discuss the matter without the collaboration of nobles and clergy, but the latter also were reticent about making a commitment. Both alternatives were unpalatable because they entailed more taxes, but Audrehem pressed for a decision and ordered the nobles and clergy to join the townsmen at Nîmes on 10 October to formulate a policy.[139] He ordered the inhabitants of all small places in Velay to take refuge from Badefol,[140] and then hastened to Avignon to confer with the pope.[141] Urban V was in no position to help, for he was concerned with protecting the left bank of the Rhone. A league of nobles was organized under papal auspices, and in November the nobles and prelates of Provence, Savoy, and Dauphiné assembled at Montélimar to discuss the crisis. The governor of Dauphiné assumed command of the coalition and a subsidy was levied in most lands east of the Rhone to pay troops.[142]

When they assembled at Nîmes, the Estates of the Beaucaire district also decided in favor of armed resistance rather than blackmail, and they authorized a force totaling 4500 troops.[143] It was yet another drain on municipal finances, and urban governments sought royal assistance in the levy and collection of local taxes that aroused resistance.[144] The inhabitants of the Velay region, whose land would be the battle ground if Badefol were met by force, were far more disposed to pay for

---

[137] *Petit Thalamus*, pp. 363–364.

[138] Prou, *Relations politiques*, p. 32.

[139] *HL* **9**: p. 759; **10**: cols. 1319–1320; AD Hérault A 5, fols. 141r–142r; BN Coll. Languedoc 85, fol. 287r; Dognon, *Institutions*, p. 609; Molinier, "Audrehem," p. 134.

[140] Monicat, *Grandes Compagnies*, pp. 28–29.

[141] Molinier, "Audrehem," p. 136; Prou, *Relations politiques*, P.J. 21.

[142] *Ibid.*, pp. 32–34; P.J. 20, 22; Dussert, *Etats Dauphiné*, p. 50; Denifle, *Désolation* **2**: p. 441f.

[143] Molinier, "Audrehem," p. 138, and P.J. 60; *Gr. Chartrier*, D-19, no. 10.

[144] AD Hérault A 5, fols. 36v–37v; 144–145; Molinier, "Audrehem," P.J. 53, 54, 56.

his withdrawal. This region was stubbornly independent in fiscal matters, and Audrehem had made repeated unsuccessful efforts to collect there the small subsidy granted in 1361 after the Pont-Saint-Esprit affair. In October, 1363, he finally canceled this tax and authorized the inhabitants to tax themselves for what was needed to buy off Badefol. Some nobles resisted even this self-imposed levy, and in December, Audrehem had to order force to compel payment. He revoked the order the following April, when a new agreement was reached with Seguin de Badefol.[145]

The *routier* chief finally was defeated near Montferrand, and on 4 April, 1364, he promised the Estates of Auvergne to evacuate Brioude in return for 15,000 florins, and no longer to trouble either Auvergne or Velay if paid another 25,000 florins by 1 November, 1365. Following this arrangement, he evacuated Brioude on 23 June, and we may assume that Velay joined Auvergne in paying him.[146]

For all his notoriety, Seguin de Badefol was not the only captain engaged in brigandage, and his withdrawal from Brioude did not rescue Languedoc from the raids of other companies. The last two months of the year 1363 were characterized by continuing incursions and no new efforts to raise money to pay for defensive forces. Brigands pouring into the seneschalsy of Beaucaire encountered little effective opposition. Audrehem, spending most of his time in the Toulouse and Carcassonne districts, did attempt a brief and unsuccessful winter siege of Peyriac, but retired with his troops to Albi before the end of December.[147] His letters indicate the gravity of the situation. The captain of one fortress was ordered not to permit any armed men to pass unless they were royal officials or carried explicit orders from the king.[148] Merchants bound for Montpellier by sea were authorized to by-pass Aigues Mortes and proceed as far as Lattes before unloading their ships, because the road from Aigues Mortes to Montpellier

[145]*Ibid.*, pp. 140f; AD Hérault A 5, fols. 38r–39r, 153r–155r; Jacotin, *Preuves Polignac* 2: pp. 33–37; Le Sourd, *Etats Vivarais*, p. 30; Delcambre, *Velay*, pp. 59–64; Monicat, *Grandes Compagnies*, pp. 28–29.

[146]*Ibid.*, pp. 30–32; Chassaing, *Spicilegium Brivatense*, nos. 134, 136; Denifle, *Désolation* 2: p. 421; *HL* 9: p. 735, note 1.

[147]Molinier, "Audrehem," pp. 142–145, and P.J. 61; Denifle, *Désolation* 2: p. 438.

[148]AD Hérault A 5, fols. 150v–151r. Because of the danger on the roads, Audrehem authorized a bourgeois to carry arms (Molinier, "Audrehem," P.J. 68).

was infested with brigands.[149] Back at Albi, Audrehem pardoned subjects of the bishop who were accused of giving aid and comfort to the *routiers*.[150] Local populations often were forced against their will to cooperate with the brigands, for the latter were known to wreak horrible vengeance on rural people who did not submit to them.

Throughout this difficult period, the government continued to collect regularly the money which was owed for the royal ransom. Various documents record the continuing collection, which was attended by none of the complaints and delays that people had placed in the way of taxation a generation earlier.[151] Yet if the taxes for the ransom encountered relatively less popular resistance, they were constantly delayed and reduced by brigandage and destruction and by diversion of the taxes to local defense. Even when special subsidies were imposed to buy off brigands, the money generally was taken from ransom receipts on hand, while collection of the special subsidy dragged on for months or years. Bernard François, who collected not only the ransom aids but also the special hearth taxes for expelling the Grand Company and Trastamara's Spaniards, recorded some telling figures regarding the seneschalsy of Toulouse. For the four years ending in February, 1364, this district owed 142,860 francs for the ransom and 33,333 francs for the other two taxes, yet by March of 1364 only 58,000 francs had been received, about one-third of the total.[152] Thus the aids, or their equivalent, provided the steady revenue that was lacking in Philip VI's reign, but not as much as they were intended to produce and at times scarcely more than was needed for essential defensive needs.

Meanwhile, the brigand menace throughout France grew more acute in the winter of 1363–1364, as Charles the Bad found a new grievance against the Valois in the Burgundian succession question and prepared for renewed hostilities. John II returned to England at the end of 1363, and Charles soon embarked on new adventures. For much of 1364, *routier* captains in many parts of France sought to give their actions a

---

[149]*Ibid.*, p. 148, and P.J. 70; AD Hérault A 5, fols. 149v–150v.

[150]Molinier, "Audrehem," pp. 145–146, and P.J. 63.

[151]*HL* 10: col. 1381; *Gr. Chartrier*, nos. 457, 460, 462; BN Doat 53, fols. 298v–312 (showing numerous sums received for the ransom at Narbonne in the 1360's).

[152]*HL* 10: col. 1231.

veneer of legality by claiming to serve Navarre.[153] On 2 March, 1364, Audrehem summoned town representatives from the seneschalsies of Toulouse and Carcassonne to meet with him at the latter city on the fifteenth. The communities of the Beaucaire district were convened separately, to Lunel on 31 March. The deliberations were to be *pro securitate patrie, regni et ipsorum,* and the seneschals were ordered to stress to their districts the urgency of the situation.[154] On 4 March, Audrehem authorized the towns of the Beaucaire district to levy taxes on themselves in order to put more troops in the field,[155] and by April the three Estates of this region had agreed to enroll and pay new forces.[156] Audrehem may also have obtained some money when he issued letters of safeguard for the Jews.[157]

It is small wonder that the people of Languedoc were coming to view the *routiers* with a desperate and frustrated hatred, comparable to the sentiments which had given birth to the *Jacquerie* in Languedoil six years before. An outburst of popular fury occurred at Narbonne in March. Some of the forces in Audrehem's employ were Spaniards who had come to France with Henry of Trastamara. The behavior of these ruffians incensed the inhabitants of Narbonne, who rose violently against them, killing several of the mercenaries. The riot appears to have taken place while the consuls were deliberating over how to eject the brigands from Peyriac.[158] Sources disagree as to whether new assemblies met for this purpose in the second half of April,[159] but by the early part of May, Audrehem had assembled the forces needed to resume the siege. The place was taken by storm on 16 June and a massacre of *routiers* followed this triumph.[160]

---

[153] Denifle, *Désolation* 2: pp. 424–425; Guigue, *Tard-Venus,* p. 107; Keen, *Laws of War,* pp. 83–85.

[154] Dognon, *Institutions,* p. 609; *HL* 9: p. 762; 10: cols. 1320–1321; AD Hérault A 5, fols. 152v–153r; BN Coll. Languedoc 85, fols. 288r–v; 86, fol. 5; Molinier, "Audrehem," pp. 152–153.

[155] *Ibid.,* P.J., nos. 67, 72; Chassaing, *Spicilegium Brivatense,* no. 133.

[156] *Gr. Chartrier,* nos. 3613, 3638; *HL* 9: pp. 762–763.

[157] BN Coll. Languedoc 86, fols. 10r–v; Molinier, "Audrehem," p. 151.

[158] *Ibid.,* pp. 153–156, and P.J. 74.

[159] *Ibid.,* p. 157; *HL* 9: p. 763, note 5.

[160] *Ibid.,* pp. 764, note 4, and 765; *Petit Thalamus,* p. 366; Denifle, *Désolation* 2: p. 438; Prou, *Relations politiques,* P.J. 38; Molinier, "Audrehem," pp. 159–162, and P.J. 83.

Occasional victories of this sort must have been heartening
to the inhabitants of Languedoc, but in the final year of John
II's reign they had been unable to do more than hold their
own, trying to keep enough troops in the field to protect the
principal towns from the worst excesses of brigandage. When
the death of his father in the spring of 1364 elevated Charles V
to the throne, the new king soon concluded that the situation
in Languedoc was unsatisfactory. A full-scale war with the
king of Navarre was now in progress, and Charles V seems to
have had little confidence that the aging Arnoul d'Audrehem
was equal to the burdens of his post. After apparently considering Gaston Phoebus of Foix as a replacement, Charles
finally decided on his able and energetic brother, Louis of
Anjou, whom he named royal lieutenant in Languedoc on 25
June, 1364.[161] Prior to this appointment, he set the stage for
vigorous new fiscal and military measures in Languedoc by
sending special commissioners to explain to the southern
towns that the struggle with Charles the Bad was a just war.
Given the Navarrese involvement with the *routiers,* the populace probably needed little persuading.[162]

Urban V once again excommunicated the *routiers* and
called for action from the league of Provencal nobles and
clergy which had been established for the defense of papal
territory with the help of crossbowmen sent by towns.[163] In the
seneschalsy of Beaucaire, another commission inspected fortresses for defensibility.[164] Ransom collections from Lyonnais
were diverted to Audrehem for military expenses.[165] The pope
asked the marshal to make certain that towns did not attempt
to fight against the companies without the leadership of an
experienced captain.[166] Charles V generally permitted towns
to establish local taxes to finance defensive measures, and he
was prepared to support municipal governments on most

---

[161] Delachenal, *Charles V* 3: pp. 104–105, 551–554.

[162]*Ibid.,* pp. 546–547. Aside from subsidizing the *routiers* at Peyriac, Charles the Bad
employed the captain known as Le Petit Meschin and sent his own brother Louis to
campaign in southern France. Their activities ranged from Bigorre to Burgundy. See
ibid., pp. 141–142, note 5, and Castro, *Catalogo* 5: nos. 270, 297–299, 368, 372, 374.

[163] Prou, *Relations politiques,* pp. 36–37, and P.J. 27, 28, 30; Michel, "Défense,"
p. 130.

[164]*HL* 9: p. 766; 10: cols. 1322–1323; Bardon, *Alais* 2: p. 71.

[165] Guigue, *Tard-Venus,* p. 209.

[166] Prou, *Relations politiques,* p. 37, note 4.

occasions when citizens tried to invoke privileges to escape these taxes.[167]

Privilege became an issue in the Velay region because Seguin de Badefol, who had still not been paid what had been promised to him, now contemplated an attack on lower Languedoc and a confrontation with Audrehem who was at Lunel (late summer, 1364). Royal commissioners hastily met with representatives of the towns of the seneschalsy of Beaucaire and obtained enough money to support 1450 troops for one month.[168] Hoping to avoid a battle altogether, Audrehem tried to speed up collection of the money promised to Badefol, but he encountered resistance because he had exempted from taxes the abbey of Saint-Chaffre which had suffered at the hands of the brigands early in 1363. This exemption added to the burdens of other communities and therefore caused resentment. Finally, on 15 September, 1364, Audrehem agreed to revoke the exemption and require that everybody contribute to buying off Badefol.[169] A few days later, he revoked permission for the Beaucaire communities to raise troops to resist the companies in Gévaudan,[170] probably because Badefol had abandoned his designs on Languedoc and had directed his attention towards Lyonnais. In November the brigand chief made his celebrated seizure of Anse.[171]

Badefol's departure from the immediate vicinity did not mean an end to brigandage in Languedoc, and later events would show that Badefol's men could still threaten the Velay region from Anse.[172] In Languedoc, the response to the challenge seemed to lack energy and direction, pending the change in royal lieutenant. Commissioners sent by Charles V in September ordered the towns of the Beaucaire district to an assembly at Nîmes, while Audrehem called the Estates of Languedoc to Béziers on 6 November.[173] On 28 October, Louis

---

[167] Wolff, *Commerces*, pp. 97, 219; Molinier, "Audrehem," p. 163 and P.J. 84; BN Coll. Languedoc 86, fols. 16r–v; AD Hérault A 5, fols. 200r–201r, 203r–204r; Gr. Chartrier, no. 288; *HL* **10**: cols. 1326–1327.

[168] Dognon, *Institutions*, p. 609; Monicat, *Grandes Compagnies*, p. 33.

[169] *Ibid.*, pp. 34–35; AD Hérault A 5, fols. 192v–194r; *HL* **9**: p. 766.

[170] *Ibid.* **9**: 766; **10**: cols. 1321–1322; Molinier, "Audrehem," pp. 165–166.

[171] *Petit Thalamus*, p. 367; Luce, *Du Guesclin*, p. 242; Denifle, *Désolation* **2**: pp. 424–425; Guigue, *Tard-Venus*, p. 105; Monicat, *Grandes Compagnies*, pp. 34–35; Delachenal, *Charles V* **3**: p. 234.

[172] Guigue, *Tard-Venus*, p. 110.

[173] Dognon, *Institutions*, p. 609; *HL* **9**: p. 766; **10**: cols. 1323–1325.

of Anjou announced that his own commissioner would precede him to Languedoc and meet the southern Estates at Carcassonne, on 30 November.[174] It is unlikely that any of these assemblies took place; Audrehem may even have left Languedoc some months before Anjou's arrival in January. In mid-November the king confirmed all acts by Audrehem as royal lieutenant and asked the towns to give their advice and assistance to his successor, Louis of Anjou.[175] Anjou summoned the representatives of Montpellier to meet with him at Beaucaire on 30 December. This meeting also may not have taken place, but Anjou was at Montpellier by 13 January and there he received a long list of grievances from the inhabitants of the seneschalsy of Beaucaire.[176] Ten days later he named *réformateurs* to investigate and correct abuses.[177]

Réformateurs were not used much in the reign of Charles V, but they remained the traditional device for dealing with grievances.[178] There is no indication that Louis of Anjou intended them for any other purpose, but as it happened, the unpopularity which some *réformateurs* had earned in the past made them useful to Louis as a bargaining point when he finally met an assembly of the southern towns. This meeting convened in Carcassonne towards the beginning of February, 1365, and on the ninth the duke of Anjou recalled the *réformateurs* at the request of the Estates. The towns subsequently agreed to support a force of six hundred men-at-arms for the three summer months and two hundred men for the ensuing six months. Their salaries would be paid by extending for a year the *gabelle* on salt.[179] Anjou also ordered collection of all unpaid back taxes from the time of the Pont-Saint-Esprit campaign of 1361; he required towns to pay the expenses of their representatives to the assembly; and he demanded a mark of silver from each royal notary.[180]

---

[174] BN MS. lat. 9175, fols. 74r–75r.

[175] Molinier, "Audrehem," p. 167 and P.J. 89, 91.

[176] *Petit Thalamus*, p. 368; *HL* 9: p. 768 and note 6; 10: cols. 1331–1332.

[177] *Ibid.* 9: p. 769–770 and notes; 10: cols. 1337–1339; AD Hérault A 5, fols. 243v–244r.

[178] Cazelles, "Réformation du Royaume," esp. p. 94; A. Molinier, in *HL* 9: 769–770, note 4.

[179] *Ibid.* 9: p. 769–770 and notes; 10: cols. 1340–1343; Dognon, *Institutions*, p. 609; Bardon, *Alais* 2: P.J. 12; BN MS. lat. 9175, fols. 62r–70v; *Gr. Chartrier*, nos. 602, 3911.

[180] AD Hérault A 5, fols. 246r–247v, 258r–v, 267r–268r; BN *Coll. Languedoc* 86, fol. 24; *HL* 9: p. 770.

By the spring of 1365 there were grounds for more concern over brigandage, for the Breton civil war and the Franco-Navarrese conflict were both nearing an end, with the prospect that many soldiers would become unemployed. The dangerous Badefol, moreover, was still at Anse, and pillaging raids from that base reached as far as the Velay region. The viscount of Polignac and the Velay nobility organized to meet the danger and were rewarded with the capture of Louis Roubaut, a captain of *routiers* who had been a terrible scourge to the inhabitants of this region. Roubaut was turned over to the duke of Anjou for execution, and with his death the Velay was delivered from brigandage for seven years.[181] In the meantime, Pope Urban V preached a crusade against the brigands which unleashed an undisciplined outburst of popular violence against isolated bands in Albigeois.[182] Discussions at Avignon centered on a scheme of sending the troublesome mercenaries on a crusade against the Turks via Hungary. This project acquired new urgency when the Franco-Navarrese peace of March, 1365, was ratified in May, for it left many soldiers unemployed.[183] With the king of Navarre no longer at war, Seguin de Badefol lost what little legal standing he had possessed, and the approach of troops assembling for the Hungarian venture further threatened his position. He therefore agreed to negotiate for the evacuation of Anse, ultimately agreeing to leave the bailiwick of Mâcon in return for 40,000 florins. This arrangement, concluded in June under papal auspices, provided that Languedoc would pay 15,000 florins, or 40 per cent of the total.[184]

While these negotiations were still pending, Louis of Anjou convened a new assembly of southern towns at Montpellier to review the military situation, but the response was unenthu-

---

[181]*Venette*, p. 135, said that the end of the Breton and Navarrese wars brought a diminution in the number of "thieves and robbers," but insofar as they did diminish in number during 1365 it was mainly as a result of efforts to lead them out of the realm. It is noteworthy that *Petit Thalamus*, p. 367, recorded the battle of Auray in far-off Brittany, as if it were realized in Languedoc that a new influx of brigands might well follow. On Louis Roubaut, see *ibid.*, pp. 367–368; Monicat, *Grandes compagnies*, pp. 36–41, 43; Guigue, *Tard-Venus*, pp. 112, 114; *HL* 9: p. 776; Molinier, "Audrehem," p. 151 and P.J. 69.

[182]*HL* 9: p. 772, note 4; 10: cols. 1332–1335; Prou, *Relations politiques*, P.J. 42; Guigue, *Tard-Venus*, pp. 144–145.

[183]Prou, *Relations politiques*, pp. 46–47.

[184]*Ibid.*, pp. 54–55, P.J. 44, 57; *HL* 9: pp. 774–775; Guigue, *Tard-Venus*, pp. 118–122; Denifle, *Désolation* 2: 425–427 and notes.

siastic and another assembly had to meet around the end of
June to consider the treaty with Seguin de Badefol. This time
the towns granted 50,000 florins, of which 40,000 were for the
defense of Languedoc and only 10,000 for Badefol.[185] Languedoc showed little enthusiasm for this latest effort to appease a
brigand chief. Only in extreme northeastern Languedoc,
Velay, had the *routiers* at Anse posed a threat, and the capture
of Roubaut largely eliminated this danger. There was little
incentive to pay for the evacuation of Anse, especially since it
was possible that Badefol's next haunt would be closer and
more dangerous. In resisting the payment of their share of
what was owed to Badefol, the consuls of Montpellier may
have expressed the sentiments of some of their neighbors.
They argued that Lyonnais, as part of *Lingua Gallicana,* was
no concern of Languedoc, and that the earlier extension of the
gabelle excused them from paying the *fouage* of two *gros*
levied for the evacuation of Anse. In 1366 a court decision
upheld this claim and the tax was canceled.[186] Badefol had
finally evacuated Anse the previous September,[187] and the
burden of paying him fell mainly on those most directly
threatened. In its effort to collect money from other districts,
the government employed the curious tactic of convening an
assembly of southern towns at Rodez, as if the deliberations
there might persuade Rouergue to contribute, even though it
was now in English hands. It is highly doubtful that anything
came of this plan.[188]

4. Bertrand du Guesclin and Louis of Anjou

Languedoc remained subject to the taxes adopted as equivalent to the aids, but because of lagging collections and
diverted receipts, not much money could be applied to the
ransom. Charles V's accession seems to have marked a more
strenuous royal effort to meet the obligations of the ransom.
Bernard François, the royal receiver, resumed collection of 12
d./l. on merchandise during the second half of 1364. He was to

[185]*HL* **9**: p. 774; **10**: cols. 1344–1345; Dognon, *Institutions,* p. 610.

[186]*Gr. Chartrier,* no. 191; BN MS. lat. 9175, fol. 96.

[187]Guigue, *Tard-Venus,* pp. 123–125, 129, 131, 336–344. On the ability of the
English to keep Aquitaine free of brigands, see Delachenal, *Charles V* 4: p. 20.

[188]AD Hérault A 5, fols. 286v–288r; Prou, *Relations politiques,* pp. 56–57, and P.J.
59; *HL* **9**: p. 775; **10**: cols. 1343–1344.

levy it on goods leaving the kingdom and in the lands of any barons who were not contributing to the ransom, but he started collecting it on a more general basis and soon aroused complaints. Louis of Anjou ordered him to halt collections in all places that were already contributing to the ransom.[189] The major towns continued to pay, as best they could, their shares of the taxes that replaced the aids,[190] but outdated hearth counts made them burdensome.

The last enumeration of taxable hearths in Languedoc as a whole antedated the Black Death of 1348. For fifteen years after that plague, *fouages* had been assessed "according to the old number of hearths," but recurrent warfare and plague made them seriously outdated. Considerable debate had arisen in 1362 over the amount to be paid as an equivalent tax,[191] and in the wake of these discussions the crown began to proceed with its long-deferred renumbering of hearths. Perhaps the pope, who was greatly concerned about the hearth count in the diocese of Mende, persuaded John II to speed up the new census when the king was in Avignon.[192] In any case, a new enumeration was completed throughout Languedoc in 1364, and the three seneschalsies were found to have 87,770 taxable hearths, a decline of 58 per cent from the earlier total.[193] The royal ransom payments were, of course, fixed by treaty, but subsequent *fouages* for other purposes could now be assessed more realistically.

Taxation continued to be dominated by the problem of brigandage, which seemed to defy solution. The *routiers* who left Anse proceeded to ravage Burgundy, and the crusade to Hungary, on which they were supposed to be employed, foundered in Alsace when imperial troops prevented the expedition from proceeding further. The combined effects of the evacuation of Anse, the Franco-Navarrese peace, and the Breton settlement were potentially explosive: thousands of soldiers were unemployed, and when Philip of Burgundy

---

[189]*HL* 10: col. 1243; *INV AM Toulouse*, p. 537 (AA 45, nos. 56, 57); AD Hérault A 5, fols. 228v–229r; 288r–289r; *Gr. Chartrier*, nos. 1796–1800, 3334.

[190]*Ibid.*, no. 500; *INV AM Pézenas*, nos. 14, 17.

[191]See above, part 1 of this chapter.

[192]Prou, *Relations politiques*, P. J. 23, 40. After considerable correspondence, Gévaudan was assessed 4510 hearths: BN Doat 255, fols. 442, 460r; AD Hérault A 5, fols. 224v–225v, 232–233. For other evidence of new hearth counts in the Beaucaire district, see *ibid.*, fols. 30r–v, 191r–v.

[193]*Petit Thalamus*, p. 365, note *a*.

moved to expel them from his lands, there was danger that a new Grand Company would take form.[194]

In the summer of 1365, the French crown moved to avert disaster by proposing a new expedition to Spain, which was a more attractive target than Hungary in the eyes of most *routier* captains. Charles V saw the advantage of installing Henry of Trastamara on the Castilian throne, and the cooperative pope was ready to proclaim a crusade against the Moors that would require a march across Castilian territory. Leadership of the expedition would be entrusted to one of the most respected captains in France, Bertrand du Guesclin. His troops were scarcely less brutal than those who followed Badefol or Cervole, but the Breton warrior differed from the others in one important respect: he had consistently remained in the service of the Valois monarchy and the pro-French party in Brittany. Having gradually gained the confidence of the king and dauphin, Du Guesclin had won a decisive victory over the Navarrese at the moment of Charles V's accession.[195] Subsequent setbacks have proved that he was no military genius, but he had given France a victorious hero when one was sorely needed, while his temperament and background made him an excellent choice to lead the companies out of France.

In August, three weeks before the evacuation of Anse, Du Guesclin agreed to lead the Spanish expedition, after receiving royal funds to pay a ransom he owed in Brittany. By October, he and Audrehem were at Auxerre, heading south with a growing force of mercenaries; a month later they were near Avignon.[196] Du Guesclin was not able to maintain complete discipline over the troops, but he had the prestige to negotiate agreements with their captains.[197] The pope granted the *routiers* absolution for their past transgressions and

---

[194] Prou, *Relations politiques*, p. 57; *HL* 9: pp. 776–778, and Molinier's note 1, p. 777. See also below, chap. VI, at notes 210–215.

[195] On Du Guesclin's career before 1365, see next chapter and also R. Cazelles, "Du Guesclin avant Cocherel," *Actes du Colloque International de Cocherel 1964:* pp. 35–40, where Bertrand's anti-Evreux tradition is stressed.

[196] L. Labande, "Bertrand du Guesclin et les Etats pontificaux de France," *Mémoires de l'Académie de Vaucluse* 4 (1904): p. 46; Prou, *Relations politiques*, p. 58; Guigue, *Tard-Venus*, pp. 152–153; Lehoux, *Jean de France* 1: p. 189; Molinier, "Audrehem," pp. 170–171; Delachenal, *Charles V* 3: pp. 294–295.

[197] *HL* 9: p. 777, note 1.

handled the main financial arrangements. Details of these are lacking, but the *routiers* may have been promised as much as 200,000 francs, about half being contributed by the pope. Urban V drew upon his own resources and also diverted the clerical tenth to the project. He also obtained sizable sums from the inhabitants of Provence and the Comtat Venaissin, who wished to keep the brigands on the right bank of the Rhone. Money was advanced from the papal treasury, to be repaid by subsequent tax collections.[198] After spending about a month in the seneschalsy of Beaucaire awaiting their money, the *routiers* passed Montpellier and Uzès around the beginning of December and were crossing the Pyrenees by the end of 1365. At both Montpellier and Perpignan, they stopped long enough to extort more money.[199]

Not only did both the pope and Charles V dislike Peter of Castile, but his ouster might bring France a valuable naval ally as well as disposing of the *routiers*. His war with Aragon had left Peter I little time in which to strengthen his position at home against dissident nobles, while his ally, the Prince of Wales, failed to prevent some Anglo-Gascons from joining Du Guesclin.[200] Peter IV of Aragon met Du Guesclin and Trastamara in Barcelona at the beginning of 1366, but despite careful preparations aimed at getting his dangerous allies across his territory quickly,[201] he found it hard to prevent brigandage and had to pay them 20,000 florins in "chivalrous blackmail."[202] Du Guesclin's forces crossed Aragon, ravaged part of Navarre, and entered Castile, where they were quickly victorious. After failing to rally his forces in the Southwest, Peter I fled the kingdom and Henry of Trastamara was proclaimed king.[203]

---

[198] As early as May, 1365, the pope had sent Du Guesclin to discuss the problem of the companies with the Prince of Wales and his advisers: Prou, *Relations politiques*, P.J. 53. On the organizing and financing of the Spanish expedition, see *ibid.*, pp. 58–61, and P.J. 62–53; Labande, "Du Guesclin," pp. 43–44, 52, 54–58; Molinier, "Audrehem," pp. 170–171; *Chron. Jean II et Charles V* 2: pp. 10–12.

[199] *Petit Thalamus*, pp. 369–370; Molinier, "Audrehem," p. 172; *HL* 9: p. 779; Labande, "Du Guesclin," pp. 58–59.

[200] Russell, *English Intervention*, pp. 35–39; Prou, *Relations politiques*, p. 57. On the other hand, the pope complained that some English captains did in fact refuse to participate because they did not wish to displease their own king (*ibid.*, p. 61).

[201] Russell, *English Intervention*, p. 40; *Chron. Jean II et Charles V* 3: P.J. 12–14.

[202] Russell, *English Intervention*, pp. 41–42.

[203] *Ibid.*, pp. 42–46; *Petit Thalamus*, p. 371; Molinier, "Audrehem," p. 173; *Chron.*

The mass exodus of *routiers* from France thus achieved much greater success than the similar project three years earlier. Because of subsequent events in Spain, the relief was to be only temporary, but at least for the moment brigandage in Languedoc abated greatly. Two renowned captains who did not go to Spain, Arnaud de Cervole and Seguin de Badefol, both met death at the hands of assassins in 1366, and their removal from the scene proved to be another blessing to the inhabitants of southern France.[204]

The decline of brigandage was accompanied by a reduced need for special taxation, with the result that there are fewer fiscal documents for 1366 than for any other year of our period. Nevertheless, the payments on earlier financial obligations were lagging badly, particularly the royal ransom which, in theory, should have been paid off by the end of 1366. The towns of the seneschalsy of Beaucaire faced renewed pressure to pay at the annual rate of 70,000 *moutons,* their original promise, instead of the reduced rate of 50,000 *moutons* that had been arranged in the face of opposition from the royal collectors. In view of the added burdens created by the companies, Urban V begged the king not to force payment of the larger sum, and in June, 1366, Charles agreed to accept 40,000 florins from the Beaucaire district to cancel all arrears.[205]

The southern towns remained willing to contribute to projects meeting their own definition of necessity, and in 1365 they had extended the *gabelle* and agreed to levy 40,000 florins for their own defense, even while they resisted paying for the evacuation of Anse. Montpellier's share of this total was 1500 florins payable in three installments,[206] a trifling sum compared with the 10,000 francs that the *routiers* exacted from the town on their way to Spain.[207]

On 22 January, 1366, the duke of Anjou assembled the towns of Languedoc at Nîmes, to deliberate on the *gabelle,*

Jean II et Charles V 2: pp. 16–17; 3: P.J. 16.

[204]*Petit Thalamus,* p. 372; Luce, *Du Guesclin,* p. 243; A. Thomas, "Arnaud de Cervole et le drame de Glaizé," *Annales du Midi* 3 (1891): pp. 255–256.

[205]BN MS. lat. 9175, fol. 87; *HL* 9: p. 796.

[206]See above, note 190; for Montpellier's final payments, *Gr. Chartrier,* Dviii, nos. 83, 86.

[207]Labande, "Du Guesclin," p. 58; *Petit Thalamus,* p. 369. Evidence of Montpellier's serious indebtedness is found in *INV AM Montpellier* 11: p. 21.

which was soon to expire.[208] Perhaps no conclusion was reached, for a new assembly met at Béziers in April and extended the *gabelle* in return for exemption from the *fouage* levied for the evacuation of Anse.[209] One of the assemblies evidently agreed to support a force of two thousand lances to oppose "enemies and rebels" who were committing "horrible disorders."[210] These enemies were *routiers* who had not yet gone to Spain and others who had returned. The excessively quick victory in Castile was to blame for their presence, and Urban V tried to persuade them to go crusading to Cyprus or face excommunication.[211]

Still other taxes were needed to cope with the continuing deterioration of the port facilities at Aigues Mortes, where the silting up of the harbor led Charles V to write his brother in April with instructions to remedy the situation.[212] On 19 June, townsmen of the Beaucaire district convened at Montpellier to discuss the problem. After moving to Aigues Mortes for a first-hand assessment of conditions there, the assembly offered 60,000 l.t. for port facilities, provided that the king contribute another 20,000.[213]

The town of Pézenas claimed to have paid three subsidies in 1366 besides contributions to the royal ransom.[214] One of these must have been that already cited, for the upkeep of 2000 lances.[215] Another was a special local tax to pay for a new count of taxable hearths, which would presumably reduce the share of later *fouages* payable by Pézenas.[216] The third subsidy of 1366 was an assessment of eight *gros tournois* per hearth which exempted the county of Pézenas from "impositions and finances."[217] This could be evidence of a new tax in Langue-

---

[208]*HL* **9:** p. 779; **10:** cols. 1345–1346; AD Hérault A 5, fols. 271v–272v; Dognon, *Institutions,* p. 610.

[209]*Ibid.*

[210]*INV AM Pézenas,* no. 1672.

[211]Prou, *Relations politiques,* p. 62; *Petit Thalamus,* p. 372; *HL* **9:** pp. 781–782 and note 6.

[212]BN MS. lat. 9175, fols. 80r–v.

[213]*HL* **9:** p. 781; BN Coll. Languedoc 86, fols. 62r–v; Dognon, *Institutions,* p. 610.

[214]*INV AM Pézenas,* no. 19.

[215]*Ibid.,* no. 1672.

[216]*Ibid.,* no. 20.

[217]*INV AM Pézenas,* no. 18.

doc for regional defense, since a *fouage* was also levied in Vivarais in 1366 to raise 133 francs.[218]

There was reason enough to be concerned with new defensive measures, because *routiers* returning from Spain defeated French forces at Montauban on 13 August when the seneschals of Carcassone and Toulouse tried to prevent them from re-entering Languedoc.[219] These *routiers* were not numerous, for the majority had remained with Du Guesclin in Castile, but their return was an ominous sign of things to come. Confident that the brigand menace had been removed, Charles V had been granting pardons to those who had been forced to cooperate with them.[220] Yet the menace had not been removed. As early as August, 1366, Charles the Bad was negotiating with Castile,[221] and in 1367 the ousted Peter I made an alliance with Navarre and the Prince of Wales, aimed at recovering his lost throne. Although his allies extracted exorbitant promises he could not fulfill, the alliance achieved its purpose, for on 3 April, 1367, the Black Prince crushed Trastamara's forces at Najera and captured both Audrehem and Du Guesclin. *Routiers* from both armies were soon streaming back into France.[222]

For the first half of 1367, taxation in Languedoc was mainly for the king's ransom, although Montpellier did raise some crossbowmen for the duke of Anjou in March.[223] Pierre Scatisse and his fellow treasurers-general persisted in trying to collect 40,000 francs from the Beaucaire district as arrears owing on the ransom. Montpellier made a series of payments towards the ransom,[224] but also received a new hearth count that left the town assessed at 2300 taxable hearths (worth 10 l. t. or more) and 2200 that were below the minimum taxable value.[225]

---

[218] Le Sourd, *Etats Vivarais*, p. 24.

[219] *Petit Thalamus*, p. 372; Prou, *Relations politiques*, p. 62.

[220] *HL* **10**: cols. 1360–1361, 1363–1373; Chassaing, *Spicilegium Brivatense*, no. 143.

[221] Tucoo-Chala, *Gaston*, p. 394, no. 240.

[222] *Petit Thalamus*, p. 376; Russell, *English Intervention*, pp. 65, 84f; *HL* **9**: p. 787; Molinier, "Audrehem," pp. 178–179; Labande, "Du Guesclin," p. 60.

[223] *Gr. Chartrier*, no. 3593.

[224] *Ibid.*, nos. 501, 507, 569, and Dviii, nos. 72, 73.

[225] *Ibid.*, no. 1725. Evidently the second new hearth count in four years, this one did not enumerate doctors, lawyers, law students, monks, and priests, all of whom are described as being exempt from taxation. The document is therefore not very useful for demographic purposes, but it does suggest the economic decline of Montpellier, which appears to have been assessed at 6000 hearths before the Black Death.

At Toulouse, accounts show that the annual payments for the ransom came to 4107 francs, 4549 francs, and 4500 francs respectively in 1365, 1366, and 1367, about 70 per cent of what the town had been able to pay earlier in the decade.[226] The ransom was to have been fully paid by 1366, and when this year passed with payments sadly in arrears, Charles V took action to rectify the situation. The aids were restored in the Midi during 1367. Since texts mention only the 12 d./l. sales tax and the thirteenth on wine, we may infer that the *gabelle* was not included.[227] The tax on salt had become a regularly renewed regional tax for purposes of defense, and for this reason the government probably did not impose an additional tax on salt for the ransom. It is clear, in any case, that the equivalent taxes adopted in 1361–1362 were not producing enough money. Reimposition of the indirect taxes meant that Languedoc now joined Languedoil in a single customs area and that goods leaving the Midi for foreign countries became subject to the 5 per cent *imposition foraine*. In August, 1368, however, Charles V accepted the argument that it was burdensome on commerce, and agreed to cancel it. Restoration of the aids also made necessary some machinery for dealing with disputes, and historians think that this period marked the beginning of the *Cour des Aides* for Languedoc.[228]

As soon as the companies returned from Spain, the ransom once again began to be eclipsed by the urgencies of local defense. Louis of Anjou, an energetic and effective royal lieutenant, was determined to prevent the brigands from ravaging Languedoc again. He called on local communities to raise troops for their defense and promised royal financial assistance.[229] He convened an assembly at Nîmes in June, 1367, to consider the new menace. The representatives of the towns requested and received a delay in which to respond to Anjou's request for aid. When they failed to give their answer at the appointed time, Louis imposed a hearth tax of 3 *gros*. Given the new figures for taxable hearths which had

---

[226] AM Toulouse CC 1847, pp. 7–9.

[227] *HL* **9:** p. 796; BN Coll. Languedoc 86, fol. 92; *INV AM Toulouse*, pp. 468–469 (AA 36, no. 14); AD Hérault A 6, fols. 60v–61v; *Gr. Chartrier*, nos. 131, 1641, 1802, 2079, 2595, 2596.

[228] *HL* **9:** p. 796; **10:** cols. 1389–1391; BN MS. lat. 9175, fols. 119r–120v.

[229] BN Coll. Languedoc 86, fol. 68.

been established in much of Languedoc, this tax was very small, but Anjou needed whatever money he could get and probably was determined to assert the principle that he could collect in time of necessity without explicit consent if the interested parties had been given a suitable opportunity to raise objections. When a new assembly met at Béziers at the end of the summer, the duration of this *fouage* was reduced from three months to two and made subject to various conditions.[230] The *gabelle* on salt was re-enacted for a year at still another assembly, this one held at Beaucaire in November.[231] The *jugeries* of the Toulouse district tried to evade it and had to pay an extra 4 *gros*.[232]

The *routiers* kept coming. Late in April, 1367, Anjou ordered prompt payment of money which some communities had promised the brigands to keep them from engaging in pillage.[233] By July the papal authorities feared that they soon would cross the Rhone, and ordered the bridges to be closed.[234] By September, a large number of *routiers* were around Montpellier, and the town employed troops from one company to protect workers in the vineyards and to guard several essential roads.[235] By early 1368 Anjou ordered the imprisonment of anyone found guilty of pillaging the land.[236] The government busily went about raising troops and rebuilding fortifications.[237]

It was now that Louis of Anjou developed the ingenious strategy which was to have an important effect on the military and fiscal position of Languedoc in the next few years. Anjou was a most ambitious man, who exploited every opportunity to increase his own wealth and power. When the Franco-Navarrese treaty had assigned the barony of Montpellier to Charles the Bad in 1365, Louis held up the transfer, arguing that Montpellier had once been promised to him. He contin-

---

[230]*INV AM Toulouse*, p. 537 (AA 45, no. 60); Dognon, *Institutions*, p. 610.

[231]*Ibid.*

[232]*HL* 10: cols. 1386-1387; AM Toulouse CC 1847, p. 15.

[233]AD Hérault A 6, fols. 2r-v; AM Toulouse AA 36, no. 25.

[234]Labande, "Du Guesclin," p. 62. In Dauphiné, fear of the companies induced the Estates to grant 30,000 florins by a *fouage* of 9 gros: *Ord.* 5: p. 84.

[235]*Petit Thalamus*, p. 381; Labande, "Du Guesclin," p. 63.

[236]AD Hérault A 6, fols. 8v-9r, 14v-17v.

[237]AM Toulouse CC 1847, p. 27; AM Albi CC 77, no. 3; AD Hérault A 6, fols. 11r, 19r; *HL* 10: cols. 1378-1379.

ued to harass Navarrese officials there.[238] Also in 1365, Anjou took advantage of the emperor's presence in Provence to obtain from Charles IV the latter's rights over the kingdom of Arles. For over a century, the French royal house had encroached on these imperial lands at every opportunity, but Louis seems to have been acting on his own behalf. Whether he actually acquired very meaningful rights has been questioned, but he began to cast covetous eyes on the county of Provence, which belonged to the queen of Naples, of the older Angevin house.[239] Louis also expected, and hoped for, an early renewal of hostilities with England and he was determined to be prepared militarily.[240] Finally, he was bent on excluding the *routiers* from Languedoc, just as they had been kept out of Guyenne.

It was this combination of motives which led the duke of Anjou to develop his new policy. Trusted commanders would assemble the *routiers* and lead them across the Rhone to conquer Provence for Louis. The towns of Languedoc would be asked to pay for the expedition, since it would keep the companies occupied elsewhere. Meanwhile, a seasoned army would be available, just across the Rhone, if it was needed for a campaign against the English in Guyenne.

Provence was particularly vulnerable to attack in 1368, not only because the queen of Naples was far away, but also because she was diverted by a quarrel with Aragon. The pope had returned to Rome, and the strenuous defensive efforts of recent years had lost their momentum. All that was needed was a commander, and, on 17 January, Bertrand du Guesclin left Bordeaux a free man after negotiating his ransom with the victor of Najera.[241] On 7 February, 1368, Du Guesclin and Audrehem were at Montpellier, en route to Nîmes. They

---

[238] Prou, *Relations politiques*, pp. 42, 45–46, and P.J. 45; *Petit Thalamus*, pp. 370–371, 376; *HL* **9**: p. 772; Delachenal, *Charles V* **3**: pp. 12–15; 4: pp. 195, 201, 202, 207. Louis of Anjou had once been granted Montpellier for himself, before being given other lands. Early in 1365 he had run afoul of the pope by stopping Navarrese envoys en route to Avignon and despoiling them of a considerable sum of money. In 1367 he had the seneschal of Beaucaire seize Montpellier for a time.

[239] V. Bourilly, "Du Guesclin et le duc d'Anjou en Provence (1368)," *Revue historique* **152** (1926): p. 162; Prou, *Relations politiques*, p. 69; Molinier, "Audrehem," p. 183.

[240] Delachenal, *Charles V* **3**: pp. 428–429.

[241] *HL* **9**: pp. 790–793; Bourilly, "Du Guesclin," pp. 162–164.

summoned the *routier* chieftains and in a few weeks had accumulated a force of about 2000 men. On 4 March, this army crossed the Rhone and besieged Tarascon.[242]

Approximately four weeks elapsed between Du Guesclin's arrival at Montpellier and the beginning of the siege of Tarascon. During this period the towns of Languedoc were asked to send representatives to an assembly which convened first at Nîmes and then at Beaucaire, directly across the Rhone from Tarascon. The staging of this assembly testifies to the political skill of the duke of Anjou. To be sure, he himself wanted to be near the scene of the coming campaign, and the assembly had to meet in his presence, but it also happened that many hundreds of *routiers* were in the vicinity of Nîmes and Beaucaire, a constant reminder of the menace which threatened if these men-at-arms were not speedily paid to cross the Rhone. The assembly was relatively small, as the deputies of a few large towns seem to have represented each seneschalsy. The meeting agreed to a tax of one franc per hearth, as well as the *gabelle*. The shares to be paid by the three seneschalsies were 40,000 francs for Beaucaire, 42,000 for Toulouse, and 52,000 for Carcassonne. The Toulouse district was allowed to defer payment until the summer.[243] Louis of Anjou also taxed the notaries.[244]

The attack on Provence outraged the pope, for Du Guesclin extorted money from pontifical territory.[245] Urban V asked the king of France and the emperor to exert pressure on Anjou to halt the campaign.[246] Tarascon, meanwhile, proved stubborn, and after a month Du Guesclin made a truce and turned towards Arles, frightening the rest of Provence. He returned to capture Tarascon late in May. The Genoese sea-captain, Ranier Grimaldi, deserted the Provençals and took service under Louis of Anjou as admiral of Languedoc.[247] After

---

[242]*Ibid.*, pp. 164–165; *Petit Thalamus*, p. 382; Prou, *Relations politiques*, p. 69; Labande, "Du Guesclin," p. 65; Delachenal, *Charles V* 3: pp. 459–462.

[243]*HL* 9: pp. 792–793, 798–799, note 5; 10: cols. 1380–1385, 1380–1391; Dognon, *Institutions*, p. 610; BN Coll. Languedoc 86, fols. 83r–86v, 99r–v; AD Hérault A 6, fols. 12v–13v, 17v–18r, 21v–22r; AM Toulouse, CC 1847, p. 15; AM Albi CC 72, nos. 6, 7; *Gr. Chartrier*, nos. 3961–3962; *INV AM Pézenas*, no. 1127.

[244]*HL* 9: p. 798.

[245]Labande, "Du Guesclin," pp. 66–67, 69, 71; Prou, *Relations politiques*, p. 73.

[246]*Ibid.*, P.J. 78.

[247]Bourilly, "Du Guesclin," pp. 165, 170; Labande, "Du Guesclin," pp. 66–67; Prou, *Relations politiques*, p. 72.

taking Tarascon, the *routiers* were without a specific objective. Some pillaged the Venaissin, for which the pope excommunicated Du Guesclin.[248] Others drifted back into Languedoc during the summer.[249] Anjou, in residence at Beaucaire, also had to repel raids by the Provencals.[250] A truce with Naples was finally concluded in November, 1368,[251] and the *routiers* were sent on a new Spanish expedition.

For almost a decade, Languedoc had undergone a continuing ordeal of war, plague, and endless taxation. The peace proclaimed in 1360 had been a mockery, for the Midi had paid heavy taxes to secure a peace which brought no safety. Rising taxes and growing misery were accompanied by the new realization that evident necessity and the common profit bore little relationship to a formal state of war or peace, and that permanent defensive forces might be worth paying for. During these same years, the inhabitants of Languedoil were making a similar discovery.

---

[248]*Ibid.*, p. 72, P.J. 80, 81, 83; Bourilly, "Du Guesclin," pp. 171-177; Labande, "Du Guesclin," pp. 74-75, 79; Michel, "Défense," p. 135.

[249]*Petit Thalamus*, pp. 382-383.

[250]Bourilly, "Du Guesclin," p. 174; E. Labande, "Louis Ier d'Anjou, la Provence, et Marseille," *Le Moyen Age* 54 (1948): p. 298, note 4, and p. 299.

[251]*Ibid.*, p. 301; *Petit Thalamus*, p. 383.

VI. The Aides, Gabelle, and Fouage in Languedoil, 1361–1368

1. Raising the Ransom and Recovering Fortresses

IN LANGUEDOIL, where indirect taxation was traditional, the establishment of the aids in December, 1360, produced only a few scattered requests for alternate forms of payment. On the other hand, the full implementation of the treaty of Brétigny began to encounter difficulties. Hoping to speed things up, the kings had separated from the treaty the mutual renunciations of Edward's claim to the French throne and John's suzerainty over Edward's French lands, and these renunciations were not even completed by the end of 1361.[1] Edward's apathetic attitude towards the renunciations has puzzled French historians who view the treaty as a French defeat and consider the retention of suzerainty in Guyenne a victory of French diplomacy.[2] If, however, Edward valued his claim to the throne above all else, the treaty was not so favorable for him and his delay in making the renunciations becomes more understandable.[3]

Even in taking over the ceded territories, however, Edward III appeared dilatory. Not until the summer of 1361 did he appoint John Chandos his representative in this process, and the actual transfer did not begin until the fall. It was not completed until March of 1362, and even then there remained

---

[1] P. Chaplais, "Some Documents regarding the Fulfillment and Interpretation of the Treaty of Brétigny, 1361–1369," *Camden Miscellany* 19 (1952): p. 6. Le Patourel, "Treaty of Brétigny," p. 37.

[2] Le Patourel, "Edward III and France," p. 178; E. Perroy, "Charles V et le traité de Brétigny," *Le Moyen Age* 29 (1928): pp. 255–281. See citations above, chap. III, note 122.

[3] Le Patourel, "Treaty of Brétigny," p. 38; Chaplais, "Documents," pp. 6–7.

disputes over a few minor places.[4] The new English subjects were left in an anomalous legal position, for until the renunciations were completed, they had no clear overlord to whom to appeal. Perhaps this fact influenced the king's decision to send the Prince of Wales to France as prince of Aquitaine.[5]

The treaty also called for the evacuation of all fortresses by English troops and the withdrawal of these troops from French soil. Here too Edward III was ineffectual, for the evacuation was entrusted to an officer who lacked enough prestige with the *routiers* to compel their obedience.[6] Quick to forget their own deficiencies in this regard, the French denounced the English for the ensuing brigandage, but peripheral wars involving Brittany or Navarre so clouded the issue as to make it difficult to assign responsibility for the bands that began to live off the country.[7]

The English expedition of 1359–1360 had left Champagne and Burgundy infested with fighting men, and these districts could not contribute to the initial ransom payment.[8] James Win, a Welsh adventurer, ravaged Nivernais in the fall of 1360, while another brigand, Garcicot du Chastel, pillaged Charolais. They had to be paid seven and five thousand *écus* respectively to withdraw.[9] Lyon hastened the rebuilding of fortifications, in the face of opposition from those who did not wish to help pay for them.[10] The soldiers stranded in eastern France began to form a dangerous coalition. The "Archpriest," Arnaud de Cervole, left royal service and formed a new company that joined others in pillaging the Rhone valley. Because Cervole and others had been that way before, the brigands of the 1360's were called the "late-comers" (*tard-*

---

[4]BN NAF 7612, fols. 90–99; AN JJ 91, nos. 204–209; *Arch. hist. Poit.* 17: p. 310; Lehoux, *Jean de France* 1: pp. 167, 169, note 5. See also R. Favreau, "Comptes de la sénéchausée de Saintonge, 1360–1362," *Bib. Ec. Chartes* 117 (1959): pp. 73–88; J. Viard, "Documents français remis au gouvernement anglais à la suite du traité de Brétigny," *Bib. Ec. Chartes* 58 (1897): pp. 158–161; P. Shaw, "The Black Prince," *History* 24 (1940): p. 7.

[5]*Ibid.*; Luce, *Du Guesclin*, pp. 393–394; Chaplais, "Documents," pp. 51–52.

[6]*Chron. Jean II et Charles V* 3: P.J. 17; Luce, *Du Guesclin*, pp. 344–345, 353.

[7]See *ibid.*, p. 318; Fowler, *King's Lieutenant*, p. 170; Coville, *Etats Norm.*, p. 100; Martène, *Thesaurus* 2: cols. 893–896.

[8]See above, chap. III. On the companies in Champagne and Brie, see *Chron. Jean II et Charles V* 1: pp. 327–328; AN JJ 89, no. 755.

[9]Cherest, *Archiprêtre*, pp. 87–88, and P.J. 8 *bis*.

[10]Guigue, *Tard-Venus*, pp. 268–270.

venus). For most of them, the first objective late in 1360 was Pont-Saint-Esprit, but many would be present later at Brignais, and the term "Grand Company" is sometimes used to describe them as early as 1360.[11]

In Auvergne, meanwhile, Thomas de la Marche, who had distinguished himself resisting Knolles in 1357,[12] was himself greatly feared by 1361. In January, the nobles of Haut-Auvergne and the inhabitants of Aurillac granted a *fouage* to Thomas if he would evacuate the district.[13] Still another major center of *routier* activity, as we shall see, was Normandy, where English, Breton, and other captains occupied vital fortresses.

It goes without saying that this brigandage, which had so interfered with earlier taxes and had prevented some regions from contributing to the first ransom payment, seriously complicated the task of collecting the aids. As in Languedoc, local initiatives and supplementary taxes would be needed in order to buy back fortresses and expel the *routiers*, and the proceeds of the aids periodically were obstructed or diverted. From the very beginning, the ransom payments were behind schedule. As we have seen, only two-thirds of the down payment had been collected by the time of John II's release, with the remainder due by early February, 1361. Payment of this first installment of 600,000 *écus* seems to have been completed by March, but according to Delachenal nothing more was paid in 1361, and only in September did John II finally acquit the abbot of Saint-Bertin of his responsibilities for supervising the collection of this initial installment.[14] Thus none of the installment for 1361 had been paid by the time it was due on 1 November. The total of one million *écus* owed by this date was not reached even by the time of John II's death in 1364, although it very nearly was.[15] Before he died,

---

[11]*Ibid.*, pp. 44f; Cherest, *Archiprêtre*, pp. 92–97, P.J. 9, 10; Delachenal, *Charles V* 2: p. 315f.

[12]*Ibid.*, p. 37.

[13]Boudet, *Thomas de la Marche*, P.J., nos. 31, 32, 36, 38–40, 46; *INV AM Riom* (CC 2); Lehoux, *Jean de France* 1: 167–168. For more evidence of brigandage in central France in early 1361, see Castro, *Catalogo* 3: no. 632.

[14]D. Haigneré, *Les chartes de Saint-Bertin* (4 v., Saint-Omer, 1886–1899) 2: no. 1710; AD Lot F 37 (copies of documents in AN J 641); Broome, "Ransom," p. xix; Delachenal, *Charles V* 2: 326–328.

[15]*Ibid.*; Mouradian, "Rançon," p. 156; Broome, "Ransom," p. xxiv; Luce, *Du Guesclin*, pp. 366–367.

Pope Innocent VI made a substantial contribution to the ransom, including a levy on the English clergy.[16]

By 1361, the *aides pour la délivrance* were in force. They were collected everywhere, even in the lands of the apanaged princes, and they were farmed under the supervision of *élus* whose normal geographical circumscription was the diocese. They are known to have been in at least twenty-four dioceses in 1361[17] and probably were in all of them. Mouradian has counted 53 different farms for the aids at Paris and 23 in the diocese of Langres. In farming the taxes on many different products separately, the crown was hoping to discourage monopolistic practices, but it appears that seven bourgeois of Paris were able to control 70 per cent of the farmed imposition of 12 d./l. in the capital.[18] These indirect taxes naturally were influenced by economic conditions, and they tended to decline in value, especially in 1362 after the plague.[19] The different commodities that were taxed fluctuated a good deal in their relative importance. The local economy of a place determined whether foodstuffs, cloth, or some other product accounted for the greatest part of the proceeds.[20] Exemptions from contributing to the aids were rare indeed. Only foreign merchants, the Carthusians, and the University of Paris were excused.[21] On the other hand, the receipts were often diverted to other purposes and almost from the outset they began to be shared with princes or towns.[22] Diversion of the receipts, like the problem of brigandage, was common to both parts of the kingdom, but unlike Languedoc, Languedoil had to bear the burden of supporting the households of the king and dauphin. The latter shared the Valois fondness for luxury and he found the domainal revenues of Dauphiné and Normandy insufficient. In 1362 the king allowed Charles to retain half the

---

[16]*Ibid.*, pp. 236, 366–367; Broome, "Ransom," p. xvii.

[17]Mouradian, "Rançon," p. 153.

[18]*Ibid.*, pp. 153–154.

[19]*Ibid.*, pp. 154–155. *Cf. Mandements*, no. 33.

[20]Mouradian, "Rançon," p. 155.

[21]*Ibid.*, p. 156.

[22]BN MS. fr. 25700, nos. 124, 129, 130, 134; 20581, no. 71. Most of the apanaged princes were, of course, loyal to the monarchy, but an exception was Charles the Bad, and he seems to have regularly levied the aids in his *apanage* for his own profit without making any contribution to the ransom of his father-in-law. See E. Izarn, *Le compte des recettes et dépenses du roi de Navarre en France et en Normandie de 1367 à 1370* (Paris, 1885), especially the introduction by G. Prévost.

receipts of the aids in his lands. Delachenal criticized this gift as typical of John's imprudent generosity.[23]

The almost universal collection of the *aids,* or their equivalent, contrasts with the collection of the down payment, to which many parts of France escaped contributing. Among the places where the aids are known to have been collected during the first half of 1361 are the dioceses of Langres and Chartres,[24] and Auvergne, Lyonnais, Beaujolais, Maine, and Vermandois.[25] Some texts dealing with the aids do not make clear the region being taxed,[26] but a good many receipts and pay orders indicate collections in Normandy,[27] notably in the diocese of Rouen.[28] This part of the duchy experienced less trouble with *routiers* than did the district around Caen, but the city of Rouen had to pay not only the aids of 1361 but also a high municipal tax levied to repay 20,000 *moutons* which the count and countess of Namur had advanced for the first ransom payment in 1360.[29] Only a few places in Languedoil seem to have shown an interest in replacing the ransom aids with lump sum payments. The town of Lille arranged to pay 3000 florins annually for six years instead of the indirect taxes, an agreement ratified on 16 June, 1361.[30] A similar transaction was made with Lyon, whose first offer of 4000 florins in lieu of the aids was raised in 1361 to an annual *finance* of 5000 florins.[31] In Artois and Boulonnais the desire to substitute an equivalent tax for the aids proved to be the principal *raison d'être* for the provincial Estates which emerged during the 1360's. The three Estates of the two counties assembled at Hesdin on 16 May and granted 14,000 *écus* to replace both the ransom aid and the clerical tenth for one year. To meet the continuing ransom installments, these Estates had to convene again on 23 July, 1362, to renew their grant. Thereafter they

[23] Delachenal, *Charles V* 2: p. 300, and notes. *Cf.* Mouradian, "Rançon," p. 156.
[24] BN MS. fr. 25700, no. 134; AN KK 10, fols. 1–26.
[25] Perroy, "Fiscalité," p. 39; Le Maire, *St. Quentin* 2: no. 684; *INV AM Montferrand* 1: pp. 313–314 (CC 3); Guigue, *Tard-Venus,* p. 208.
[26] BN MS. fr. 25700, no. 141; 26003, no. 1056; 26004, nos. 1154, 1165–1167, 1196.
[27] BN Clairambault 214, no. 13; BN MS. fr. 26004, nos. 1153, 1161, 1199, 1247–1249; Luce, *Du Guesclin,* P.J. 24.
[28] BN MS fr. 26004, nos. 1162, 1172.
[29] Martène, *Thesaurus* 1: cols. 1434–1436; BN MS. fr. 26004, nos. 1201–1221, 1238, 1251–1253, 1255, 1256, 1258, 1266, 1275.
[30] *Ord.* 3: pp 503–504.
[31] Guigue, *Tard-Venus,* pp. 208–209.

met annually for this purpose and thus in Artois a permanent representative institution resulted directly from the ransom requirements.[32]

The county of Flanders was beyond the reach of royal taxation, even for the ransom, but John II did try to collect from Nevers, another fief of Louis II of Flanders. For two years, Nevers had experienced the dubious blessing of Arnaud de Cervole as royal lieutenant. Now that the count of Tancarville had replaced him, it proved difficult to dislodge Cervole's company from the fortresses they held. Tancarville ultimately arranged a transaction whereby Cervole's evacuation would be completed, for a payment of 16,000 *royaux*. This arrangement included the promise that the royal ransom aids would be levied henceforth in the county of Nevers. Louis of Flanders, however, continued to obstruct collection as much as possible.[33]

In certain parts of Languedoil, the fiscal situation was gravely complicated by the presence of armed men, whether they were properly salaried troops or merely brigands. A well-documented example is lower Normandy, where English and Navarrese captains demanded a price before evacuating certain vital fortresses. From the beginning of 1361, the king's lieutenant in Normandy, Louis d'Harcourt, had the responsibility of recovering these strongholds.[34] Whereas prior to 1360, the Normans had generally levied regional taxes to raise troops, they now raised money to buy back castles from the companies who held them. In time this policy would prove unsatisfactory and would be reversed. Yet it was cheaper than trying to besiege every stronghold, and people understood the point of view of captains who regarded the castles as legitimate spoils of war from which they were entitled to claim a profit. In January, 1361, Louis d'Harcourt convened representatives of the three Estates from the region around the occupied stronghold of Neubourg and offered a tax equal to part of the sum needed to ransom the place. A document of 16

[32] P. Bertin, *Une commune flamande-artésienne: Aire-sur-la-Lys des Origines au XVIe siècle* (Arras, 1947), pp. 250, 398; C. Hirschauer, *Les états d'Artois* (2 v., Paris, 1923) 1: pp. 18-19, 111-112; Guesnon, *Inv. Arras*, pp. 127-128; *INV AD Pas-de-Calais* 2: p. 70 (A 696).

[33] Cherest, *Archiprêtre*, pp. 92-93, and P.J. 11. Tancarville's commission is in AN JJ 89, no. 698.

[34] Coville, *Etats Norm.*, pp. 100, 376-377.

January mentions a "subsidy and imposition" of two *sols* per pound at Caen.[35] This tax was double the sales tax levied for the ransom, and the extra 12 d./l. may be the tax levied for Neubourg.

When the English concluded the treaty of Brétigny, they agreed to evacuate all Norman fortresses, except for the important lordship of Saint-Sauveur, which had been bequeathed to Edward III by the rebellious Godefroy d'Harcourt. Edward now gave this seigneurie to John Chandos, and for another fifteen years it provided the English with a port of entry into Cotentin. Chandos levied substantial sums on the adjacent populations, both French and Navarrese subjects, and the English at Saint-Sauveur remained able to support Charles the Bad when his conflict with the Valois resumed.[36]

Meanwhile, the English charged ransoms for every fortress that they did evacuate. They received 2000 *écus* for Graffart and over 15,000 *royaux* for Barfleur, and turned these places over to the Navarrese in July, 1361.[37] They charged the French 16,000 *écus* for the strongholds of Saint-Vaast and Lingèvres, and to complete this transaction Louis d'Harcourt assembled the Estates of the bailiwick of Caen on 1 February. To raise the money, this assembly established a special sales tax to be levied for three months. It came to 6 d./l., and since it was levied in addition to the aids, the inhabitants of this district had to pay a total sales tax of 7½ per cent during this period. The Estates named as collectors some burghers of Caen who were paid two florins per day from the proceeds.[38] Although the levy should have been completed by early May, it was continued into June and perhaps even later, for the English captain at Saint-Sauveur, John Stoke, was still receiving payments as late as 23 July.[39] A number of documents indicate collection of this special tax between 6 February and mid-

---

[35] BN P.O. 2886, *dossier* 64120, no. 11.

[36] Secousse, *Charles le Mauvais* 1: p. 190; Delisle, *St. Sauveur*, pp. 113, 118–122, and P.J. 96, 97, 99, 100.

[37] *Ibid.*, p. 118.

[38] Saint-Vaast and Lingèvres had been taken by the English in 1357 and an effort to regain them in 1359 had failed (*ibid.*, p. 119). On the taxes for their recovery in 1361, see *ibid.*, p. 120; Coville, *Etats Norm.*, pp. 100–101, 377–379.

[39] BN Clairambault 214, nos. 17–18; Delisle, *St. Sauveur*, P.J. 92–94.

June.[40] One local lord made a "gift" to help recover the two fortresses. It was later repaid by Caen.[41]

In Picardy, Beauvaisis, and Vermandois, a somewhat similar process was going on. After consulting the local notables, a royal councillor agreed to pay 3000 *moutons* for the evacuation of certain strongholds. Some places resisted paying their shares of the money, and the levy had to be suspended while the crown investigated. A new and more representative assembly, which included non-nobles from both towns and countryside, then authorized the necessary tax, but Saint-Quentin still avoided it because the town was not in the immediate area of the fortresses to be recovered.[42] Saint-Quentin already suffered financially because of the reduction of its municipal revenues. Establishment of the aids had meant cancellation of all other sales taxes, apparently including municipal ones, but in February, 1361, Saint-Quentin obtained royal permission to levy a tax on wine for one year and to retain for municipal use one-sixth (2 d./1.) of the sales tax being levied for the ransom.[43] Other towns in different parts of Languedoil were also allowed to retain one-sixth of the aids for the municipal budget.[44] This practice became more widespread in future years, but it would be erroneous to say that the crown made a sweeping grant to all the towns. It appears only that this sharing of the aids was authorized for a year at a time to those towns that requested it.[45]

We have seen that the first ransom payment seems not to have been collected in the vast region of central France, extending from the Loire valley southward to upper Languedoc. Undoubtedly it was brigandage that was largely responsible. Although the aids were now being levied in these lands, they continued to suffer terribly from the *routiers*. When those

---

[40] BN MS. fr. 26004, nos. 1149, 1150, 1159, 1173, 1180, 1181, 1198, 1233; BN Clairambault 214, nos. 21, 23, 24.

[41] Coville, *Etats Norm.*, p. 101, citing BN MS. fr. 26005, no. 1325.

[42] Le Maire, *St. Quentin* 2: no. 683.

[43] *Ibid.*, nos. 684, 686.

[44] BN MS. fr. 20581, nos. 3–5; 20583, no. 44; 25700, no. 144; *INV AM Montferrand* 1: pp. 313–314 (CC 3).

[45] Mouradian, "Rançon," p. 156, conveys the impression that John II authorized all the towns to retain part of the aids. In fact, more towns every year were allowed to keep 2 d./1., but the grants seem to have been for a year at a time, judging from the many renewals.

at Pont-Saint-Esprit threatened Avignon at the beginning of
1361, Innocent VI wrote urgently to the princes of France,
asking them not to let the brigands pass through their
territories.[46] Doubtless they were anxious to comply, but it
was no easy matter to do so. In the westernmost part of central
France, a captain named Robert Markaunt led a contingent of
Gascon and Breton troops who managed to capture the count
of Vendôme and exact a ransom of 40,000 florins for his
release.[47]

In the Massif Central, the brigand problem was most acute
throughout the 1360's. The topography of this region made it
suitable to those who wished to establish haunts from which
to terrorize the adjacent towns and the valley settlements. In
the absence of effective royal military power, the bourgeoisie
of Auvergne had little choice but to accept a steadily spiraling
tax burden in order to resist the *routiers* or buy them off. We
are informed of these taxes by the towns of Auvergne, who
agitated for the cancellation of taxes in 1380 and listed all the
taxes paid by the *pauvre pays d'Auvergne* since 1356.[48] The
region continued to be plagued by Thomas de la Marche, who
still called himself lieutenant of the duke of Berry late in
January, 1361. He refused to evacuate a fortress in the mountains of Auvergne until the local populace levied a tax of 3
francs per hearth to buy him off. From March until September
he was at war with the Estates of Auvergne, who failed to
dislodge him from his castle of Nonette. His men occupied
seventeen fortresses and terrorized the local inhabitants. He
exacted tribute from the towns, and only his early death
brought some measure of relief.[49] To carry on their struggle
against him, the Auvergnats adopted a hearth tax in 1361 —
one florin in the walled towns and one-half florin in the rural
communities.[50]

At the eastern extremity of this troubled belt of lands in
central France lay Burgundy, Nivernais, and Lyonnais. These
districts were threatened by the companies based in Auvergne,

[46] Martène, *Thesaurus* 2: cols. 851–852, 854–855.
[47] *Venette*, p. 107; Luce, *Du Guesclin*, p. 382, note 4.
[48] *INV AM Riom*, resumé of CC 2, gives a summary of the taxes paid.
[49] Boudet, *Thomas de la Marche*, P.J. 46, 47, pts. 1 and 8, 48. Chassaing, *Spicile-gium Brivatense*, no. 130.
[50] *INV Am Riom, CC 2*. This tax is also mentioned in *HL* 10: col. 1248.

as well as by those who remained from the English campaign of early 1360. In January, 1361, the *tard-venus* split into three groups, one threatening Beaujolais; another, Lyonnais; and a third (the largest), Mâcon.[51] The pope was especially anxious to prevent them from joining those who had already descended the Rhone, and the cathedral chapter at Lyon urged its commanders to maintain their defenses.[52]

Both royal finance and military defense in Burgundy were complicated by politics and factions among the nobles. Since 1349, the region had lacked political authority, with the counties of Nevers and Burgundy subject to the absentee rule of the house of Flanders, while ducal Burgundy belonged to young Philip of Rouvres, whose widowed mother had married John II. A kind of loose royal regency existed in the duchy, but various outside influences were injected into Burgundian politics: Charles the Bad's claim to be the young duke's heir; the English invasion of 1359–1360; and recurrent appearances by Arnaud de Cervole, who had married into the Burgundian aristocracy. The Burgundians had promised 200,000 florins to obtain Edward III's withdrawal from the duchy in 1360, but many *routiers* stayed behind.[53] In November, 1361, the Burgundian Estates agreed to royal collection of the aids in the duchy, with the understanding that the crown would pay the rest of their debt to Edward III.[54] Then, on 21 November, Duke Philip died,[55] perhaps of the plague, which had spread northward as far as Artois.[56] The ducal government continued to administer the duchy, but was not certain on whose behalf it was acting, since the succession was disputed.[57] Charles the Bad's claims went back several generations and, legalities aside, it was imperative for John II to prevent him from acquiring a new power base. John ordered the count of Tancarville into Burgundy as his lieutenant, and obtained the services of Arnaud de Cervole, an old enemy of

---

[51] Guigue, *Tard-Venus*, p. 50.

[52] *Ibid.*, pp. 276–277; Marténe, *Thesaurus* 2: cols. 880–881.

[53] Cherest, *Archiprêtre*, pp. 105–112, 125f.

[54] Vuitry, *Régime financier* 2: pp. 175–176.

[55] *Chron. Jean II et Charles V* 1: p. 335.

[56] Haigneré, *St. Bertin* 2: no. 1710. *Venette*, p. 107, mentions the plague at Paris in 1361.

[57] Cherest, *Archiprêtre*, pp. 136–137.

Charles the Bad.[58] On 5 December, John himself left for Burgundy to take possession as duke.[59]

These swift actions effectively secured Burgundy for the Valois and also produced a brief respite from the ravages of the companies.[60] The king soon reached an accord on the succession with the dowager countess of Flanders, and he reaffirmed his promise to pay the 57,000 florins still owed to Edward III by the Burgundians.[61] For the next two years, Burgundy would be directly subject to the king and relatively more accessible to royal taxes, but at the same time the absence of a strong local ruler left the Burgundian lords without discipline. In October, 1361, John II had taken the unusual step of prohibiting private war at a time when the realm was at peace,[62] but this measure did little to restore public order and eliminate the brigandage that drained and disrupted tax receipts.

Brigandage also disrupted the collection of the aids in Normandy. The dauphin had to order that funds earmarked for the royal ransom be used instead to pay Bertrand du Guesclin, who was commanding ducal troops in Cotentin.[63] Du Guesclin was captured in a skirmish on the Breton border late in 1361,[64] but he soon gained his release and was joined by Robert de Fiennes early in 1362 for an attack on the abbey of Saint-Martin-de-Séez. This monastery had been seized and fortified by the English who had been paid to evacuate Saint-Vaast, Lingèvres, Graffart, and Barfleur the year before.[65] The laborious collection of special local subsidies in order to buy back fortresses was thus already beginning to display weaknesses.

---

[58]*Ibid.*, pp. 143–144, 207–208, 395–397; Luce, *Du Guesclin*, p. 408.

[59]*Chron. Jean II et Charles V* 1: p. 335.

[60]Cherest, *Archiprêtre*, p. 157.

[61]U. Plancher, *Histoire générale et particulière de Bourgogne, avec des notes, des dissertations, et les preuves justificatives* (4 v., Dijon, 1739–1781) 2: nos. 306, 307, 309.

[62]R. Cazelles, "La réglementation de la guerre privée de Saint Louis à Charles V et la précarité des ordonnances," *Rev. hist. droit fr. et étr.* 1960: p. 544. The prohibition of private war, never well observed, had hitherto been attempted only in wartime, and the prohibition of 1361 was canceled in December, 1363, at the behest of the Estates General. However short-lived, the action of 1361 offers evidence of the concern being caused by brigandage.

[63]AD Lot F 37; Luce, *Du Guesclin*, P.J. 28.

[64]*Ibid.*, pp. 347–350, 357. By early 1362, Du Guesclin had attained the rank of banneret and was called a royal councillor.

[65]*Ibid.*, pp. 358–359; Coville, *Etats Norm.*, pp. 102–103.

At the same time, however, the Normans found no readily acceptable alternative to ransoming the more strategic castles. Throughout the middle months of 1361, a number of documents from upper Normandy indicate the levy of a "subsidy" recently granted to the duke, and one indicates that the bailiwicks of Caux and Rouen were paying a *fouage* of one-quarter *royal*. Coville suggested that it was to finance the evacuation of Honfleur.[66] In lower Normandy, meanwhile, the residents had barely finished paying for the recovery of Saint-Vaast and Lingèvres when the bailiff of Caen convened a new assembly of the three Estates of the district on 18 July, 1361. It is not certain that they adopted a new subsidy or prolonged the special local sales tax; Coville supposed that their concern was the recovery of Rupierre.[67]

This place was held by James Pipe, an English captain whose troops occupied a number of Norman fortresses in this period.[68] He finally agreed to leave Rupierre in February, 1362, for a ransom of 15,000 *royaux*, but he soon created a new crisis when, on 17 April, he seized the abbey of Cormeilles. From Cormeilles, Pipe could menace both upper and lower Normandy, including the important naval arsenal at Rouen.[69] Du Guesclin and Fiennes, who were besieging La Vignée, interrupted their operations and hastened to Cormeilles when they learned of its capture.[70] The Estates of upper Normandy, convened on 22 May, failed to take decisive action, so the dauphin summoned the Estates of the entire duchy to meet at Rouen on 9 June.[71] This assembly finally agreed to a *fouage* of 5 s. t., to be levied in each of the next three months, and by late August the money for ransoming Cormeilles had been collected. Du Guesclin secured Pipe's withdrawal and left to return to the service of his Breton lord.[72]

---

[66]*Ibid.*, p. 102; Luce, *du Guesclin*, P.J. 23; BN MS. fr. 25701, no. 209; 26004, nos. 1158, 1192, 1267.

[67]Coville, *Etats Norm.*, pp. 102, 379.

[68]Delachenal, *Charles V* 2: p. 313.

[69]Delisle, *St. Sauveur*, p. 123f; Coville, *Etats Norm.*, pp. 103–104. By the time he took Cormeilles, Pipe may have learned of the battle of Brignais and concluded that he could act more boldly.

[70]Luce, *Du Guesclin*, p. 361.

[71]*Ibid.*, P.J. 32; Coville, *Etats Norm.*, pp. 104, 380–381; Delisle, *St. Sauveur*, pp. 126–127.

[72]Luce, *Du Guesclin*, pp. 369–371; BN MS. fr. 26005, nos. 1403, 1427; Delachenal, *Charles V* 2: p. 313; Coville, *Etats Norm.*, pp. 104, 385.

Although granted by the Estates of the whole duchy in order to meet a common threat, the special *fouage* was administered separately in the two parts of Normandy. A letter of 17 June to the viscount of Falaise stated that the tax had been granted by the three Estates and the *plat pays* of the bailiwicks of Rouen, Caux, and Gisors, for reason of *très grant necessité*. A second document, dated four days later, concerned the establishment of treasurers-general to collect it in Caen and Cotentin.[73] For nearly a decade now the division between upper and lower Normandy for fiscal purposes had become established as regular practice. The Valois-Evreux conflict and the proximity of lower Normandy to the English bases in Brittany caused the districts of Caen and Cotentin to face problems not shared by their neighbors to the east. Now the occupation of Cormeilles threatened both parts of the duchy, but when the joint Estates met, it seems that upper and lower Normandy granted the tax separately. In the generation from the 1350's to 1380, the Normans held numerous assemblies, but few involved the entire duchy. Smaller regions convened to deal with local problems, and it seems inaccurate even to speak of the Estates of Normandy.

In upper Normandy, administration of the *fouage* was entrusted to three governors-general.[74] It was probably collected by existing fiscal personnel, since the great bulk of the Norman documents from mid-1361 to late-1362 concern officials charged with collecting the *aides pour la délivrance*. Some documents mention the aids in the bailiwicks of Caen and Cotentin,[75] while many more are not specific as to geographical area.[76] Other texts specify sums collected in the diocese of Rouen,[77] or taxes levied in the town of Rouen to

---

[73]*Ibid.*, pp. 381–383.

[74]*Ibid.*, p. 384.

[75] BN MS. fr. 26005, nos. 1349, 1375, 1410. Another document, BN Clairambault 214, no. 30, mentions the aids in the bailiwicks of Caen and Caux, a most unusual reference since Caen (in lower Normandy) and Caux (in upper Normandy) normally utilized separate fiscal administrations in this period.

[76] BN MS. fr. 25700, no. 146; 26004, nos. 1304–1306; 26005, nos. 1323, 1324, 1326, 1328–1331, 1335, 1340, 1351, 1352, 1356, 1364, 1370, 1385, 1389; BN P.O. 1522, *dossier* 34634, nos. 21, 22; P.O. 2169, *dossier* 48800, nos. 7, 15. P.O. 493, *dossier* 11104, no. 17; Clairambault 73, no. 63. Many of these documents merely refer to Normandy.

[77] BN MS. fr. 26004, nos. 1230, 1237, 1245, 1273, 1279, 1286, 1287, 1292, 1313; 26005, nos. 1394, 1466; BN Clairambault 214, nos. 19, 20.

repay the loan from the count of Namur.[78] Aside from Normandy, the continuing collection of the aids during 1362 can be documented at Tournai, Arras, Pontoise, and the dioceses of Noyon and Langres.[79] In Burgundy, John II levied them as duke rather than as king.[80] Lyon paid 6000 florins, perhaps indicating a second increase in the *finance* paid by that city in lieu of the aids.[81] The aids were also levied in Anjou, Maine, and Touraine,[82] and in Auvergne, where Riom retained one-sixth of the sales tax to help pay its local military expenses.[83]

One of the most trying provisions of the treaty of Brétigny, from the standpoint of the towns, was the requirement that the leading towns of France send hostages to London as guarantors of the ransom.[84] Their maintenance in England had to be paid for by the communities that sent them, but since only the larger towns had to send hostages, the lesser ones in the area were expected to contribute to the costs. Considerable debate and litigation arose over this requirement. *Parlement* had to decide how much the towns of Picardy would contribute to the upkeep of hostages.[85] Chalons-sur-Marne sought and finally obtained royal permission to extend its municipal taxes and receive contributions from neighboring towns. After considerable correspondence, four of these places each were assessed 150 pounds annually to help support the hostages from Chalons.[86] The sizable sum of 1000 francs per year was needed to maintain the hostages from Lyon. This money was appor-

[78] BN MS. fr. 26004, nos. 1236, 1266, 1283, 1303; 26005, nos. 1355, 1357, 1361, 1363, 1368, 1369, 1373, 1377, 1379–1383, 1413, 1416, 1471; J. Tardif, *Monuments historiques* (Paris, 1866), nos. 1388, 1389, 1409.

[79] BN MS. fr. 25700, no. 144; 26005, no 1342; BN NAF 7612, fols. 168r–169r; BN Moreau 235, fol. 62; AN KK 10, fols. 54r–81r; Secousse, introduction to *Ord.* 3: p. xcvii.

[80] Billioud, *Etats Bourgogne*, p. 154.

[81] Guigue, *Tard-Venus*, p. 209.

[82] BN Clairambault 31, nos. 140–142, 144.

[83] AM Riom CC 14, nos. 15, 884, 1312.

[84] The names of the four bourgeois of Paris who had to serve as hostages are given in AN P 2294, p. 107.

[85] See, for instance, Thierry, *Recueil* 1: 615–617; Le Maire, *St. Quentin* 2: no. 693.

[86] *INV Am Chalon-sur-Marne*, pp. 164–165 (CC 5).

tioned among nine communities, apparently without too much acrimony.[87]

We can only speculate as to how the support of hostages may have affected bourgeois opinion in France. Like the *routiers,* they may have served as a constant reminder of war and defeat that the treaty could not erase. The bourgeois hostages themselves were in an unfortunate plight, for the money to support them must rarely have reached them on schedule. According to a chronicler, many of them died in an epidemic that ravaged London late in 1363.[88]

The hostages of noble or princely rank played a far different role, for they were in a position to influence diplomacy. Led by Louis of Anjou and John of Berry, they viewed with impatience the leisurely way in which the kings were executing the treaty. As the two governments exchanged lengthy notes over matters still at issue in 1362,[89] the French court began to fear that the princely hostages might bargain for their freedom with new concessions. The fear was not unfounded; when new French emissaries went to England, Edward demanded a French renunciation of suzerainty without any accompanying renunciation of his own claim.[90] As he may have expected, the talks broke down, and Edward then negotiated a new treaty with the princely hostages, who agreed to surrender more land and money to gain their freedom. John II refused to accept this treaty, but he agreed to submit it to the Estates General. There were no immediate plans for this body to meet, however, and John was about to leave for an extended visit to Avignon.[91]

The ransom payments were falling behind because the French crown's resources, other than the aids, were inadequate. For a generation the royal domain had proven increasingly inadequate as a means of support, and now it was reduced territorially as well as suffering from the effects of

[87] Guigue, *Tard-Venus,* p. 40; G. Ducket, *Original Documents Relating to the Hostages of John, King of France, and the Treaty of Brétigny in 1360* (London, 1890), pp. 13. 14.

[88] *Chron. Valois,* p. 130.

[89] Chaplais, "Documents," pp. 29–38; *Chron. Jean II et Charles V* 3: P.J. 10.

[90] Chaplais, "Documents," pp. 8, 45–48; *Chron. Jean II et Charles V* 3: P.J. 11.

[91] Lehoux, *Jean de France* 1: 170–171; Delachenal, *Charles V* 2: pp. 323–324, 339–342.

plague and brigandage. Dowries, pensions, and other assignments of money diminished domainal receipts still further,[92] and the crown could not exploit most of the overworked fiscal expedients of the preceding generation. *Réformateurs*, especially in Languedoil, were concerned mainly with their original function of correcting errant officials, rather than with bringing in revenue.[93] The crown did obtain a substantial new *finance* from the Jews and briefly resumed the collection of debts owed to Lombards, but the latter effort may have been concerned only with unpaid arrears.[94] In the interest of economy, the government also took steps to improve the customs administration[95] and (in September, 1361) to reduce the salaries of *élus* and others who levied the aids.[96] Finally, on 5 March, 1362, John II announced that the cancellation of taxes other than the aids and *gabelle* had not been intended to include the unpaid arrears of taxes owed since 1355.[97] There is no way of knowing whether John now actually tried to collect the high taxes that the Estates had tried to impose on the nobility during his captivity. The crown had already had to modify the earlier cancellation of other taxes in order to let municipal governments continue certain local levies. Despite economies and expedients, government at all levels was short of funds, and receipts of the aids inevitably were diverted from the ransom.

The lack of adequate royal revenues was most apparent when it came to dealing with brigandage. Since the king was first captured, the government had let individual regions take initiatives of their own to meet local dangers when royal resources were inadequate. Yet it was not to the crown's best interest to let uncontrolled localism continue indefinitely, and it was decided to launch a strenuous royal effort against

[92] Vuitry, *Régime financier* 2: p. 114, note 2; Tardif, *Monuments historiques,* nos. 1395, 1399, 1402, 1407, 1420. One reason for the diversion of ransom money was that some dowries and other assignments had involved revenues in lands which were ceded to England by the treaty of Brétigny.

[93] BN MS. fr 25700, no. 137; 26004, no. 1200; AN JJ 91, no. 398. On the role of *réformateurs* earlier, see Henneman, "Enquêteurs," *passim.*

[94] On the Jews, see *Ord.* 3: pp. 467-471; AN JJ 93, no. 163; BN NAF 7612, fols. 211-216v; 7376, fols. 657-659. On the Lombards, see BN MS. fr. 6739; BN NAF 7612, fol. 349.

[95] AN P 2294, pp. 141-143, 463-467.

[96] *Ibid.,* pp. 203-205; *Ord.* 3: p. 522.

[97] *Ibid.,* p. 553; AN P 2294, pp. 303-304.

brigandage in 1362, the year that the Grand Company was beginning to take shape. As we have seen, the situation was very ominous in early 1362, as *routiers* began to congregate in the region from Auvergne to the Rhone.[98] Late in January, the crown began its initiatives, extending royal safeguard to the metropolitan chapter of Lyon[99] and appointing Tancarville to the vast lieutenantcy of Champagne, Burgundy, Berry, and Lyonnais. John II ordered a special tax in these regions to support troops to fight the brigands, and Lyon provided five hundred florins.[100] Despite these preparations, the *routiers* cornered at Brignais brought a dismal end to the royal effort with their victory of 6 April, 1362. The crown began to avoid pitched battles and emphasize a policy of paying brigands to leave.[101]

After the battle, Lyon hastily took emergency action to secure its defenses, and municipal taxes produced 14,285 florins to finance this effort.[102] Tancarville and Fiennes had to devote strenuous efforts to protect Burgundy from attack, and only the temporary departure of the Grand Company provided a respite.[103] The inhabitants of Auvergne continued to pay heavily to recover castles from brigands,[104] but when Henry of Trastamara's Spanish troops defeated the bastard of Breteuil, many *routiers* agreed to follow him to Spain.[105] As in Languedoc, the tax to support their exodus was a *fouage* of one-half florin.[106] It brought only partial relief, for not only did Seguin de Badefol and other captains remain in Auvergne, but thousands of brigands poured back into the region after Gaston of Foix's victory at Launac in December.[107] The pope reduced by half the assessment of the clerical tenth in badly ravaged dioceses such as Bourges, Clermont, and Lyon.[108]

---

[98] Guigue, *Tard-Venus*, pp. 59–60, and P.J. 35; Boudet, *Thomas de la Marche*, p. 345, and P.J. 51, 52. See also chap. V, part 2.

[99] Guigue, *Tard-Venus*, P.J. 34.

[100] *Ibid.*, p. 57 and P.J. 36; Delachenal, *Charles V* 2: p. 319; Cherest, *Archiprêtre*, pp. 160–161.

[101] *Ibid.*, pp. 184–187; Luce, *Du Guesclin*, pp. 365–366; *Chron. Jean II et Charles V* 1: p. 336; Guigue, *Tard-Venus*, pp. 61–75.

[102] *Ibid.*, pp. 78–82.

[103] See Cherest, *Archiprêtre*, pp. 189, 192–194; Luce, *Du Guesclin*, P.J. 35.

[104] *INV AM Aurillac* 2: pp. 9–12 (EE 2, EE 3).

[105] Cherest, *Archiprêtre*, pp. 189–190; Delachenal, *Charles V* 3: p. 261.

[106] *INV AM Riom*, CC 2.

[107] Lehoux, *Jean de France* 1: pp. 181–189.

[108] Prou, *Relations politiques*, P.J. 12.

When the company of Bertucat d'Albret occupied a fortress near Saint-Flour,[109] the towns of Auvergne took urgent defensive measures. A subsidy in January, 1363, proved inadequate, and the consuls of Riom obtained the duke of Berry's permission to apply to their fortifications four hundred pounds from the receipts of the ransom aids. The royal tax collector refused to execute the order until he received a royal confirmation of it in May.[110] Auvergne paid a *fouage* of one *écu* in 1363, apparently for the purpose of expelling the *routiers* by sending them on a crusade, but its collection at Montferrand was delayed until September, 1364, by a dispute over the number of taxable hearths.[111] The regions bordering on Auvergne were teeming with military activity in 1363: aided by Cervole, the count of Vaudemont waged war in Lorraine and Bar;[112] Navarrese companies took La Charité and menaced the middle Loire valley;[113] the bailiff of Mâcon had to request a special subsidy to deal with *routiers* at Vimy.[114]

In Normandy, the growing military strength of Du Guesclin led to a shift in emphasis, from the ransom of castles to the use of force against brigands. In replacing local action with more centralized royal direction, the royal government had failed in Auvergne, but it met with increasing success in Normandy. The growing strength of royalist forces would culminate in the defeat of the Navarrese in 1364. Coville has attributed to this revival of central authority the decline in the number of Norman assemblies during the decade after 1362.[115]

There may in fact have been assemblies in Normandy that are unknown to us only because direct documentary evidence of them is lacking. On 27 December, 1362, Robert de Warignies was given power to assemble the men of the Caen district and obtain subsidies needed to pay for men-at-arms and crossbowmen.[116] Royal forces were busy fighting *routiers*

---

[109] Boudet, *Thomas de la Marche*, P.J. 33, 1.

[110] AM Riom CC 13, unnumbered parchment, and nos. 48, 797; CC 14, no. 809.

[111] *INV AM Riom*, CC 2; *INV AM Aurillac* 2: p. 8 (EE 7); Lehoux, *Jean de France* 1: p. 187 and note 1. Lehoux cites AM Montferrand, but seems to be wrong on either the date or the document. For more on both crusading plans and new hearth counts, see above, chap. V, part 3.

[112] *Venette*, p. 114; Cherest, *Archiprêtre*, pp. 222–223.

[113] Delachenal, *Charles V* 3: p. 125.

[114] Guigue, *Tard-Venus*, P.J. 53.

[115] Coville, *Etats Norm.*, pp. 110–111.

[116] BN MS. fr. 22468, nos. 14, 23.

sympathetic to Charles the Bad, who threatened Saint-Lô and
Torigny. Du Guesclin, now the dauphin's captain of lower
Normandy, received payments from the receipts of the ransom
aids during the early months of 1363.[117] By July, however, he
was being paid by a receiver-general of "aids ordered for the
matter of the war."[118] There are numerous other indications
of a war subsidy in Normandy, beginning early in July and
continuing well into 1364.[119] Such a tax was said to have been
granted in November, 1363, and it was collected under the
direction of the same receiver who had charge of the ransom
aids.[120] Although there is no direct evidence of assemblies, the
fact that the tax was "granted" suggests that some kind of
meeting was held in November, and another probably met in
May or June to authorize the tax which began to be collected
in July.

Throughout Languedoil, in fact, the year 1363 marked a
shift in emphasis towards military expenditures and taxation.
Accompanying these measures were continuing arrangements
for repair of town fortifications and tax relief for places which
had suffered devastation.[121] The major tax of recent years had
been the royal ransom, which above all was supposed to pay
for peace. Yet this peace had not been attainable, and would
not be without the elimination of hostile companies from
vital fortresses. Local measures had provided for the ransom of
some of these places and the crown had finally attempted to
reassert its military power in order to complete the task. The
defeat at Brignais marked the initial failure of this effort in
Auvergne, but Trastamara's campaign there had partly re-
trieved the situation, and in Normandy the dauphin's commanders were gradually gaining the initiative. These military
efforts were costly and the collection of the ransom lagged ever
further behind. Of course the aids for the ransom continued to
be paid throughout Normandy,[122] and in Languedoil gener-

[117] Luce, *Du Guesclin*, pp. 382–386, and P.J. 29–31.

[118] *Ibid.*, P.J. 43, 46.

[119] BN MS. fr. 20402, nos. 8, 42, 45, 46; 25701, nos. 270, 277, 286, 287, 291, 293–295,
298; 26005, nos. 1479, 1482, 1500, 1505, 1509, 1526, 1531; P.O. 366, *dossier* 7953, nos. 4,
5; 3019, *dossier* 66913, nos. 26, 27.

[120] BN Clairambault 193, no. 55; Mandements, no. 19.

[121] AN K 48, nos. 32, 32 *bis*, 38 *bis*; Guigue, *Tard-Venus*, pp. 184–185, and notes.

[122] BN MS. fr. 20415, p. 15; 25700, no. 150; 26005, nos. 1421, 1512, 1515; Clairambault 214, no. 38.

ally.[123] The inhabitants of Rouen were still paying off their three-year-old debt to the count of Namur.[124] Yet as other priorities began to develop, the king ordered the treasurers-general of these aids to grant whatever remissions and delays in payment they might consider advisable.[125] There was a receiver general at Paris for subsidies,[126] and the overall impression is that in Languedoil, as in Languedoc at the same time, the ransom was being subordinated to the need for more aggressive action against the *routiers*. It was in this context that the king of France summoned the Estates General to meet at Amiens late in November, 1363.

2. The New Fouage for Military Defense

The Estates may have been preceded by preparatory assemblies, for we know that representatives from the town of Amiens met with the king at Reims in October "for the good of the kingdom."[127] It may have been at the request of the towns that John announced the final cancellation of his lengthy effort to collect the debts owed to Italian moneylenders.[128] We cannot know what subjects were discussed with the burghers. It is doubtful that the problem of brigandage was neglected, but the king may have wished to focus the discussion on another matter. One reason for convening the Estates General, and perhaps the most pressing one in royal eyes, was that the Treaty of the Hostages, concluded a year earlier, had become a source of embarrassment which no longer could be ignored.

In the expectation that the treaty would be ratified in France, the princely hostages had been delivered to Calais by the English. Following their arrival, Louis of Anjou broke parole and fled to French territory.[129] This action was repre-

[123] BN MS. fr 26005, nos. 1406, 1409, 1419, 1445, 1465, 1499; P.O. 470, *dossier* 10446, nos. 5; Clairambault 31, no. 143; AN K 48, no. 324.

[124] Tardif, *Monuments historiques,* no. 1419.

[125] Vuitry, *Régime financier* 2: p. 114, note 1; *Ord.* 3: p. 437; AN P 2294, pp. 533–535; Molinier, "Audrehem," P.J. 40.

[126] AN JJ 92, no. 275.

[127] Thierry, *Recueil* 1: p. 622.

[128] The cancellation of the action against debtors (AN JJ 95, no. 29) was dated 15 October, 1363. On this matter, see Henneman, "Italians," p. 41.

[129] Delachenal, *Charles V* 2: pp. 347–348.

hensible in terms of the chivalric principles espoused by the two monarchs. Edward III was outraged and John II felt dishonored. John therefore determined to return to England and take his son's place if the Estates rejected the treaty. There was, in fact, little enthusiasm for the pact in France, and the government probably urged the Estates to reject it, as in 1359. They declined to ratify it, and John II would not be dissuaded from returning to England. On 3 January, 1364, he embarked at Boulogne, never to return to France.[130] This departure was not a disaster like the king's capture in 1356, for the dauphin now was an experienced and respected prince and the crown had regular revenues. Scholars still debate the abilities of John II and the degree to which he actually governed France after 1360. It is possible that he returned to England in hope of negotiating a more favorable treaty, but a chronicler of the time said he was rumored to have gone there merely for diversion.[131]

The major significance of the Estates General at Amiens lay in the area of taxation. The assembly did not raise objections to the *aides pour la délivrance*, thereby tacitly ratifying the taxes imposed three years earlier without consent by an assembly.[132] The major task of the Estates was to come to grips with the problem of brigandage which, according to Luce, was worse than ever. Edward III had allowed Jean Jouel, a captain of *routiers*, to enter Normandy, where he seized the fortress of Rolleboise, near Mantes, and cut off communications between Paris and Rouen. Brigandage around Paris was as bad as in 1358.[133] Added to the earlier seizure of La Charité and the threat posed by Badefol at Brioude, the new menace left no part of Languedoil free of disorder. The time had come to blot out the memory of Brignais and finance military measures that would expand throughout France the successful royal initiatives that had been tried in Normandy.

To meet this challenge, the Estates adopted a second general tax which, like the aids, was to run throughout Languedoil

---

[130]*Ibid.*, pp. 349–350; *Chron. Jean II et Charles V* 1: p. 339; Luce, *Du Guesclin*, p. 409.

[131]*Venette*, p. 116.

[132]Vuitry, *Régime financier* 2: pp. 116–118. *Venette*, pp. 114–115, the only chronicler to mention the assembly, believed that its major purpose was to obtain new taxes for the ransom.

[133]Luce, *Du Guesclin*, pp. 409–410, 417, P.J. 48, 50.

without a stated time limit. It was to be a *fouage* for the defense of the realm, the kingdom's first direct tax levied regularly in peacetime, and the earliest ancestor of apportioned direct taxes called *tailles* that would be the mainstay of the fifteenth-century monarchy.[134] In determining the form of tax, the assembly rejected a new "imposition" (here clearly synonymous with indirect tax), because it might damage trade and adversely affect the receipts of the aids.[135] Instead, the Estates decided to maintain an army of six thousand men by taxing each hearth in Languedoil at the average rate of three francs per year. Payments were to be graduated from one to nine francs according to ability to pay, and would be due thrice yearly, on 30 April, 31 August, and 31 December. Walled towns were expected to pay more than the badly ravaged *plat pays*. Two reputable men from each parish would assess the hearths, and the *élus* in each diocese were placed under the supervision of *généraux élus* in Paris. The *élus* were to consult with local nobles and, with their assistance, raise the troops for which their dioceses were responsible and see to the replacement of men-at-arms who were killed or wounded.[136]

Since the taxes granted by the Estates in 1355–1358 had been resisted in many quarters, we may say that the *fouage* granted in 1363 was the first uniform tax on all Languedoil to be granted by a central assembly for a purpose unrelated to feudal aids and collected without ratification by local bodies. As a direct tax, it extended regular taxation to the large rural population as well as the towns and required wealthy landowners to bear a proportionately greater part of the burden. In effect, a central assembly had finally consented to a tax in time of peace for reasons of evident necessity, and the tax was able to be collected without reference back to local constituents. It was the weakness of the monarchy, rather than its strength, that led to this action, and this very weakness made it inappropriate for the Estates to impose conditions and restrictions on the government. Therefore, an event that might have had important constitutional implications a few years earlier did not, on this occasion, secure any important new rights for

---

[134] Vuitry, *Régime financier* 2: p. 116.
[135] *Ibid.*, pp. 117–118; *Ord.* 3: p. 646; Varin, *Reims* 3: pp. 273–276.
[136] *Ibid.* On the *généraux élus*, cf. Delachenal, *Charles V* 4: p. 237, note 2.

central assemblies. No new assemblies were planned, and no time limit was placed on the *fouage*. No austerities were imposed on the government, and the crown continued to spend money on luxuries.[137] Although John II still paid lip service to the idea of a crusade, the pope was skeptical, and he denied John's request for a loan, while agreeing to a tenth to be used in fighting the companies if John abandoned the one previously granted for the crusade.[138]

As always, the scattered fiscal documents give only an incomplete picture of the collection of the new *fouage*. A book listing towns and parishes in the diocese of Reims during the first five years of the new tax shows that the region was broken down into deaneries for fiscal purposes. Not only did the *élection* still correspond to a diocese in this period, but fiscal organization evidently paralleled the ecclesiastical at a more local level. Some places were unable to meet their assessments in 1364 and had to be given abatements.[139] An extremely hard winter in 1363–1364 surely made new taxes more difficult to collect.[140] The inhabitants of Reims were especially burdened because they were still repaying money borrowed to pay the first ransom installment.[141]

Lands of the apanaged princes were not subject to the new *fouage* but were paying roughly comparable taxes. Burgundy had been taken over in mid-1363 by Duke Philip the Bold, who immediately began levying a 1½-franc *fouage* for military purposes. This duchy, therefore, was not subject to the tax granted at Amiens.[142] In John of Berry's *apanage*, Auvergne paid a 3-florin hearth tax in 1364, slightly less than that in the royal domain.[143] Auvergne was also paying a hearth tax of ½ florin to expel Spanish soldiers, doubtless those of Henry of Trastamara. Since there is no evidence that Auvergne had been obligated to contribute to the 53,000 florins paid to

---

[137] Luce, *Du Guesclin*, p. 419.

[138] See Prou, *Relations politiques*, pp. 35–36; P.J. 24, 25, 29, 36.

[139] Varin, *Reims* 3: pp. 276–281.

[140] *Venette*, p. 116; Luce, *Du Guesclin*, pp. 412–413, and notes. Brigands crossed frozen rivers and attacked castles which normally were protected by water.

[141] Varin, *Reims* 3: pp. 282–286. Reims had to raise 16,000 *royaux* for the first ransom payment.

[142] Vuitry, *Régime financier* 2: p. 176. On the military uses of the subsidies in Burgundy, see BN MS. fr. 26005, no. 1533; Plancher, *Hist. Bourgogne* 3: no. 4.

[143] *INV AM Riom* (CC 2). Three florins equaled 36 *gros*, while three francs equaled 45 *gros*.

Trastamara by Languedoc, this tax may have been for a separate extortion.[144] The ransom aids continued to be collected in Auvergne and diverted to other purposes. Riom continued to receive for local use one-sixth of the aids levied in the town.[145]

The new *fouage* was certainly being collected during 1364 in Picardy, the county of Blois, and the lands of the countess of Flanders (evidently Artois).[146] Documents indicate collection of both the *fouage* and the ransom aids in the duchy of Orléans.[147] The Normans also were paying the ransom aids[148] and a war subsidy in 1364.[149] The latter, in most documents, is clearly identified as the tax granted at Amiens. It is not clear whether the *fouage* supplanted the subsidy granted by the Normans in November, or whether the latter was simply a short-term grant which soon expired and was then succeeded by the *fouage*. In any case, it is clear that the tax granted by the Estates General in December was not encountering the demands for time-consuming local ratification which had hindered grants by central assemblies in the later 1350's. Many other documents refer to the treasurers-general of the "aids of the kingdom." These could refer to either tax, but most probably to the aids for the ransom.[150]

The Normans, of course, had begun to levy special taxes for military purposes well before the *fouage* was granted at Amiens, and the financial effort was beginning to achieve military results during the winter of 1363–1364. The capture of Le Molay was engineered by local initiative on the part of Caen,[151] but in general, royal forces superseded those raised by local efforts. Du Guesclin, now captain-general of royal troops between the Seine and the Loire and in the Orléans

[144] Lehoux, *Jean de France* 1: p. 184, note 6.

[145] AM Riom CC 14, no. 447; *Mandements*, no. 7.

[146] BN Clairambault 29, no. 70; 78, no. 180; 214, no. 41; *Mandements*, nos. 5, 53A, 65.

[147] *Ibid.*, no. 15.

[148] *Ibid.*, nos. 8, 37, 48, 59, 70, 73; BN MS. fr. 20412, nos. 1, 2; 26005, nos. 1537, 1542; 26006, no. 34; BN NAF 20026, no. 95; BN Clairambault 214, no. 42.

[149] BN MS. fr. 26005, no. 1527; 26006, nos. 1, 4, 30, 52, 53, 58, 66; *Mandements*, no. 3.

[150] BN MS. fr. 26006, nos. 22, 23, 35–38, 40, 44, 45, 48, 49, 51, 59, 64, 65. From a text cited below, note 188, it would appear that these refer to the ransom rather than to the *fouage* for defense.

[151] Coville, *Etats Norm.*, pp. 104–105; Luce, *Du Guesclin*, P.J. 52, 62.

apanage, slowly drove back the Navarrese in Normandy.[152] The campaign used up the receipts of taxes designed to finance military operations, and funds from the ransom aids were diverted to pay Du Guesclin and his men,[153] as well as the master of artillery.[154] Fortifications in much of Normandy were maintained by sums deducted from the aids and retained locally.[155]

Indeed, the government continued to turn to the aids whenever money was needed for any purpose. The sum of 10,000 francs was diverted to the queen's household in July, 1364,[156] and the duke of Berry and other royal hostages received payments from the aids to meet their expenses.[157] More money intended for the ransom was diverted to princes and great lords in France.[158] In short, diversions of the ransom continued to escalate in 1364, paralleling the increased emphasis on military operations and continuing the trend of 1363.

On 8 April, 1364, John II died in London.[159] Since Charles V was already in charge of the government and had every reason to maintain the peace with England, the change of reign marked no difference in French policy towards the treaty or the ransom. The dauphin assumed the royal title on 17 April, when news of his father's death reached Paris. John's body arrived on 1 May and was interred at Saint-Denis on the seventh.[160]

The beginning of the new reign coincided with the reopening of formal hostilities with the king of Navarre. Charles the Bad's latest grievance had been John II's seizure of Burgundy at the end of 1361. Since that time he had been plotting revenge and had been subsidizing some of the *routier* chief-

---

[152]Delachenal, *Charles V* 3: pp. 44–45; Coville, *Etats Norm.,* pp. 104–105; S. Luce, "Du Guesclin en Normandie. Le siège et la prise de Valognes," *Rev. quest. hist.* 53 (1893): pp. 375, 397, 400–401.

[153]Delachenal, *Charles V* 3: P.J. V; Luce, *Du Guesclin,* P.J. 59, 60.

[154]BN MS. fr. 20402, no. 49.

[155]*Mandements,* nos. 18, 36, 44, 52, 60, 156.

[156]*Ibid.,* no. 54.

[157]BN MS. fr. 20412, nos. 40, 41; 20413, fol. 16; 25701, no. 307.

[158]*Mandements,* nos. 68, 71; BN MS. fr. 20412, nos. 57, 58; Delachenal, *Charles V* 3: pp. 145–146.

[159]Luce, *Du Guesclin,* p. 428; *Chron. Jean II et Charles V* 1: p. 341.

[160]*Ibid.,* p. 342; Delachenal, *Charles V* 3: pp. 7, 18–21.

tains who were troubling the French monarchy. His brother Philip, count of Longueville, exercised a moderating influence on Charles and actually helped the French fight brigandage in Normandy. In August, 1363, however, Philip of Navarre died, and even before that date Charles had designated a new lieutenant for Normandy—his cousin, Jean de Grailly, captal of Buch, whom the Prince of Wales had recommended as the man best qualified to direct a new war.[161]

Grailly had not yet reached Cherbourg when Du Guesclin entered Mantes late in March and began to besiege the *routiers* at Rolleboise.[162] Once the Franco-Navarrese war broke out, however, Blanche of Navarre's towns were closed to the French, and Du Guesclin had to interrupt his siege and reoccupy Mantes by force, on 8 April. Soon thereafter, he also took Meulan,[163] and by the end of the month Blanche had been forced to make a treaty of neutrality with Charles V, letting royal captains take control of her fortresses, while the crown granted her additional revenues.[164] The captal of Buch now assembled the Navarrese army near Evreux, hoping to make a swift attack which might disrupt the coronation of Charles V.[165] Du Guesclin, supported by several prominent *routier* captains, opposed Grailly's forces, and on 16 May at Cocherel he defeated them decisively and took Grailly prisoner. This victory, followed three days later by the coronation, gave the new reign an auspicious beginning.[166] The Navarrese remained strong in lower Normandy, but their military strength in the vicinity of Paris was destroyed, and Charles the Bad no longer was able to cripple the Valois monarchy.[167] Du

---

[161] Luce, *Du Guesclin*, pp. 408–409, 435; Delachenal, *Charles V* 3: pp. 28–34 (including a summary of Charles's Burgundian claims). For Grailly's periodic services to Charles the Bad, 1361–1364, see also Castro, *Catalogo* 3: nos. 625, 661, 1107; 4: no. 410; 5: no. 203.

[162] Luce, *Du Guesclin*, pp. 418, 421, and P.J. 53.

[163] *Ibid.*, pp. 426–428, 438; *Chron. Jean II et Charles V* 1: pp. 341–342. *Venette*, pp. 117–118. *Ibid.*, p. 130, records the final evacuation of Rolleboise in 1365.

[164] Delachenal, *Charles V* 3: pp. 3–6, and P.J. III.

[165] *Ibid.*, p. 37.

[166] *Ibid.*, p. 54; Luce, *Du Guesclin*, pp. 439–440; Secousse, *Charles le Mauvais* 1: p. 196; *Chron. Jean II et Charles V* 1: p. 345; 2: pp. 1–2; *Venette*, 121–122; Cherest, *Archiprêtre*, pp. 241–253.

[167] Delachenal, *Charles V* 3: pp. 62, 124. For the financing of a major Navarrese war effort in Normandy during the summer of 1364, see Castro, *Catalogo* 5: nos. 413–419, 437–439, 466–469.

Guesclin, now royal chamberlain, was given the county of Longueville as an additional reward.[168]

The triumphant Charles V celebrated his "joyous accession" in the traditional manner, granting pardons and privileges,[169] reappointing existing judicial and fiscal officers,[170] and promising that there would be no more gifts or assignments of royal tax revenues except for alms.[171] He also undertook to require a more efficient administration of the *gabelle* in the hope of attaining greater equity in the tax.[172] His coronation, which was very costly, proved to be a serious burden for the town of Reims since Charles did not contribute anything to help defray the expenses. The king permitted the *échevins* to adopt new local taxes.[173]

Charles V also confirmed his father's earlier decision to grant the duchy of Burgundy to Philip the Bold as an *apanage,* although the right of succession to this duchy was still in dispute. Philip was named royal lieutenant in the four dioceses of Lyon, Langres, Autun, and Chalons.[174] He agreed to permit the levy of all "impositions and subsidies" in Burgundy, but received in return the ransom aids collected in the duchy for the year beginning 1 August, 1364.[175] Philip's lieutenantcy included most of the eastern Loire valley, which was "infested with thieves and robbers,"[176] and by the fall Seguin de Badefol's occupation of Anse would add another peril. In the Franche-Comté, where Philip and Cervole had already waged a campaign against nobles who cooperated with the companies, the English were subsidizing Navarrese partisans.[177]

---

[168] Luce, *Du Guesclin,* p. 430, and P.J. 57; Secousse, *Charles le Mauvais* 1: pp. 192–195; Delachenal, *Charles V* 3: p. 118 (suggesting that the prestige of his new title was useful to Du Guesclin on his Spanish expedition of 1365).

[169] *Ibid.,* pp. 9, 120; Secousse, *Charles le Mauvais* 1: p. 195; BN Moreau 235, fols. 147r–154v; *Ord.* 4: pp. 421–440, 458–460, 482–485. Rouen paid 6000 francs for the renewal of its privileges.

[170] *Ibid.,* pp. 413f, 418f.

[171] AN P 2294, pp. 479–480, 525–528. For a new revocation of alienations of royal domain, see *Ord.* 4: p. 466.

[172] *Mandements,* no. 21.

[173] Varin, *Reims* 3: pp. 286–291. On the coronation, see Delachenal, *Charles V* 3: p. 72f.

[174] Secousse, *Charles le Mauvais* 1: pp. 197–200; Plancher, *Hist. Bourgogne* 2: no. 15.

[175] *Ibid.,* nos. 14, 16; Delachenal, *Charles V* 3: pp. 102–103.

[176] *Venette,* p. 123.

[177] Cherest, *Archiprêtre,* pp. 238f, 266–268.

In August, 1364, the duke of Burgundy levied 2500 pounds
to ransom the fort of La Vesure, which was razed as soon as it
was recovered.[178] At La Charité, the Navarrese could intimidate the inhabitants of a large region, and Louis of Navarre
showed his contempt for the French defenses by marching
from La Charité to Normandy without opposition to replace
Jean de Grailly as Charles the Bad's Norman lieutenant.[179]
Philip of Burgundy organized a siege of La Charité which
ended when the place was ransomed for 25,000 francs in
March, 1365.[180]

In Normandy, Du Guesclin's campaign against the Navarrese aimed at driving them from Cotentin. He took Valognes
and Carentan, but fell short of his main objective, Cherbourg.[181] His lieutenants were active in clearing Normandy of
marauding bands,[182] but the Normans sometimes found Du
Guesclin's men as dangerous as the enemies they were fighting.[183] The badly ravaged suburbs of Caen were excused from
paying the aids for a year,[184] but local taxes to recover
fortresses continued to be levied in parts of Normandy.[185]

Collection of the new *fouage* was well underway by the
second half of 1364,[186] and the town of Pontoise was contributing to it at the annual rate of 3000 florins.[187] Yet many more
documents indicate collection of the ransom aids. These
indirect taxes had a well-established administration and were
probably easier to collect, but the bulk of our documentation

---

[178] Plancher, *Hist. Bourgogne* 3: nos. 19, 20, 24.
[179] Delachenal, *Charles V* 3: pp. 136, 144–145. *Cf.* Castro, *Catalogo* 5: nos. 473, 798,
799. The captal of Buch was mentioned as Navarrese lieutenant in Normandy as late
as 2 November, 1364 (BN MS. fr. 26006, nos. 96, 103). From that date onwards, Louis
of Navarre acted as his brother's lieutenant in France, Normandy, and Burgundy (BN
MS. fr. 26006 nos. 104, 110, 113, 114, 136, 138).
[180] Cherest, *Archiprêtre*, pp. 259–261; Delachenal, *Charles V* 3: p. 143; Garnier,
"Fiennes," p. 44. According to Cherest, *Archiprêtre*, pp. 290–291, and Loray,
"Grandes Compagnies," pp. 279–280, Philip the Bold and Arnaud de Cervole largely
succeeded in restoring order in Burgundy by the end of 1364.
[181] Luce, "Du Guesclin en Normandie," p. 400f.
[182] *Mandements*, no. 95; Delachenal, *Charles V* 3: p. 133.
[183] *Venette*, p. 124.
[184] *Mandements*, no. 137.
[185] Luce, "Du Guesclin en Normandie," p. 402.
[186] *Mandements*, nos. 84, 86; BN Clairambault 159, no. 22; P.O. 1082, *dossier* 24901,
nos. 7, 10, 11; ms. fr. 26006, nos. 79, 89, 94, 95, 106, 108, 118–120, 124, 140, 144, 145.
[187] *Mandements*, nos. 35, 127.

arises from their diversion to military uses.[188] Not surprisingly, perhaps, nearly two years elapsed without a ransom payment to England, after 100,000 *écus* were paid in February, 1364.[189]

3. The Breton Peace and the Companies in Languedoil

Du Guesclin's successful campaign in Normandy lost its momentum towards the end of July, and about the same time a French peace mission failed to bring an end to the generation-long dispute over possession of Brittany.[190] Du Guesclin considered his first allegiance to be his fealty to Charles of Blois, the French candidate for duke of Brittany, and he now resigned his command in Normandy to return to the service of his Breton lord. The crown halted its payments from the aids to Du Guesclin but continued to use the receipts from these taxes to finance the operations of his successor in Normandy, Guillaume du Merle.[191]

The count of Longueville proved unable to save the French party in Brittany, for John of Montfort, the claimant supported by England, triumphed in the battle of Auray on 29 September, 1364. Charles of Blois was killed and Du Guesclin was captured.[192] Charles V had no choice but to negotiate with the victor, and by the treaty of Guérande (12 April, 1365) the latter was recognized as John IV, duke of Brittany. He did not render homage to Charles until the end of 1366.[193]

---

[188] Documents concerning the aids for the ransom are *ibid.*, nos. 47, 66, 87, 88, 91, 92, 100, 101, 109, 116, 122, 125, 135, 136, 141, 144, 159; BN MS. fr. 26006, nos. 81, 105, 117; P.O. 268, *dossier* 5866, no. 4; P.O. 418, *dossier* 9361, nos. 6–8; P.O. 439, *dossier* 9860, nos. 6, 8, 10–12; P.O. 524, *dossier* 11781, no. 2; P.O. 648; *dossier* 15260, nos. 10, 13; P.O. 1684, *dossier* 39199, no. 12; P.O. 1936 *dossier* 44515, nos. 6, 13; Tardif, *Monuments historiques*, no. 1430. Several texts refer simply to the "aids of the kingdom" (BN MS. fr. 26006, nos. 61, 100, 109). The last of these makes it clear that the tax in question is for the ransom.

[189] Broome, "Ransom," pp. ix-x, xiii, 35–38; Ducket, *Original Documents*, p. 62. Edward III intervened personally in the fall of 1364 to stop his subjects from committing brigandage in Normandy (Delisle, *St. Sauveur*, p. 131), possibly because he realized that brigandage was retarding ransom payments.

[190] Delachenal, *Charles V* 3: pp. 155–156, and notes.

[191] BN MS. fr. 26006, no. 62; *Mandements*, no. 117.

[192] *Venette*, pp. 126–127; *Chron. Jean II et Charles V* 2: pp. 5–8.

[193] *Ibid.*, pp. 24–25; Delachenal, *Charles V* 3: pp. 161–169; M. Jones, *Ducal Brittany 1364–1399* (Oxford, 1970), pp. 1, 2, 19, 46.

Victory in Normandy and defeat in Brittany were the main military developments in the eventful first year of Charles V's reign, but most of the kingdom was engulfed in warfare. The *routier* captains, like Badefol in the southeast, increased their boldness now that they could claim to be serving Charles the Bad in a recognized war.[194] The inhabitants of Lyonnais were especially hard-pressed. Among other expenses, they had to maintain hostages in England and pay 1000 florins to Arnoul d'Audrehem, who was raising troops for their defense. Individuals tried to avoid paying taxes, while some of the lesser communities pled inability to contribute. The royal government had to destroy buildings that obstructed urban fortifications or threatened to provide refuge for enemies. By the time Badefol finally left Anse, Lyonnais must have been too badly ravaged to pay substantial taxes to the crown.[195]

Badefol had already inflicted comparable misery on Auvergne, where his occupation of Brioude did not end until the summer of 1364, and other bands of armed men continued to infest this region. Taxes levied to combat brigandage easily fell into arrears at Montferrand, where collectors had great difficulty obtaining everything that was owed. The receipts of the aids at Montferrand in this period amounted to 2225 l. t., and the town government, like so many others in France, was permitted to retain one-sixth of the total.[196] In August, 1364, the towns of Auvergne were threatened by Louis of Navarre on his way to Normandy. In September, assemblies of the regional Estates were twice postponed because of the siege of La Charité. When another assembly was scheduled for 5 October, the consuls of Riom dared not attend because Bertucat d'Albret's company was making the roads too dangerous.[197] The towns continued to negotiate with Seguin de Badefol and other captains, and assemblies in December discussed the taxes that would be needed to pay for the evacuations of

---

[194] Prou, *Relations politiques*, p. 53; Molinier, "Audrehem," p. 168; Castro, *Catalogo* 5: nos. 441, 856. There seems no doubt that Charles the Bad had been financing some of the *routiers*.

[195] Guigue, *Tard-Venus*, pp. 105, 198–200, 209, and P.J. 23, 54; AM Lyon CC 340, for efforts by some to escape taxation. See also below, note 225.

[196] *INV AM Montferrand* 1: p. 395 (CC 167). On the *routiers* in Auvergne, see also Denifle, *Désolation* 2: p. 420.

[197] Lehoux, *Jean de France* 1: p. 186; *INV AM Montferrand* 1: p. 395 (CC 167).

Brioude, Port-du-Château, and Blot.[198] In all, the communities of Auvergne paid taxes totaling three florins per hearth
during 1364.[199] These all were granted by the regional Estates
to cope with local military threats. There is no evidence that
the *fouage* granted at Amiens was collected in the duke of
Berry's *apanage*. The local taxes served the same purpose as
the royal one and substituted for it.

The pattern continued in 1365; assemblies in January
discussed the siege of Blot, and the towns of Auvergne paid to
support three hundred lances employed against the brigands
there. Montferrand was paying the arrears of earlier *fouages*
levied to buy off Trastamara's Spaniards and some "Picards,"
and also a new *fouage* of one florin to purchase the evacuation
of Blot.[200] Riom reported paying only the last of these taxes in
1365, but in fact Auvergne was subject to two new taxes by the
summer. In April the regional Estates granted the duke of
Berry the support for four hundred troops for three months,
while still other assemblies met on 15 May and 6 July to deal
with ways of purchasing the evacuation of Blot.[201] To finance
these endeavors, the Estates established a sales tax of one franc
per *tonneau* on wine[202] and a second hearth tax of one
franc.[203] The double *fouage* of a florin and a franc was
opposed by local nobles until Berry allowed them to retain a
portion of the tax levied in their lands.[204]

Thus in Languedoil, as in the Midi, the companies of
routiers exerted a significant and continuing influence on
taxation. The diversion of the aids to military needs, the
fouage granted at Amiens in 1363, and the continuing fiscal
localism in the most threatened areas such as Auvergne—all
these were outgrowths of the apparently insoluble brigand
problem. In the winter of 1364–1365, the problem was aggravated by two factors: the continuing Franco-Navarrese war

---

[198]*Ibid.*, p. 396.

[199]*INV AM Riom* (CC 2).

[200]*INV AM Montferrand* 1: pp. 397–398. As taxes multiplied, Montferrand sought a
reduction in its taxable hearth assessment from 418 to 300 (*ibid.*, p. 399).

[201]Lehoux, *Jean de France* 1: pp. 181, 189; Rivière, *Institutions* 1: p. 313.

[202]Lehoux, *Jean de France* 1: pp. 189–190, and notes; R. Lacour, *Le gouvernement
de l'apanage de Jean, duc de Berry, 1360–1416* (Paris, 1934), pp. 234, 381.

[203]*Ibid.*, p. 250.

[204]*Ibid.*, pp. 78–81, 320–331. On Berry's use of *réformateurs* to pacify Auvergne, see
ibid., p. 197, and Lehoux, *Jean de France* 1: pp. 190–191.

which gave the *routiers* some legal justification for their actions, and the decisive battle of Auray which promised early unemployment for the troops engaged in the Breton conflict. These factors forced the French crown to develop two main policies during 1365. First, it was desirable to undermine the legal basis for brigandage by making peace with Navarre. Secondly, it was necessary to devise a policy which would draw the unemployed soldiers out of the kingdom.

The Norman campaign of 1364 having fallen short of its objectives, the French could not dictate a victor's peace to Charles the Bad. The desire to end the war quickly also weakened the negotiating position of Charles V, but the king of Navarre was woefully short of funds himself and had suffered military defeat, so his own position was not strong. The pope was available, as always, to act as mediator,[205] and the captured Navarrese commander, Jean de Grailly, was an important figure in the peace talks.[206] In March, 1365, a truce was concluded at Paris and a draft treaty drawn up. It confirmed the French conquests of Mantes, Meulan, and the county of Longueville, but compensated Charles the Bad with the barony of Montpellier. The new possession may have had some value in terms of revenue, but it was isolated geographically and useless politically.[207] Charles received additional revenues in compensation for his Burgundian claims, and certain fortresses and prisoners were exchanged. Supporters of either side were to receive pardons and regain confiscated property.[208] Because it ratified the Burgundian succession and the ouster of the Navarrese from the environs of Paris, the treaty must be counted a French victory, but Navarrese power remained strong in Cotentin under Eustache d'Auberchicourt, a *routier* captain with powerful marriage connections in England.[209]

---

[205] Delachenal, *Charles V* 3: pp. 177–182; Secousse, *Charles le Mauvais* 1: pp. 200–208; Prou, *Relations politiques*, P.J. 32, 41. Louis of Anjou, then en route to Languedoc, was asked by the king to explain the French point of view to the pope.

[206] Secousse, *Charles le Mauvais* 1: pp. 243–246; Delachenal, *Charles V* 4: pp. 185–187.

[207] See chap. V, note 238, for the difficulties which Louis of Anjou created for Charles the Bad in Languedoc.

[208] Secousse, *Charles le Mauvais* 1: pp. 214–232, 239–242; *Mandements*, nos. 219, 219A, 225A; Delachenal, *Charles V* 4: pp. 189, 191; BN MS. fr. 26006, no. 165.

[209] Luce, "Du Guesclin de Normandie," p. 388; Delisle, *St. Sauveur*, pp. 134f; Castro, *Catalogo* 5: nos. 313, 962. See also above, note 167.

The Franco-Navarrese treaty was ratified in Pamplona early in May, not long after the conclusion of peace in Brittany.[210] It was now essential to find employment for the companies of soldiers that had participated in the two wars just concluded. The first project to be considered was the crusade against the Turks in the Balkans. It was to be led by Arnaud de Cervole and was to traverse the empire and the kingdom of Hungary. Urban V may have genuinely hoped to contribute to the serious crusading efforts of certain Christian princes in the Levant,[211] but the emperor seems to have been interested mainly in having the *routiers* intimidate the Alsatian city of Strasbourg.[212] Although those who did join the Archpriest may have helped induce Seguin de Badefol to evacuate Anse,[213] the project did not arouse great enthusiasm among the *routiers*. Cervole's troops entered Alsace, ravaged the region, and then were pushed back into France by the emperor's show of force.[214] Perhaps skeptical of the Balkan crusade, Charles V had already revived the proposal for an Iberian campaign, since a Castilian alliance would be a valuable asset. With the aid of a new clerical tenth, Charles helped Du Guesclin pay the ransom he had incurred when captured at Auray, and by the fall of 1365 the Breton warrior was in Languedoc at the head of the companies.[215]

The end of the Breton and Navarrese wars made 1365 a year of transition in French fiscal and military history. These localized conflicts, both intermittent and both antedating the battle of Poitiers, had created grave difficulties for the monarchy. Their termination simplified the political situation while aggravating the remaining fiscal/military problem— that posed by the *routiers*. It was hoped, of course, that the

---

[210] Secousse, *Charles le Mauvais* 1: pp. 243–246, 254–258; *Chron. Jean II et Charles V* 2: pp. 9-10.

[211] On the emperor's visit to Avignon and the negotiations over this crusading scheme, see Prou, *Relations politiques*, pp. 49–53, and *Petit Thalamus*, p. 368. On the crusading efforts of the 1360's in the Levant, see A. S. Atiya, *The Crusade in the Later Middle Ages* (London, 1938), pp. 319–397.

[212] R. Reuss, "La première invasion des 'Anglais' en Alsace: épisode de l'histoire du quatorzième siècle," *Mélanges . . . Bémont* (Paris, 1913), pp. 281–303.

[213] Prou, *Relations politiques*, p. 56, note 1.

[214] *Ibid.*, p. 56 and P.J. 54; Cherest, *Archiprêtre*, pp. 304–323; *Venette*, p. 131; Delacherral, *Charles V* 3: pp. 246–247.

[215] *Ibid.*, pp. 282–286; Prou, *Relations politiques*, p. 48 and P.J. 58. See above chap. V, at notes 195–199.

Spanish expedition would provide a solution to this last problem.

It appears that little, if any, money was paid to England for the ransom during 1365.[216] Opposition to taxes, while much less evident than a decade earlier, had not disappeared,[217] and part of the aids increasingly had to be diverted to the towns for their own defensive needs.[218] The crown remained closely concerned with urban fortifications and sought to supervise the manner in which municipal taxes for this purpose were used.[219] When royal taxes were diverted to the towns, it was always the ransom aids that were involved. The *fouage* for defense was employed exclusively by the crown. This *fouage* seems to have grown in importance during 1365, judging from the increased number of documents relating to it,[220] but the ransom aids continued to be mentioned more frequently in the texts.[221] It is likely that the hearth tax was more widely collected in 1365 as military disruptions were reduced, but being designed for defense it produced fewer documents than did the ransom aids, which could not be diverted to military purposes without written instructions. Charles V assigned some of the receipts from the aids to his brother John of Berry.[222] In the Evreux possessions, where Louis of Navarre was serving as his brother's lieutenant, the aids continued to be levied by the Navarrese and diverted to their own projects.[223]

Above all, it was warfare which continued to cause diver-

---

[216] Broome, "Ransom," pp. ix-xiii; Ducket, *Original Documents*, p. 62.

[217] One example of resistance is in AN P 2294, p. 577.

[218] *Mandements*, nos. 181-183, 196, 208, 222, 223, 225, 234, 243.

[219] *Ibid.*, no. 271; Le Maire, *St. Quentin* **2:** no. 695.

[220] *Mandements*, nos. 162, 207, 210, 227, 235, 244, 250, 255, 270, 271; BN MS. fr. 26006, nos. 154, 155, 162, 166, 177, 179, 180, 203, 206-209, 215, 244, 247-250; P.O. 358, *dossier* 7761, nos. 8, 20, 21, 32; P.O. 1082, *dossier* 24901, no. 8; P.O. 3019, *dossier* 66913, no. 28; Tardif, *Monuments historiques*, nos. 1425, 1436.

[221] See citatons above, note 218, as well as *Mandements*, nos. 163, 166, 169, 173, 212, 258, 271; BN MS. fr. 20415, nos. 24-26; 26006, nos. 128, 131, 134, 135, 139, 142, 143, 146, 147, 152, 157, 161, 172, 173, 178, 191, 193, 198-201, 217, 220, 221, 227, 228, 235-237, 241, 253, 254, 260; P.O. 1936, *dossier* 44515; nos. 12, 18; P.O. 2777, *dossier* 61826; Clairambault 154, no. 24; Varin, *Reims* **3:** pp. 293-294. In Artois, the Estates annually granted a tax as an equivalent to the aids for the ransom. See *Ord.* 4: pp. 589 and 690 for the grants of 1365 and 1366. Other documents, referring only to the "aids of the kingdom," are in BN MS. fr 26006, nos. 182, 194, 204, 223.

[222] *Mandements*, nos. 163, 169, 174.

[223] BN MS. fr. 26006, nos. 151, 156, 195, 197, 226, 232, 245, 246, 251, 264.

sions of receipts. The ransom aids were employed for urban defenses in Normandy.[224] At Lyon, all receipts had to be used to buy off Seguin de Badefol, and the land was so devastated that tax collections were insufficient and the town had to borrow money.[225] The ransom of fortresses in lower Normandy also required forced loans as well as special taxes in both French and Navarrese lands and the diversion of receipts from the aids.[226] No less than 36,000 francs had to be paid to companies in the Seine and Yonne valleys during the spring of 1365.[227] In 1366 the aids at Saint-Lô had to be diverted to defense,[228] while the proximity of enemy strongholds continued to disrupt tax collection in parts of Normandy. *Routiers* in the area caused collection of the *fouage* to fall behind schedule in the diocese of Lisieux, and Cotentin continued to be a battleground, despite the efforts of Guillaume de Merle, the royal captain.[229]

Overall, however, France probably suffered less from brigandage in 1366 than in any year in the past decade, thanks to Du Guesclin's Spanish campaign and the deaths of Badefol and Cervole.[230] The aids for the ransom were collected in most places, and Charles V managed to make a payment to England, the first since early 1364.[231] Many communities were allowed to retain a fraction of the aids for local needs,[232] but the *fouage* for defense had begun to produce revenue steadily, reducing the need to divert ransom funds.[233] Some money still was diverted to royal princes, however,[234] and Charles the Bad

---

[224]*Mandements*, nos. 192, 264; BN MS. fr. 20398, fol. 25.

[225]Guigue, *Tard-Venus*, pp. 113–114, 210, and P.J. 57. The last of these shows that the chapter of Lyon was still paying in 1367 its share of the money owed for Badefol's evacuation of Anse.

[226]*Mandements*, nos. 236, 237, 266; Coville, *Etats Norm.*, pp. 111–112, 385–386.

[227]Varin, *Reims* 3: p. 295.

[228]BN MS. fr. 26007, nos. 277, 278.

[229]*Mandements*, nos. 287, 308, 309.

[230]Chap. V, note 204; Cherest, *Archiprêtre*, pp. 349f, P.J. 21.

[231]*Mandements*, nos. 338, 356; BN MS. fr. 26007, nos. 274, 279, 288, 294, 300, 326, 349, 360, 393, 426, 430, 473, 475; BN P.O. 2169, *dossier* 48880, no. 9. These are fewer documents than for 1365, suggesting fewer diversions of receipts. Charles V's claim to have paid nearly 400,000 *écus* to England by the end of 1366, supported by Delachenal, is strongly doubted by Broome, "Ransom," pp. ix-x, 35–38, because of evidence that only 100,000 were received in England.

[232]*Mandements*, nos. 274, 283–285, 291, 292, 337, 339.

[233]*Ibid.*, nos. 276, 286, 306, 310; BN MS. fr. 26006, nos. 265–267; 26007, nos. 302, 305, 341.

[234]Lacour, *Gouvernement*, p. 235; *Mandements*, no. 314.

levied the aids in his lands for his own profit wherever he was able to do so.[235] A fragmentary account shows that the aids at Laon yielded an average of 225 l. p. per month during the winter of 1366–1367 and 504 l. p. per month during the summer of 1367, when the volume of trade was normally higher.[236] These indirect taxes were subject to considerable fluctuation, and a recent student has found that they tended to decline in value during the 1360's.[237]

The *gabelle*, established as a 20 per cent *ad valorem* tax on salt, presented continuing administrative problems. Norman merchants who by-passed the salt *grenier* at Caen to avoid the tax were penalized in 1366 by having some of their stock confiscated for sale.[238] A new ordinance of 7 December aimed at curbing corruption and reducing transportation hazards. Henceforth the tax would be assessed by royal officers who would determine a fair price for salt at the warehouses and then add twenty-four francs per *muid* as the tax.[239]

The defending, supplying, and recovering of fortresses continued to affect taxation in Normandy during 1366. A special assessment was required to ransom the castle of Lyvarot, and another special tax was imposed to help defend the critical stronghold of Mantes.[240] Fighting continued in lower Normandy, and the new cathedral at Coutances was ordered to be fortified as a refuge for the inhabitants.[241] In various towns of Languedoil, the need to continue supporting hostages in England caused a continuing financial burden.[242] All these types of expense afflicted the finances of Reims, and Charles V authorized the captain of the town to assemble the inhabitants in order to adopt a new tax to meet municipal expenses without prejudice to the ransom aids and the tax for the war (i.e., the *fouage*).[243]

In Auvergne, the high tax level of 1365 was not reduced in 1366. The inhabitants paid a double hearth tax of two *écus*

---

[235] Izarn, *Comptes des recettes*, introduction, p. liii.
[236] BN MS. fr. 26007, no. 397.
[237] Mouradian, "Rançon," p. 156.
[238] *Mandements*, no. 326.
[239] *Ord. 4*: p. 694. *Cf.* discussion by Vuitry, *Régime financier* 2: pp. 122–123, note 1.
[240] *Mandements*, nos. 344, 358, 362.
[241] Luce, *Du Guesclin*, P.J. 63 *Cf.* Delisle, *St. Sauveur*, pp. 142–143.
[242] *Mandements*, nos. 311, 315; Ducket, *Original Documents*, pp. 54–55.
[243] Varin, *Reims* 3: p. 304.

and one florin, a sales tax amounting to 16 d./l., and two wine taxes—one for the king's ransom and one for the duke of Berry. For 1367, however, the duke replaced the hearth taxes and the sales tax with a single *fouage* of three *écus*. The tax on wine which had been granted to Berry was the subject of considerable negotiation during 1367, with an assembly of towns convening at Clermont in May.[244] On 13 February, meanwhile, the duke had been permitted by Charles V to keep the aids for defense collected in the diocese of Clermont. Since he had already been granted the ransom aids in his *apanage*, the king may have received no money at all from the taxes paid in Auvergne in 1367.[245]

From the standpoint of the royal government, 1367 was in fact a difficult year. Since late 1365, the Spanish expedition had removed the worst of the brigands from the realm, and the taxes levied for defense had served their purpose well enough to permit a resumption of ransom payments to England. In 1367, however, it was becoming difficult to collect the *fouage*. At Reims, collections fell seriously into arrears,[246] and the same must have been true in areas which had suffered militarily. While the taxes were high, only a part of the receipts can have been available to the government in Paris, for much of the money had to be employed locally to pay troops or buy off brigands. When money was available to the crown, it was supposed to be used for the royal ransom, but the maintenance of hostages in England, the expedition to Spain, and the regular costs of government also made demands on tax receipts. The worst problem of 1367, however, was created by the battle of Najera, which sent thousands of *routiers* heading back towards France.[247] Fearing the imminent new incursion, Charles V determined to arrange new financial and defensive measures in consultation with an assembly of the Estates.

The meetings which followed were not, strictly speaking, Estates General representing all of Languedoil, but they were large enough to belong to the tradition of central, rather than

---

[244]*INV AM Montferrand* 1: p. 399 (CC 168).

[245]*Mandements*, no. 376. This is the first evidence of *royal* taxes for defense in the duke of Berry's *apanage* in the 1360's. The other taxes, being granted by the regional Estates for local defensive needs, were, in effect ducal taxes from the outset.

[246]Varin, *Reims* 3: pp. 282–285, note.

[247]On this French defeat in Spain early in April, see above, chap. V, at notes 221–222; also *Chron. Jean II et Charles V* 2: pp. 35–37; Guigue, *Tard-Venus*, p. 168.

provincial, assemblies. The first one met at Compiègne in June of 1367. This assembly appears to have been devoted mainly to an exchange of views and a discussion of people's grievances. Complaints evidently revolved around three main issues—the mounting debts and financial difficulties of town governments, impoverishment of the *plat pays*, and general objections to the *gabelle*. These at least were the questions with which the king attempted to deal. He allowed all walled towns to keep for their own expenses (mostly fortification maintenance) one-fourth of the *fouage* for defense and one-fourth of all unpaid arrears.[248] This concession was in addition to the increasingly general authorization for towns to retain a portion of the ransom aids.[249] The inhabitants of the countryside, for their part, were allowed to keep one-half the current *fouage* and one-half the unpaid arrears. As an economy measure, restrictions were placed upon the salaries paid to the unpopular sergeants who served the *élus*. As for the *gabelle*, this matter was deferred to a new assembly scheduled to meet at Chartres on 1 July, 1367.[250]

Since it is not clear who attended the Compiègne assembly, we cannot know whether the meeting at Chartres represented the same regions. Since, however, objections to the *gabelle* expressed at the first assembly were to be dealt with at the second, it seems probable that most of the districts represented at Compiègne were again represented at Chartres. It appears that Normandy, Picardy, and much of the Ile-de-France were not represented, so again we are dealing with "non-general" Estates. The meeting did contain a certain number of barons and prelates, as well as representatives from the towns of Champagne, Burgundy, Berry, Auvergne, Bourbonnais, and Nivernais. All these lands had suffered badly from brigandage and were vulnerable to the companies returning from Spain. Except for Champagne, all were *apanages* rather than part of the royal domain. The king had explained to the preliminary gathering at Compiègne that the brigand problem made it necessary to retain the *fouage*,[251] and he may have been

---

[248] Varin, *Reims* **3**: pp. 318–321; Vuitry, *Régime financier* **2**: pp. 119–120.

[249] Varin, *Reims* **3** p. 317; AM Lyon CC 368, no. 5; Tardif, *Monuments historiques*, no. 1453; *Mandements*, nos. 370, 388, 415, 417, 424; BN MS. fr. 26007, no. 355.

[250] Varin, *Reims* **3**: pp. 318–321.

[251] Coville, *Etats Norm.*, p. 107; Delachenal, *Charles V* **3**: p. 443; Picot, *Etats* **1**: p. 200.

dissatisfied with the way in which defenses had been organized and tax receipts utilized in the *apanages*. Perhaps also, he had deliberately deferred action on the *gabelle* in order to have a stronger bargaining position at Chartres; yet his greatest bargaining point was, as always, provided by the *routiers*, for it was now nearly three months since the battle of Najera. In any case, it took several weeks to work out the needed agreements on taxes and military measures. During this period, the assembly may have recessed in order to consult with local constituents or gain broader representation. Ultimately, the Estates were reassembled at Sens.

Finally, in two ordinances of 19 and 20 July, 1367, the government announced the results of the consultations. They indicate that in circumstances of evident necessity people were prepared to accept a considerable degree of royal intervention. Charles V sought to modernize and improve the French military posture and organize more effectively the defense of exposed rural areas. Fortresses were to be made fully defensible or else torn down. Structures interfering with fortifications or providing potential shelters for brigands were to be demolished. People were encouraged to practice archery.[252] Some of these measures had been attempted on a more modest scale in the past, and they sometimes involved a more substantial intrusion into property rights than taxation itself.[253]

The fiscal measures in the July ordinances reaffirmed the earlier promises made at Compiègne and also declared that the price of salt paid by consumers, as well as the royal tax on salt, would be reduced by half. The king also agreed to have *enquêteurs* look into the conduct of royal fiscal officers. Outside of the reduction in the *gabelle*, the aids originally ordered for the royal ransom were left intact, although their primary purpose now was to pay for defense. Small retail transactions of less than five *sols* were made exempt from the sales tax. The *fouage* granted for defense in 1363 also was renewed, with strict prohibition against its diversion to any non-military purposes. In return, all unpaid arrears on previous taxes were officially canceled. The list of royal taxes

---

[252]*Ibid.*, p. 201. The ordinances in question are in *Ord.* 5: pp. 14f, 19f. with the first of these being largely devoted to the defensive measures.

[253]See Timbal, *Guerre*, pp. 107f, 184f, and (for some of the legal problems arising from the struggle with the companies) 468–495.

preserved at Riom indicates a *fouage* of 2 francs and 4 francs paid in 1368, with the higher rate doubtless applying in the towns and the lower rate in the *plat pays*.[254]

The towns of Auvergne had to hold several assemblies after the Estates at Sens, not only for local defensive concerns but also, apparently, to seek reduction in the tax being paid to John of Berry.[255] The resolution of these matters seems to have delayed collection of the royal *fouage* until the beginning of 1368. The town of Reims continued to pay the hearth tax by means of an annual *finance* or equivalent of 4000 francs.[256] A few pay orders indicate disbursal of *fouage* receipts in Languedoil during 1367,[257] but there is very little documentation for the ransom aids, perhaps because it was less necessary to divert them, to other (i.e., military) purposes.[258] The ransom, of course, was to have been paid in full by the end of 1366, and it is possible that there may have been some uncertainty as to whether to continue to collect them.

Although we have few documents for 1367, what we know of the assemblies of that summer suggests that the government was making a strenuous effort to deal with the reviving *routier* menace and to ease the burden on poorer taxpayers, especially those in the countryside. The effort to be prepared against brigandage came not a moment too soon, for the *routiers* had entered Bourbonnais and Nivernais by late September.[259] In October the pope granted a new clerical tenth to Charles V for the defense of the realm.[260] It is said that those returning from Spain numbered 4000 combattants and five times that number of "pillagers."[261] Languedoc, on this

---

[254]*Ord.* 5: pp. 14f, 19f. *Cf.* the discussion of these texts by Picot, *Etats* 1: pp. 201–202; Vuitry, *Régime financier* 2: pp. 120–123. Arrears since the imposition of the aids were not cancelled, and royal officers still undertook to collect them (*Mandements*, no. 393). See also *INV AM Riom* (CC2).

[255]*INV AM Montferrand* 1: pp. 400–401 (CC 168).

[256]Varin, *Reims* 3: p. 303f.

[257]*Mandements*, nos. 379, 391, 397, 399, 402, 410, 411; BN MS. fr. 26007, nos. 348, 399, 436.

[258]References to the aids are found in *Mandements*, no. 384, and the documents cited above, note 249. Artois again renewed its annual equivalent tax in 1367 (*Ord.* 5: p. 82).

[259]Delachenal, *Charles V* 3: pp. 441–442.

[260]Prou, *Relations politiques*, P.J. 75.

[261]E. Fréville, "Des Grandes Compagnies au quatorzième siècle," *Bib. Ec. Chartes* 3 (1842–1843): p. 271f.

occasion, was better prepared than usual, and many of the *routiers* were also forced out of Aquitaine and into Limousin, whence they entered central France.[262] These troops were mostly English and Gascon, and their return to French territory was resented in Paris as a violation of the promises of the treaty of Brétigny. The returning brigands poured into Champagne and Gâtinais, which they terrorized until nearly the middle of 1368, demanding the enormous sum of 1.4 million francs as a bribe to depart. Unwilling to consider such a proposition, the king sent the two aging marshals, Audrehem and Boucicaut, to help protect Burgundy.[263] As quickly as the threat materialized, it began to dissipate somewhat, for the *routiers* lacked the cohesiveness of an organized, disciplined army. The Gascons turned away to the South, while those described as "English" moved northwestward, avoiding Paris. They ravaged Anjou and then entered Normandy, taking Vire.[264] The royal commander in lower Normandy, Guillaume du Merle, arranged to pay 2200 francs for the evacuation of this place, and the king ratified the agreement in September.[265]

Charles V, meanwhile, took action to upgrade the defensive capabilities of the kingdom. Two younger men, Louis de Sancerre and "Mouton" de Blainville, replaced the old marshals.[266] At the end of September, Charles ordered that all fortresses and walled towns be well stocked with provisions and able to withstand a siege at any time.[267] By this time, however, the issue no longer was brigandage alone, for political events in Gascony had made the renewal of the Hundred Years' War all but certain.

---

[262] Delachenal, *Charles V* 3: p. 441.
[263] *Ibid.*, pp 444–447; Fréville, "Grandes Compagnies," pp. 272–273.
[264] *Ibid.*, pp. 274f; Delachenal, *Charles V* 3: pp. 449–450.
[265] Fréville, "Grandes Compagnies," pp. 276–277; *Mandements*, no. 465.
[266] Delachenal, *Charles V* 3: p. 448.
[267] *Mandements*, no. 469.

VII. Financing the Victories of Charles V

1. *The Gascon Appeals*

WE have seen that the main territorial cessions required by the treaty of Brétigny had been made between the fall of 1361 and the spring of 1362. John Chandos received the lands on behalf of Edward III, who soon named his son Prince of Aquitaine.[1]

The Black Prince, to his great credit, proved able to keep his vast Aquitainian territory largely free of brigandage during the next five years, a period when the *routiers* were sorely troubling the rest of France. In performing this basic function of defense and protection, Edward succeeded where the king of France failed. He also took care to respect the privileges of the towns. As a result, the communities of Rouergue, Quercy, and Périgord, which had been transferred to English rule, were able to overcome their initial unhappiness and accept the treaty of Brétigny. It was difficult with the nobles, however.[2]

Because their feudal tradition provided for changes in suzerain and their principal interests had usually been selfish or at least narrowly local, they might have been expected to acquiesce more readily than the towns in the new territorial arrangements. In fact, however, they soon became discontented, for largely economic reasons. Peace meant unemployment, at a time when economic and demographic factors were placing serious strains on seigneurial revenues. In this situation one privilege above all was vital to them, the exemption of their subjects from ducal taxation.[3] Although he did not tax

---

[1] Delachenal, *Charles V* 4: p. 3.

[2] *HL* 9: pp. 796–797, and Molinier's comments 797–798, note 1; Breuils, "Jean d'Armagnac," p. 75.

[3] If unable to secure the exemption of their subjects, the nobles desired at least to collect the taxes themselves and, presumably, retain a portion of the receipts for themselves. See Shaw, "Black Prince," p. 8.

Guyenne heavily, the Black Prince was not prepared (and indeed probably could not afford) to acquiesce in this exemption of seigneurial subjects. The lords most deeply concerned about this financial question were those who formed the coalition which had been so disastrously defeated at Launac in 1362. These lords had to pay large ransoms to the count of Foix. Hardest hit was John I, count of Armagnac and Rodez, now an English vassal after years of service as French lieutenant in Languedoc. John of Armagnac had to pay 300,000 florins to Gaston Phoebus.[4]

It was Armagnac's financial straits that first brought him into conflict with the Prince of Wales. In 1364, when the Estates of Guyenne granted Edward a *fouage*, Armagnac resisted efforts to levy it on his subjects.[5] The seeds were planted for a rupture between the prince and his principal subjects. At the same time, other factors tended to keep Armagnac loyal to his English suzerain for the time being. Charles V did not share the strong sympathy for the count that the other Valois princes displayed. If anything, he favored Gaston of Foix, although he preferred to maintain an even balance of power between the greater Gascon lords.[6] The Prince of Wales, on the other hand, favored Armagnac to the extent of lending him the money needed to pay his ransom.[7] In 1367 he also offered potentially lucrative employment to the Gascon lords by enlisting them for the Spanish expedition to fight against Du Guesclin and Henry of Trastamara in Castile.[8]

This expedition, which culminated in the battle of Najera, was, on the face of it, a triumph for English policy, but this triumph proved only temporary and the campaign had very unfortunate consequences for the Black Prince and his régime in Aquitaine. Some of his principal advisers had opposed the expedition, and their misgivings proved to be justified, for both Edward's health and his finances were ruined. The prince found it difficult to control the unpaid *routiers* who returned

[4] Delachenal, *Charles V* 4: pp. 64–66, and above, chap. V. Breuils, "Jean d'Armagnac," pp. 76–77, described Armagnac's efforts to tax his territories to raise the money.
[5] Delachenal, *Charles V* 4: pp. 66–67.
[6] *Ibid.*, p. 65.
[7] Breuils, "Jean d'Armagnac," pp. 74–75, 85.
[8] Delachenal, *Charles V* 4: p. 66.

with him in August of 1367.[9] In addition, of course, the Gascon aristocracy, like the *routiers,* found itself too quickly deprived of opportunities for lucrative employment and booty.

Faced with financial difficulties, the Black Prince had to resort to taxation, and to this end he convened the Estates of his principality at Angoulême on 18 January, 1368. The assembly granted a *fouage* of 10 s. per hearth, to be collected for five years without a new assembly.[10] This tax encountered opposition, especially from nobles who resented having it levied on their subjects. Armagnac and other seigneurs began to realize certain important practical distinctions between French and English rule. Before 1361, their immediate feudal superior had been an absentee king of France represented by a lieutenant or an absentee king of England represented by a seneschal, depending on where their fiefs were located. In either case contentious matters could be appealed to the distant but still fairly accessible *parlement* in Paris. Now, however, the immediate lord was a vigorous prince residing in Bordeaux, and it was not at all clear whether, and to whom, his actions could be appealed. The mutual renunciations of English claims and French sovereignty, provided for in the treaty of Brétigny, had not taken place, but pending execution of this clause, the French court was refraining from exercising its old appellate jurisdiction. Did Armagnac and his fellow malcontents therefore have the right to appeal to Edward III, whose sovereignty over Guyenne had not yet been established?[11] Presuming that they did, they appealed the Gascon *fouage* to England.

The circumstances surrounding this appeal are still debated. It appears that an important factor was the lack of goodwill and understanding between London and Bordeaux. To justify his subsequent actions, Armagnac claimed later that his appeal to London had been subject to long delays and treated with indifference. Friction within the English government may explain this indifference, but the friction may have

---

[9]*Ibid.* **3:** p. 441; **4:** pp. 5, 17; Breuils, "Jean d'Armagnac," p. 79; Shaw, "Black Prince," p. 9; *HL* **9:** pp. 788–789, note 4.

[10]Delachenal, *Charles V* 4 pp. 55–59; Breuils, "Jean d'Armagnac," p. 81; *Chron. Jean II et Charles V* **2:** p. 46, note 1.

[11]Delachenal, *Charles V* **4:** pp. 83–84.

already persuaded the appellant lords to address themselves to Paris. Whether the appeal to London was sincere, or whether it was merely contrived for the sake of form, it seems incontestable that one of the most crucial politico-judicial questions of the fourteenth century was badly mishandled by the Plantagenets. Perroy maintains that Edward III wanted to conciliate the Gascons while the Black Prince took the obstinate position.[12]

Throughout the 1360's, the French government had maintained an officially correct position while trying to take advantage of whatever frictions arose in Aquitaine. Since French interests in Languedoc were seriously threatened by the Armagnac-Foix war in 1362, John II had offered his good services to the conflicting seigneurs. The continuation of this policy naturally reinforced the old tradition of looking to Paris for justice.[13] At the same time, anti-English sentiments were fairly well ingrained among the people of Quercy and Agenais after a generation of war. Although some of the benefits of English rule had reconciled them to the treaty of Brétigny, it appears that the Prince of Wales had not pursued a concerted policy of binding the newly acquired territories to his cause.[14]

The Gascon revolt which now developed was fundamentally feudal, however.[15] The principal lords may have retained some lingering fidelity to their former suzerain, but their main concern was financial, since most of them had been impoverished by their defeat at the hands of the count of Foix.[16] Perhaps the most acquisitive of the Gascon seigneurs was Arnaud Amanieu, lord of Albret, whose ties to the English were stronger and of much greater antiquity than Armagnac's. Albret began negotiating with the French early in 1368, and on 4 May he married the queen's sister. Several weeks later, he became the vassal of Charles V and received a royal pension of 10,000 pounds. While not relinquishing his homage to the Plantagenets, Albret nevertheless complained about the con-

[12] E. Perroy, "Edouard III d'Angleterre et les seigneurs gascons en 1368," *Annales du Midi* 51 (1948): pp. 93, 95; E. Perroy, "Franco-English Relations 1350–1400," *History* 21 (1936–1937): pp. 148–154.

[13] Delachenal, *Charles V* 4: pp. 50–51.

[14] Shaw, "Black Prince," pp. 7–8.

[15] Breuils, "Jean d'Armagnac," p. 82.

[16] Tucoo-Chala, *Gaston*, p. 105.

duct of the Prince of Wales, and these actions were certainly not a secret.[17]

Meanwhile, the count of Armagnac turned to Paris, asking Charles V to consider his appeal against the *fouage* demanded by the Black Prince. The failure to complete the mutual renunciations agreed to at Brétigny gave Charles a legal basis for accepting the appeal, but to do so would involve a citation of the Black Prince before the royal court, and this action could only bring war. Late in June, thirty-six princes, prelates, and senior royal officials convened at Paris in a great council to discuss the matter. Somewhat hesitantly, they took the fateful decision. In an agreement containing thirteen articles, the royal government said it would accept the appeals of John of Armagnac, Arnaud Amanieu of Albret, and Archambaud, count of Périgord, in their names only. The appellants would be excused from extraordinary taxes for a decade and would be furnished 200,000 francs annually from the aids in Languedoc. Supplied with such funds, they would reciprocate by giving military service to Charles V anywhere in France south of the Loire. The king promised never again to relinquish suzerainty over their lands.[18]

The next five months were marked by little significant change in Anglo-French relations, but the French government busily encouraged more people to join in the appeals. If the great majority of towns and seigneurs in Gascony could be induced to oppose the *fouage* and appeal to Paris, France could claim broad support in the coming war and the Prince of Wales would have badly depleted resources in money and men. In the early summer of 1368, a regional council of the clergy from the three provinces of Auch, Toulouse, and Narbonne gave considerable support to the appeals, and the towns began to give their adherence as the year wore on.[19] On 8 September the lord of Albret formally submitted his appeal to Paris.[20] The town of Rodez supported the appeal on 17

[17]G. Loirette, "Arnaud Amanieu, sire d'Albret, et l'appel des seigneurs gascons en 1368," *Mélanges . . . Bémont* (Paris, 1913), pp. 320-325; Perroy, "Edouard et les seigneurs," p. 93; Delachenal, *Charles V* 4: pp. 83-84; Breuils, "Jean d'Armagnac," pp. 86-87.

[18]*Ibid.*; Delachenal, *Charles V* 4: pp. 85-90, and notes; *Chron. Jean II et Charles V* 2: pp. 45-47, and notes; 3: pp. 138-139 (P.J. 17).

[19]Breuils, "Jean d'Armagnac," p. 84.

[20]*Ibid.*, p. 87; Loirette, "Arnaud Amanieu," pp. 326, 331-333; BN Doat 196, fols. 287r-290v; Delachenal, *Charles V* 4: p. 95; *Chron. Jean II et Charles V* 2: p. 46, note 1.

September and other communities of Rouergue and Quercy soon followed suit.[21] Later in September, John of Armagnac paid back the remainder of what he had borrowed from the Black Prince for his ransom in 1363. Having discharged this obligation, he was ready for a formal break with Edward.[22]

Events began to move rapidly in mid-November, 1368. Charles V summoned the Prince of Wales to appear in the *parlement* at Paris on 2 May, 1369, instructed the seneschal of Toulouse to have the summons delivered, and ordered the three southern seneschals to take the appellant lords under French protection should Edward try to retaliate against them.[23] Soon afterwards, Charles assumed certain debts of the appellant lords and authorized the annual pensions promised in June, to be taken from the receipts of the aids in Languedoc.[24] Evidently these pensions were to begin on 15 January, 1369.[25]

On 3 December, 1368, the French king issued letters to the towns of Guyenne, explaining his acceptance of the appeals and justifying the French position.[26] This effort at propaganda proved highly successful, for we are told that by March of 1369 some 900 towns and fortified places had declared against the Prince of Wales.[27] The letters to the towns were issued on a triumphant day for the Valois dynasty, for on 3 December the queen presented Charles with a son and heir.[28] It was an increasingly confident monarch who convened another assembly of several dozen great magnates and royal advisers on 28 December. This group ratified the action taken six months earlier and declared that Charles V possessed suzerainty over Guyenne and had every right to accept the

[21] Breuils, "Jean d'Armagnac," pp. 89–90.

[22] *Ibid.*, pp. 88–89. Delachenal, *Charles V* 4: pp. 68–69, implied that Armagnac repaid this debt early in 1368.

[23] Loirette, "Arnaud Amanieu," P.J. 24; Breuils, "Jean d'Armagnac," p. 89.

[24] *Mandements*, nos. 478, 480; Loirette, "Arnaud Amanieu," pp. 338–340; Delachenal, *Charles V* 4: pp. 99–101, and notes. The 200,000 francs from the aids in Languedoc were to be divided as follows: 100,000 to Armagnac, 60,000 to Albret, and 40,000 to Périgord.

[25] *Chron. Jean II et Charles V* 3: P.J. 20.

[26] Delachenal, *Charles V* 4: pp. 101–104; Fowler, *Plantagenet and Valois*, pp. 66–69; Roquette, *Rouergue*, pp. 148–150; G. Tessier, "L'activité de la chancellerie royale française au temps de Charles V," *Le Moyen Age* 48 (1938): p. 27.

[27] Shaw, "Black Prince," p. 10. Cf. Breuils, "Jean d'Armagnac," p. 91, note 4.

[28] Delachenal, *Charles V* 3: pp. 536–537.

appeals.[29] By this date, in Languedoc, Louis of Anjou had ratified the accord of 30 June in the presence of John of Armagnac.[30]

The English, of course, did not view these events with indifference. In January, 1369, when the Black Prince had received his summons and was asked to respect the property of the appellants, he imprisoned the messengers of the French king.[31] Edward III sent a long complaint to Paris, noting arrears on the ransom and the failure of the French to transfer certain minor territories in accordance with the treaty of Brétigny. This document also attacked the French position on the Gascon appeals and warned of the possible consequences. Charles V justified his position on all these points in a lengthy reply which, among other things, rightly blamed the *routiers* for the slow collection of money for the ransom.[32]

Elsewhere on the international front, France achieved some important triumphs during the first few months of 1369, notably in the Netherlands and Spain. The daughter of Louis II of Flanders was the most important heiress in Europe, since she was to inherit Artois and the county of Burgundy as well as Flanders and Nevers. With considerable papal assistance, Charles V was able to circumvent a proposed marriage between this princess and a son of Edward III. Instead, she married Philip the Bold, duke of Burgundy and the youngest brother of Charles V. The marriage was celebrated in June, 1369, following treaties in mid-April which effectively secured Flemish neutrality in the Anglo-French war in exchange for the return of the bailiwick of Lille to Flanders.[33]

The French victory in Spain was more military than diplomatic. Louis of Anjou had made a treaty with the persistent count of Trastamara, and as the campaign in Provence drew to a close in the summer of 1368, Bertrand du

[29] Breuils, "Jean d'Armagnac," p. 90; Delachenal, *Charles V* 3: p. 537. On 6 December, Charles wrote to Louis II of Flanders setting forth his position on the appeals, but Louis sent an unpleasant reply (*ibid.*, p. 105).

[30] Breuils, "Jean d'Armagnac," p. 89; *HL* 10: cols. 1404–1406.

[31] *Ibid.* 9: pp. 800–801; Breuils, "Jean d'Armagnac," p. 91; Delachenal, *Charles V* 4: p. 106.

[32] Dessales, "Rançon," pp. 155–159; *Chron. Jean II et Charles V* 3: pp. 123–143 (P.J. 17, 18).

[33] *Mandements*, nos. 523, 532; Prou, *Relations politiques*, P.J. 61; L. Mirot, *Une grande famille parlementaire aux XIVe et XVe siècles: les d'Orgemont* (Paris, 1913), p. 14.

Guesclin and a large force of *routiers* crossed into Roussillon en route to Castile.[34] This time Aragon was on the side of England, but Peter IV could not hold the passes of the Pyrenees and Du Guesclin entered Aragon in December. His forces marched through Aragon and into Castile, joining Henry of Trastamara near Toledo. The governments at London and Bordeaux failed to realize the grave threat to their interests in Castile, and in March, 1369, Peter I was defeated, captured, and murdered. The count of Trastamara mounted the Castilian throne as Henry II.[35] By June, France and Castile had concluded the treaties which secured for Charles V the invaluable alliance of a major naval power.[36]

The Valois monarchy therefore was in an unusually strong position when the day approached for the Prince of Wales to appear at the *parlement* in Paris. Since it was evident that he would not respond to the summons, Charles V prepared for a judicial proceeding which had political, military, and financial implications. The action of the royal court would create a situation of "evident necessity" requiring immediate measures for the defense of the realm. Consequently, the king convened a most unusual assembly. Charles and his great magnates were present in a session of *parlement* that resembled those ceremonial occasions later known as *lits de justice*.[37] When the Black Prince failed to appear, the court adjourned for a week to permit the arrival of town representatives who must have been summoned previously. When the proceedings resumed on 9 May, 1369, they amounted to an assembly of the Estates General, convened in *parlement*. Such a gathering would not have been unusual for the "High Court of Parliament" in England, but it was only the first of three occasions in fourteenth-century France when the Estates and *parlement* held a joint assembly. To prepare the country for the inevitable war subsidies, Charles V broke with the French tradition of separating consultive and judicial assemblies.

[34] Russell, *English Intervention*, pp. 127, 138–141; Delachenal, *Charles V* 3: pp. 428–429, 557–562.

[35] Russell, *English Intervention*, pp. 141–142, 147, 162–165; *Petit Thalamus*, p. 383.

[36] Martène, *Thesaurus* 1: cols. 1500–1505.

[37] Delachenal, *Charles V* 4: pp. 136–137. The account of the meeting, in AN X 1a 1469, has been published by Delachenal in *Chron. Jean II et Charles V* 3: P.J. 19.

The most important judicial action of the fourteenth century was executed in the presence of the three Estates.[38]

The assembly replied to the complaints of Edward III regarding the Gascon appeals.[39] When he received this reply, Edward III reassumed the title of king of France, and in the fall of 1369 the English lands in France were declared confiscate.[40] The Hundred Years' War had resumed.

2. Rising Taxes in Languedoc

Not surprisingly, the renewal of hostilities had its first impact on Languedoc, which lay adjacent to many of the lands which England had acquired by the treaty of Brétigny. In addition, of course, the defecting Gascon lords had their lands in the Midi and were drawing their pensions from the aids in Languedoc. Taxation for military purposes had become a habit in the south well before the Prince of Wales was due to make his appearance in Paris. Because the duke of Anjou was shrewdly determined to be prepared for the coming conflict, the resumption of war subsidies really began with the *fouage* of one franc which was granted for the Provençal campaign in March, 1368.[41]

This hearth tax, being collectable in installments over a six-month period, was not very burdensome, particularly in view of the new hearth figures. Nevertheless, it encountered some of the usual difficulties. Anjou had to issue special orders to levy it on the nobles in the Beaucaire district, following customary opposition from the seigneurs of Velay and Gévaudan.[42] In the fall, he also had to order the notaries and lawyers with urban property to contribute to the municipal *tailles*.[43] Impa-

---

[38]*Ibid.* 2: pp. 72–76, 103–116 3: P.J. 19. See the remarks of modern historians: Coville, *Etats Norm.*, p. 108; Picot, *Etats* 1: pp. 204–205; Vuitry, *Régime financier* 2: p. 124; Delachenal, *Charles V* 4: pp. 141–143. Delachenal, *ibid.*, pp. 138–139, differs with Picot as to whether the meeting qualified as an "Estates General," suggesting that it was merely a meeting of the king's council in *parlement*.

[39]*Chron. Jean II et Charles V* 2: pp. 81–116; 3: pp. 139–143.

[40]Fowler, *Plantagenet and Valois*, pp. 66–69.

[41]See above, chap. V, at note 243.

[42]AD Hérault A 5, fols. 163v–164r; BN Coll. Languedoc 86, fols. 95r–v; *HL* 9: p. 795; Delcambre, *Velay*, p. 60.

[43]*Gr. Chartrier*, nos. 2449, 2612.

tient at the slow receipts, he borrowed money [44] and invoked a curious fiscal expedient, collecting unpaid arrears from a tax promised twelve years earlier. In 1356 the southern towns had made a grant subject to the condition that the heir to the throne come to Languedoc as royal lieutenant. As heir to the throne through most of 1368, Louis of Anjou felt entitled to claim the remainder of this tax. [45] Meanwhile, the towns of the Beaucaire district imposed a small hearth tax of ¾ *gros* upon themselves in order to finance an embassy of eight men to the royal court in Paris. [46]

The last installment of the money granted in March was payable in September, 1368. By this time the Provençal venture had largely come to an end, but the war with England had not resumed and Anjou was determined to continue his policy of keeping the *routiers* on his payroll. In September he convened the Estates of Languedoc at Toulouse, and after a lengthy session the assembly granted 160,000 francs, to be raised by a *fouage* of 2 francs per hearth, once again payable over a six-month period. An additional levy of one *gros* per hearth was earmarked for Bertrand du Guesclin, who was still entrusted with the task of keeping the *routiers* occupied, [47] and was about to lead them on the successful expedition to Spain. In effect, the three seneschalsies granted twice as much as they

---

[44]*Ibid.*, no. 3594; *INV AM Pézenas*, no. 1673.

[45] BN Coll. Languedoc 86, fol. 101; *Gr. Chartrier*, nos. 2451, 3918; and above, chap. IV, at notes 5 and 6.

[46]*HL 9*: p. 795; BN Coll. Languedoc 86, fol. 94. Another regional assembly in 1368 was held in Dauphiné, where the Estates met to supervise the administration of their earlier grant: Dussert, *Etats Dauphiné*, p. 67. Regarding the embassy which the towns of the Beaucaire district wished to send to Paris, the archives of Montpellier suggest a number of issues that could have been involved: the problem of paying off municipal debts (*Gr. Chartrier*, no. 2667); violations of royal safeguard by Anjou's officers (*ibid.*, no. 363); and the conduct of royal officers towards those accused of violating royal monetary ordinances (BN MS. lat. 9175, fols. 115r-v). Subsequently, Montpellier received the right to levy local taxes on external commerce (*Gr. Chartrier*, no. 3915), and the king renewed privileges granted by Louis X (*Ord. 5*: pp. 120-121).

[47]*HL 10*: cols. 1396-1399; Dognon, *Institutions*, pp. 610-611. It is not clear how the total of 160,000 francs was to be raised if the seneschalsy of Carcassonne paid only 52,000, as the sources indicate. This figure represents only 1½ francs per hearth according to the hearth figures established for the district in the mid-1360's (*Petit Thalamus*, p. 365, note *a*: 35,700 hearths). It would seem (see below, note 57) that this assessment of hearths was still in effect in 1368-1369, or that only minor reductions had occurred. Dognon claimed that the seneschalsy of Toulouse was to pay 42,000 francs, but his source for this figure seems to refer to the share owed by this district for the earlier one-franc hearth tax plus the *gabelle*.

had six months earlier, agreeing to their largest peacetime subsidy up to this time (if one excludes the ransom aids, which continued to be collected). Once again, this grant had only the most indirect connection with the defense of the realm. It seems clear that the towns of Languedoc, however reluctantly, had learned the lesson of a decade of brigandage preceded by a generation of unsuccessful war. Louis of Anjou's policy of keeping the *routiers* employed and developing a war chest for the coming struggle with England was beginning to win support. As a result, in 1369, the southern lieutenancy would be prepared for military action, in dramatic contrast with the days of Philip VI.[48]

The subsidy granted in the fall of 1368 was needed for a variety of purposes—to finance the Castilian campaign, to provide funds for the pensions of the Gascon lords,[49] and to repay money which Louis of Anjou had borrowed from various towns and moneylenders.[50] By February, 1369, the Black Prince had already reacted with hostility to his summons to the royal court, and the outcome of the Spanish campaign was still in doubt. Anjou's troops had already entered Rouergue and Quercy, where many towns adhered to the appeals and welcomed the French forces.[51] In this situation, Louis felt a need for additional money and the southern towns again were assembled at Toulouse. They agreed to raise the existing tax by 25 per cent, to 200,000 francs (2½ per hearth). They also extended the *gabelle* for two years, with some of the money reserved to the personal use of the royal lieutenant.[52] Thus in the final year before the formal resumption of Anglo-French hostilities, the towns of Languedoc had granted taxes equal to 3½ francs per hearth, over and above the *gabelle* and the aids. In this year the *fouage* alone exceeded Languedoc's share of the first ransom payment in 1360.

With this financial backing, Louis of Anjou was able to be

---

[48] See *HL* **9**: pp. 799–800.

[49] On payments to the Gascon lords, the *dossiers* for Albret and Armagnac in the *Pièces Originales* furnish most of our information: BN P.O. 24, *dossier* 603, no. 8; P.O. 93, *dossier* 1958, nos. 17, 26, and others.

[50] See above, note 44, and *Gr. Chartrier*, no. 3596.

[51] *Chron. Jean II et Charles V* **2**: p. 67; *HL* **9**: pp. 805–806, note 3; Chaplais, "Documents," p. 55.

[52] *Gr. Chartrier*, nos. 603, 3597; BN MS. lat. 9175, fols. 108–111v; Dognon, *Institutions*, p. 611; *HL* **9**: p. 804.

prepared militarily at a time when the Black Prince was financially and politically embarrassed. This state of affairs represented a complete reversal of the situation which had prevailed in 1345 and 1355, when the English had built up their forces during the periods of truce and had defeated the unprepared French armies. Now the brigandage of the *routiers* had forced the French taxpayers to accept a burden in time of peace which would have been inconceivable a generation earlier, and the French were ready when the war resumed.

The effects of this military preparedness, and the propaganda campaign which had accompanied it, were dramatic. Most of the towns in Rouergue and Quercy were in French hands by the end of February, 1369, and the occupation of these districts was completed with the capitulation of Millau in December.[53] This community was the object of considerable propaganda from both sides, and the consuls consulted a number of Bolognese jurists before deciding to support the Gascon appeals and open their gates to the French.[54] By this time the French were occupying Périgord and Agenais and the English had lost some of their long-time possessions in Gascony proper.[55] To counter the rapid advance of Anjou's forces, John Chandos led an Anglo-Gascon raid into Albigeois and the Toulousain in April, 1369, but this diversion failed to halt the French reconquest and it gave Charles V an excuse to order the confiscation of Chandos's possessions in France.[56]

These French successes could not be sustained without a steady stream of funds from taxation. Victory, however, had the virtue of persuading taxpayers that their money was well spent, and by the time the Estates of Languedoc reconvened at Toulouse on 28 April, 1369, impressive triumphs had been recorded in both Guyenne and Castile. The assembly granted

---

[53]*Ibid.*, pp. 805–806, note 3; Delachenal, *Charles V* 4: p. 187; Chaplais, "Documents," p. 55; Artières, *Annales de Millau*, pp. 157–158.

[54]Chaplais, "Documents," pp. 58–61; Delachenal, *Charles V* 4: p. 170.

[55]*Ibid.*, pp. 187, 252; *Petit Thalamus*, p. 384; *HL* 9: pp. 802–803, 806. Delachenal attributes the rapid French success in Agenais to the skill of John of Armagnac. For privileges extended to the recovered southern towns, see *Ord.* 5: pp. 255–260, 263–268, 288, 291–296, 406, 408, 499, 692–694.

[56]*Mandements*, no. 540; Delachenal, *Charles V* 4: p. 177. Wolff, *Commerces*, notes that Toulouse was permitted to employ money from the aids to repair its fortifications, presumably to resist the attack by Chandos.

a new subsidy in the form of a loan equal to 2½ francs per hearth, presumably about 200,000 francs in all. This loan would be repaid from subsequent tax receipts. Evidently the *gabelle* would be applied to this purpose, for the new *fouage* was to be only two francs and one *gros*. Although sources differ as to actual amounts, it appears that the seneschalsy of Carcassonne was to raise 67,000 francs by this method.[57] This arrangement was confirmed by still another assembly at Toulouse in midsummer.[58]

Collection of these subsidies in Languedoc was in the hands of receivers-general named by the Estates.[59] The aids, now largely applied to the pensions of the appellant lords, continued to be collected simultaneously.[60] The taxes in Languedoc were now higher than ever before, yet the victorious duke of Anjou used up the money rapidly and constantly required more. Money which should have been used to repay the loan from the Estates had to be spent on military salaries as soon as it was collected.[61] The pensions promised to the Gascon lords were of high priority and had to be paid promptly whether or not the receipts from the aids were adequate.[62] Anjou did prohibit forced loans and requisitions of food at Toulouse,[63] but the need for money led him to send Pierre Scatisse to seek loans from the important towns of the seneschalsies of Toulouse and Carcassonne during September.[64]

To meet his financial needs, Louis convened the Estates of Languedoc for the fourth time in 1369. The assembly met at Carcassonne in September, then adjourned and reconvened at

---

[57]*HL* **10:** col. 1048; AM Albi CC 77, no. 5; *HL* **9:** p. 804, note 3. Dognon, *Institutions*, p. 611, found sources which quoted Carcassonne's share as 71,000 francs, a figure which could include the shares of seigneurial enclaves within the district. Whichever figure is used, the total probably does not include the *gabelle*, but only the hearth tax of 2 francs, 1 *gros* (or 31 *gros*). This *fouage* indicates that the seneschalsy had between 32,400 and 34,400 taxable hearths, only slightly fewer than the 35,700 reported in *Petit Thalamus*, p. 365, note *a*, where Languedoc as a whole was assessed at over 87,000 hearths, rather than 80,000. References to a *fouage* of 2½ francs at Narbonne in BN MS. *fr.* 20582, nos. 80, 81, probably refer to the earlier grant, since they are dated late April and early May.

[58]Dognon, *Institutions*, p. 611.

[59]BN P.O. 2661, *dossier* 59050, no. 8.

[60]*Gr. Chartrier*, no. 2613; *INV AM Toulouse*, p. 538 (AA 45, no. 67).

[61]See *HL* **10:** cols. 1409–1412, 1414–1415.

[62]See BN P.O. 24, *dossier* 603, nos. 10, 11, 17.

[63]*INV AM Toulouse*, pp. 86, 538 (AA 5, AA 45).

[64]*Gr. Chartrier*, no. 3919; *HL* **9:** p. 810, and notes.

Toulouse, where it completed its deliberations in November. To induce them to make a large grant, Louis promised the Estates that he would maintain a strong enough force to keep the three seneschalsies free of brigandage.[65] After the experiences of the past decade, the promise was a compelling one, and the Estates knew well that Anjou was prepared to deal ruthlessly with undisciplined men-at-arms. In May he had executed a number of famous *routier* chiefs on charges of treason.[66]

The result of the long deliberations was an enormous new tax of 430,000 francs, easily the largest granted in Languedoc heretofore. In return for this subsidy, the royal lieutenant published an ordinance of fifty-eight articles that virtually recapitulated the history of tax negotiations in Languedoc since 1300. Commissioners of reform were to be suppressed; no fines were to be levied for the acquisition of noble fiefs; no force was to be used to compel people to pay their taxes. Careful regulations were established to deal with criminal cases, commerce, and the raising and paying of troops. The ransom aids, no longer required for their original purpose, were canceled, so the new grant was to provide both a war subsidy and the funds required to finance the Gascon seigneurs. The principal new tax was a *fouage* of 3 francs per hearth, to be supplemented by indirect taxes, notably a half-franc per *tonneau* of wine and a levy on grapes.[67] The promised concessions were not always executed, particularly those regarding the vexing question of franc-fief,[68] nor were the indirect taxes collected without opposition.[69]

Since this heavy set of taxes was to last for a full year, it is hard to explain the action of the next assembly, which convened at Toulouse late in February, 1370, and also granted a *fouage* of 3 francs and a tax on wine. Some texts say that this grant was intended to produce 330,000 francs (implying that some of the indirect taxes were not retained).[70] Others say that the amount in question was 430,000 francs, the same sum

---

[65] *HL* **10**: cols. 1378–1379.
[66] *Petit Thalamus*, pp. 383–384.
[67] *HL* **9**: pp. 811–812, and notes; **10**: cols. 1415–1416; Dognon, *Institutions*, p. 611; BN MS. lat. 9175, fols. 130–149; *Gr. Chartrier*, nos. 3920–3922.
[68] *Ibid.*, nos. 2094, 2095, 2098.
[69] *HL* **9**: pp. 811–812, note 7.
[70] See Dognon, *Institutions*, p. 611; *Gr. Chartrier*, no. 2621.

granted in November.[71] Since a second grant of this magnitude within three months would have imposed a remarkably heavy burden on the populace, it seems likely that this assembly merely confirmed the earlier tax. This view is reinforced by the fact that the next assembly met in November to grant a new tax, just one year after the original grant of 430,000 francs. It is possible, however, that the assembly of February, 1370, did reduce its total grant to 330,000 francs by eliminating some of the indirect taxes, for there is evidence that the 12 d./l. originally imposed for the ransom was again in force in July, 1370.[72] The tax of ½ franc on wine remained in effect,[73] but nobles rendering military service were excused from paying it.[74] Nobles did not always render this service, and their failure to respond to one summons caused Louis of Anjou some exasperation.[75]

Since early 1368, the taxes imposed on Languedoc had steadily risen, attaining a level far higher than anything known previously in this region. The archives of Montpellier document this process in considerable detail. In the second half of 1368, Montpellier paid 2300 francs for a one-franc *fouage* granted in March.[76] The town also lent 2500 francs to Louis of Anjou and paid 3250 florins to settle an old tax.[77] In return, it was allowed to deduct 1600 francs from the town's quota of 4400 francs for the *fouage* of 2 francs granted in the fall of 1368.[78] As we have seen, this *fouage* was raised to 2½ francs early in 1369 and was followed by a new assessment of 2½ francs in the spring. The latter took the form of a loan to be repaid from later taxes, and Montpellier, which should have owed 5750 francs, made a prompt advance of 5000 francs and was excused from paying the rest.[79] Nevertheless, when *réformateurs* approached the towns for additional loans, the consuls of Montpellier offered 10,000 francs in September, provided that the government excuse them from further

[71]*HL* **9**: pp. 816–817; Delachenal, *Charles V* **4**: p. 252.
[72]*Gr. Chartrier*, nos. 2469–2471.
[73]AD Hérault A 5, fols. 89r–90r.
[74]*Ibid.*, fols. 91r–92v.
[75]AD Hérault A 5, fols. 84v–89r.
[76]*Gr. Chartrier*, no. 3634.
[77]*Ibid.*, nos. 3594, 3918.
[78]*Ibid.*, nos. 3592, 3595, 3596.
[79]*Ibid.*, nos. 476, 3601, 3917.

subsidies for a year.[80] Two months later, the Estates made
their large grant of 430,000 francs, and Montpellier, which
should have been excused from contributing, agreed to pay,
provided that its loan of a year earlier (2500 francs) be
deducted from the total.[81] In July, 1370, the town received its
quittance for the 6900 francs owed for the *fouage,* after
wealthy citizens had been forced to advance money to meet the
total.[82] Possibly the 10,000 franc loan of September, 1369, was
canceled, or the 6900 francs included in it, but the *Grand
Chartrier* provides no information on this point.

It is not easy to convert these documents into meaningful
figures, but if a total can be established for the period from
mid-1368 to mid-1370, it will offer some basis for comparing
the level of taxation in this period with that in the earlier
fourteenth century. Until the fall of 1369, the ransom aids
continued to be levied. In promising pensions to the Gascon
lords, the government calculated that at least 200,000 francs
were being collected annually from this source. Such estimates
were often overly optimistic, but when the Estates granted
430,000 francs in the fall of 1369, the *fouage* of 3 francs would
have produced only about 240,000. The remaining 190,000
francs, to be raised by indirect taxes, represented a substitute
for the aids. Since *gabelle* receipts are not known, and may not
have been included in this total, it is probably not unreason-
able to say that indirect taxes produced about 200,000 francs
annually in Languedoc at this time, the equivalent of $2\frac{1}{2}$
francs per hearth. At Montpellier they would have been worth
5750 francs per year, or 11,500 francs for the two-year period
under consideration.

In the same period, the town received a number of quit-
tances for the *fouages:* 2300, 1100, 5000, 4650, 1600, 3143, and
6900 francs.[83] These may not be complete, and the documents
are somewhat confusing about what may have been deducted.
If, however, we subtract the 1600 francs deducted from the
subsidy of late 1368 and the 2500 francs previously loaned to

[80]*Ibid.,* no. 3919. These commissioners, a noble and a law professor, arrived early in
August with "full financial and coercive powers" and demanded full payment of $2\frac{1}{2}$
francs per hearth (*ibid.,* no. 475). This must have been done in violation of the earlier
abatement given to Montpellier.

[81]*Ibid.,* no. 3920.

[82]*Ibid.,* nos. 2460, 3606.

[83]*Ibid.,* Dviii, no. 77; and nos. 3601, 3604, 3606, 3615, 3630, 3631, 3634.

the duke of Anjou, we arrive at a figure of more than 20,500 francs.[84] Added to the 11,500 francs estimated for Montpellier's share of the indirect taxes, the total exceeds 32,000 francs for this two-year period. This appears to be a conservative estimate, if only because it does not take into account the 10,000-franc loan promised by the consuls in the fall of 1369 and the 3250 florins paid in 1368 for an earlier tax.[85] Since Montpellier possessed 2300 taxable hearths at this time, the citizens were paying taxes totaling 14 francs per hearth between mid-1368 and mid-1370, an annual average of 7 francs.

For purposes of comparison, it is convenient to use 1328 and 1348, when the *livre tournois* was about the same value as it was in 1368–1370 (6 l. t. per mark) and therefore equal to the franc of the latter period.[86] In 1328 Montpellier paid a subsidy of 2000 l. t. with considerable protest, claiming adverse economic conditions. In 1348 the town promised 6000 l. t. before the Black Death, when the proposed subsidy (which was not collected) amounted to five times as much as the largest tax previously collected in France.[87] In the reign of Philip VI, Montpellier seems to have been assessed at 6000 taxable hearths, so the levy of 1328 was equivalent to one-third *livre* per hearth and that of 1348 equaled one *livre* per hearth. Given these figures, the comparison with 1368–1370 is very striking. The total tax paid in 1368–1370 was sixteen times as much as that collected in 1328 and more than five times as much as that promised in 1348. The annual tax per hearth was twenty-one times as much as it had been in 1328. In the *fourteen-year* period, 1320–1333, Montpellier's total subsidies to the crown amounted to 4000 l. t., while in the *two-year* period, 1368–1370, the town paid eight times as much, and twenty-one times as much per hearth. In short, there seems little doubt that royal taxation in Languedoc had experienced an increase of revolutionary proportions since the beginning

---

[84]*Ibid.*, no. 3632 and Dviii no. 80, concern repayment of the 2500 franc loan. If it was actually repaid and not deducted from taxes, our total would be 23,000 francs. Other texts (*ibid.*, nos. 3597, 3629) indicate a deduction of 900 francs ordered on 2 March, 1369, and a quittance for 90 francs two days later. If this second figure is an error for 900, then this total should probably be deducted from the estimated total payments, but the documents leave one uncertain.

[85]See above, note 45.

[86]*RTF 1322–1356*, pp. 339–340.

[87]*Ibid.*, pp. 71, 236–237.

of Philip VI's reign. Most of this increase seems to have occurred during the lieutenancy of Louis of Anjou, but this hypothesis cannot be tested because of the delay between the Black Death in 1348 and the new hearth counts of the 1360's.

The rate of taxation did not slacken in the early 1370's. After asking Anjou not to make the clergy pay the indirect taxes granted by the Estates, Urban V granted Louis a tenth in October, 1370.[88] The duke also obtained a *fouage* of two francs from Dauphiné,[89] and in the fall of 1370 the Estates of Languedoc met at Toulouse to grant a *fouage* of one and one-half francs for four months. In January, 1371, they reconvened and granted another two francs per hearth.[90] In August they granted a *fouage* of three francs, followed five months later by a renewal of the *gabelle* and still another three-franc *fouage*.[91] Thus in the two-year period 1370–1372, the *fouages* alone amounted to nine and one-half francs—slightly more than in 1368–1370. The pace continued through most of the decade. *Fouages* of two francs in October, 1372, and three francs in March, 1373, were followed by grants of two and three francs in the spring of 1374, a terrible year of famine and plague in which Louis of Anjou had to order a new hearth count.[92] A recurrence of brigandage in 1375 made matters worse and occasioned a new hearth tax in the summer; additional sales taxes and *fouages* were levied in 1376, and in these two years the hearth taxes came to six francs in all.[93] In 1377 the Estates of Rouergue and Quercy imposed taxes to combat brigandage, and Anjou obtained two grants from the three large seneschalsies in the last months of the year, totaling seven and one-half

---

[88] Prou, *Relations politiques*, pp. 78–80, P.J. 86.

[89] Dussert, *Etats Dauphiné*. p. 72.

[90] *HL* 9: p. 821; 10: cols. 1416–1417. *Gr. Chartrier*, nos. 683, 3607, refer to a hearth tax of 1¼ francs in the fall of 1370. While this could be an error, it could also mean that the Estates had granted 1½ florins (18 *gros*). For early 1371, AM Albi CC 77, no. 6, refers to a grant of one franc in January instead of three, but the document could be referring to a local tax levied in addition to that granted by the Estates.

[91] *HL* 9: pp. 828–829; *Gr. Chartrier*, no. 3666. The grant of August, 1371, was actually for 350,000 l. t., and the 3 franc hearth tax could have produced only about two-thirds of the total. Parts of the tenth and the *gabelle* were to make up the rest (*INV AM Toulouse*, p. 470).

[92] *HL* 9: pp. 831–847; Wolff, *Commerces*, p. 628; AM Albi CC 75, nos. 2, 4; *Ord.* 6: p. 184. By this time the payments from the aids that were due the count of Armagnac had fallen 132,400 francs into arrears (*HL* 10: cols. 1523–1525).

[93] *HL* 9: pp. 846–855.

francs.[94] Since all these taxes were in addition to the aids, it is clear that the inhabitants of the Midi had been forced to undergo an extremely high level of taxation.

3. War Financing in Languedoil

In the regions of northern and central France, the two basic taxes collected during 1368 and 1369 were the *fouage* for military defense[95] and the aids originally imposed for the royal ransom.[96] The former amounted to four francs in the walled towns and one and one-half in the country. The latter consisted of the indirect taxes levied since 1361, with the *gabelle* at the revised rates of 1367. When the war with England resumed, these aids continued to be levied, now as a war subsidy, and the crown continued to let towns keep a portion of the aids for their own defensive needs. Normally, this was one-sixth of the 12 d./l. sales tax,[97] but Rouen was permitted to retain one-third.[98] The king diverted to defensive purposes some funds from the aids in the viscounty of Bayeux which had been earmarked for his household expenses; he similarly diverted 1700 francs per month from receipts at Rouen, evidently the equivalent of half the Norman *gabelle* receipts.[99] The duke of Berry was authorized to keep the aids for 1369 in the four dioceses of central France where he was royal lieutenant,[100] and other receipts from indirect taxes were diverted to the count of Charolais.[101] The sum of 40 francs which the town of Orchies had been paying for the maintenance of hostages in England was diverted to maintaining the town's *château*.[102] The crown also collected the tax on Italian

---

[94]*Ibid.* **9:** pp. 855–863; **10:** cols. 1602–1606.

[95]BN MS. fr. 26008, nos. 501, 650, 652, 664, 743, 777, 788; *Mandements*, nos. 445, 460, 488, 499, 513, 514; AN K 49, nos. 24, 25, 30, 37 *ter*, 38, 38 *bis*; BN P.O. 493, *dossier* 11104, no. 23; P.O. 789, *dossier* 17879, no. 2; P.O. 1936, *dossier* 44515, nos. 9, 27, 30. Many of these documents refer to the tax as the "aids for defense," the term applied to extraordinary revenues in the 1370's.

[96]*Mandements*, no. 545; BN MS. fr. 26007, nos. 463, 470; 26008, nos. 505, 625, 630, 658, 673, 682; BN Clairambault 73, no. 65; BN P.O. 1936 *dossier* 44515, nos. 25, 29.

[97]*Mandements*, nos. 437, 459, 482, 487, 543, 548.

[98]*Ibid.*, no. 492; AN K 49, no. 36.

[99]*Mandements*, nos. 432, 447.

[100]*Ibid.*, nos. 486, 495, 527. Berry, in turn, allowed his towns a portion of the tax: Lacour, *Gouvernement*, pp. 239, 359.

[101]*Mandements*, no. 536.

[102]*Ibid.*, no. 450.

merchants known as the *boîte aux Lombards*, and a loan of 1000 francs was obtained from Jews.[103] On 21 July, 1369, Urban V authorized the collection of a two-year subsidy from the French clergy outside Languedoc.[104] The towns of Crotoy and Abbeville, recovered from the English in April, were promised that they would not have to pay any tax to which they had not consented.[105]

The royal government, meanwhile, stepped up its military preparations. Charles V named a new war treasurer, ordered naval supplies stockpiled at the arsenal at Rouen, and instructed his Norman commander to assist Navarrese troops who were fighting Breton *routiers*.[106] Normandy continued to be the scene of warfare against brigand companies. For 3000 francs, a contingent of *routiers* had agreed to evacuate Château-Gontier early in 1369,[107] but then they joined the English garrison at Saint-Sauveur. The captain of this fortress collected a heavy ransom during the second half of 1369 to stop molesting the neighboring region, but brigandage continued.[108]

As all these actions proceeded, the crown's major concern was to find an adequate basis for financing the war over an extended period. Neither the ransom aids nor the *fouage* for defense were designed to finance an Anglo-French war, and the inclusion of town representatives in the assembly in *parlement* in May, 1369, doubtless was part of an effort to impress the bourgeois with the need for further taxation. Three months later, in early August, Charles V convened his next assembly. It met at Rouen, and it has been subject to the usual scholarly debate as to whether it should be called a true Estates General.[109] As always, this dispute seems unimportant, if only because the term "Estates General" was not used in the fourteenth century. Like the Estates of 1367, the meeting contained barons, prelates, and townsmen from a large part of Languedoil but probably not all of it. They met to consider

---

[103]*Ibid.*, no. 512; AN P 2294, pp. 679–680.
[104]Prou, *Relations politiques*, P.J. 85.
[105]*Chron. Jean II et Charles V* 2: p. 67; *Ord.* 5: pp. 183, 689.
[106]*Mandements*, nos. 503, 507, 515.
[107]C. Samaran, "Pour l'histoire des grandes compagnies. Le videment de Château-Gontier par les Anglais (1369)," *Mélanges . . . Halphen*, pp. 641–643.
[108]Delisle, *St. Sauveur*, pp. 151, 153; *Mandements*, no. 570; AN K 49, no. 46.
[109]Delachenal, *Charles V* 4: p. 201.

specific taxes. Their meeting place, Rouen, not only was the capital of the Norman duchy which had been the king's *apanage,* but, still more important, was also the site of the major naval arsenal in northern France. The king adopted a tactic which had rarely failed to loosen the purse strings of the Normans in the past: he proposed an invasion of England. The presentation of the royal case emphasized the state of readiness of the fleet and the "army of the sea." We cannot speculate as to the impact of the proposal on representatives from the inland districts, but perhaps it is not too fanciful to imagine that guided tours of the *Clos des Galées* were arranged for those who were skeptical.[110] This discussion of offensive warfare, staged at Rouen, must have involved considerable propaganda, and perhaps we should infer that the carefully managed proceedings in the *parlement* in May had not generated the desired enthusiasm for new taxation. The point at issue seems to have been the *fouage,* which had been collected for more than five years, although modified in 1367. Unlike the aids, which were levied on commerce and affected the towns primarily, hearth taxes bore upon the rural population, which was far more numerous, if less wealthy, and which included most of the nobles and their subjects. Perhaps the lay and ecclesiastical seigneurs led the opposition to the *fouage;* in any case, it was now abandoned. The assembly adopted new indirect taxes which must have affected urban consumers primarily. Wine and other beverages sold in large lots were to be taxed at one-sixth of their value. Beverages sold in taverns or at retail were to be subject to a high tax of 25 per cent. In addition, the assembly adopted a tax on cereal grains *(molage).*[111]

The assembly at Rouen was not followed by an invasion of England. The war in Languedoil resembled in form the struggle against *routiers* during the 1360's. Hostile troops took refuge at Saint-Sauveur and in Brittany, and when other companies were dislodged from Harfleur, they moved to the Oise valley and created danger for the inhabitants of that region.[112] Still faced with this kind of warfare, the government

---

[110]*Ibid.,* pp. 202, 226; Coville, *Etats Norm.,* pp. 108–111.

[111]*Ibid.;* Delachenal, *Charles V* 4: pp. 203–204, 226; Vuitry, *Régime financier* 2: pp. 125, 127; AN K 49, no. 40; *Mandements,* nos. 562, 563.

[112]*Ibid.,* no. 598.

encouraged the continuation of local initiatives in matters of defense. Towns were permitted to retain 10 per cent of the new aids, sometimes in addition to their usual portion of the sales tax.[113]

The new indirect taxes soon ran into trouble, and on 7 November, Charles V ordered the *élus* and other fiscal personnel to let the farmers of these taxes in ravaged rural areas abandon their agreements.[114] In all probability, the crown found that it could not wage war without levying taxes on the thousands of rural hearths. In any case, the king soon announced that the new levies had aroused such complaints that he intended to replace them at the beginning of December with the *fouage* which had been levied prior to 1367.[115] This decision could only be provisional, and Charles again summoned the Estates of Languedoil to provide a more workable plan.

Ordered to assemble on 7 December, 1369, the Estates convened a day or two later, and the deliberations continued until the nineteenth. As in May, the king met with this assembly in *parlement*.[116] The purpose of this meeting was to decide on specific taxes, while the earlier assembly had been a political-judicial proceeding. The *parlement* had been a logical, if not obvious, setting for the assembly in May, even though there was no recent tradition of combining a representative assembly and a high court. The reasons for adopting a similar setting in December are much less evident. As dauphin, Charles V had had some bad experiences with the Estates General, and perhaps he hoped to diminish the power and pretensions of large assemblies. He had dealt with limited assemblies of the three orders in 1359, 1367, and at Rouen in 1369, but he may have felt that larger meetings should be treated as ceremonial sessions of the *parlement* rather than as consultive bodies. In this way, the decisions that were reached could be treated as enactments of the king in his court, without any admission that large consultive assemblies had a right to act as consenting bodies when taxation was imposed.

[113]*Ibid.*, nos. 582, 585, 593–597, 599, 601, 602, 633.

[114]*Ibid.*, no. 603.

[115]*Ibid.*, no. 609; Coville, *Etats Norm.*, p. 109.

[116]*Ibid.*, pp. 109–110; Picot, *Etats* 1: pp. 206–207; Delachenal, *Charles V* 4: pp. 227–228, citing AN X 1a 1469, fol. 388.

The long negotiations of December, 1369, conducted in an atmosphere of "great necessity," led to the adoption of a new *fouage:* 6 francs per hearth in the walled towns and 2 francs in the *plat pays*. The king, in return, promised to reduce the salaries of officers, which this assembly, like all others, regarded as excessive. The *quatrième* on wine was retained, so the new hearth tax replaced only the *molage*.[117] The clergy received exemption from the *fouage*, but only those nobles who served personally in the army were excused. They were at least able to preserve their identity as a separate class in fiscal matters.[118] The count of Alençon replaced the tax in his lands with a separate *composition* of 2000 francs, and a number of towns also preferred to pay by means of lump-sum payments.[119]

The royal tax structure now consisted of the heavy *fouage* and the *quatrième* on wine, both of which were to support the war, and the *gabelle* on salt and the general 5 per cent sales tax, both of which were intended mainly for the maintenance of the king. The last of these continued to be shared with localities concerned with their own defenses.[120] Since ransom payments had been halted with the renewal of war, the old distinction between the aids and *gabelle* on the one hand and the *fouage* on the other became rather blurred, and the same administration dealt with all the extraordinary taxes. They were collected under the immediate direction of *élus* and the ultimate direction of *généraux* in Paris. The latter now were called "councillors-general," and collectively they were the forerunner of the *Cour des Aides* of the next generation.[121]

The first half of 1370 was marked by a certain hesitancy on the part of the crown regarding the taxation of Languedoil. On the one hand, the *fouage* aroused considerable discontent, while on the other hand the government was unable to wage war without taxing the vast rural population in this way. On

---

[117]*Chron. Jean II et Charles V* 2: pp. 137–139; Coville, *Etats Norm.*, pp. 108–110; Tessier, "L'activité de la chancellerie," p. 27; Delachenal, *Charles V* 4: pp. 229–230, and notes; Vuitry, *Régime financier* 2: pp. 127–128; *Mandements*, no. 625.

[118]Vuitry, *Régime financier* 2: pp. 127–128; G. Prevost, introduction to Izarn, *Compte de recettes*, p. lxiii.

[119]*Ibid.*, p. xxxvii; Guigue, *Tard-Venus*, p. 210.

[120]*Ibid.; Mandements*, nos. 627, 628.

[121]Delachenal, *Charles V* 4: pp. 229–232. See also *Mandements*, nos. 613, 616, 621–623.

25 January, Charles V reduced the *fouage* to 4 francs per urban hearth and 1½ francs in the country.[122] With hearth counts often becoming outdated rapidly, there were communities, like Mantes, whose war losses left them unable to pay even at the reduced rate.[123] On 26 April, 1370, however, Charles V finally restored the higher *fouage* of 6 and 2 francs, citing the decision of the assembly held in Paris the preceding December. Unable to manage with lower taxes, he reaffirmed the principle that taxes must be based on ability to pay: the strong must carry the weak.[124] After this decision, the taxes were left unchanged for a decade. Confirmed in an ordinance of April, 1374, they remained in effect without new central assemblies.[125]

By the middle of 1370, therefore, Languedoil, like Languedoc, was paying the highest taxes in its history. Everywhere in France the average urban hearth was being taxed at an annual rate of more than six francs. Yet even now the taxes did not always prove sufficient for local military needs. Peter of Alençon, the royal lieutenant in Normandy, had to assess a special surtax of one-third on the inhabitants of five Norman dioceses.[126]

To direct the French war effort, Bertrand du Guesclin was recalled from Spain.[127] The Breton captain was back in France by the end of July, 1370, and on 2 October he was named constable of France. He enlisted the aid of Olivier de Clisson, another Breton seigneur, whose troops now joined the French side. The task of the royal commanders was formidable, for Robert Knolles was leading English forces in the northwest and Charles the Bad was at Cherbourg, ready to fish in troubled waters. Du Guesclin maintained his forces by paying them out of his own pocket, since tax receipts were collected too slowly for the needs of military salaries. At the constable's behest, a forced loan was levied in Normandy and at Paris during the latter part of 1370, the money to be repaid from the

---

[122] *Ibid.*, no. 637; Vuitry, *Régime financier* 2: p. 129.

[123] AN K 49, no. 444

[124] *Mandements*, no. 679.

[125] *Ord.* 6: p. 2; Vuitry, *Régime financier* 2: pp. 146–147. The tax on wine remained high: one-fourth on retail sales, one-sixth on many bulk sales, and one thirteenth in certain cases where large amounts of wine changed hands.

[126] Coville, *Etats Norm.*, pp. 112–113, 387–388.

[127] Russell, *English Intervention*, p. 161.

tax receipts as they were collected.[128] Receipts continued to be depleted by reduced assessments for the *fouage* [129] and sums set aside for towns to use for their own needs.[130] The military summons, so widely used in the past, was still employed occasionally as a device for accelerating payments.[131]

The war in Languedoil was largely settled by two important French victories, the first in 1372 and the second in 1375. In 1372 the Castilian alliance, which the Valois had patiently cultivated for nearly a decade, finally brought its reward when galleys from Castile intercepted a large English fleet carrying troops and money for Aquitaine. The English were defeated off La Rochelle and their fleet destroyed. The French took that city in August and again made Jean de Grailly a prisoner.[132] In December, 1372, Poitou, Saintonge, and Angoumois formally returned to the obedience of Charles V.[133]

The second important triumph was the recovery of Saint-Sauveur in lower Normandy, eventually by negotiation rather than assault. In 1372 the Norman Estates began to meet fairly frequently, to urge action against Saint-Sauveur and to provide additional financial support for this project. Assemblies in July and September granted small sums to Du Guesclin, and in January, 1373, the Normans voted 40,000 pounds to aid the campaign. In 1374 the able Jean de Vienne, admiral of France, was named lieutenant in lower Normandy for the campaign against Saint-Sauveur. Assemblies in August and October each granted taxes equal to two-thirds of the *fouage,* with the result that the Normans, in 1374, were paying fourteen francs per hearth in addition to the aids. This great financial sacrifice continued into 1375, when the Normans had to grant additional sums, but in that year the fortress was reacquired.[134]

By the middle 1370's, the French had won back most of their earlier territorial losses, but the victory was incomplete and

---

[128] Delachenal, *Charles V* 4: pp. 220, 328–333, and notes.

[129] *Ibid.,* p. 334, note 1; Varin, *Reims* 3: p. 358.

[130] *Ibid.,* p. 338.

[131] Thierry, *Recueil* 1: pp. 650–651 (4 June, 1371).

[132] Russell, *English Intervention*, pp. 193–194; *Chron. Jean II et Charles V* 3: P.J. 23.

[133] *Ord.* 5: p. 557.

[134] Coville, *Etats Norm.*, pp. 113–119; BN MS. fr. 20415, no. 37; Tardif, *Monuments historiques*, no. 1529.

the momentum was gradually lost. The English retained the Bordelais for another eighty years. Charles the Bad, whose intrigues had won him a new and somewhat more favorable treaty with France in 1371,[135] rebelled again in 1378, apparently hoping for English help in protecting Navarre against France's Castilian ally. The English obtained access to his Norman port of Cherbourg and the French failed to take this stronghold.[136] As the level of warfare declined, the old *routier* problem reappeared with its former intensity.[137] Despite the efforts of Charles V, the crown would not be able to eliminate brigandage for another seventy years.

As the high taxation continued through the 1370's, certain regions made special arrangements which marked the beginning of that inequality and lack of uniformity which would characterize royal taxation until the end of the old régime. Dauphiné, which lay outside the kingdom, had a separate fiscal history,[138] while newly recovered lands were less heavily taxed than those in French hands during the 1360's. Artois, Boulonnais, and Saint-Pol escaped the regular taxes by granting an annual *finance* through their regional Estates.[139] The county of Ponthieu was promised the right to consent to all taxes and regularly received letters of non-prejudice for its grants.[140] Burgundy and Brittany paid relatively little in royal taxes, although Du Guesclin did impose a *fouage* on Brittany in 1373.[141] The king continued to collect money from other sources: over 11,000 l.p. from an inquest into the waters and forests that began in 1372,[142] and 20,000 francs from the Jews of Languedoil in 1378.[143]

The financing of Charles V's victories thus was accomplished by a variety of methods. Although the major territo-

---

[135] Delachenal, *Charles V* 4: pp. 356–384.

[136] See Secousse, *Charles le Mauvais* 1: pp. 373–437; *Chron. Jean II et Charles V* 2: pp. 284–317; 3: P.J. 28; Martène, *Thesaurus* 1: cols. 1529–1569; Russell, *English Intervention*, pp. 255–257, 264f; Coville, *Etats Norm.*, pp. 119–120.

[137] L. Mirot, *Les insurrections urbaines au début du règne de Charles VI (1380–1383). Leurs causes, leurs consequences* (Paris, 1906), p. 14; Rey, *Domaine*, pp. 125, 181; Michel, "Defense," p. 130.

[138] Dussert, *Etats Dauphiné*, pp. 74f.

[139] *Ord.* 5: p. 651; 6: pp. 68, 88, 164, 362, 449, 600; 7: pp. 4, 75, 111, 144, 166; Rey, *Domaine*, p. 182. The payment was 14,000 francs annually.

[140] *Ibid.*, pp. 243, 355, 451, 586.

[141] Vuitry, *Régime financier* 2: p. 178.

[142] Rey, *Domaine*, p. 152.

[143] *Ord.* 6: p. 339.

rial distinction in fiscal policy and administration continued to be that between Languedoil and Languedoc, both of these large areas were subject to regional distinctions of their own. Centralization and uniformity in matters of taxation were as absent in time of victory as in the earlier years of defeat. At the same time, it is clear that taxes were much heavier and more regular than in earlier generations. After 1370, it is no longer possible to distinguish between those levied for the royal ransom and the *fouage* established for defense. The documents regularly refer to both as the "aids ordered for the war." A multitude of pay vouchers, receipts, and other documents attest to their continued collection, not only in 1370 and 1371,[144] but also during the remaining years of Charles V's reign.[145] It was this continuous and regular taxation that made his reign successful and victorious. The distinction between direct and indirect taxation was of political significance, as future events would demonstrate, but one finds little evidence of it in the documents of the 1370's.

---

[144] Varin, *Reims* 3: p. 349; *Mandements*, no. 629; *Ord.* 5: p. 348; Delachenal, *Charles V* 4: p. 277, note 1; p. 354, note 3; BN MS. fr. 20583, no. 13; 20586, nos. 39, 40; 26009, nos. 819–826, 843, 852, 862, 930, 931, 933, 935, 938, 944, 946, 950, 953, 956, 957, 959, 962, 970, 975–977, 999, 1016, 1025, 1047; 26010, nos. 1110, 1116, 1124, 1125, 1149, 1153, 1154, 1218, 1220, 1222, 1237, 1246, 1251, 1257, 1276; BN NAF 23634, no. 154; BN Clairambault 12, nos. 172, 173; BN Clairambault 73, nos. 132, 133; BN P.O. 493, *dossier* 11104, nos. 24, 29, 31; P.O. 1474, *dossier* 33408, nos. 36, 37; P.O. 2624, *dossier* 58366, no. 14; P.O. 2812, *dossier* 62547, no. 21; P.O. 3019, *dossier* 66913, nos. 30, 31; AN K 49, nos. 53, 55. Among all these documents, a few still mention the ransom: BN MS. fr. 26009, nos. 837, 961; 26011, no. 1280. Others describe a special tax in 1371 for the evacuation of the fortress of Thimy: BN MS. fr. 26010, nos. 1177, 1193, 1195, 1197–1206, 1214, 1249.

[145] Between 1372 and 1380, many scores of vouchers and receipts document the collection and disbursement of the "aids ordered for the war." Some are in AN K 50 and 51. Others may be found in the following volumes of manuscripts: BN Clairambault 12, 17, 20, 34, 35, 47, 53, 73, 105; P.O. 366, 447, 493, 549, 1082, 1134, 1433, 1849, 1936, 2030, 2236, 2624, 3019; BN NAF 20027, 23634; BN MS. fr. 20414–20416. By far the largest number of such documents may be found in BN MS. fr. 26011–26017, and it is in this series that the cancellation of the aids in 1380 (see next chapter) is vividly documented by the sudden and almost complete cessation of vouchers and receipts.

VIII. Royal Taxation Comes of Age: Conclusions

1. Politics and Privilege

W HEN the future Charles V, as the young dauphin, was thrust into power in 1356, the French government had been virtually bankrupt for about two years. The royal collaboration with the Estates General in 1355–1356 had been a failure, as resistance to taxes forced the crown into fiscal expedients that led reformers to suspect the king of bad faith. Yet as long as John II was present and the nation's plight was evident, it remained possible that king and Estates would work out a policy of taxation and reform with potential constitutional significance. John's capture ruined this possibility, as both taxation and reform became subordinated to political factionalism. The very officials on whom the dauphin had to depend became the target of a loose coalition of genuine reformers and anti-Valois agitators. The latter, led by men like Le Coq, appeared strong late in 1356, were eclipsed for some months in 1357, and then became dominant in the nine months following the release of Charles the Bad, the party's true leader.

The two great antagonists of 1357–1358, the dauphin and Etienne Marcel, cannot easily be assigned to any faction. Strongly motivated by personal jealousies and ambitions, Marcel seems to have begun as a reformer and to have moved into the anti-Valois camp of Charles the Bad only gradually, towards the end of 1357. The dauphin, compelled by inexperience if not inclination to support the unpopular officials, was not insensitive to proposals for reform, and after securing Paris in 1358 he became conciliatory. Perhaps the greatest achievement of Charles "the Wise" was to distinguish between constructive reformers and mere political agitators and to win to the Valois camp many members of the reform party of 1356.[1] With their indispensable support, he was able to neutralize and then defeat the Evreux faction, while building the fiscal régime and reformed government that would bring France the long-awaited victories of the 1370's.

For much of 1357, there remained a chance for the Estates to assume leadership through the execution of the Grand Ordinance of early March, but this chance was more apparent than real. Already jeopardized by factionalism, it was killed by the progressive alienation of the nobility and the failure to collect the promised taxes. If the liberation of Charles the Bad ensured the victory of self-seekers over reformers in the assemblies, the murder of the two marshals in February, 1358, permanently compromised Marcel and drove a wedge between the nobility and the reform-minded bourgeoisie.[2] The conservative reaction began immediately and, politically speaking, the *Jacquerie* was but a passing episode. As the constitutional struggles in England demonstrate, the aristocracy was the decisive factor in any medieval political equation. When circumstances threw the nobles into his camp, the dauphin Charles knew how to reward and retain their support. Here, the stereotypes of the chivalrous John II and the frail, studious Charles V are misleading, for it was John who had dangerous enemies among important segments of the French nobility, while Charles was the one who conciliated this important class.[3]

The form of taxation in Languedoil offers some indication of the *rapprochement* between the Valois and the aristocracy. The Estates of 1356–1358 sought to collect taxes on the non-noble population according to hearths. The highest of these, 180 *écus* per year on every seventy urban hearths, was only slightly less than the three-franc *fouage* later adopted in 1363, but it imposed a much lighter burden on the towns than did the subsequent *fouage* of 1370. On the other hand, the same assemblies undertook to tax nobles and clergy on the basis of income, the highest rate being 15 per cent, much more than a wealthy bourgeois would have to pay. Once the dauphin (and with him the nobility) regained the ascendancy in 1358, the

---

[1] Cazelles, "Parti navarrais," p. 868.
[2] See Avout, *Meurtre*, pp. 263–264; Luce, *Jacquerie*, pp. 121–122.
[3] Cazelles, "Jean II," pp. 12–13.

government returned immediately to indirect taxation, which affected primarily the urban population and the poor consumer. Up to 1360, substantial *monnayage* was collected, but this affected all people with movable wealth and did not spare bourgeois fortunes. Much the same can be said about the forced loans used for the first ransom payment.

It seems clear that the tax structure of 1358–1360 was more favorable to the nobles than that proposed by the Estates in the two preceding years. More favorable still was the fiscal régime set up at the end of 1360. Reform of the currency meant an end to heavy *monnayage*. The new *aides* and *gabelle* were heavy indirect taxes—5 per cent on most products, somewhat more on salt and, initially, slightly less on wine. The burden, again, was on the consumer; the beneficiaries of this arrangement must have been the rich, especially the rural rich.

It is not so easy to relate class interests to the form of taxation when considering Languedoc. Most assemblies of Estates in Languedoc consisted only of deputies from the towns, but nobles and clergy played a role in these towns, and assemblies of urban representatives were consistently more conservative than their northern counterparts. They followed a tradition that went back to 1346, meeting several times a year to grant short-term taxes, usually apportioned among the communities according to the number of *roturier* (generally, urban) hearths. Early in 1356, Languedoc abandoned these *fouages* in favor of unpopular emergency measures such as the *capage* and property taxes of that year and the *gabelle* on salt, which was reinstated in 1359. The latter became too useful to be abandoned for long, and it became the regular tax for local defense. *Fouages* reappeared in Languedoc to meet the first ransom payment in 1360 and to buy off the companies in 1362 and 1363. They served as the equivalent taxation that replaced the aids from 1362 to 1367. Soon after the aids were reestablished, *fouages* again made their appearance (early 1368), this time to finance the armed forces that Louis of Anjou wished to maintain on a regular footing. For the next decade the hearth taxes became steadily higher and more frequent.

If the aids marked the first sharp increase in the general level of taxation, the *fouages* marked the second. Their real impact in Languedoc came only after 1368, when they were levied *in addition to* the aids. They were, moreover, a traditional form of tax assessment in the Midi and affected all who held *roturier* property. In Languedoil, on the other hand, the general hearth tax first established late in 1363 was an important landmark. Except for the unpopular experiments of the Estates between 1356 and 1358, *fouages* had been very rare in northern France, and they were assessed on the basis of actual households rather than a certain type of property. As opposed to the aids, which in practice were mostly urban taxes, the *fouage* bore heavily on the countryside—on the nobles and their subjects. Even when they were levied at a much higher rate in the towns, the hearth taxes drew most of their revenue from the countryside because most people lived there. It is significant that this tax, which was established to combat brigandage, bore largely on the *plat pays,* where the population was most vulnerable to brigandage and the lords were thought to be implicated in it. The direct taxation of the countryside, moreover, was (and continued to be) tied closely to the maintenance of an army and the payment of military salaries to lords. The history of the *fouage,* like the tax structure generally in Languedoil, suggests Charles V's desire to cultivate the nobles. The towns soon were required to pay it at a higher rate; then, in 1369, an attempt was made to replace it with the sharply regressive new indirect taxes on wine and cereals. When the *fouage* was found indispensable and was reimposed, the towns were assessed at six francs per hearth, triple the rural rate. Finally, it was the *fouage* that Charles V chose to cancel when he lay dying in 1380.[4]

The political influence of the nobles, which affected the failure of the Estates General in the 1350's and the subsequent successes of Charles V, thus also affected the form taken by royal taxation in Languedoil. It was once again demonstrated that a medieval government could not collect taxes successfully without the cooperation of the important men, especially the nobles. Regressive taxes authorized by conservative

---

[4] See below at note 83. The relationship between the political power and economic interests of the nobles and the form taken by royal taxes is a subject that needs careful study. The views expressed in this chapter are necessarily preliminary conclusions, and I have been heavily influenced by the ideas of Charles M. Radding, expressed in private correspondence and also in his unpublished doctoral dissertation, "The Administration of the Aids in Normandy" (Princeton, 1972). See also C. M. Radding, "The Estates of Normandy and the Revolts in the Town of the Beginning of the Reign of Charles VI," *Speculum* 47 (1972): pp. 79-90.

assemblies were easier to collect than progressive taxes forced on the privileged classes by reformers.

The term "privileged classes" must, however, be used with great caution when discussing the fourteenth century. Individuals or corporate groups who hoped to escape taxation often invoked claims of privilege, but one is not impressed by the success of their efforts. The nobles had made the most use of fiscal privilege during the age of the war subsidy, but by the 1350's they were being forced to pay taxes more regularly.[5] Despite the tendency of Charles V to conciliate the nobles, this trend was not reversed.

For the most part, nobles and their subjects paid the aids for the king's ransom without question because of their feudal obligations.[6] Nobles were liable to the *fouages* if they did not bear arms personally, although they were treated separately and sometimes found ways to obtain exemptions or reductions. At the same time, it had become established that seigneurs, like towns, could not tax their own subjects without royal permission.[7]

In Languedoc, the question of noble privilege revolved around two issues—royal taxation of their tallageable subjects and municipal taxation of their *roturier* possessions. The crown usually supported nobles who demanded that their subjects be excused from taxes,[8] but usually upheld municipal authorities in their efforts to tax the urban property of nobles.[9] Sometimes nobles were required to pay municipal taxes only in certain circumstances;[10] on some occasions they managed to escape these taxes altogehter.[11] In general, however, nobles

---

[5] *RTF 1322–1356*, chap. IX, part 2.

[6] On this subject, see Henneman, "Ransom Aids." It should be noted, however, that the indirect taxes did not weigh very heavily on rural *seigneuries*, and that nobles still sometimes had to be ordered to contribute to the ransom, as in AD Hérault A 5, fols. 118r–119r. In another case, nobles who claimed fiscal privileges waived them to permit the collection of the aids in their lands: AN JJ 93, no. 73.

[7] G. Dupont-Ferrier, "Les institutions de la France sous le règne de Charles V," *Journal des Savants* 1932: p. 438; AD Hérault A 5, fols. 275v–276v.

[8] *Ibid.*, A 4, fols. 428r–429v; A 5, fols. 163–164, 310v–312v; 322r–323v; A 6, fols. 118v–119v; BN Coll. Languedoc 86, fols. 95r–v; *HL* 9: pp. 707–708; Delcambre, *Velay*, p. 67.

[9] AD Hérault A 4, fols. 297r–298r; A 5, fols. 82v–84v, 180v–182r; *HL* 9: p. 7078; 10: cols. 1166–1167; *Ord.* 5: pp. 430–431; 7: p. 28; BN Coll. Languedoc 86, fols. 16r–v; *Gr. Chartrier*, no. 2607.

[10] AD Hérault A 5, fols. 29r–v.

[11] *Ibid.*, A 5, fols. 20v–21v, 27r–v; A 6, fols. 1v–2r.

other than the greatest magnates seem to have been subject to most royal taxes in the period 1356–1370. As in the earlier period, they were somewhat more successful than other classes in escaping taxes, but privilege does not seem to have played a major role in reducing their fiscal burden. The most important "privilege" of the nobles continued to be their *de facto* political influence, which was more valuable financially than any theoretical exemption from taxation. Reform of the currency, largely a political issue, probably brought greater tax relief to the nobles in this period than any of the privileges they claimed. Other "privileged" groups, who were less important politically, derived less practical benefit from their privileges.

The clergy continued to pay clerical tenths authorized by the pope during John II's captivity, and they contributed to the first ransom payment.[12] Clerics also paid the aids, and during the nominal peace of the 1360's the tenth ceased to be a regular tax. It reappeared from time to time as an extraordinary papal measure to combat brigandage or promote a crusade that would employ the *routiers,* and it was sometimes limited to a part of the kingdom. Used in this way, it began to serve as the clergy's counterpart of the *fouages,* and clerics normally were not subject to the hearth taxes.[13] When the latter were succeeded by the occasional direct taxes called *tailles* under Charles VI, churchmen paid their counterpart in the form of occasional tenths.[14] After the aids were canceled and then restored in the 1380's, the clergy maintained a special status and the right of consent by going through the formality of granting the aids or their equivalent every two or three years.[15] Clerical incomes suffered from economic problems in the fourteenth century, and by the 1390's a tenth produced only about half as much as it had under Charles IV.[16] The tenths were levied only on ecclesiastical benefices, and these

---

[12] See above, chap. III, part 2.

[13] Vuitry, *Régime financier* 2: pp. 209–210; Prou, *Relations politiques*, P.J. 86.

[14] Rey, *Domaine*, pp. 341, 346.

[15] *Ibid.,* pp. 228–229, and notes.

[16] *Ibid.,* p. 341. According to J. Favier, "Temporels ecclésiastiques et taxation fiscal: le poids de la fiscalité pontificale au XIVe siécle," *Journal des Savants* 1964: p. 109, the real revenue of the bishopric of Cahors declined from 15,000 francs in 1368 to 1000 francs in 1387.

were exempt from *fouages* or *tailles*,[17] but the *roturier* lands of the clergy remained subject to debate.

Before 1356, when most taxes were based on military service, the clergy's claims of privilege were derived from the fact that clerics did not render personal service. The main debate over privileges involved taxes imposed by the towns, which often were shared by the crown, or were levied to pay royal subsidies, or served royal purposes by paying for troops or fortifications. With so obvious an interest in these taxes, the crown regularly supported municipal efforts to tax the urban property of clerics.[18] After 1356, commutation of military service passed out of use as a primary basis for taxation, and the new fiscal machinery enabled the crown to collect its taxes with less recourse to the municipal governments as intermediaries. With the clergy now contributing to the aids but paying tenths in lieu of the *fouages* and later *tailles*, the church maintained a separate identity in fiscal matters. Disputes between municipal authorities and clerics claiming privileges seem to have been less numerous, except in Languedoc, where most taxes still were apportioned among the towns.

By the same token, the crown had a less obvious interest in intervening on behalf of urban governments, although Charles V usually insisted that clerics pay municipal taxes on their *roturier* property.[19] There sometimes were exceptions to this rule,[20] although the only religious order excused from the aids was the Carthusian order.[21] The crown sometimes supported special privileges for prelates,[22] and the upper clergy undoubtedly was able to evade taxation more easily than the lower clergy.[23]

Certain other groups claimed to have fiscal privileges, and again most of the disputes involved municipal taxation in southern France. As various people tried to find excuses for

---

[17] Dupont-Ferrier, *Inst. financières* 2: pp. 166–167.

[18] *RTF 1322–1356*, chap. IX, part 2. When churches or abbeys did owe military service or its equivalent in money, they often had great difficulty in forcing their subjects to contribute what they owed. See Timbal, *Guerre*, p. 30f.

[19] BN Coll. Languedoc 86, fols. 16r–v; AD Hérault A 5, fols. 74v–76v, 82v–83v; A 6, fol. 11r; *Gr. Chartrier*, no. 2607. Guigue, *Tard-Venus*, p. 189.

[20] Tardif, *Monuments historiques*, no. 1412; BN MS. fr. 22469, no. 73; AD Hérault A 1, fols. 39v–41v; A 5, fols. 345v–346r.

[21] AN JJ 93, no. 218; Mouradian, "Rançon," p. 156.

[22] AD Hérault A 5, fols. 196r–200r, 289v–292r; A 6, fols. 3v–4v.

[23] Dupont-Ferrier, *Inst. financières* 2: p. 136.

escaping taxes, their fellow citizens demanded measures to prevent the evasion that would increase their own fiscal burden. An order of 1367 named nobles, clergy, doctors, lawyers, and moneyers as privileged persons who had to contribute to municipal *tailles*.[24] In the case of the moneyers, their privileges covered the emoluments of their offices, but if they engaged in other commercial activity they were taxable. The same rule was applied to royal notaries and sergeants.[25] These officials, as well as people in military garrisons or *bastides,* were often excused from regular taxes but required to pay special ones.[26] When they held property in a town and sought to evade its taxes, the crown regularly required them to pay.[27]

Taxes levied in towns for local defense and repair of fortifications often encountered resistance, and the crown supported the consuls in their efforts to obtain payment.[28] Outlying communities could be forced to contribute to the upkeep of representatives sent to provincial Estates.[29] On the other hand, the consuls of Montpellier did not win royal support when they tried to tax people who had fled to the town seeking refuge from warfare.[30] Some towns received relief from taxation because of special circumstances,[31] while the ravages of war and plague created a general demand for the new hearth counts that began in the 1360's.[32] Even these could give rise to bitter disputes, however, and at Montpellier there were charges of inequity and violation of fiscal privileges.[33]

The whole question of urban privilege and tax evasion remained a complex and contentious one. Although the crown was becoming less directly interested in municipal

[24]*Gr. Chartrier*, no. 2607.

[25]*Ibid.*, nos. 1803, 2571.

[26]AD Hérault A 4, fols. 380v–381v, 393v–394v; A 6, fols. 60v–61v.

[27]*Ibid.*, A 5, fols. 36r–v, 87v–88r, 165r–v; A 6, fols. 25r–26v, 28r–46v; *Gr. Chartrier*, no. 2611. For years after 1370, see BN MS. lat. 9176, fols. 127r–129r.

[28]AM Albi CC 71, no. 1; BN Doat 119, fols. 215r–216v; BN MS. lat. 9175, fols. 47–52; AD Hérault A 4, fols. 426v–428r; A 5, fol. 164r; A 6, fol. 11r.

[29]*Ibid.*, fols. 12v–13v.

[30]*Gr. Chartrier*, no. 1973. In 1380, Lunel had trouble getting royal support in compelling people to pay *tailles* (BN MS. lat. 9176, fols. 13–20v).

[31]AD Hérault A 5, fols. 28r–29r; *Ord.* 5: p. 421.

[32]*Ibid.* 4: pp. 486, 582–584; 6: p. 494. See also chap. V.

[33]*Gr. Chartrier*, no. 2462.

taxation, it normally upheld consuls or *échevins* in their efforts to tax recalcitrant citizens and royal officials. Yet there remained various kinds of privileged people, and efforts to evade taxation did not cease. People with claims to special rights never hesitated to seek the utmost fiscal advantage from such rights. As long as the king opposed these efforts, the claims were merely an irritant to municipal governments, but their continuing existence left open the possibility that privilege might, in the future, give rise to significant inequities in taxation.

Although political influence proved more lucrative in the fourteenth century than fiscal privilege, the two were not completely separate, for the former could help create the latter. In terms of political influence, the most privileged of all people were the small number of great lords who might be called territorial princes. One of the most vexatious political problems to confront the fifteenth-century monarchy was the ability of these princes to divert significant amounts of royal revenue to their own use. In part, this practice grew out of certain "revenue-sharing" practices that the crown found expedient in the fourteenth century.

In the age of the war subsidy, royal financial officers did not enjoy full access to the *apanages* and some great fiefs, such as Flanders, Burgundy, Brittany, and Blois. As a result, subsidies levied in these lands often were divided between the king and the territorial lord.[34] During the 1360's, when large new *apanages* had been created in Anjou, Berry, and Burgundy, a somewhat similar system prevailed, not as a matter of right but as a result of arrangements between the king and his brothers. The aids in the *apanages* produced relatively little revenue, and the king often allowed his brothers to retain all or part of the receipts in a given year.[35] Burgundy seems to have been treated more generously than Berry, for Charles V maintained his right to collect and retain the aids in the latter's *apanage*.[36] After Charles was dead, however, and the regular *fouage* had been supplanted by the periodic direct tax called the *taille*, the princes began to declare that direct

---

[34] *RTF 1322–1356*, pp. 9, 317; *cf.* Vuitry, *Régime financier* 2: p. 113, note 1.

[35] On the aids in the *apanages*, see Rey, *Domaine*, p. 243. See above, chap. VI, for various concessions of the aids to the apanaged princes.

[36] Lacour, *Gouvernement*, p. 312.

taxation abridged the value of their *apanages* and that they should share in the collection and receipt of the funds.[37]

Diversion of tax receipts to the great lords took several other forms. The dukes of Anjou and Berry, as successive royal lieutenants in Languedoc, obtained the use of domainal revenues from their lieutenancy as well as occasional special grants from the local Estates.[38] The Gascon lords who appealed to the crown in 1368—Armagnac, Albret, and Périgord—received large annual pensions from the aids in Languedoc and privileges regarding the taxation of their subjects, in return for aiding the war effort against England.[39] It soon became the practice to abandon to important lords a fraction of the aids collected in their lands, generally one-third, because of their special contribution to the national interest in defending their lands.[40] This practice really was part of a much broader royal policy, one that capitalized on the strong spirit of localism in France.

2. Localism, Necessity, and Consent

Local or regional particularism is so deeply rooted in the French past that one could write a plausible political history of the entire millennium before 1789 by concentrating on the way in which successive governments dealt with localism. With respect to taxation, Philip the Fair had given up his attempt to impose uniform taxes on the whole realm, finding it expedient to let individual regions substitute forms of payment that were compatible with local customs and politics. His successors continued this practice until local variations in taxes reached their greatest diversity around 1339 or 1340. Thereafter, uniformity gained some ground, although Languedoc and Languedoil developed separate fiscal traditions. In the north, localism remained strong enough to frustrate the Estates General of 1355 and 1356, and throughout the country we find a resurgence of it in the later 1350's, inspired by the fear that a corrupt or inept central government would squander taxes and leave localities undefended.[41]

---

[37] Rey, *Domaine*, p. 338.
[38] *Ibid.*, p. 48.
[39] See above, chap. VII, part 1.
[40] Rey, *Domaine*, pp. 198–199.
[41] *RTF 1322–1356*, chap. IX, part 3.

The disaster at Poitiers cut two ways with regard to localism. On the one hand, it made people begin to think of evident necessity in national terms, perhaps for the first time, and gave rise to a heightened royalism and a desire for strong leadership that Charles V eventually would exploit.[42] On the other hand, it sharply amplified the existing fear that individual regions could not look to the central government for protection. Forced to provide for their own defense, individual regions took many initiatives. Provincial Estates multiplied and assumed responsibilities not contemplated in previous years. Where localism had once obstructed royal efforts to mobilize resources for national defense, it now served the constructive function of organizing defense regionally and financing effective measures that the crown was too weak to direct.

This trend could not continue indefinitely without grave danger to the embryonic French state. People terrified by brigandage could not afford to be unselfish towards their neighbors, and the inhabitants of Auvergne were not concerned that the *routiers* they ejected turned their wrath on Lyonnais. The crown, however, regained control before the particularism got out of hand. The new tradition of higher taxes imposed locally for local defense facilitated the collection of higher royal taxes in the later 1360's. The royal government continued to let towns raise taxes for their own defense and retain a portion of the aids for the same purpose. It was in much the same spirit that the king shared royal tax revenues with the great territorial lords. Charles V avoided a direct assault on local particularism, finding it more effective to conduct the defense of the realm through decentralized efforts.

If the tribulations that followed 1356 affected French localism, they also affected the public response to such legal concepts as "common profit," "evident necessity," and *quod omnes tangit*. People still associated the common profit mainly with countering military danger, but they no longer were so rigid as to believe that taxes for the common profit were irrelevant in time of truce. The *routiers* proved more

---

[42] See below, at note 46. See also Mirot, *Insurrections*, p. 60, for a similar reaction in the 1380's.

persuasive than the lawyers of Philip IV or Philip VI. When heavy taxes were levied to ransom castles, send soldiers to remote parts of Europe, or further Louis of Anjou's ambitions in Provence, their justification was not challenged. The ransom aids, almost by definition, were peacetime taxes, but the lack of opposition to them suggests that people considered peace with England and the king's return to be necessary for the common profit.[43]

Well before 1356, it has been argued, the French accepted the principle that "necessity knows no law." The "necessity," however, had to be "evident," and mere royal assertions of necessity were not sufficient in the years of intermittent skirmishing during the first half of the century.[44] The capture of John II, however, created an undeniable state of "evident necessity" that was national in character. No doubt people still considered local criteria first when defining necessity, but the events that followed Poitiers placed every region in peril and left no doubt that the king's captivity was a local as well as national calamity. The truce of 1357 left thousands of soldiers unemployed; open war with the king of Navarre in the summer of 1358 gave *routiers* a legal basis for their operations. The English invasion of 1359, serious enough in itself, was doubly so because it left Champagne and Burgundy infested with brigands. The militance of Gaston Phoebus in Languedoc was another consequence of the king's captivity, and the very treaty that secured John's release left virtually every part of France exposed to *routiers*. At the time he imposed the aids, John II could rightly claim that the taxes were necessary not merely to pay his ransom but to prevent the very destruction of the kingdom.[45]

The dauphin Charles, meanwhile, had gained some first-hand experience with "evident necessity," and he was quick to perceive that royal interests could be served by perpetuating within the country a sense of crisis. He possessed a sense of the majesty and sacred purpose of French kingship that was fully in the tradition of Louis IX and Philip IV, and he never failed to emphasize his devotion to the *chose publique* and his belief that the nation would be in peril if the *chose publique* were

---

[43] Henneman, "Ransom Aids," pp. 628–629.
[44] See above, chap. I, part 3.
[45] Henneman, "Ransom Aids," note 62.

improperly administered.[46] A student has recently argued that "the most astute propaganda device of Charles V is to be found in his creation of a timeless state of emergency. The very meaning of 'necessity' shifts from an outer limited state of emergency to an inner timeless administrative need."[47] This observation is based on a reading of the preambles to the king's ordinances, and it would seem that Charles outdid his predecessors in stressing the common profit and the existence of threats to the general welfare. One must conclude that Charles understood the mood of the country and knew how to exploit it. He was successful in collecting high taxes and in rebuilding royal power; by contrast, his sons and brothers would fail to present themselves as credible upholders of the common welfare.[48]

We have said that a striking characteristic of the age of the war subsidy was the apparent lack of interest in the doctrine of *quod omnes tangit*. Consent as such was not unimportant, for taxation in any community required the cooperation of the powerful men. Rarely, however, did people claim a fundamental right to give even procedural consent to measures that might suspend their rights.[49] At first glance, consent seems to have been taken more seriously after 1356. Ordinances mention actions taken with *commune assentment*[50] or require that future actions be taken only with consent.[51] Oresme may have helped to popularize the principle, for his treatise on the coinage dealt with a subject of great contemporary political interest that clearly touched everybody. Significantly, the Grand Ordinance of 1357 gave the Estates General the right to consent to any alteration of the *pied de monnaie*.[52]

It is equally significant, however, that these Estates, which actually had given consent on a number of other matters, did not claim a *right* to do so except with respect to the coinage.

---

[46]G. Dodu, "Les idées de Charles V en matière de gouvernement," *Rev. quest. hist.* 110 (1929): pp. 20, 24–27.

[47]S. H. Madden, "Charles V and Royal Propaganda, 1364–1380," unpublished seminar paper, University of Iowa (Iowa City, 1970).

[48]See the comments of Radding, "Estates," p. 79.

[49]See above, chap. I, part 3.

[50]*Ord.* 4: pp. 589, 690; 5: pp. 614, 652; 6: pp. 68, 164, 362. These documents are discussed by Madden (*cit. supra*, note 47).

[51]*Ord.* 5: pp. 183, 689.

[52]See the discussion of the Grand Ordinance above, chap. II, at notes 38–50.

To the modern historian, consent is especially interesting when it relates to the potential constitutional role of representative assemblies, and although assemblies assumed a greater role as consenting bodies in practice during the years 1356–1370, one finds little evidence that they claimed any right to consent to taxes. In Languedoil, the Estates General regularly consented to specific taxes after 1355, but only the *fouage* of 1363 was collected without some form of additional consultation. Taxes imposed by central assemblies in the 1350's met great opposition unless ratified locally. The assemblies of 1367 and 1369 appear to have consulted with the localities before taking final action. The Estates of Languedoc, which began as a branch of the Estates General but became more like a provincial assembly after 1360, regularly consented to taxes that their constituents, with a few exceptions, considered binding. Other assemblies that were more clearly provincial in character often gave binding consent to taxes. Nevertheless, a recent study shows that Normandy (so often the pacesetter on matters of finance) paid taxes regularly to Charles V, whether or not the Estates had met to grant them.[53] Evidently formal consent still was not considered an essential prerequisite to the payment of taxes. Opposition, when it occurred, still did not focus on a failure to obtain consent. Consent to taxation by assemblies was more widespread in practice, but still not important in principle.

For assemblies, the late 1350's marked something of a turning point. The period of crisis from the battle of Crécy through the Black Death had spawned many regional and bailiwick assemblies. These somewhat *ad hoc* meetings had enabled the crown to obtain the cooperation of important local people in levying taxes, and to do so more easily than through laborious negotiation with individual localities. They were small enough to safeguard regional interests, while permitting taxpayers to negotiate with the crown from a less vulnerable position. The appearance of these regional assemblies was accompanied by a decline in the oppressive tactics of *réformateurs,* and all parties must have welcomed them as an improvement over earlier procedures. The big question, by 1355, was whether these effective regional assemblies could be

---

[53] Radding, "Estates," p. 79.

"nationalized," or assimilated into a single assembly for all of Languedoil if not the whole kingdom. In the long run, such a development might have led to limitations on royal power, but in the medieval context it was far more likely to be a benefit to the crown. In any case, efforts in this direction met with setbacks in 1355–1356, and as already pointed out, the king's capture further reduced their chances of success.

For the Estates General to survive as an institution of enduring significance, the right conditions were necessary, since the assemblies had to meet several potentially conflicting requirements. They had to be able to (1) produce taxes and be useful to the crown without alienating the forces of localism; (2) press for reforms without assuming so hostile a stance as to pose a threat to royal power itself; (3) maintain a spirit of cooperation, if not common interest, between the nobles and the upper bourgeoisie; and (4) meet with enough frequency to preserve continuity. The last of these requirements had not been met before the 1340's, but it was between 1343 and 1369, and had the Estates satisfied the first three requirements, the fourth would have followed as a matter of course, barring extraordinary circumstances of an external nature. Such a circumstance was the Black Death; the Estates of late 1347 seem to have met the first three requirements (certainly the first two), but because of the plague their program did not receive an adequate trial. In 1355 the Estates failed to meet the first requirement, and this fundamental failure to produce taxes ultimately brought down the Estates of October, 1356, and February, 1357. Those of later 1357 and early 1358 failed to meet any of the first three requirements, and by the time the dauphin regained Paris, the Estates were in disrepute. Even then, however, their potential usefulness could not be ignored, and the Estates General of the 1360's seemed to meet all the requirements for success.

It was too late, however. If central assemblies were sometimes useful, they had clearly failed to make themselves indispensable. There was still no great interest in the principle of consent, and the experiences of his youth doubtless made Charles V suspicious of large meetings. He was able to collect substantial taxes without them. Knowing how to exploit local particularism, he was discovering the value of a decentralized approach to the problem of brigandage, thanks to the constructive initiatives of regional assemblies.

Where the local negotiations of the 1330's and 1340's had given way to regional assemblies in the 1350's, the latter did not in turn become amalgamated into a central assembly. Instead, these regional meetings proliferated after 1356 and developed into the provincial Estates. Although they would temporarily recede in importance after 1370, they proved to be a more enduring and significant institution than the Estates General. In the critical years of the king's captivity, the provincial Estates proved more effective than central assemblies in providing money, and the struggle against brigandage enhanced their importance further. It was no longer a question of giving counsel as to the existence of an emergency, or even of giving passive consent to some royal program. These assemblies taxed their regions to cope with a manifest emergency; they hired and equipped troops, ransomed fortresses, and concluded treaties. The populace came to view the provincial Estates as the appropriate bodies for safeguarding local interests, apportioning taxes, obtaining alternative forms of taxation if desirable, and giving such consent as was thought necessary.[54]

In serving the interests of their regions during these years of trouble, these assemblies were also serving royal interests, just as did towns that repaired their own ramparts or great lords who defended their lands against the English. It was essential to the crown that it maintain some control over these local initiatives, and Charles V was able to do so. At the same time, it became clear that both royal finance and national defense could be conducted with more efficiency and less friction when most of the work was left in local hands. This policy was pursued in collecting the down payment on the king's ransom in 1360;[55] it appears to have been what was intended by the

---

[54] See A. Thomas, "Le Midi et les Etats généraux sous Charles VII," *Annales du Midi* 4 (1892): p. 18; Lewis, *Later Medieval France*, pp. 280–281; Major, *Representative Institutions*, p. 25; Wolfe, *Fiscal System*, p. 42f. It should be emphasized, of course, that even in the 1370's many regions paid taxes regularly without assemblies at any level, and the tendency, in the next century, was for the *pays d'états* to become less numerous. These facts do not, however, detract from the significant proliferation of regional assemblies in the period after 1356. Even where such assemblies had occasionally met previously, their increased frequency was in most cases directly attributable to the king's capture. See for instance, the case of Artois: Hirschauer, *Etats d'Artois* 1: pp. 18–19, 111–112.

[55] That is, each locality could determine what tax it wished to use in repaying the forced loans collected for the king's release. See Richard, "Instructions," and the discussion in chap. III, above.

Estates General of late 1347. People were more willing to support measures that were carried out by men of their own region. They had distrusted and resisted the aggressive commissioners of Philip VI and the centralized decision-making of the Estates General in the later 1350's.

We probably should not credit the kings with conscientiously adopting the most effective policy. It seems safe to say that the provincial Estates and regional initiatives became important not because the crown preferred them, but because the circumstances created by John II's capture made a centralized national policy impossible. At the very time that Charles V was cultivating an exalted view of kingship and a sense of continuing national emergency, the weakness of the monarchy in dealing with the *routiers* forced it to encourage regional initiatives. Surely, however, we can credit Charles (or the reformers that he drew into his camp) with making the best of the situation that was imposed on the government. The victories of the 1370's were founded on a system which resembled that "certain local autonomy" to which Cazelles has referred, and foreshadowed the "bureaucratic decentralization" by which Major has characterized the fifteenth-century monarchy.[56]

3. Fiscal Administration and the Level of Taxation

Although Joseph Strayer has criticized the European monarchies of the late Middle Ages for failing to adjust to change and devise the new institutions that they needed,[57] it is difficult to accept this generalization when considering France. The fourteenth century was a period of great institutional development. Not only did the Chamber of Accounts,

---

[56] See above, chap. I, at notes 66 and 67. Major's expression is intended to describe the somewhat paradoxical situation in which the monarchy had more highly developed institutions than in the thirteenth century, but exercised less direct control from Paris. It is my contention that this state of affairs began to be evident under Charles V, but admittedly one major aspect of "bureaucratic decentralization"—the development of provincial *parlements* and other sovereign courts—came only in the fifteenth century. Dupont-Ferrier, "Institutions sous Charles V," p. 397, said that centralization made great progress under Charles V, but to say this is to miss the significance of the *routiers* and the provincial Estates. The way in which Charles V encouraged localism but brought it effectively under ultimate royal control is revealed more accurately by Contamine, *Guerre*, pp. 146-147, 162.

[57] J. R. Strayer, *On the Medieval Origins of the Modern State* (Princeton, 1970), pp. 77-84.

the *parlement*, and the Estates at different levels experience significant growth, but Maurice Rey is probably correct in saying that the monarchy's most original administrative creation in the second half of the century was the machinery for extraordinary revenues.[58] When considering it, one must bear in mind that the new machinery was the product of a gradual evolution and that all forms of tax continued to be regarded as temporary expedients long after regular taxation was established. These facts influenced institutional development.[59]

Through the age of the war subsidy, little progress was made in developing a financial administration, and the Chamber of Accounts had to supervise extraordinary as well as ordinary revenues.[60] The rapid growth in the power and influence of this body came under attack in the mid-1340's, and the crown began to search for alternative ways of administering finances. A separate body was established to administer the currency, and in 1345 the government first proposed a nationwide tax computed in men-at-arms, with the money to be administered, not by royal officials, but by persons named by the taxpayers of each region.[61] Such local appointees had been employed in Vermandois and Picardy as early as 1340, and when the royal plan was finally adopted by the Estates General of 1347, local assemblies throughout France named *élus* to collect the subsidy. This new system did not survive the Black Death, but the Estates General of Languedoil in 1355 and 1356 revived the *élus* and added the supervisory officials called *généraux*.[62]

When, therefore, the age of the war subsidy was succeeded in 1356 by the period of the king's captivity and ransom, the precedents were available on which to build a new financial administration. The disordered years of the later 1350's saw more experimentation; then, with the establishment of the

[58] Rey, *Domaine*, p. 231. As Contamine, *Guerre*, pp. 219-222, points out, it is significant that the *arrière-ban* was not used on a general scale between 1356 and 1410, after its extensive use as a fiscal device in the age of the war subsidy.

[59] Rey, *Domaine*, p. 197f; Mouradian, "Rançon," p. 153; G. Dupont-Ferrier, *Les origines et le premier siècle de la chambre ou cour des aides de Paris* (Paris, 1933), pp. 14-15.

[60] On the Chamber of Accounts and its influence in the government from 1335 to 1345, see Cazelles, *Soc. politique*, pp. 107f, 431-432.

[61] *RTF 1322-1356*, p. 181f.

[62] *Ibid.*, pp. 149, 151, 225, 229-231, 286, 291f.

aids in 1360, the crown organized the first fully developed machinery for extraordinary revenues. *Élus*, now salaried royal officers, were established in every diocese to supervise farming and collection of the aids. They were responsible to treasurers-general at Paris. Establishment of the *fouage* in Languedoil three years later led to further changes, including separate *généraux* at Paris, but in many places the same administration handled both the aids and the hearth tax.[63] When the war with England resumed and the aids no longer were specifically for the ransom, the extraordinary taxes were collected by a single administration— the *élus* in every diocese and the *généraux*, now called councillors-general, at Paris. The *élus* were employed throughout Languedoil, even in *apanages* and in regions that had provincial Estates. Only gradually were the dioceses broken down into the smaller financial districts that became known as *élections*.[64] The *géneraux* may have been given some judicial functions under Charles V,[65] but it was only towards 1390 that the councillors-general began to exercise judicial powers as a corporate body, the Court of the Aids.[66] Languedoc, which continued to be administered separately, had no *parlement* in the fourteenth century, and the treasurers-general who supervised the receivers in each seneschalsy began to exercise judicial powers much earlier.[67] When the *fouages* of Charles V were replaced in subsequent reigns by the apportioned direct taxes called *tailles*, Languedoc assessed these in the same manner as the former *fouages*. In Languedoil, the apportionment was carried out by *élus* in consultation with local notables.[68]

The actual weight of taxation—how much people had to pay and how much the government collected—is largely a matter of speculation. So few financial figures survive for the period 1350–1370 that one is limited to a few approximations. The recurrent plagues and new enumerations of hearths create

---

[63] Dupont-Ferrier, *Inst. financières* 2: pp. 25–26; Rey, *Domaine*, pp. 186–187.

[64] Dupont-Ferrier, "Institutions sous Charles V," p. 198; see also Radding, "Administration," chap. 2.

[65] Dupont-Ferrier, "Institutions sous Charles V," p. 440; Dupont-Ferrier, *Origines . . . cour des aides*, pp. 17–18.

[66] On the councillors-general, see *Ord.* 6: p. 705; p. 762f. See also Rey, *Domaine*, p. 250f; Dupont-Ferrier, "Institutions sous Charles V," p. 440.

[67] Rey, *Domaine*, pp. 122, 226, 334.

[68] *Ibid.*, p. 331.

an added complication. Fortunately, the coinage remained fairly stable, with silver fluctuating between the 21st and 25th *pied* between 1361 and 1385. In such years as 1304, 1328, and 1348, the *pied* had been in the same general range, and the gold franc established late in 1360 represented one *livre tournois*. These facts permit us to express certain totals in francs/*livres tournois* for purposes of rough comparison, and in this way it was possible to show the startling increase in the annual tax burden per hearth at Montpellier. It would be more desirable, if figures were available, to convert all totals to silver marks based on the price paid for specie at the mints, but even these results would be distorted because they would ignore fluctuations in the purchasing power of the precious metals.[69]

The yield of taxes must have been affected by a variety of external factors. The plagues of 1348, 1361, and 1374 reduced the taxpaying population, as did the territorial cessions to England. The *routiers* must have disrupted the collection of taxes and the dispatch of revenues to Paris, but the economic impact of plunder, ransoms, and military salaries has not yet been described satisfactorily. If it is uncertain how these factors may have aggravated or mitigated the economic depression, it is equally difficult to describe their effect on taxation. Indirect taxes on salt, wine, and other consumer goods were collectable mainly in the towns, where most commerce was concentrated and evasion was most difficult. Consequently, they could be affected adversely by plagues and other disruptions of urban life. Direct taxes, which bore on rural as well as urban areas, presumably suffered from war and brigandage. For further enlightenment, we must await studies of local economic and fiscal conditions.[70]

For the present, we are left with Rey's estimate that the taxes in Languedoil produced 1,650,000 pounds in 1372–1373. Although he separates the aids from the *gabelle*, Rey seems to include the *fouage* with the aids, presumably because both taxes in the 1370's were called the "aids for the war" and were

---

[69] For variations in the *pied* and other remarks on the currency, see below, appendix I, and notes. For a somewhat more detailed treatment of the subject, with reference to the years before 1356, see *RTF 1322–1356*, appendix I.

[70] Publication of the theses of Mouradian, Radding, and certain American graduate students currently working in this field, should offer historians valuable details about the effects of different forms of taxation.

collected by the same administration.[71] The *fouage* seems to have accounted for perhaps a third of the total in the towns and as much as half in less urbanized areas like Anjou.[72] The indirect aids may thus have produced between 900,000 and 1,000,000 pounds in Languedoil in the 1370's, 30 per cent more than Philip IV had collected from a much larger and more prosperous population in 1304. The receipts were swelled, perhaps considerably, when the *quatrième* (25 per cent) was established on wine in 1369, and they may in any case have been higher than they were in the disordered 1360's. Radding suggests that the *fouages* and aids in Languedoil during the 1360's produced a little more than half the receipts from these sources in the 1370's.[73] This would imply a total of around 850,000 pounds, so that even if the *fouage* accounted for as much as half, the aids should have been sufficient to meet the annual ransom payments if not diverted to other purposes.

In the absence of more documentation, none of these figures inspire great confidence. The aids, being based on trade, fluctuated with economic conditions, and their importance

---

[71] Rey, *Domaine*, p. 260.

[72] Radding, "Administration," chap. 2, has analysed AN KK 350 in order to establish the relative importance of different taxes in the Norman towns between 1371 and 1375. He also compares these receipts with what is known from other surviving accounts, including information from the lands of the duke of Anjou.

[73] *Ibid.* Radding finds that taxes on wines produced about one-third of the royal taxes in the 1370's, with by far the largest part coming from the *quatrième* on retail sales, first established in 1369. He thinks that Rey's figures for the aids under Charles VI are too high, because receipts in Normandy seem to have dropped about 40 per cent when the *fouage* was canceled in 1380. Rey's figures do present some difficulties. He states (*Domaine*, p. 242) that few towns in Languedoil paid as much as 25,000 francs for the aids in Charles VI's reign, while some of the greater towns of Langeudoc were able to pay 45,000 annually. If Montpellier was one of these, it would imply an average contribution of twenty francs per taxable hearth, an enormous figure even when compared to the high level of 1368–1372 (above, chap. VIII, at notes 76–92). In terms of rate, one of the higher taxes was the *gabelle*, and by 1370 the crown was requiring all parishes to buy a minimum amount of salt subject to this tax (Rey, *Domaine*, p. 184; Dupont-Ferrier, *Inst. financières* 2: p. 119). If we may infer (chap. VII, note 99) that half the *gabelle* in Normandy approximated 1700 francs per month in 1370, then this tax produced over 41,000 francs, or about 10 per cent of Radding's estimate for all tax receipts in Normandy. Again, however, the documentation is so limited as to raise doubts as to the validity of such a figure. In estimating the size and cost of the royal army in the 1370's, Contamine, *Guerre*, p. 136 and notes, concluded that the crown had about 825,000 l. t. annually available for military purposes. For the subsidy of 1304 (at least 735,000 l. t. in money on the 26th *pied*), see Strayer and Taylor, *Studies*, p. 74.

relative to the *fouage* must have varied. The *fouages,* moreover, were not constant; in Languedoc they were short-term
grants by assemblies and they sometimes fluctuated more than
the indirect taxes. At Montpellier between 1368 and 1370, they
were worth considerably more than the aids or their equivalent if our estimates are correct, but this was not necessarily
the case in other periods.[74] Finally, it is clear that the few
surviving treasury registers do not reveal the extent of royal
income from extraordinary revenues. For 1374, receipts from
subsidies, loans, etc., were recorded as 88,000 l.t., while the
comparable figures for 1384 were substantially lower.[75] Both
totals are absurdly low, particularly in view of a special surtax
on the aids that was imposed in 1384.[76] Evidently receipts
from the major taxes were not recorded in the traditional
treasury documents, and these registers cannot be used as an
indication of the ·relative importance of ordinary and extraordinary revenues.

In terms of its relative importance in the royal budget, the
royal domain declined drastically during the fourteenth century. The cessions to England and the creation of large
apanages had reduced the extent of the domain, while the
ravages of war, plague, and depression also took their toll.
Considerable territory had been recovered by 1374, but in that
year the country was beset by plague and famine, and the net
domainal receipts at the treasury are said to have been less
than 50,000 pounds.[77] By contrast, Charles IV and Philip VI,
in the 1320's, had enjoyed average annual net domainal
revenues of about 442,000 l. t. and 647,000 l. t. respectively in
comparable currency.[78] Of course, 1374 was an unusually bad
year, and Rey has concluded that an economic improvement
took place in the last quarter of the century. Between
1369–1370 and the end of the century, revenue from indirect
taxes at Paris increased 16 per·cent on cloth and 9 per cent on

---

[74] See above, chap. VII, at notes 76–87.

[75] Rey, *Domaine,* pp. 91–92.

[76] See the discussion below, note 81. On the special tax of 1384, see below at note
108.

[77] Rey, *Domaine,* p. 91.

[78] These are artificial figures derived from the material in *RTF 1322–1356,* appendix
I. The estimated average in marks of silver has been converted to *livres tournois* using
the *pied de monnaie* in order to facilitate comparison with figures from the last third
of the century, when the *pied* is known, but not the mint price of silver in all cases.

grain.[79] The net ordinary revenues of Charles VI were up to 101,000 l. t. in 1384; 125,000 in 1388; and around 190,000 in 1389, 1394, and 1395.[80] These figures, however, were slightly inflated by a new weakening of the currency to the 27th *pied*. Where the domain produced more than 40 per cent of Philip VI's revenue in the first years of his reign, it is doubtful that it produced more than 10 per cent of Charles VI's revenue. In the troubled 1360's, moreover, domainal receipts may well have approached more closely the low figure of 1374.[81]

Without adequate figures, we can say no more about the weight of taxation in the years 1356–1370. We are left with two safe conclusions: the drastic decline in the relative importance of the royal domain, and the equally drastic increase in the fiscal burden of the average taxable household that the figures from Montpellier demonstrate.

4. Continuity and Change

During the age of the war subsidy, taxes had been light but had encountered resistance. The opposition had been based on precedent or privilege or the absence of evident necessity, but not on the principle of consent. Taxes were collectable only in cases of "necessity," which people defined in such a way as to mean military danger to the taxpayers' locality. By 1370, however, taxes were regular, annual, and relatively heavy, collected in time of peace as well as war, and yet significant opposition did not materialize between the late 1350's and the late 1370's. Clearly, a major change had taken place.

At the same time, there was much that did not change dramatically. People had come to define "common profit" more broadly than before, yet a sense of necessity remained far

---

[79] Mouradian, "Rançon," p. 154, indicates that receipts from the aids declined in the 1360's. On the subsequent rise in these revenues, see Rey, *Domaine*, p. 235.

[80] *Ibid.*, p. 92.

[81] On the domain under Philip VI, see *RTF 1322–1356*, appendix I. On the changing *pied* under Charles VI, see below, appendix I. Wolfe, *Fiscal System*, p. 20, cites the tables of Rey, *Domaine*, pp. 81–99, to show that the domain was still the main source of income and that taxes produced less than 30 per cent of the total revenue in the later fourteenth century. This conclusion, however, is erroneous, since Rey's other figures for the *aides* and *tailles* show that taxes produced far more than the receipts in the treasury journals indicate.

more important than the formality of consent when it came to paying taxes. Localism now took the form of constructive efforts on behalf of regional defense, but it remained a strong sentiment, and the crown merely displayed greater skill in dealing with it. Those who claimed exemption from taxes appeared to be losing ground, but privilege continued to be invoked. A regular administration, rather than domainal officers, now collected the extraordinary taxes, but the taxes still were extraordinary in principle. The fiscal expedients so familiar in the 1320's and 1330's were much less common, but they had not disappeared completely.

In many respects, therefore, the changes were gradual and consisted mainly of modifications of traditional practice rather than a sharp break with the past. The similarities between the political events of 1345–1348 and those of 1355–1358 make it tempting to adopt a periodization that stresses a transitional phase from 1345 to 1360. This period began with the Chamber of Accounts' fall from power and the government's proposal for a national tax expressed in men-at-arms. It ended with the reform of the coinage and the establishment of the aids. At the same time, it lacked real unity because it was interrupted by two events of crucial importance: the Black Death, which ruined the first serious attempt to accomplish taxation and reform through the Estates General; and the capture of John II at Poitiers, without which many subsequent developments would be inconceivable.

With the king a captive, the Estates General became more vulnerable to destructive factionalism, unpaid soldiers resorted to brigandage, and the country faced the need to raise a large royal ransom. The *aides pour la délivrance* combined the features of a feudal aid and a tax levied out of evident necessity. France's first peacetime taxes were regular, heavy, and imposed without bargaining with assemblies. At this very moment, the threat of brigandage was forcing people to change their thinking about taxation. The routiers taught them that "evident necessity" and the "common profit" were not determined by a formal state of peace or war. The *routiers* taught provincial assemblies to assume responsibility for their own defense, and they forced the royal government to welcome local, decentralized action in the areas of finance and defense. Above all, it was the *routiers* who persuaded local inhabitants that it was cheaper in the long run to pay for a standing army than to suffer the brutality and blackmail of unemployed soldiers in time of peace. This bitter lesson laid the first foundations for the rise of absolutism in early modern France.

Even while conceding the many elements of continuity between the early and late fourteenth century, we must conclude from these facts that the history of French taxation was permanently and irrevocably altered by the events set in motion by the battle of Poitiers. Yet if the year 1356 marked a significant break with the past, were there not other moments of dramatic change in the years ahead? To what extent are we really justified in saying that the financial basis for the early modern French state was laid in the years 1356–1370? To deal with these questions, we must consider, in broad outline, the evolution of royal taxation from the 1370's to the 1440's.

5. From Charles V to Charles VII: The Legacy of the 1360's

A notable feature of the high taxes under Charles V was the fact that they encountered much less opposition than did the much lower taxes of an earlier generation. The new fiscal burden was not, however, accepted cheerfully. It was a matter of grave necessity to pay the ransom, to suppress the brigands, and to finance a victorious renewal of the war, but once it was suspected that the taxes were not achieving the desired results, a reaction against them set in. The momentum of the French recovery had slackened notably by 1378. Cherbourg and Bordeaux remained firmly English. Edward III had been succeeded by a minor, and with Charles V in failing health there was reason to think that France also would soon have a child king. New peace negotiations were underway, and with them came a growing feeling that taxes should be reduced.

In Languedoc, Louis of Anjou had well-known foreign ambitions, and there was fear that his rigorous administration would maintain high taxes to support his private schemes. A serious rebellion broke out at Montpellier in 1379, after which the southern towns jointly levied a *fouage* of one and one-third francs in order to finance an embassy to Paris in the spring of 1380. This mission secured the recall of Anjou late in April, and the king sent *réformateurs* to the Midi with wide powers to redress grievances.[82]

This crisis in Languedoc was the first phase of a major reaction against taxation that briefly appeared to threaten the royal financial edifice constructed in the 1360's. Considerable speculation has surrounded the motives and behavior of Charles V, who died in September, 1380, after issuing a famous "last ordinance" canceling the *fouage*.[83] The royal chancellor did not mention this ordinance in his chronicle, and may indeed have disapproved of it, but the text was not suppressed, and copies were known in several localities within a few weeks.[84]

Nationalist historians have deplored this action as an aberration, a blemish on the career of a king who had led the monarchy from degradation to victory in less than twenty years. Yet the fact that Charles was successful does not entitle us to judge him by the standards of modern secular politics. The majesty of medieval kingship involved more than power alone, and Elizabeth Brown has argued that the theologians' writings on fiscal morality and their influence on the consciences of kings played a significant role in the French royal tradition. Philip IV, whose government is often associated with ruthlessness, had assumed a posture of great moral rectitude; and he was not the only previous French king to return a tax whose collection he had concluded was unjustified. When Charles V faced death, a favorable peace with England seemed attainable, and he may well have doubted his moral right to continue the *fouage*. Cancellation of the tax

---

[82]*HL* **9**: pp. 872-879, 892-893. It is notable that Languedoc, which had asked for a royal prince as lieutenant in 1356, was eager to be rid of one a generation later. The immediate cause of the rebellion at Montpellier seems to have been a *fouage* at the very high rate of twelve francs, obtained by officers of Louis of Anjou in 1379 when the duke was absent from the land. On these events see also *Ord.* **6**: p. 465f; Mirot, *Insurrections*, pp. 15-16; Dussert, *Etats Dauphiné*, p. 89f (on Anjou's Mediterranean ambitions); A. Blanc, "Le rappel du duc d'Anjou et l'ordonnance du 25 Avril 1380," *Bull. hist. et phil. du comité des trav. historiques et scientifiques* 1899: pp. 191-195, 197-201, 205-212; H. Miskimin, "The Last Act of Charles V: The Background of the Revolts of 1382," *Speculum* **38** (1963): pp. 437-439.

[83]*Ord.* **7**: p. 710; *Mandements*, no. 1955.

[84]L. Finot, "La dernière ordonnance de Charles V," *Bib. Ec. Chartes* **50** (1889): pp. 164-167.

would have been consistent with the best traditions of French kingship as he saw them.[85]

Other modern historians are inclined to credit Charles with more pragmatism than conscience. Harry Miskimin believes that the taxes of the 1370's had filled the treasury and that Charles V considered the aids to be sufficient for a peacetime budget. Suspecting the bellicosity and foreign ambitions of his brothers, the king canceled the *fouage* to compel his successor to adopt a policy of peace and frugality and relieve royal subjects of an unnecessary burden.[86] Charles Radding has recently suggested that the tax was canceled because it was unpopular with the nobility, whose support would be valuable if the new king was a minor.[87]

In a sense, Brown, Miskimin, and Radding may all be right, for it is unlikely that Charles V was impelled by any single motive. Miskimin cannot prove that the treasury was full in 1380, but royal finances surely were in better condition than implied by Léon Mirot, who believed that the Estates General were summoned in November because the government was in financial distress. It was rather that the late king's brothers, who were jealous of each other and wanted to appropriate royal revenues for their own purposes, had to confront the growing discontent towards all taxation.[88]

Whether or not the cancellation of the *fouage* was intended to appease the nobles, it certainly produced a sharp reaction from the townspeople, who demanded an end to the aids as well, and bullied tax collectors in some regions.[89] After his coronation in November, Charles VI proceeded to Paris, where the Estates were convened in *Parlement* to honor him.[90] Louis of Anjou's request for more taxes did not impress the assembly (which probably suspected his foreign projects), and

[85] E. Brown, "Taxation and Morality in the Thirteenth and Fourteenth Centuries: Conscience and Political Power and the Kings of France," *French Historical Studies* **8**, 1: pp. 24–25. A will and codicil of Charles V are found in *Chron. Jean II et Charles V* **3**: P.J. 25, 30.

[86] Miskimin, "Last Act," pp. 436–437, 439–441. *Cf.* Mirot, *Insurrections*, pp. 15–16.

[87] Radding, "Administration," esp. chap. 6.

[88] Mirot, *Insurrections*, pp. 9, 21–25, 25n. On the rapacious princes, also see Radding, "Estates," p. 80; Miskimin, "Last Act," pp. 441–442.

[89] Radding, "Estates," p. 80, note 4; Coville, *Etats Norm.*, p. 123; Mirot, *Insurrections*, pp. 20–21, 80.

[90] *Ibid.*, pp. 27, 29 (note 1), 31 (note 1), 34.

the Parisians agitated for the cancellation of the aids.[91] Anjou's power was soon curtailed by his brothers, and John of Berry was named lieutenant in Languedoc, where he quickly resumed his old quarrel with Gaston of Foix and antagonized the southern population.[92] Meanwhile, the divided government bowed to the public clamor and abolished all extraordinary taxes levied since the reign of Philip IV.[93] It hoped to obtain new taxes from regional assemblies, but despite a widespread *routier* threat, the provincial Estates did not prove generous. They followed the lead of Normandy in refusing a grant until they should learn the reactions of other regions.[94]

Reconvening on 20 December, 1380, the Estates General of Languedoil presented their grievances, and a new ordinance in January, 1381, reaffirmed old privileges as well as the recent cancellation of taxes.[95] Now the provincial Estates were prepared to make grants, and the Normans, who had rejected new indirect taxes, met in February to authorize a *fouage* graduated according to the wealth of each household. Collectable by *élus* of the Norman Estates for fifty-four weeks, it was to produce from $1\frac{1}{8}$ to $6\frac{3}{4}$ l. t. per hearth for this period.[96] As on other occasions, the rest of Languedoil followed the Norman lead. By the spring of 1381, the government had obtained hearth taxes generally, perhaps following a new meeting of the Estates General.[97]

The reaction against taxation, however, did not abate. The new subsidy was to expire in a year, and well before this time it encountered trouble in Normandy, where nobles obstructed collection.[98] Before the end of 1381, the crown ordered the levy of a surtax.[99] Louis of Anjou failed to persuade the magnates

---

[91]*Ibid.*, pp. 27–28 and notes, 34f.

[92]*Ord.* **6:** pp. 529–532; *HL* **9:** pp. 881–883, 897; C. Portal, "Les insurrections des Tuchins dans le pays de Langue d'Oc vers 1382–1384," *Annales du Midi* 4 (1892): p. 437.

[93]Mirot, *Insurrections*, pp. 37–40; *Ord.* **6:** pp. 527–528; Coville, *Etats Norm.*, P.J. 40. The crown soon ordered, however, that the aids up to 15 November and all arrears were to be collected: *Ord.* **6:** p. 534.

[94]Mirot, *Insurrections*, pp. 39–44.

[95]*Ibid.*, pp. 45–49; *Ord.* **6:** pp. 552–554, 564–565; *Chron. Valois*, p. 294.

[96]*Ibid.*, p. 293; Coville, *Etats Norm.*, pp. 124, 127–128, 192, 391–393; Radding, "Estates," p. 80; Mirot, *Insurrections*, pp. 40, 52 (note 3).

[97]*Ibid.*, pp. 53–61.

[98]*Ibid.*, pp. 87–90; Radding, "Estates," pp. 80–81.

[99]Mirot, *Insurrections*, pp. 64–65.

to support additional levies to finance his quest for the Neapolitan throne, but in January, 1382, the government reimposed the aids after meeting representatives of the guilds of Paris.[100] The response of the towns was immediate and hostile: Paris, Rouen, and other northern communities rose in spontaneous revolt. The risings were not coordinated, and the crown was able to suppress them, first by conciliation and later by force. By 1383, municipal franchises were curtailed sharply and royal *réformateurs* were able to levy substantial fines on the rebellious communities.[101] A similar pattern prevailed in Languedoc, where the duke of Berry was confronted by a wave of urban uprisings, followed by a widespread revolt of landless and impoverished *Tuchins* who were abetted by a few renegade lords.[102]

Like earlier reactions against royal taxes and financial officers, the ill-coordinated uprisings of the early 1380's began to lose their momentum. By the spring of 1382, the crown was negotiating with assemblies in each ecclesiastical province, and despite a few pockets of bitter opposition, new taxes were generally granted.[103] In the summer, an expedition against rebels in Flanders occasioned a new increment or surtax (*creue*) on these levies,[104] and opposition amounted to little more than efforts to substitute direct taxes for indirect ones where possible.[105] The nobles and upper bourgeoisie were aligned again with the crown, and after Charles VI's victorious return from Flanders, all remaining opposition was suppressed. In 1383 the government reimposed the *aides* and *gabelle*, and these taxes, which had originally been levied for the ransom of John II, were collected annually until 1418.[106] The Estates of Languedoc, at Lyon in July, 1383, agreed to the re-establishment of the aids in the Midi as well. Languedoc

---

[100]*Ibid.*, pp. 68–70, 75, 87–89, 111 and notes.

[101]*Ibid.*, pp. 91, 94–95, 109 (note 1), 113–115, 179, 189, 197–198, 209–213; Radding, "Estates," pp. 81–83.

[102]*HL* **9:** pp. 899–913; Portal, "Insurrections des Tuchins," pp. 438–439, 465, 470, 473–474.

[103]Mirot, *Insurrections*, pp. 67, 146–150; Radding, "Estates," p. 82. Some places, such as Reims, firmly refused to pay.

[104]*Ibid.*; Mirot, *Insurrections*, pp. 158–164, 176–177.

[105]*Ibid.*, pp. 165–169.

[106]*Ibid.*, pp. 213–217; *Ord.* **7:** pp. 705, 746–751; Radding, "Estates," p. 82; Rey, *Domaine*, p. 167. In April, the *généraux* of the aids were given wide powers to interpret their instructions as they saw fit (*Ord.* **7:** p. 752).

ROYAL TAXATION COMES OF AGE: CONCLUSIONS 303

also had to endure heavy new *fouages* to pay 800,000 francs in fines for the *Tuchin* uprising.[107]

By 1384, therefore, the crisis had been weathered. The aids were back in force; Languedoc was paying the heaviest *fouage* in history; and other regions were levying supplementary taxes to pay royal fines or combat *routiers*. The revenue from these sources might well have been sufficient, had the government made peace with England and been directed by disinterested officials, but the apanaged princes retained their influence and diverted money to their own projects. Under such circumstances, the crown sorely missed the revenue from the *fouage* in Languedoil that Charles V had canceled. Soon it became necessary to return to direct taxation.

During the crisis of the early 1380's, the towns had repeatedly sought to replace the aids with direct taxes. Reestablishment of the aids, rather than the *fouage,* can only be seen as a triumph for wealthy and rural interests at the expense of the bulk of the urban population. Not wishing to offend these interests unnecessarily, the government used evident caution in imposing new direct taxes beginning in 1384. They were assessed as lump sums representing a percentage of the anticipated revenue from the aids, and thus were somewhat like the surtaxes already imposed in 1381 and 1382. Several direct taxes of this sort were collected from 1384 to 1387, each as an emergency expedient intended for a specific (usually military) purpose.[108]

Introduced in this cautious, piecemeal manner, the new direct taxes remind one of the war subsidies imposed a half-century earlier, but they actually were the true descendents of the canceled *fouage*. They were known as *grandes tailles* because they were based on the principle formerly employed in the levy of seigneurial tallages—the apportionment (*répartition*) of a lump sum. The *fouages* of Charles V had never been assessed at a flat rate: a rate of three francs meant that this was the *average* to be collected from each taxable hearth, but actual payments were apportioned according to ability to pay ("the strong carrying the weak"). The new *tailles,* which were

---

[107] Rey, *Domaine*, pp. 166, 350; Portal, "Insurrections des Tuchins," p. 434. See also *Ord.* 7: p. 28; *HL* 9: pp. 914–917; AD Hérault A 6, fols. 23v–24v.

[108] Rey, *Domaine*, pp. 236–244, 325–326; *HL* 9: p. 933, *Ord.* 7: p. 759; Radding, "Administration," chap. 6; Radding, "Estates," pp. 83–84, 87–90.

to become the major royal tax in early modern France, followed the same principle.[109]

For years, *fouages* in Languedoc had been expressed as lump sums that were then divided among the seneschalsies and towns on the basis of their taxable hearths. By 1396, if not earlier, this principle was applied to the whole kingdom in the levy of the *taille,* but outside Languedoc the apportionment was based on a variety of criteria and gradually became enveloped in privileges and exceptions until Frenchmen of later centuries came to regard the *taille* as a burdensome tax, capriciously and inequitably assessed.[110] Even under Charles VI, more kinds of people were exempt from the *taille* than from the aids—clerics, nobles bearing arms, and numerous officials—and it is probable that privilege became truly important only when the *taille* became a heavy and regular tax in the fifteenth century.[111]

Introduction of the *tailles* did not eliminate regional taxes, which were needed for a long time to cope with recurrent brigandage. In 1387, an assembly of Estates at Rodez assessed 250,000 francs on Languedoc and Auvergne; while between 1387 and 1389 the Estates of Forez, Mâconnais, Lyonnais, and Nivernais met five times to make financial arrangements to deal with *routiers.*[112]

The next royal *taille* on the whole kingdom, levied in 1388 for an expedition to the Low Countries, was largely squandered by the king's uncles,[113] and the twenty-year-old Charles VI ousted them from power. For the next four years, Charles ruled with the aid of veteran officials who had served his father, men known as the Marmousets. The government avoided *tailles* and economized by cutting pensions and salaries. *Réformateurs* were sent through the realm, and in 1389 the king visited Languedoc personally to enlist popular support and correct governmental abuses. He subsequently removed the duke of Berry as royal lieutenant and replaced him with three *réformateurs.* About the same time, the crown organized the *Cour du Trésor* in Paris to oversee financial

---

[109]Rey, *Domaine,* pp. 166–167; Wolfe, *Fiscal System,* pp. 7, 305.

[110]On the levy of the *taille* and the abuses connected with it in the future, see *ibid.,* pp. 307–316. *Cf.* Rey, *Domaine,* pp. 324, 330–332.

[111]*Ibid.,* p. 332.

[112]*HL* **9**: pp. 926–932; Rey, *Domaine,* pp. 351, 353.

[113]*Ibid.,* pp. 326–327.

matters.[114] A decade after the death of Charles V, his system of government and finance was still essentially intact, despite the troubles of his son's minority. If the *fouage* was no longer levied in Languedoil, the *taille* had made its appearance as a tax that could be imposed by the government when needed, without recourse to assemblies. The personal rule of Charles VI and the influence of the Marmousets were, however, short-lived, for in 1392 the king became insane.

The long period from 1392 to 1435 was one of the darkest in the history of medieval France. The monarchy was at the mercy of competing princes, foreign enemies, and royal favorites. Individuals pursuing their own private interests plundered the treasury. Royal officers were vulnerable as scapegoats during financial crises, and even the best of them sought the protection of powerful princes and became the creatures of faction.[115] It was an age of civil strife, political assassination, and religious schism. When the English renewed the Hundred Years' War, they crushed the French army, conquered Normandy, and in 1420 imposed the treaty of Troyes, which effectively partitioned France among the English, the Burgundians, and the disunited followers of the dauphin Charles.[116] Valois fortunes could not revive significantly until 1435, when Burgundy abandoned its alliance with England.

Such a prolonged time of trouble inevitably placed a severe strain on governmental institutions. What is striking about the period is not the breakdown of these institutions but the degree to which they survived and the speed with which Charles V's system was reconstituted after 1435. For nearly twenty-five years after the king's insanity set in, the fiscal machinery functioned without a serious breakdown. The aids were collected annually,[117] and the French re-acquired Cher-

---

[114]*Ibid.*, pp. 63, 100–103, 175–176. See G. Dupont-Ferrier, *Les origines et le premier siècle de la Cour du Trésor* (Paris, 1936), chap. 2.

[115]Rey, *Domaine*, pp. 100, 110.

[116]Perroy, *Hundred Years War*, pp. 238–244.

[117]Just as in the 1370's, the councillors-general of the "aids ordered for the war" issued and received numerous pay vouchers and receipts after the restoration of these taxes in 1382. For the ensuing twenty-year period, many such documents are found in AN K 53 and 54 (Tardif, *Monuments historiques*); BN Clairambault 23, 35, 47, 53, 82, 83, 88, 99; BN MS. fr. 20416, 20586, 20589, 20599; P.O. 24, 232, 359, 366, 384, 418, 439, 447, 455, 650, 789, 795, 875, 1082, 1280, 1474, 2030, 2149, 2474, 2624, 2889, 3015. See especially BN MS. fr. 20618 and the next twenty volumes of that series.

bourg in 1394 with additional financing from a special subsidy in Normandy.[118] The government soon revived the periodic levy of *tailles*, never seeking consent to these taxes but generally trying to minimize controversy by associating them with the venerable tradition of feudal aids or war subsidies. The *taille* of 600,000 francs in 1396 was to help pay the dowry of Charles VI's daughter when she married Richard II of England; that of 400,000 francs in December, 1397, was justified by the needs of Christendom following the crusaders' defeat at Nicopolis.[119] *Tailles* in 1404 (800,000 pounds), 1406 (400,000 francs), and 1411–1412 (900,000 francs) were based on military necessity.[120] Throughout the period, individual regions adopted local taxes to maintain order in the face of recurrent brigandage.[121]

Eventually, however, the accumulating strains brought about financial collapse. A last attempt at massive reform through the Estates General in Languedoil proved abortive in 1413; Languedoc suffered from urban social strife; and the army had to recruit an increasing number of foreign adventurers as French nobles began to avoid military service.[122] Half a century of relatively stable coinage came to an end. The crown had weakened the currency to the 29th *pied* in 1405 and the 32nd *pied* in 1411, but these relatively minor adjustments were followed in 1417 by drastic new mutations that placed the coinage on the 60th *pied* by the end of the year. [123] In 1418 the dauphin and the duke of Burgundy, who were competing for popular favor, abolished the aids in their respective parts of France, and the government lost the revenues of this essential tax which had been levied in all but two of the preceding fifty-seven years.[124] The most available alternative revenue was *monnayage*, and by 1420 the coinage was weakened to the 160th *pied*. In the dauphin's part of France, the currency was

---

[118] Rey, *Domaine*, pp. 348–350.

[119] *Ibid.*, pp. 326–327.

[120] *Ibid.*, pp. 327–330.

[121] *Ibid.*, pp. 354–358.

[122] Perroy, *Hundred Years War*, pp. 232–234; Wolff, "Luttes," p. 449; Contamine, *Guerre*, pp. 210, 228, 247–248, 255–261.

[123] J. Lafaurie, *Les monnaies des rois de France de Hugh Capet à Louis XII* (2 v., Paris, 1951–1956) 2: pp. 68–70, 95–102. See below, appendix I.

[124] *HL* 10: cols. 1984–1985; C. Petit-Dutaillis, in Lavisse, *Historie* 4, 2: pp. 28f, 239f; Rey, *Domaine*, p. 370.

all but worthless by 1422, and despite efforts at reform, it fluctuated considerably until well into the 1430's.[125]

The disastrous years after 1417 occasioned a new interest in central assemblies. The Estates General, or assemblies representing most of Languedoil, had met some twenty times between 1343 and 1369, but in the next fifty-one years the only meetings were those of 1380–1381 and one in 1413. Except for the first months of Charles VI's reign, the classes whose cooperation was essential to taxation showed little interest in acting through the Estates General, and the government had collected high taxes without the assemblies.[126] Such taxes had made possible the victories of the 1370's, which contrasted with the defeat and disorder that had characterized the efforts of the Estates in the later 1350's. In the 1420's, however, Charles VII needed not only money, but also counsel and moral support from the regions that still recognized his authority. Not only did central assemblies appear potentially useful, but the diminished size of his realm led Charles to attempt a reunification of the Estates of Languedoil and Languedoc.[127] The patterns established in the 1360's, however, proved to be so well-ingrained as to frustrate this effort.

An assembly of combined Estates granted a *taille* of 800,000 l. t. in 1421, but few representatives from Languedoc were present and some districts refused to accept as binding the quotas assigned by the assembly. In 1422 Charles VII obtained grants directly from provincial Estates, but he still hoped to induce central assemblies to give the binding consent that would produce taxes more speedily. Early in 1423, the Estates of Languedoil met at Bourges and granted a million pounds, of which nearly half were to come from Languedoc. When regional assemblies in the Midi convened, however, they refused to pay the full amounts assigned to their districts. Later in the year, the king obtained a new *taille* of 200,000 l. t. from the Estates of Languedoil, as well as an *aide* (indirect tax) that was converted to an equivalent *taille* when it met serious local resistance. The Estates of Languedoil met twice in 1424, each time granting large *tailles*. The southern Estates

[125]Lafaurie, *Monnaies* 2: pp. 95–102.
[126]Rey, *Domaine*, p. 325; *cf.* Wolfe, *Fiscal System*, pp. 20–21 and note 24.
[127]Petit-Dutaillis, in Lavisse, *Histoire* 4, 2: pp. 239–242; Major, *Representative Institutions*, p. 25; Thomas, "Le Midi" 1: p. 290; Gilles, *Etats Languedoc*, pp. 40–47.

convened after each of these assemblies to agree to their share
of these grants. Languedoc remained reluctant to send
representatives ouside the Midi. Charles VII summoned his
sixth central assembly in the fall of 1425, hoping to convene
the Estates jointly at Poitiers, but again the Estates of Languedoil and Languedoc met separately. The latter were unwilling
to act, while the regions of Languedoil rejected an aid in favor
of an apportioned *taille*. This pattern was repeated in 1426,
when the Estates of Languedoil proposed an alternative to the
taille and local resistance, for the third time in four years,
compelled its conversion to a *taille*.[128]

Political strife at the royal court delayed the next assembly
until September, 1428, when the combined Estates General
held a famous meeting at Chinon. This body granted 500,000
francs plus the equivalent of a tenth on the clergy, and some of
the money was to be raised by indirect taxes. For the first time
in a decade, the crown was able to collect an *aide* from a large
part of the realm, but 1428 did not establish a new pattern,
since subsequent aids in the 1430's were repeatedly converted
into *tailles*.[129] The representatives of Languedoc were clearly
unhappy at this summons to Chinon and they asked the king
not to convene them outside the Midi in the future. Charles
VII did not agree to this request, but assemblies of the whole
realm that were summoned in 1432 and 1434 did not take
place.[130]

It is clear that this last sustained effort to turn the medieval
Estates General into an effective consenting body for taxation
was foundering in the face of local particularism. The successful decentralization under Charles V had become too well
established to be uprooted. The provincial Estates had been
less active during the last quarter of the fourteenth century,
but they retained enough continuity to resume a constructive

---

[128] Thomas, "Le Midi" 1: pp. 292-295, 300-303, 306-312; Major, *Representative Institutions*, pp. 25-29. By this time, it should be noted, the *livre tournois* and the franc were not equal anymore.

[129] *Ibid.*, pp 29-30; Thomas, "Le Midi" 4: pp. 1-4. Wolfe, *Fiscal System*, p. 29, attributes great importance to the grant and collection of an aid in 1428, but it seems to have been an isolated occurrence of indirect taxes.

[130] *Ibid.*, pp. 29-31; Major, *Representative Institutions*, pp. 30-31; Thomas, "Le Midi" 4: pp. 8-9, 12-15. On the failure of the Estates to assume a major role despite the repeated assemblies of this period, see P.S. Lewis, "The Failure of the French Medieval Estates," *Past and Present* 23 (1962): pp. 3-24.

role in the new crisis of the early fifteenth century. As long as they could effectively overrule the actions of a central assembly, the latter could not become a vital institution. A major factor in the failure of central assemblies was the local hostility to indirect taxation. It would appear that local interests (presumably bourgeois) were determined to prevent a repetition of what had occurred in 1382–1383, when the advocates of indirect taxes had prevailed. A careful scholarly study of this question is urgently needed.

However much indirect taxation was opposed, the fact remains that the aids originally established for the ransom of John II had proven extremely valuable. They had provided the royal government with a regular annual revenue in time of peace or war, and had made possible half a century of stable coinage. The crown persisted in its effort to restore these taxes, and in 1435, when the treaty of Arras detached Burgundy from its English alliance, the Estates of Languedoil consented to a restoration of the aids for four years. Once again, local assemblies converted these to a *taille*, but only for one year, and when a central assembly reaffirmed the grant in 1436, the government resumed collection of indirect taxes. They were levied annually thereafter without further consultation with assemblies, and as in 1360, their collection permitted a new reform of the currency.[131]

In Languedoc, the aids were restored by an assembly at Béziers in 1437, and here too they were collected year after year, even though they were supposed to be temporary. Languedoc, however, had a venerable tradition of direct taxation, and in 1443 the southern Estates proposed to replace the aids with an equivalent tax, as had been done more than eighty years before. The new substitute, actually called the *équivalent*, was to be a lump sum of 83,000 l. t. per year, and although it was raised by indirect taxes, these soon fell short of providing the promised sum. To make up the difference, Languedoc had to adopt an extra *taille*, apportioned among the hearths of the region, just like the *fouage* that served as equivalent to the aids in the 1360's.[132]

---

[131] Wolfe, *Fiscal System*, p. 30; Petit-Dutaillis, in Lavisse, *Histoire* 4, 2: pp. 242–243; Lafaurie, *Monnaies* 2: pp. 108–111.

[132] *HL* 10: cols. 2198–2204; Wolfe, *Fiscal System*, p. 32; A. Spont, "L'équivalent aux aides en Languedoc de 1450 à 1515," *Annales du Midi* 3 (1891): pp. 232–240.

The treaty with Burgundy in 1435, like that with England in 1360, thus was followed by the establishment of the aids on a regular basis and the stabilization of the coinage. It resembled the earlier treaty in another important respect, for it gave rise to a serious new wave of brigandage. The *routiers* of the 1430's were known as the *écorcheurs* to the terrified populace of eastern France. To respond to this danger, the government adopted measures based on the precedents of the 1360's: sending brigands on a dangerous foreign expedition, putting them on the royal payroll as a kind of standing army, and levying regular direct taxes to pay military salaries and maintain domestic order.[133]

The last of these measures is of particular relevance to this study, for it involved a regularization of the *taille* that was comparable to the establishment of the royal *fouage* at the end of 1363. In 1439 the Estates of Languedoil granted a *taille* for one year and endorsed a royal ordinance that set up regular companies of paid troops. The Estates of the entire realm were scheduled to meet in 1440, but a revolt of the princes prevented the meeting and disrupted the military reform. Nevertheless, Charles VII continued to levy the *taille* annually,[134] and after his truce with England in 1444 he succeeded in establishing the standing army based on regular *compagnies d'ordonnance*.[135] This effort was more sophisticated, successful, and enduring than that of Louis of Anjou and Charles V in the previous century, but it was very similar otherwise.

The achievements of Charles VII's government in taxation and military organization between 1435 and 1445 laid the basis for the early modern French state and they have justly been described as "great reforms."[136] It should be clear, however, that they amounted largely to a re-enactment of

---

[133]Contamine, *Guerre*, p. 249; Perroy, *Hundred Years War*, pp. 294-296, 303, 310-311; A. Tuetey, *Les écorcheurs sous Charles VII* (2 v., Montbéliard, 1874) 1: pp. 4, 36, 42-43, 123f; E. Cosneau, *Le connétable de Richemont (Artur de Bretagne) (1393-1458)* (Paris, 1886), pp. 237-238, 259-262, 307, 314, 341-355, 566-567, and P.J., nos. 66, 81, 82.

[134]*Ibid.*, pp. 297-298; *Ord.* 13: pp. 306-313; Contamine, *Guerre*, pp. 142-144, 278; Wolfe, *Fiscal System*, pp. 34-35; Thomas, "Le Midi" 4: pp. 16-17; Petit-Dutaillis, in Lavisse, *Histoire* 4, 2: pp. 243-245.

[135]On the military reform and its consequences, see Cosneau, *Connétable*, pp. 356-357, 614-616; Contamine, *Guerre*, pp. 277, 400-403, 532; Petit-Dutaillis, in Lavisse, *Histoire* 4, 2: pp. 95-110, 304-306.

[136]The quoted words are from Wolfe, *Fiscal System*, p. 24.

what had been done in the 1360's. Charles VII secured for the crown an enduring fiscal absolutism, but only by building on the precedents of Charles V, who had first achieved this power, and only by accepting the decentralization that Charles V had been forced to accept.[137] Charles VII was more fortunate in his successor, and he is remembered as the ruler who established permanent taxation and a standing army without being limited (or helped!) by central assemblies. Yet the real breakthrough, when France first accepted regular royal taxation and a regularly paid army, came in the years 1356–1370. It was the capture of John II at Poitiers that led to decisive changes in the financial structure of the French monarchy. The many disruptions of the early fifteenth century, far from reversing these changes, underscored the need for them and led to their re-establishment on a permanent basis.

---

[137]On the question of decentralization, see Major, *Representative Institutions*, pp. 5–6, 34f, and the comments above in note 56. On the question of when the crucial breakthrough in French royal taxation actually occurred, see Wolfe, *Fiscal System*, p. 24, where it is argued that "dramatic breaks in the continuity of the king's right to levy imposts at his own discretion," such as in 1380–1382, and again after 1417, proved that the kings did not have the "absolute" power over taxes that was available to Charles VII after 1440. In fact, however, Charles V had this power. The civil wars of the next generation disrupted its exercise, just as the Wars of Religion would do in the sixteenth century (*ibid.*, pp. 147–205). The important question is not when, or whether, fiscal absolutism became permanent, but when it was first asserted successfully. It was in the 1360's that the crown began to levy regular annual taxes without consent and had a permanent organization to administer them.

Appendix

I. NOTE ON THE COINAGE

THE royal currency is a complex subject which can be understood only by scholars trained in both history and numismatics. Writings on the subject to date would seem to have aroused controversy without answering questions, and more research into this difficult specialty is surely called for. The role of the coinage as a political issue in the 1350's has been discussed above in chapters I and II, where the *pied de monnaie* and the ways of altering it were briefly explained. In addition, the appendix of an earlier book has dealt at some length with some of the difficulties posed by fluctuations in the silver coinage, especially insofar as these difficulties affect our interpretation of the royal financial documents.[1] The following table summarizes the principal fluctuations in the silver coinage from mid-1356 onwards, indicating the periods when the *rate* of the crown's *monnayage* was greatest without, however, offering any clue as to the *amount* of *monnayage*.

Languedoil

Date	Value of silver mark established by the king ($\frac{1}{4}$ of *pied*)[2]	Price of silver brought to the royal mints[3]	% of difference
Aug.–Sept. 1356	12 l. t.[4]	6.5 l. t.	54.2%
Sept.–Oct. 1356	15	7.25	51.7

[1] *RTF 1322–1356*, pp. 331–353.

[2] The figures in this column are derived from those published by Miskimin, *Money*, pp. 176–198, supplemented by Lafaurie, *Monnaies* 2: pp. 69–74, and L. F. J. C. de Saulcy, *Recueil de documents relatifs à l'histoire des monnaies frappées par les rois de France* (4 v., Paris, 1879–1892) 1. I have simplified and modified Miskimin's list by omitting figures for minor issues of coins, correcting some figures in the light of De Saulcy's documents, and combining some figures in periods when different mints were striking coins simultaneously at different *pieds*. For useful graphs and commentary on the coinage mutations, see also E. Fournial, *Histoire monétaire de l'occident médiéval* (Paris, 1970), pp. 100–134.

[3] These figures are taken from an excerpt of BN MS. fr. 18500 entitled *valor marche argenti* and published by De Saulcy, *Documents* 1: pp. 10–14. This table represents a continuation of that published in *RTF 1322–1356*, pp. 339–341.

[4] During this period, the mint at Poitiers struck a considerable number of coins at 15 l. t. to the mark (60th *pied*): Miskimin, *Money*, p. 176.

312

Date	Value of silver mark established by the king ($\frac{1}{4}$ of *pied*)[2]	Price of silver brought to the royal mints[3]	% of difference
Oct.–Nov. 1356	15	8.5	43.3
Dec. 1356–Jan. 1357	12	7.4	38.3
Feb.–July 1357	7	6.2	11.4
Aug. 1357–Jan. 1358	11.25	6.2	55
Jan.–May 1358	11.25	8.2	27
May–June 1358	13.5	10	25.9
July 1358	13.5	12	11
Aug. 1358	20	14	30
Sept.–Oct. 1358	8	6.75	10
Oct.–Nov. 1358	11.25	7–8	33.3
Dec. 1358–Feb. 1359	15	8.69–9.5	about 40
Feb.–Mar. 1359	10	7	30
Mar.–Apr. 1359	10	7.5	25
May–June 1359	15	9	40
June–July 1359	17.5	12	31.4
Aug. 1359	28	16.6	40
Sept.–Oct. 1359	34[5]	22.15	34.9
Oct.–Nov. 1359	43[5]	29.4	31.6
Nov.–Dec. 1359	24	15	37.5
Jan. 1360	36[6]	24.63	31.6
Jan.–Feb. 1360	54	34.47–42	?[7]
March 1360	75–125	53.88–102	?[7]
Apr.–July 1360	12–16	7–10.5	33–41[7]
July–Aug. 1360	16–25	15–17	?[7]
Aug.–Sept. 1360	30	18.5	38.3
Sept.–Oct. 1360	8.25	6.5–7	18
Oct.–Nov. 1360	13.2	8–9	35.6
Dec. 1360–Mar. 1361	6	4.9	18.3
Apr. 1361–Apr. 1365	5.25	4.25	19
Apr. 1365–1384	6	5	16.7
1384–1389	6.25	?	
1389–1405	6.75		
1405–1411	7.25		

---

[5] *Ibid.*, pp. 182–183, indicates simultaneous coinages of different *pieds*, and since the amount of each issue is known, I have averaged the figures to obtain a composite *pied* for the period.

[6] Some mints struck stronger money (20 or 24 l. t. per mark), but the great majority of the coins minted were at 36 l. t. to the mark (144th *pied*): *ibid.*, p. 183.

[7] The monetary anarchy of this period makes one hesitate to attribute much significance to any of these figures. The rate and amount of royal *monnayage* cannot even be approximated, and several minor coinages at *pieds* falling outside the indicated range have not even been listed here.

Languedoc

Date	Value of silver mark established by the king ($\frac{1}{4}$ of *pied*)[2]	Price of silver brought to the royal mints[3]	% of difference
Feb.-Nov. 1356	same as in Languedoil		
Nov. 1356-Jan. 1357	8		
Jan. 1357-June 1358	same as in Languedoil		
June-Oct. 1358	8[8]		
Oct.-Dec. 1358	11.25		
Dec. 1358-Jan. 1359	7.5-7.8		
Jan.-Mar. 1359	18		
Mar.-Apr. 1359	10		
Apr 1359-Dec. 1360	8		
After 1361	same as in Languedoil		

These figures show that Languedoc was able to avoid the worst excesses of the monetary anarchy which characterized the years 1359 and 1360 in the north. I have stressed in this study the close connection between coinage reform and regular taxes,[9] and it seems evident that Languedoc was able to achieve a greater measure of monetary stability because it possessed Estates who were prepared to grant taxes and able to deliver them. Such a body could bargain with the crown for concessions because it could fulfill its promises to the crown.

After 1360, the coinage ceased to be a significant source of royal revenue for more than half a century. The *pied* crept slowly upward, by a total of 21 per cent between 1361 and 1411, but these changes were insignificant compared with the fluctuations of the late 1350's, and they were no doubt determined by the need to attract bullion rather than by any royal desire to gain a profit.

For the historian of taxation, the silver coinage does not pose a serious problem in the years under consideration in this study. There are not enough financial figures to justify a serious attempt to determine royal revenues, and for much of

---

[8] During this period, a minor coinage was issued at 20 l. t. per mark (80th *pied*). See Miskimin, *Money*, p. 179.

[9] This is not a novel conclusion, for Miskimin, *ibid.*, p. 47, called attention to it a decade ago.

the period the coinage was relatively stable. It is rather the
gold coinage which poses problems when dealing with this
period. The era of frequent mutations had caused a change in
the fiscal documents in the years following the Black Death of
1348. Instead of quoting figures in money of account (*livres,
sols, deniers*), they tend to refer to real coins, like the gold *écu,
mouton,* florin, or *royal,* and the silver *gros.* Sums expressed in
these currencies have been mentioned frequently in these
pages, but without much certainty as to their value in money
of account. One old study which does give such values for the
gold coins appears to be riddled with errors and therefore
untrustworthy.[10] A brief discussion of these gold and silver
coins therefore seems necessary here.

The florin was not really a French coin at all, but a
Florentine piece which enjoyed such international popularity
that it was widely copied.[11] In Languedoc, it seems to have
been interchangeable with the *mouton,* and it was equal to 12
silver *gros.* The franc, a new gold coin authorized with the
reform of late 1360, contained 15 *gros,* and four francs
equalled five florins. The franc is known to have been intended
to equal one *livre tournois* in money of account,[12] so it would
seem that one *gros* equalled 16 d. t. and one florin or *mouton*
equalled 16 s. t. In establishing the ransom of John II, the
treaty of Brétigny expressed the amount to be paid in *écus,* and
we have seen that in computing the down payment on this
ransom, five *écus* equalled four *royaux.* The question which
remains unclear is what relation the *écu* had to the franc or
florin. Delachenal appears to equate the *écu* with the florin, in
which case the *royaux* of 1360 would have been the equivalent
of the francs issued from the following year onwards.[13] On the
other hand, there is some reason to think that the *écu* of 1360
was supposed to be reckoned at six to the silver mark, in
which case it would not equal the florin but rather the future
franc. If the *écu* equalled the franc and the pound *tournois* of

---

[10] See *RTF 1322-1356,* p. 332, note 5, discussing N. de Wailly, "Mémoire sur les
variations de la livre tournois depuis le règne de Saint Louis jusqu'à l'établissement
de la monnaie decimale," *Mémoires de l'Institute Imperial de France* 21, 2 (1857):
p. 234f.

[11] J. B. Giard, "Le Florin d'or au Baptiste et ses imitations en France du XIVe
siècle," *Bib. Ec. Chartes* 125 (1967): pp. 134-137.

[12] See above, chap. V, note 27. *Cf.* Rey, *Domaine,* p. 39.

[13] Delachenal, *Charles V* 2: p. 221. *Cf.* chap. III, above, at note 143.

the reformed currency, then it also equalled 15 *gros*, and the royal was worth more than 18 *gros* or half again as much as the florin. It is hoped that experts in this field will be able to clarify this question in the future.

II. TABLE OF PRINCIPAL TAXES LEVIED

Year	Languedoil	Languedoc
late 1356	Deadlock between dauphin and Estates, who propose tax for men-at-arms	fouage of one *agnel*; *capage*; property tax of 2 d. per week
1357	15 per cent income tax on nobles & clergy; 180 *écus* (annual salary of a soldier) per 100 non-noble hearths; some local taxes	continuation of the above taxes for four months, then cancellation because of truce
1358	until May, the above taxes, despite opposition and slow collection; after May, 5 per cent income tax on nobles, tenth on clergy, and 180 *écus* for every 70 non–noble hearths; resumption of high *monnayage*; indirect taxes in some regions	arrears and temporary renewals of the *capage*; temporary grant of troops for defense against brigandage; *fouage* of one *mouton* for ransom (in anticipation of treaty with England)
1359	royal and regional sales taxes; increased *monnayage*; grant of troops by Estates in June; reinstatement of *gabelle* on salt	reinstatement of *gabelle* to finance local defense; continue one *mouton* hearth tax; 2 d./l. municipal sales taxes; some grant for abortive Danish alliance
1360	high *monnayage* early in year; forced loans and other taxes for 1st ransom installment. Establishment of aids and reform of coinage, December	continuation of *gabelle* and one mouton *fouage*; then, extension of the *fouage* for ransom payment; large sums promised to Foix and Armagnac
1361	*Aides pour la délivrance*: 12 d./l. (5 per cent) general sales tax, *gabelle* on salt, "thirteenth" on wine; local taxes to ransom fortresses	Continuing *fouage* for 1st ransom payment; continued *gabelle* for local defense; establishment of the ransom aids; special taxes to fight brigands at Pont-Saint-Esprit

II. TABLE OF PRINCIPAL TAXES LEVIED (*cont.*)

Year	Languedoil	Languedoc
	Establishment of 12 d./l. *imposition foraine* as extension of aids, to be collected on goods shipped out of regions where aids were in effect	
1362	aids and *gabelle* for ransom; local taxes to ransom castles; *fouage* of ½ florin to send Grand Company to Spain (Auvergne & vicinity)	aids replaced by equivalent *fouage* equal to roughly 0.7 francs per hearth (pre-1348); special ½ florin *fouage* to send Grand Company to Spain
1363	aids and *gabelle* for ransom; special regional taxes for brigandage (1 florin *fouage* in Auvergne)	*fouage* in lieu of aids; renewed *gabelle* for regional defense; 4 *gros fouage* to obtain withdrawal of Spaniards
1364	*Fouage* for defense (average, 3 francs); aids and *gabelle* for ransom; special levies to buy off brigands locally (Auvergne)	*fouage* in lieu of aids; *gabelle* for regional defense; special contributions to buy off Seguin de Badefol
1365	*fouage* for defense; aids and *gabelle* for ransom; tax in Auvergne to buy off Seguin de Badefol	*fouage* in lieu of the aids; *gabelle* for defense; special levy to finance Du Guesclin's Spanish expedition
1366	*fouage* for defense; aids and *gabelle* for ransom	*fouage* in lieu of the aids; *gabelle* for defense; special local taxes for repair of Aigues Mortes and resistance to brigandage
1367	*fouage* for defense; aids for ransom; restructured *gabelle*; substantial sharing of taxes by local districts	re-imposition of the ransom aids; arrears of *fouage*; *gabelle* for defense; small special *fouage*
1368	*fouage* for defense; aids and *gabelle* for ransom; new increase in local taxes to combat brigands	Ransom aids; *gabelle*; 1-franc *fouage* for Provençal campaign; new 2-franc *fouage* in September

II. TABLE OF PRINCIPAL TAXES LEVIED (*cont.*)

Year	Languedoil	Languedoc
1369	Aids for the war: 12 d./l. sales tax and *gabelle*, as for the ransom; *fouage* replaced by *molage* on cereals and thirteenth replaced by *quâtrième* on retailed wine. Then *molage* replaced by *fouage* of 6 francs in towns, 2 in country	hearth tax raised to 2½ francs (Feb.); aids and *gabelle*; loan of 2½ francs per hearth (Apr.); new loans in Sept.; 3 franc *fouage* in Nov. and indirect taxes in lieu of aids
1370 to 1380	aids for the war: 12 d./l. sales tax; *gabelle, quâtrième,* and *fouage*	aids and *gabelle*; plus following *fouages*: 1½ francs (fall 1370); 2 francs (Jan., 1371); 3 francs (Aug. 1371); 3 francs (Jan., 1372); 2 francs (Oct., 1372); 3 francs (Mar., 1373); 2 and 3 francs (spring, 1374); total of 6 francs in 1375–1376; 7½ francs in 1377; etc.

Bibliography

I. MANUSCRIPT SOURCES

Paris: Archives Nationales

Inventories: Series 1, numbers 33–41 (Godefroy and Dupuy), 62–68 (Curzon). Series 2, number 59 *bis*.
Series JJ: numbers 86–95, 97–100.
Series K: numbers 47, 48, 49, 51.
Series KK: numbers 7, 10.
Series P: numbers 2292–2294.
Series PP: number 117.
Series Z lb: numbers 55, 56.

Paris: Bibliothèque Nationale

Manuscrits français: numbers 6739, 7350–7365, 7375, 7377–7379, 7381, 7383, 7384, 7386–7392, 20398, 20402, 20410–20416, 20579–20589, 20599, 20683–20685, 21407, 21408, 22295, 22468, 22469, 24120, 25700, 25701, 26001–26020.
Nouvelles acquisitions françaises: numbers 1433, 3654, 7373–7376, 7389, 7430, 7610–7612, 20026, 20075.
Pièces originales: numbers 24, 25, 78, 93, 118, 142, 159, 164, 187, 213, 232, 246, 268, 358, 359, 366, 382–384, 418, 439, 447, 455, 456, 470, 493, 524, 539, 542, 549, 599, 638, 648, 650, 651, 669, 751, 789, 795, 875, 1065, 1066, 1082, 1134, 1151, 1172, 1270, 1273, 1280, 1433, 1474, 1522, 1539, 1603, 1675, 1684, 1826, 1849, 1935, 1936, 2030, 2130, 2149, 2169, 2209, 2218, 2236, 2268, 2330, 2419, 2474, 2477, 2624, 2661, 2777, 2809, 2812, 2866, 2886, 2889, 2892, 2900, 3015, 3016, 3019–3021.
Manuscrits latins: numbers 9146, 9175–9177, 10002.
Collection Baluze: number 87.
Collecton Clairambault: numbers 11, 12, 15, 17, 20, 23, 27, 29–31, 33–35, 44–47, 53, 60, 61, 63, 64, 73, 78, 80, 82, 83, 88, 95, 99, 101, 105, 108–110, 154, 156, 158, 159, 162, 164, 192, 193, 213, 214.
Collection Doat: numbers 8, 53, 60, 81, 109, 119, 192–196, 249–255, 257.
Collection Languedoc: numbers 85–88, 159.
Collection Moreau: numbers 233–235.

Archives Municipales/Communales

Albi: Series AA, number 44; series CC, numbers 69, 72, 73, 75, 77.
Alès: I S, series 3, 12, 13, 16.
Cordes: Series CC, number 29.
Gourdon: Series CC, number 1.
Lyon: Series BB, number 368; series CC, number 340.
Millau: Series CC, numbers 349–353; series ee, numbers 9, 32; *archives non classées*, selected pieces.
Nîmes: Series CC, number 1; series LL, number 1; series NN, number 1; series RR, number 1.
Riom: Series AA, numbers 15, 16, 21 31; Series CC, numbers 13, 14.
Toulouse: Series AA, numbers 6, 35, 36, 45 (selected microfilmed documents); series CC, numbers 1847, 1849.

319

Archives Départementales

Aveyron: Series C, numbers 1519, 1520; series 2E, number 178; series G, numbers 10, 28, 31.
Hérault: Series A, numbers 1, 4, 5, 6.
Lot: Series F, numbers 35-37, 114.
Basses-Pyrenées: Series E, no. 408.

II. PUBLISHED DOCUMENTS, CHRONICLES, AND INVENTORIES

ALBE, E. 1920-1924. "Cahors: Inventaire raisonné et analytique des archives municipales," 2e partie. *Bulletin de la Société des Etudes Litteraires, Scientifiques et Artistiques du Lot* **41**: pp. 1-48; **43**, 2: pp. 1-28; **45**, 2: pp. 28-99.

Archives historiques du Poitou. 1872-. (52 v., Poitiers).

Archives historique du Rouergue **6, 7, 17** (Rodez).

ARTIÈRES, J. 1894-1899. *Annales de Millau* (Millau).

―――― 1930. *Documents sur la ville de Millau* (*Archives historiques du Rouergue* **7**, Millau).

BERTHELÉ, J. 1907. *Archives de la ville de Pézenas, Inventaires et documents: Inventaire de F. Ressequier* (Montpellier).

―――― 1925. *Repertoire numerique des archives de l'Hérault, série E supplement* (Montpellier).

BERTHELÉ, J., and F. CASTETS. 1895-1899. *Archives de la ville de Montpellier, Inventaires et documents: Inventaire du Grand Chartrier* (Montpellier).

BOCK, F. 1931. "Some new Documents Illustrating the Early Years of the Hundred Years War (1353-1356)." *Bulletin of the John Rylands Library* **15**: pp. 60-99.

BOUDET, M. 1903. "Nouveaux documents sur Thomas de la Marche, seigneur de Nonette et d'Auzon, bâtard de France (1318-1360)." *Le Moyen Age* **16**: pp. 283-302.

BOYER, F. 1892. *Ville de Riom: Inventaire sommaire des archives communales antérieures à 1790* (Riom).

BROOME, D. M. 1926. "The Ransom of John II, King of France, 1360-1370." *The Camden Miscellany* **14**.

CASTRO, J. R. 1952-1967. *Diputacion foral de Navara, Catalogo del Archivo General. Seccion de comptos. Documentos* (46 v., Pamplona).

CHAPLAIS, P. 1952. "Some Documents Regarding the Fulfillment and Interpretation of the Treaty of Brétigny, 1361-1369." *The Camden Miscellany* **19**: pp. 1-78.

CHASSAING, A. 1886. *Spicilegium Brivatense. Recueil de documents historiques relatifs au Brivadois et à l'Auvergne* (Paris).

COMBARIEU, L. 1900. *Inventaire sommaire des archives départementales antérieures à 1790: Lot* **3** (Cahors).

COMPAYRÉ, C. 1841. *Etudes historiques et documents inédits sur l'Albigeois, le Castrais, et l'ancien diocese de Lavaur* (Albi).

COVILLE, A. 1893. "Les Etats de 1332 et de 1357." *Le Moyen Age* **6**: pp. 57-59.

DAINVILLE, M. O. DE 1955. *Archives de la ville de Montpellier, Inventaires et documents* **2** (Montpellier). This work supplements that of Berthelé and Castets listed above, and together the two volumes make up the inventory cited in the notes as *Gr. Chartrier*.

―――― 1959. *Documents Comptables. Archives de la Ville de Montpellier* **11** (Montpellier).

DELACHENAL, R. 1900. *Journal des états généraux réunis à Paris au mois d'octobre 1356* (Paris).

—— 1910. *Chronique des règnes de Jean II et de Charles V* (3 v., Paris).

DELISLE, L. 1874. *Mandements et Actes Divers de Charles V (1364-1380), recueillis dans les collections de la Bibliothèque Nationale* (Paris).

DESSALLES, J. 1850. "Rançon du roi Jean." *Mélanges de litterature et d'histoire recueillis et publiés par la Société des bibliophiles français* (Paris).

DOUËT D'ARCQ. 1840-1841. "Acte d'accusation contre Robert le Coq, evêque de Laon." *Bibliothèque de l'Ecole des Chartes* 2: pp. 350-353.

DUCKET, G. F. 1890. *Original Documents Relating to the Hostages of John King of France and the Treaty of Brétigny in 1360* (London).

DUMAS DE RAULY, C. 1881. "Documents inédits sur Saint-Antonin pendant la guerre de Cent Ans, extraits de l'inventaire sommaire des archives de cette ville." *Bulletin archéologique et historique de la Société Archéologique de Tarn-et-Garonne* 9: pp. 273-301.

ESQUIER, G. 1906-1922. *Inventaire des archives communales de la ville d'Aurillac antérieures à 1790* (2 v., Aurillac).

Foedera, conventiones litterae et cujuscunque generis acta publica inter reges Angliae et alios quosvis imperatores, reges, pontifices, principes vel communitates. 1727-1735. (2nd ed., 20 v., London).

FROISSART. See below, Kervyn de Lettenhove.

FURGEOT, H. 1920-1960. *Actes du Parlement de Paris, 2e série* (2 v., Paris).

GUÉRIN, P. *Recueil de documents concernant le Poitou. . . . (Archives historiques de Poitou* 17).

GUESNON, A. 1862. *Inventaire chronologique de chartes de la ville d'Arras* (Arras).

HAIGNERÉ, D. 1886-1899. *Les Chartes de Saint-Bertin* (4 v., Saint-Omer).

HONORE-DUVERGE, S. 1941. "Un fragment de compte de Charles le Mauvais." *Bibliothèque de l'Ecole des Chartes* 102: pp. 292-297.

IZARN, E. 1885. *Le compte des recettes et dépenses du roi de Navarre en France et en Normandie de 1367 à 1370* (Paris).

JACOTIN, A. 1898-1906. *Preuves de la Maison de Polignac* (5 v., Paris).

JOLIBOIS, E. 1869. *Inventaire sommaire des archives communales antérieures à 1790, ville d'Albi* (Paris).

KERVYN DE LETTENHOVE, H. 1876-1877. *Oeuvres de Froissart* (18 v., Brussels)

LEDOS, E. 1890. "Deux Documents relatifs aux Compagnies en Auvergne après 1360." *Revue d'Auvergne* 7: pp. 41-59.

LEMPEREUR, L., B. DE GAULEJAC, and J. BOUSQUET. 1958. *Archives de L'Aveyron, Inventaire sommaire série G, 2G, 4G 4* (Rodez).

LE MAIRE, E. 1888-1910. *Archives ancienne de la ville de Saint-Quentin* (2 v., Saint-Quentin).

LEMOINE. 1896. *Chronique de Richard Lescot, moine de Saint-Denis (1328-1334). Continuation de cette chronique (1334-1344)* (Paris).

LUCE, S. 1860. "Pièces inédits relatives à Etienne Marcel et à quelques-uns de ses principaux adherents." *Bibliothèque de l'Ecole des Chartes* 21: pp. 73-92.

—— 1862. *Chronique des quatre premiers Valois (1327-1393)* (Paris).

—— 1879. "Documents nouveaux sur Etienne Marcel." *Mémoires de la Société de l'Histoire de Paris* 6: pp. 305-324.

MAHUL, A. 1857-1882. *Cartulaire et archives des communes de l'ancien diocese et de l'arrondisement administratif de Carcassonne* (6 v. in 7, Paris).

MARCHAND, J. 1927. "Un compte inédit de Bertrand du Guesclin." *Bibliothèque de l'Ecole des Chartes* 88: pp. 260-265.

MARTENE, E., and U. DURAND. 1717. *Thesaurus nouvus anecdotorum* (5 v., Paris).

MEYER, P. 1902. "Lettre de Jean Chandos et de Thomas de Felton aux consuls et habitants de Millau (2 janvier 1368)." *Le Moyen Age* 15: pp. 1-4.

MORANVILLÉ, H. 1888. "Une lettre à Charles le Mauvais." *Bibliothèque de l'Ecole des Chartes* 49: pp. 91-94.

MOUYNES, G. 1877. *Ville de Narbonne, Inventaire sommaire des archives communales antérieures à 1790, série AA* (Narbonne).

NEWHALL, R. 1953. *The Chronicle of Jean de Venette* (tr. J. Birdsall, New York).

Ordonnonances des roys de France de la troisième race recueillies par ordre chronologique. 1723-1849. (21 v., Paris).

PETIT, J., M. GAVRILOVITCH, *et al.* 1899. *Essai de restitution des plus anciens mémoriaux de la chambre des comptes de Paris* (Paris).

Le Petit Thalamus de Montpellier. 1836. *Société archéologique de Montpellier* (Montpellier).

PORTAL, C. 1903. *Inventaire sommaire des archives communales antérieures à 1790, ville de Cordes* (Albi).

REDET, *et al.* 1839. *Table des manuscrits de D. Fonteneau conservés à la bibliothèque de Poitiers* 1 (Poitiers).

RICHARD, J. M. 1875. "Instructions données aux commissaires chargés de lever la rançon du roi Jean." *Bibliothèque de l'Ecole des Chartes* 36: pp. 81-90.

——— 1878-1887. *Inventaire sommaire des archives départementales antérieures à 1790: Pas-de-Calais, Archives civiles, série A* (2 v., Arras).

RIGAL, J. L., and P. A. VERLAGUET. 1913-1926. *Notes pour servir à l'histoire de Rouergue* (2 v., Rodez).

ROSCHACH, E. 1891. *Ville de Toulouse, Inventaire des archives communales antérieures à 1790, série AA* (Toulouse).

ROSSIGNOL, M., and J. GARNIER. 1863-1894. *Inventaire sommaire des archives départementales antérieures à 1790: Côte-d'Or, Archives civiles, série B* (6 v., Paris and Dijon).

SAULCY, L. F. J. C. DE 1879-1892. *Recueil de documents relatifs à l'histoire des monnaies* (4 v., Paris).

SECOUSSE, D. F. 1755. *Recueil de pièces servant de preuves aux Mémoires sur les troubles excités en France par Charles II dit le Mauvais, roi de Navarre et comte d'Evreux* (Paris).

SOLENTE, S. 1940. *Le livres des fais et bonnes meurs du sage roy Charles V par Christine de Pisan* (2 v., Paris).

TARDIF, J. 1866. *Monuments historiques* (Paris).

TEILHARD DE CHARDIN, E. 1902-1922. *Inventaire sommaire des archives communales antérieures à 1790, ville de Clermont-Ferrand: Fonds de Montferrand* (Clermont-Ferrand).

THIERRY, A. 1850-1859. *Recueil de monuments inédits de l'histoire du tiers état, première série* (4 v., Paris).

VARIN, P. 1843. *Archives administratives de la ville de Reims* (4 v., Paris).

VIDAL, A. 1900. *Comptes consulaires d'Albi (1359-1360)* (Toulouse).

——— 1906. *Douze comptes consulaires d'Albi du XIVe siècle* (Albi).

III. SECONDARY WORKS CITED IN THE FOOTNOTES

ARRIAZA, A. 1971. "Henry Trastamara, the *Routiers*, and Iberian Politics, 1356-1363." Unpublished graduate seminar paper, University of Iowa (Iowa City).

ATIYA, A. S. 1938. *The Crusade in the Later Middle Ages* (London).

AVOUT, J. D'. 1960. *Le meurtre d'Etienne Marcel* (Paris).

BALAS, L. 1928. *Une tentative de gouvernement représentatif au XIVe siècle. Les états-généraux de 1356-1358* (Paris).

BARDON, A. 1891-1896. *Histoire de la ville d'Alais* (2 v., Nîmes).

BEAUVILLÉ, V. DE. 1875. *Histoire de la ville de Montdidier* (2nd ed., Paris).

BERTIN, P. 1947. *Une commune flamande-artésienne: Aire-sur-la-Lys, des Origines au XVIe siècle* (Arras).

BILLIOUD, J. 1922. *Les états de Bourgogne aux XIVe et XVe siècles* (Dijon).

BLANC, A. 1899. "Le Rappel du duc d'Anjou et l'ordonnance du 25 avril 1380." *Bulletin historique et philologique du comité des travaux historiques et scientifiques*, 1899.

BOUDET, M. 1900. *Thomas de la Marche, bâtard de France, et ses aventures (1318-1361)* (Riom).

BOURILLY, V. L. 1926. "Du Guesclin et le duc d'Anjou en Provence (1368)." *Revue historique* 152: pp. 161-180.

BREUILS, A. 1896. "Jean Ier, comte d'Armagnac, et le mouvement national dans le Midi au temps du prince Noir." *Revue des questions historiques* 59: pp. 44-102.

BRIDREY, E. 1906. *La théorie de la monnaie au XIV siècle, Nicole Oresme* (Paris).

BROWN, E. 1971. "Subsidy and Reform in 1321: The Accounts of Najac and the Policies of Philip V." *Traditio* 27: pp. 399-432.

——— 1972. "*Cessante causa* and the Taxes of the Last Capetians: The Political Applications of a Philosophical Maxim," *Studia Gratiana* 15: pp. 565-587.

——— 1973. "Taxation and Morality in the Thirteenth and Fourteenth Centuries: Conscience and Political Power and the Kings of France." *French Historical Studies* 8, 1: pp. 1-28.

CALLERY, A. 1879. "Histoire du pouvoir royal d'imposer depuis la féodalité jusqu'au règne de Charles V." *Revue des questions historiques* 26: pp. 419-492.

CALVET, M. 1850. "Prise de possession par le roi d'Angleterre de la ville de Cahors et du Quercy en 1361." *Recueil des travaux de la Société d'agriculture, de sciences, et d'arts d'Agen* 5: pp. 167-209.

CASTELNAU, J. 1956. "Etienne Marcel a-t-il trahi?" *Revue des Deux Mondes* 1956: pp. 297-312.

CAZELLES, R. 1958. *La société politique et la crise de la royauté sous Philippe de Valois* (Paris).

——— 1960. "Le parti navarrais jusqu'à la mort d'Etienne Marcel." *Bulletin philologique et historique* 1960: pp. 839-869.

——— 1960. "La réglementation de la guerre privée de Saint Louis à Charles V et la précarité des ordonnances." *Revue historique de droit français et étranger* 1960: pp. 530-548.

——— 1962-1963. "Une exigence de l'opinion depuis Saint Louis: La réformation du royaume." *Annuaire Bulletin, Société de l'histoire de France* 1962-1963: pp. 91-99.

——— 1964. "Du Guesclin avant Cocherel." *Actes du Colloque International de Cocherel*, pp. 33-40.

——— 1965. "Etienne Marcel au sein de la haute bourgeoisie d'affaires." *Journal de Savants* 1965: pp. 413-427.

——— 1966. "Quelques réflexions à propos des mutations de la monnaie royale française (1295-1360)." *Le Moyen Age* 72: pp. 83-105, 251-278.

——— 1974. "Jean II le Bon: quel homme? quel roi?" *Revue historique* 509: pp. 5-26.

CHEREST, A. 1879. *L'Archiprêtre: episodes de la guerre de cent ans au XIVe siècle* (Paris).

CONTAMINE, P. 1971. *Guerre, état, et société à la fin du moyen âge* (Paris).

COSNEAU, E. 1886. *Le connétable de Richemont (Artur de Bretagne) (1393-1458)* (Paris) [see p. 310, n. 133].

COVILLE, A 1894. *Les Etats de Normandie, leurs origines et leur developpement au XIVe siècle* (Paris).

——— in *Histoire de France* 4, 1. See Lavisse.

CUTTINO, G. 1956. "Historical Revision: The Causes of the Hundred Years' War. *Speculum* 31: pp. 463-472.

DELACHENAL, R. 1909-1931. *Histoire de Charles V* (5 v., Paris).

DELISLE, L. 1867. *Histoire du château et des sires de Saint-Sauveur-le-Vicomte* (Valognes).

DENIFLE, H. 1899. *La désolation des églises, monastères et hôpitaux en France pendant le guerre de Cent Ans* (2 v., Paris).

DEPREZ, E. 1908. "Une conférence anglo-navarrais en 1358." *Revue historique* **99**: pp. 34-39.

DODU, G. 1929. "Les idées de Charles V en matière de gouvernement." *Revue des questions historiques* **110**: pp. 5-46.

DOGNON, P. 1896. *Les institutions politiques et administratives du pays de Languedoc du XIIIe siècle aux guerres de Religion* (Toulouse).

DUBY, G. 1968. *Rural Economy and Country Life in the Medieval West* (tr. C. Postan, London).

DUPONT-FERRIER, G. 1930-1932. *Etudes sur les institutions financières de la France à la fin du moyen âge* (2 v., Paris).

—— 1932. "Les institutions de la France sous le règne de Charles V." *Journal des Savants* 1932: pp. 385-400, 433-445.

—— 1933. *Les origines et le premier siècle de la chambre ou cour des aides de Paris* (Paris).

—— 1936. *Les origines et le premier siècle de la cour du trésor* (Paris).

DUSSERT, A. 1915. *Les états du Dauphiné aux XIVe et XVe siècles* (*Bulletin de l'Académie Delphinal*, sér. 5, **8**, Grenoble).

FARAL, E. 1945. "Robert le Coq et les états généraux de 1356." *Revue historique de droit français et étranger*, 4e sér, **23**: pp. 171-214.

FAVIER, J. 1964. "Temporels ecclésiastiques et taxation fiscal: le poids de la fiscalité pontificale au XIVe siècle." *Journal de Savants* 1964: pp. 102-127.

FAVREAU, R. 1959. "Comptes de la sénéschausée de Saintonge, 1360-1362." *Bibliothèque de l'Ecole des Chartes* **177**: pp. 73-88.

FINOT, L. 1889. "La dernière ordonnance de Charles V." *Bibliothèque de l'Ecole des Chartes* **50**: pp. 164-167.

FOURNIAL, E. 1970. *Histoire monétaire de l'occident médiéval* (Paris).

FOWLER, K. 1967. *The Age of Plantagenet and Valois* (New York).

—— 1969. *The King's Lieutenant: Henry of Grosmont, First Duke of Lancaster, 1310-1361* (New York).

FREMAUX, H. 1903. "La famille d'Etienne Marcel, 1250-1397." *Mémoires de la Société de l'histoire de Paris* **30**: pp. 175-242.

FRÉVILLE, E. DE. 1841-1842. "Des Grandes Compagnies au quatorzième siècle." *Bibliothèque de l'Ecole des Chartes* **3**: pp. 258-281.

FUNK, A. L. 1944. "Robert le Coq and Etienne Marcel." *Speculum* **19**: pp. 470-487.

GARNIER, E. 1852. "Biographie de Robert de Fiennes connétable de France (1320-1384)." *Bibliothèque de l'Ecole des Chartes* **13**: pp. 23-52.

GAUJAL, M. DE. 1858-1859. *Etudes historiques sur le Rouergue* (4 v., Paris).

GERMAIN, A. 1855. "Projet de descente en Angleterre concerté entre le gouvernement français et le roi de Danemark Valdemar III, pour la délivrance du roi Jean." *Mémoires de la Société archéologique de Montpellier* **4**: pp. 5-28.

GIARD, J. B. 1967. "Le florin d'or au Baptiste et ses imitations en France du XIVe siècle." *Bibliothèque de l'Ecole des Chartes* **125**: pp. 94-141.

GILLES, H. 1965. *Les Etats de Languedoc au XVe siècle* (Toulouse).

GORE, R. H. 1973. "The French Customs System: The Impact of Royal Policy." Unpublished Masters' Essay. University of Iowa (Iowa City).

GUIGUE, G. 1886. *Les Tard-Venus en Lyonnaise, Forez, et Beaujolais* (Lyon).

HENNEMAN, J. 1968. "The Black Death and Royal Taxation in France, 1347-1351." *Speculum* **43**: pp. 405-428.

—— 1968. "*Enquêteurs-Réformateurs* and Fiscal Officers in Fourteenth Century France." *Traditio* **24**: pp. 309-349.

—— 1969. "Taxation of Italians by the French Crown, 1311-1363." *Mediaeval Studies* **31**: pp. 15-43.

——— 1970. "The French Estates General and 'Reference Back' to Local Constituents." *Studies Presented to the International Commission for the History of Representative and Parliamentary Institutions* **39:** pp. 31-52.

——— 1971. *Royal Taxation in Fourteenth Century France: The Development of War Financing, 1322-1356* (Princeton).

——— 1972. "The French Ransom Aids and Two Legal Traditions." *Studia Gratiana* **15:** pp. 615-629.

HIRSCHAUER, C. 1923. *Les Etats d'Artois* (2 v., Paris).

HONORÉ-DUVERGÉ, S. 1947-1948. "Des partisans de Charles le Mauvais: les Picquigny." *Bibliothèque de l'Ecole de Chartres* **107:** pp. 82-92.

JONES, M. 1970. *Ducal Brittany 1364-1399* (Oxford).

JOURDAIN, C. 1878. "L'université de Paris au temps d'Etienne Marcel." *Revue des questions historiques* **24:** pp. 548-566.

KEEN, M. 1965. *The Laws of War in the Later Middle Ages* (Toronto).

LABANDE, E. R. 1948. "Louis Ier d'Anjou, la Provence et Marseille." *Le Moyen Age* **54:** pp. 297-325.

LABANDE, L. H. 1901. "L'occupation du Pont-Saint-Esprit par les Grandes Compagnies (1360-1361)." *Revue historique de Provence* 1901.

——— 1904. "Bertrand du Guesclin et les Etats pontificaux de France." *Mémoires de l'Académie de Vaucluse* **4:** pp. 43f.

LACABANE, L. 1839-1840. "Mémoire su la mort d'Etienne Marcel (1358)." *Bibliothèque de l'Ecole des Chartes* **1:** pp. 79-98.

LACOSTE, G. 1873-1876. *Histoire générale de la province de Quercy* (4 v., Cahors).

LACOUR, R. 1934. *Le gouvernement de l'apanage de Jean, duc de Berry, 1360-1416* (Paris)

LAFAURIE, J. 1951-1956. *Les monnaies des rois de France de Hugh Capet à Louis XII* (2 v., Paris).

LANGMUIR, G. 1958. "Counsel and Capetian Assemblies." *Studies Presented to the International Commission for the History of Representative and Parliamentary Institutions* **18:** pp. 21-34.

LAVISSE, E. (ed.). 1900-1911. *Histoire de France* (9 v., Paris).

LEDOS, E. G. 1895. "L'imposition d'Auvergne en janvier 1357." *Mélanges Julien Havet* (Paris): pp. 429-450.

LEHOUX, F. 1966-1968. *Jean de France, duc de Berri: Sa vie, son action politique (1340-1416)* (3 v., Paris).

LE PATOUREL, J. 1953. "Edward III, 'roi de France et duc de Normandie,' 1356-1360." *Revue historique de droit francais et étranger,* 4e sér, **31·** pp. 317-218.

——— 1958. "Edward III and the Kingdom of France." *History* **43:** pp. 173-189.

——— 1960. "The Treaty of Brétigny, 1360." *Transactions of the Royal Historical Society* 5th ser., **10:** pp 19-39.

——— 1965. "The King and the Princes in Fourteenth Century France." *Europe in the Later Middle Ages* (ed. J. Hale, J. Highfield, and B. Smalley, London), pp. 155-183.

LE SOURD, A. 1926. *Essai sur les Etats de Vivarais depuis leurs origines* (Paris).

LEWIS, P. 1962. "The Failure of the French Medieval Estates." *Past and Present* **23:** pp. 3-24.

——— 1968. *Later Medieval France: The Polity* (London and New York).

LOIRETTE, G. 1913. "Arnaud Amanieu, sire d'Albret, et l'appel des seigneurs gascons en 1368." *Mélanges historiques offerts à M. Charles Bémont* (Paris), pp. 317-340.

LORAY, T. DE. 1881. "Les Grandes Compagnies et l'Archiprêtre en Bourgogne, 1360-1366." *Revue des questions historiques* **29:** pp. 264-285.

LOT, F., and R. FAWTIER. 1957-1963. *Histoire des institutions françaises au Moyen Age* (3 v., Paris).

LUCE, S. 1857. "Du rôle politique de Jean Maillart en 1358." *Bibliothèque de l'Ecole des Chartes* 18: pp. 415-426.

—— 1860. "Examen critique de l'ouvrage intitulé Etienne Marcel et le gouvernement de la bourgeoisie au XIVe siècle, par M. Perrens." *Bibliothèque de l'Ecole des Chartes* 21: pp. 241-282.

—— 1875. "Negociations des Anglais avec le roi de Navarre pendant la révolution parisienne de 1358." *Mémoires de la Société de l'Histoire de Paris* 1: pp. 113-131.

—— 1876. *Histoire de Bertrand du Guesclin et de son epoque* (Paris).

—— 1890. *La France pendant la guerre de Cent Ans* (Paris).

—— 1894. *Histoire de la Jacquerie* (2nd ed., Paris).

MADDEN, S. H. 1970. "Charles V and Royal Propaganda, 1364-1380." Unpublished graduate seminar paper, University of Iowa (Iowa City).

MAJOR, J. R. 1957. "The Renaissance Monarchy: A Contribution to the Periodization of History." *Emory University Quarterly* 13: pp. 112-134.

—— 1960. *Representative Institutions in Renaissance France, 1421-1559* (Madison).

MÉNARD, L. 1744-1758. *Histoire civile, ecclésiastique, et littéraire de la ville de Nismes, avec des notes et des preuves* (7 v., Paris).

MEYER, E. 1898. *Charles II, roi de Navarre, comte d'Evreux, et la Normandie au XIVe siècle* (Paris).

MEYNIAL, E. 1922. "Etudes sur la gabelle du sel avant le XVIIe siècle en France." *Tijdschrift Voor Rechtsgeschiendenis* 3: pp. 119-162.

MICHEL, R. 1910. "La défense d'Avignon sous Urbain V et Grégoire XI." *Mélanges d'archéologie et d'histoire de l'Ecole française de Rome* 1910: pp. 129-154.

MILLEROT, T. 1879. *Histoire de la ville de Lunel depuis son origine jusqu'en 1789* (Montpellier).

MIROT, L. 1906. *Les insurrections urbaines au début de règne de Charles VI (1380-1383). Leurs causes, leurs conséquences* (Paris).

—— 1913. *Une grande famille parlementaire aux XIVe et XVe siècles les d'Orgemont* (Paris).

MISKIMIN, H. 1963. "The Last Act of Charles V: The Background of the Revolts of 1382." *Speculum* 38: pp. 433-442.

—— 1963. *Money, Prices, and Foreign Exchange in Fourteenth-Century France* (New Haven).

—— 1969. *The Economy of Early Renaissance Europe, 1300-1460* (Englewood Cliffs, N.J.).

MOLINIER, A. See Vic, C. de and J. Vaissete.

MOLINIER, E. 1883. "Etudes sur la vie d'Arnoul d'Audrehem, maréchal de France (1302-1370)." *Mémoires presentées par divers savants à l'Académie des Inscriptions et Belles Lettres*, 2e sér. 6, 1: pp. 1-359.

MONICAT, J. 1928. *Les Grandes Compagnies en Velay* (Paris).

MORANVILLÉ, H. 1895. "Le siège de Reims, 1359-1360." *Bibliothèque de l'Ecole de Chartes* 56: pp. 90-98.

MOURADIAN, G. 1970. "La rançon de Jean II le Bon." *Positions des Thèses, Ecole des Chartes* 1970: pp. 151-156.

NICHOLAS, D. M. 1971. *Town and Countryside in Fourteenth-Century Flanders* (Bruges).

PEROUSSE, G. 1898. "Etude sur les origines de la gabelle et sur son organisation jusqu'en 1380." *Positions des Thèses, Ecole des Chartes* 1898: pp. 89-98.

PERROY, E. 1928. "Charles V et le traité de Brétigny." *Le Moyen Age*, 2e sér., 29: pp. 255-281.

—— 1928. "La fiscalité royale en Beaujolais au XIVe et XVe siècles." *Le Moyen Age*, 2e sér., 29: pp. 5-47.

—— 1936-1937. "Franco-English Relations, 1350-1400." *History* 21: pp. 148-154.

—— 1948. "Edouard III d'Angleterre et les seigneurs gascons en 1368." *Annales du Midi* **61**: pp. 91–96.

—— 1951. *The Hundred Years War* (tr. W. B. Wells, London).

PETIT-DUTAILLIS, C., in *Histoire de France* 4, 2. See Lavisse, E.

PETIT-DUTAILLIS, C., and P. COLLIER. 1897. "La diplomatie française et le traité de Brétigny." *Le Moyen Age* 2e sér., **1**: pp. 1–35.

PICOT, G. 1872. *Histoire des Etats-Généraux, considerés au point de vue de leur influence sur le gouvernement de la France de 1355 à 1614* (4 v., Paris).

PLANCHER, U. 1739–1781. *Histoire générale et particulière de Bourgogne, avec des notes, des dissertations, et les preuves justificatives* (4 v., Dijon)

PORTAL, C. 1892. "Les insurrections des Tuchins dans les pays de Langue d'Oc, vers 1382–1384." *Annales du Midi* **4**: pp. 433–474.

—— 1902. *Histoire de la ville de Cordes, 1222–1799*·(Albi).

POST, G. 1964. *Studies in Medieval Legal Thought: Public Law and the State, 1100–1322* (Princeton).

PREST, T. R. 1971. "Policy and Protest: The Search for Monetary Reform in France, 1343–1365." Unpublished M.A. thesis, University of Iowa.

PROU, M. 1888. *Relations politiques du Pape Urbain V avec les Rois de France Jean II et Charles V, 1362–1370* (Paris).

RADDING, C. M. 1972. "The Administration of the Aids in Normandy, 1360–1389." Unpublished doctoral dissertation, Princeton University.

—— 1972. "The Estates of Normandy and the Revolts in the Towns at the Beginning of the Reign of Charles VI." *Speculum* **47**: pp. 79–90.

REGNÉ, J. 1918. "La levée du capage et l'emuete Toulousaine du 9 mai 1357." *Annales du Midi* **30**: pp. 421–428.

REUSS, R. 1913. "La première invasion des 'Anglais' en Alsace: èpisode de l'histoire du quatorzième siècle." *Mélanges historiques offerts à M. Charles Bémont* (Paris), pp. 281–303.

REY, M. 1965. *Le domaine du roi et les ressources extraodinaires sous Charles VI, 1388–1413* (Paris).

RIVIÈRE, H. F. 1874. *Institutions historiques de l'Auvergne* (2 v., Paris).

ROQUETTE, J. 1887. *Le Rouergue sous les Anglais* (Millau).

RUSSELL, P. E. 1955. *The English Intervention in Spain and Portugal in the Time of Edward III and Richard II* (Oxford).

SAMARAN, C. 1951. "Pour l'histoire des Grandes Compagnies: Le 'videment' de Château-Gontier par les Anglais (1369)." *Mélanges d'histoire du Moyen Age dédiées à la mémoire de Louis Halphen* (Paris), pp. 641–644.

SHAW, P. 1940. "The Black Prince." *History* **24**: pp. 1–15.

SPONT, A. 1891. "L'équivalent aux aides en Languedoc de 1450 à 1515." *Annales du Midi* **3**: pp. 232–253.

STRAYER, J. R. 1970. *On the Medieval Origins of the Modern State* (Princeton).

STRAYER, J. R. and C. H. TAYLOR. 1939. *Studies in Early French Taxation* (Cambridge, Mass.).

TAYLOR, C. H. 1968. "French Assemblies and Subsidy in 1321." *Speculum* **43**: pp. 217–244.

TEMPLEMAN, G. 1952. "Edward III and the Beginnings of the Hundred Years' War." *Transactions of the Royal Historical Society*, 5th ser., **2**: pp. 69–88.

TESSIER, G. 1938. "L'Activité de la chancellerie royale française au temps de Charles V." *Le Moyen Age* **48**: pp. 14–52, 81–113.

THOMAS, A. 1889–1892. "Le Midi et les Etats Généraux sous Charles VII." *Annales du Midi* **1**: pp. 289–315; **4**: pp. 1–24.

—— 1891. "Arnaud de Cervole et le drame de Glaizé." *Annales du Midi* **3**: pp. 255–256.

TIMBAL, P. C. *et al.* 1961. *La guerre de Cent Ans vue à travers les registres du Parlement (1337–1369)* (Paris).

Tucoo-Chala, P. 1960. *Gaston Fébus et la vicomté de Béarn, 1343–1391* (Bordeaux).

Tuetey, A. 1874. *Les écorcheurs sous Charles VII* (2 v., Montbéliard).

Vaissete, J. See Vic, C. de.

Valois, N. 1883. "La revanche des frères Braque." *Mémoires de la Société de l'Histoire de Paris* 10: pp. 100–126.

——— 1885. "Le gouvernement représentatif en France au XIVe siècle." *Revue des questions historiques* 37: pp. 63–115.

Viard, J. 1897. "Documents français remis au gouvernement anglais à la suite du traité de Brétigny." *Bibliothèque de l'Ecole des Chartes* 58: pp. 155–161.

Vic, C. de, and J. Vaissete. 1872–1904. *Histoire générale de Languedoc avec des Notes et les pièces justificatives* ed. A. Molinier, *et al.* (16 v., Toulouse).

Viollet, P. 1895. "Les Etats de Paris en fevrier 1358." *Mémoires de l'Académie des Inscriptions et Belles Lettres* 24, 2: pp. 261f.

Vuitry, A. 1878–1883. *Etudes sur le régime financier de la France avant la Révolution de 1789, nouvelle série* (2 v., Paris).

Wailly, N. de 1857. "Mémoire sur les variations de la livre tournois depuis le règne de Saint Louis jusqu'à l'établissement de la monnaie decimale." *Mémoires de l'Institut Imperial de France* 21: pp. 177–427.

Wilkinson, B. 1925. "A Letter to Louis de Mâle, Count of Flanders." *Bulletin of the John Rylands Library* 9: pp. 177–187.

Wolfe, M. 1972. *The Fiscal System of Renaissance France* (New Haven).

Wolff, P. 1947. "Les luttes sociales dans les villes du Midi française, XIIIe-XVe siècles." *Annales: Economies, sociétés, civilisations* 2: pp. 443–454.

——— 1954. *Commerces et marchands de Toulouse (vers 1350–vers 1450)* (Paris).

Zacour, N. 1960. "Talleyrand: The Cardinal of Périgord (1301–1364)." *Transactions of the American Philosophical Society* 50, 7 (Philadelphia).

Index

DATE DUE
